HITMAN

FORGE BOOKS BY HOWIE CARR

Hitman

Hard Knocks

HITMAN

The Untold Story of
Johnny Martorano:
Whitey Bulger's Enforcer
and the Most
Feared Gangster
in the Underworld

HOWIE CARR

A TOM DOHERTY ASSOCIATES BOOK | NEW YORK

HITMAN

Copyright © 2011, 2012 by Frandel LLC

A Forge Book
Published by Tom Doherty Associates, LLC
175 Fifth Avenue
New York, NY 10010

www.tor-forge.com

Forge® is a registered trademark of Tom Doherty Associates, LLC.

ISBN 978-0-7653-6531-6

Tor books may be purchased for educational, business, or promotional use. For information on bulk purchases, please contact Macmillan Corporate and Premium Sales Department at 1-800-221-7945 extension 5442 or write specialmarkets@macmillan.com.

First Edition: April 2011
First Mass Market Edition: June 2013

Printed in the United States of America

0 9 8 7 6 5 4 3 2 1

Once again, to Kathy,
and to my mother

Contents

Acknowledgments

First of all, thanks to my beautiful wife, Kathy, and our three daughters—Carolyn, Charlotte, and Tina—for their forbearance during the writing of this book. And Carolyn, thank you for your assistance in bailing me out of whatever computer difficulties I was grappling with from day to day.

Obviously, this book could not have been written without the cooperation of Johnny Martorano. I sought him out on his return to Boston, and eventually he came around to the idea that his life story could serve as the framework for a larger tale, a history of organized crime in Boston over the past half century.

We spent hours together, much of it in the city room of the *Boston Herald* early Sunday mornings. He talked, I listened. Everything that has been said about his memory is true. Not only does he have a near-photographic recall of details, but he's also a first-class raconteur. As one of my *Herald* colleagues who got to know Johnny on those Sunday mornings put it, "If only he wasn't so damned likable." He also introduced me to a number of his friends and associates, who had their own stories to share and whose memories refreshed Johnny's recollections, as a lawyer might say in court. I appreciate everyone who shared their stories with me, although I won't name them, for obvious reasons.

I hope that the photographs will add a different dimension to this book. I would like to thank everyone at the *Herald,* where I have worked for so many years, for their assistance. For allowing me to print many of the photographs, I owe a particular debt of gratitude to Pat Purcell, the owner and publisher of the *Herald.* Thanks also to the staff of the *Herald*'s library, which came up with clippings about ancient crimes. Photographer Mark Garfinkel also provided invaluable assistance.

As for the mug shots, most of them were made available to me by people who probably wouldn't appreciate being identified here. But I hope they know how much gratitude I have for their assistance. The organizational chart of the Winter Hill Gang from 1975 was made available to me by the Drug Enforcement Administration (DEA) and the Massachusetts State Police (MSP). Many thanks, especially to DEA agent Dan Doherty.

My great friend Larry Bruce spent what must have seemed to him like endless hours getting the mug shots into publishable form, and I appreciate it more than I can express. I would also like to thank my radio producer, Nancy Shack, for all her help on the book in so many ways.

Much of this book is based on public records and police reports. To break up the text, I occasionally used transcripts of Johnny's testimony at the two Zip Connolly trials, in Boston in 2002 and in Miami in 2008. He was asked many of the same questions at both trials, and I used what I considered the more compelling of his answers.

I am grateful to all who provided me with the FBI reports quoted in the book, and also thanks to the Boston Police Department's public-information unit, from which I obtained the official accounts of murders sometimes dating back more than forty years.

Thanks also to my Florida neighbor, Steve Lewinstein, for coming up with the title, *Hitman*.

Bob Gleason, my editor at Forge, has been a pleasure to work with. He and his staff, especially his assistant Ashley Cardiff and editor Eric Raab, did yeoman's work molding the book's various elements into a coherent whole. Along with Larry Bruce, Eric's skillful handling of the photos gave this book its unique look. George Tobia, my agent as well as Johnny's, put together the deal in his usual professional matter.

Finally, for introducing me to Bob Gleason, I owe my friend Bill Martin, the bestselling novelist, more than one gift certificate to Fleming's Steak House or the Hanover Street Chophouse, whichever he so desires.

WINTER HILL ORGANIZATION CIRCA 1975

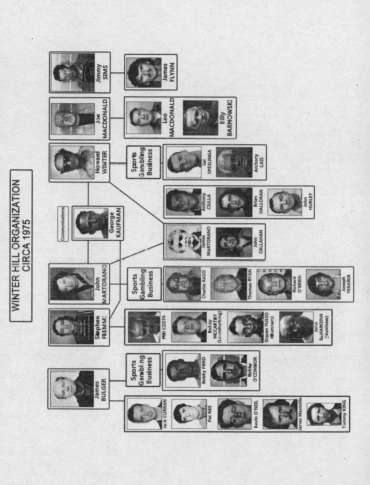

HITMAN

Prologue: Miami 2008

Johnny Martorano was choosing his words carefully. It was September 17, 2008, and he was sitting in the witness stand in a state courtroom in Miami. The sixty-seven-year-old hitman was being cross-examined in the murder trial of a corrupt FBI agent from Boston, John Joseph Connolly, Jr.—better known as Zip, the nickname bestowed upon him by his underworld paymaster, the legendary gangster Whitey Bulger.

Zip Connolly was already more than five years into a ten-year federal sentence for racketeering. And now in Florida he was facing life for the 1982 murder of a businessman who'd made the fatal mistake of throwing in with the Hill—the Winter Hill Gang of Boston—of which Johnny Martorano was a founding member.

Martorano had actually pulled the trigger on the businessman, John Callahan, a good friend of his—the twentieth and final murder of his career. But state prosecutors were contending that the murder at the airport in Fort Lauderdale had actually been orchestrated by the "highly decorated FBI agent," as Zip Connolly was invariably described in the newspapers.

Zip was accused of convincing the Hill that Callahan could implicate all of them, gangsters and FBI agents alike, in an earlier string of murders involving the take-over of a jai-alai company.

At Zip Connolly's first trial for racketeering, in Boston, Martorano had been the prosecution's chief witness, and Zip's attorneys hadn't been able to lay a glove on him. Now, in Miami, another high-powered defense lawyer was having a go at Martorano, and he, too, was flailing. The lawyer, Manuel Casabielle, had already told the judge during a sidebar conference that simply being in the presence of Martorano was intimidating him.

"It feels scary when you are close to him," Casabielle whispered. The Dade County jurors didn't seem frightened, though. They appeared mesmerized by his tales of the Winter Hill Gang, a collection of unusually murderous mobsters.

At its peak, the Hill's cast of killers had included Martorano, admitted murderer of nineteen men and one woman, as well as Stevie "the Rifleman" Flemmi. The Rifleman was now doing life for ten murders, and in various other court appearances Flemmi had taken the Fifth Amendment when asked about nine other slayings he'd never been formally charged with.

Finally there was James "Whitey" Bulger, a fugitive since 1994, number two on the FBI's Ten Most Wanted List behind only Osama bin Laden. Just two weeks earlier, on his seventy-ninth birthday, the FBI had doubled the reward for his capture to $2 million. Whitey, who hadn't been seen in the United States since 1996, was charged with twenty-one murders.

What Johnny Martorano hadn't known during his gangster days was that both Whitey Bulger and Stevie Flemmi were informants for the FBI—rats, as Johnny would put it. And for that he could never forgive them.

Whitey and Stevie hadn't been just Johnny Martorano's partners, they were among his closest friends. Stevie was the godfather of Johnny's middle son, christened in 1970 when Stevie was a fugitive from murder and car-bombing raps in Boston. Whitey was the godfather of Johnny's youngest son, Jimmy, born in 1986, when Johnny himself was on the lam, in Florida, living less than thirty miles from the courthouse where he was now testifying.

But Johnny Martorano was an even more fearsome killer than his two Winter Hill cohorts. In a few days, Stevie Flemmi would testify that after Martorano had become a fugitive in 1979, he had always kept the FBI informed of Johnny's whereabouts. But the FBI never moved to arrest him, Stevie explained, because Johnny was a life insurance policy of sorts for the feds' star underworld informants Bulger and Flemmi. The Mafia in Boston would never dare move against the two "independent" gangsters as long as Johnny was still out there . . . somewhere, capable of avenging his two sons' godfathers, the two guys he thought were his best friends.

"Johnny Martorano was a boogey-man to the Mafia," Stevie Flemmi would testify. In fact, Stevie's older brother, another notorious Boston hitman known as Jimmy the Bear, had once taken—and botched— a Mafia contract on Johnny's life. The Bear was another of Martorano's closest friends—he'd been the godfather of Johnny's oldest son. But like so many of Johnny's old pals, the Bear was gone now, dead of a drug overdose in state prison.

IN THEIR DIRECT examination, the state prosecutors had already gone over the complete list of Martorano's twenty murders, hit by hit. Between 1965 and 1982, he'd killed fifteen whites and five blacks, in three states. Their bodies had been dumped in alleys, in ditches, or left in the trunks of stolen cars. One corpse had never been found. Johnny Martorano killed them in telephone booths, at airports, at stop signs, on the open highway, and in

coffee shops, as they left barrooms drunk or snorted cocaine in a parked car.

The jury now knew that he had mostly used a .38-caliber
snub nose revolver, although he'd killed three others with
a carbine, two more with a grease gun, and one with a
sawed-off shotgun. One time he was the driver when
Whitey and Stevie took out a guy in a phone booth. And
then there was the pimp that Martorano had stabbed to
death while out on a date with a nurse.

It was standard procedure in these kinds of cases for
the prosecution to put onto the record everything that
seemed even vaguely unseemly, before the defense could
do so and make it appear to the jury that the government
was hiding something.

So all Connolly's defense lawyer could do was re-ask
as many of the same questions about Martorano's blood-
soaked past as the judge would permit, and hope for an
opening. Casabielle was reading aloud from Martorano's
plea agreement with the state of Florida to testify in any
and all prosecutions. The lawyer asked him if that was
why he had come to Miami.

"I'm keeping my word to the government and I'm
being honest," Martorano said. "That's it."

Casabielle instantly looked up from his notes. "You're
honest?"

"Yes."

"You are an honest man?"

"I try to be."

An honest man—this might be the crack that Casabielle had been probing for. Now the lawyer had to decide
which of the twenty murders to use to pry some holes in
Martorano's testimony.

He picked Richie Castucci, a middle-aged hustler from
Revere, who Martorano had shot in the head in Somer-
ville in 1976. Castucci died after the Hill got a tip that
Castucci was an FBI informant. Castucci had told the

FBI where two fugitive Winter Hill mobsters, Joe Mc-Donald and Jimmy Sims, were hiding out in New York City. Zip Connolly had been convicted in Boston of tipping off Whitey Bulger that Castucci had given up Mc-Donald, but that was something the Florida jury hadn't been told. They also hadn't been told at the time of the Castucci murder that Joe McDonald had been on the FBI's Ten Most Wanted List.

When the Hill decided to kill Castucci, they had owed a New York bookie $150,000 in lost football bets. Castucci was collecting for the New York bookmaker.

Just after Christmas 1976, the Hill called Castucci and told him to come over to the mob's headquarters in a garage on Winter Hill to pick up a down payment of the money they owed the bookie in New York. It was a two-birds-with-one-stone deal: by killing the informant, they were also canceling the six-figure debt to the Mafia-protected bookie in New York.

If Casabielle was going to undercut Martorano's testimony, the Castucci murder was as good a place as any to start. Casabielle's strategy was to keep hammering that one word to the jury: *honest*.

"When you lured any of the victims that you shot and killed," he asked Martorano, "were you being honest with them?"

"Well, I didn't think so at the time."

"I see. When you told Mr. Castucci to go to an apartment with the $60,000—"

"I thought you were talking about here," Martorano interrupted. "I'm telling you that's true."

Casabielle shook his head. "But your statement is, you are an honest man. You didn't qualify that by saying, 'I am an honest man today.' You qualified it by saying, 'I am an honest man.' So let's explore that."

"Yes," said Martorano, warily.

"When Mr. Castucci met with you at the garage to pick

up his money, did you tell him you were going to shoot him in the head?"

"No, I lied to him and then shot him in the head."

"So you weren't honest then?"

"No, I was honest to someone else."

"So it's okay to lie to somebody, shoot them in the head, and you can justify that by being honest to some other person?"

"Usually if somebody gets killed," Martorano explained, "somebody gets helped."

"Who was helped by killing Castucci?"

"Joe McDonald felt better. I felt better. I felt better at the time. Whitey and Stevie felt better. Everybody felt better."

"So you helped them by making them feel better?"

"I killed a rat."

"So the only reason that you killed someone you know, like Mr. Castucci, is because it made you feel good."

"No, it was because he was an FBI informant."

The unmentioned irony, of course, was that two of the Winter Hill mobsters who "felt good" about Castucci's murder, Whitey and Stevie, were themselves FBI informants—"Top Echelon," as the feds described them. The third Winter Hill gangster who felt good, Joe McDonald, had already become so suspicious of Whitey and Stevie that he refused to meet with them while he was on the lam.

And there was another, larger irony—Johnny Martorano, lifelong hater and exterminator of any rats that he came across, real or imaginary, was now himself a witness for the government. But whenever Martorano was asked now about how he could hate rats and yet testify against his former partners in crime, he always had the same answer. He would mention Judas, the faithless apostle, and how the nuns at St. Agatha's parochial school in Milton back in the early 1950s had drummed into him that there was no worse person in the Bible, Old Testament or New, than Judas Iscariot, who sold out his Savior for forty pieces of silver.

Whitey Bulger and Stevie Flemmi—what were they in their own way but Judases who had sold out their friends, and for considerably more than forty pieces of silver? Johnny Martorano knew better than anyone that he was no saint, but he felt comfortable describing Whitey and Stevie as Judases. It wasn't a hard decision to turn on them—it was his obligation, dammit. Sure, sometimes when he suggested that he was doing something noble now by testifying against the crooked FBI agent, he'd get ripped in the Boston newspapers, or by Zip's lawyers, but Johnny Martorano knew one thing.

The nuns at St. Agatha's would have understood.

"You can't rat on a rat. That's the way I see it."

JOHNNY MARTORANO LOOKED dapper on the witness stand. He was wearing one of his trademark double-breasted pinstripe suits. After his arrest in Boca Raton in 1995, his common-law wife had put all his clothes into storage for him, and after his release from prison in 2007, he'd had them shipped north to Boston.

The jury couldn't see them, but Martorano was wearing the most expensive shoes in the courtroom: $700 alligator loafers, custom-made, imported from Italy. In the old days, Johnny would drive across the state to Sarasota, to buy them from a high-end haberdasher, a friend of his. He always paid cash.

Johnny had always tried to dress appropriately—in the gang's garage in Somerville, he had favored leather jackets, like Whitey and Stevie. But in his nightclubs in Boston, Johnny wore suits—the police reports sometimes mentioned his meticulous taste in clothes. Cashmere in the winter, silk during the warmer months. His suits he'd buy wherever he could—Filene's Basement or the swanky

Louis of Boston, it didn't matter to him, off the rack was fine as long as they were properly tailored.

It was in the accoutrements and the accessories where Johnny Martorano tried to make his fashion statements. For close to twenty years, he'd worn a five-carat diamond pinkie ring, a gift from "the boys" in the gang. But shortly before his arrest in Boca Raton, he impulsively took the ring off his finger and handed it to a fellow fugitive from Boston who was short of cash. Johnny told him to pawn it.

"I liked the kid," Johnny Martorano would explain later.

It was all about the lifestyle. Johnny understood that the Miami and Boston reporters covering his testimony would routinely if imprecisely identify him as a "hitman," as if any other kind of person could have survived—let alone flourished—in the treacherous Boston underworld of the 1960s and 1970s. But even in those bloody years, there had been another Johnny Martorano—the affable nightclubber, the connected businessman whose first wedding the lieutenant governor of Massachusetts had attended.

Martorano's trade—the rackets—bankrolled a lavish lifestyle. He went to Vegas every other month to gamble. Staying at the top hotels and watching the best floor shows, Johnny Martorano was a high-roller, and the casinos comped everything. In the winter, he would fly to Miami to enjoy the beaches and to bet on the horses at Hialeah. He was a ladies' man. Everyone in his circle knew he had shady business connections, but he was loyal, friendly, quick to pick up a check, and invariably left a big tip. He was fun to be around.

Back then, on his left wrist he'd worn a Presidential Rolex watch, featuring emerald-cut diamonds around the face, inlaid with authentic mahogany that matched the dashboard of his black Mercedes 560 SEL, which he parked next to his thirty-three-foot Holiday Rambler RV.

Everything was of course long gone now—sold off to pay his legal fees.

THE UNSEEN PRESENCE in the Miami courtroom, day after day, was Whitey Bulger. He was the Winter Hill hoodlum who had captured the imagination of the general public, at least until the cops started digging up the bodies he'd buried around Boston over the years.

Unlike Martorano and the rest of the Hill, Whitey and Stevie had enjoyed police protection for more than twenty years. FBI agent Connolly, now sitting at the defense table, was their go-to guy in law enforcement. Growing up in South Boston, Zip had always worshipped Whitey's younger brother, Billy Bulger, who with the assistance of the FBI had become the president of the state senate, the most powerful politician in Massachusetts.

After fortuitously timed federal investigations had eliminated Billy Bulger's rivals in the legislature, Billy Bulger had asked Zip for one last favor. "Mr. President," as Billy preferred to be called, wanted Zip to keep Whitey "out of trouble"—or so Whitey had told Martorano. At the time it had seemed a reasonable enough story. But now Casabielle was asking Martorano why he never got suspicious as everyone in the Winter Hill Gang kept getting arrested, except for two guys.

Whitey and Stevie.

IN FEBRUARY 1979, the entire hierarchy of Winter Hill was indicted for running a multistate conspiracy to fix hundreds of horse races. Everybody was charged except Whitey and Stevie. On cross-examination, Martorano told Zip's lawyer that he was "happy" when Whitey told him that he'd managed to avoid the federal indictment.

"Did you not wonder why [Whitey and Stevie weren't arrested]?"

"They told me why. Whitey said because John Connolly was able to keep him out of it."

"Did you wonder why John Connolly would do such a thing for Mr. Bulger?"

"Because one of his promises was to help Billy Bulger maintain his position by keeping his brother out of the trouble."

"Today, do you still believe the same thing?"

"I sort of believe it still, but I think there was more to it than that."

"But you are not so clear, are you?"

Martorano thought for a moment about his old friend Whitey. "There was a lot of truths that he said to me, not just all lies."

"You didn't really know who Mr. Bulger was, did you?"

"Well, I felt I knew him. We were partners. I mean, we had a lot of crimes we committed together. I felt he was a stand-up guy."

IN MIAMI, JOHNNY Martorano was back in familiar territory, where he'd spent sixteen years. After he fled Boston in 1979, just before he was indicted in the race-fixing case, he lived mostly in South Florida until his arrest in January 1995. Then he'd been shipped back to Massachusetts. At the Plymouth County House of Correction, he'd lived for more than two years with his codefendants—all except Whitey, of course, who had already vanished.

The rest of them had been charged in a racketeering indictment—nothing about any of the dozens of murders they'd committed collectively, and individually. But Johnny Martorano had only been arrested on the old race-fixing charges. He was looking at four to five years, tops. So he just sat tight in the jail as the lawyers wrangled over the usual arcane pretrial legal issues in court. Every day he spent in the Plymouth County House of Correction before the trial would count as part of his eventual sentence.

But in 1997, Stevie and Whitey were disclosed as informants. As part of pretrial discovery, the FBI began turning over its informant files to the defendants. Johnny Martorano suddenly learned that for all those years he and Whitey and Stevie had been committing crimes together, they'd been informing on him, and on the rest of the gang, to the FBI. Whitey and Stevie—his sons' godfathers even had their own personal informant numbers, just like the numbers the cops had on their badges. That fact alone bothered Martorano enough to mention it, unsolicited, during the cross

"I never believed they were informants," Martorano told Casabielle, "when we were out shooting people."

"Obviously they were with you when you were out shooting people?"

"Obviously."

"So they know you had shot people. Can you tell how many people they were present for that you had shot?"

"I don't know."

As far back as the 1960s, Johnny Martorano learned from the yellowing FBI reports, his friend Stevie Flemmi was calling him a pimp behind his back, and trying to frame him for murders Stevie himself was planning to commit. It was all right there in the FBI reports—the 209s and 302s, many of them written by agents who were being paid off by the gang, including Martorano himself. But neither Whitey nor Stevie had ever mentioned any of the murders to their G-man handlers. So Stevie still had one card left to play against Johnny: he could rat him out for all the murders they'd committed together. After living large all these decades, with his immunity from prosecution, now Stevie Flemmi could betray Johnny one final time.

But this time Johnny Martorano understood what was happening, and he was determined to stop the rat. He had to act quickly, though, before Flemmi could move against him.

"I was concerned," Martorano was telling Zip's lawyer. "Now I know they could possibly implicate me, my brother, all my friends."

"You did it for your friends?"

"I did it for a lot of them, yeah."

"So you did the right thing?"

"I still believe I did. I mean, I didn't think anybody else got hurt by Flemmi or Bulger after the fact."

"You did the right thing, Mr. Martorano?"

"Yes."

"Did you always do the right thing?"

"I tried. But I don't think I always did the right thing."

JOHNNY'S NEGOTIATIONS WITH the feds took more than a year, part of which he spent in the hole at the federal prison in Otisville, New York, but in the end Johnny Martorano was finally offered a sweet deal by the feds. As Casabielle told him, "They wanted you really bad." Because Johnny Martorano had the goods on Stevie and Whitey and Zip Connolly, and because he knew just how solid his information was, he held out.

For forty years, even when he was a fugitive, Martorano had moved easily among all the crews and factions in the Boston underworld, Irish and Italian, black and white, Mafia and independents. He was the one fish the feds couldn't afford to let slip through the net. And so eventually they cut him exactly the plea bargain he had held out for: he would testify, but only against Whitey, Stevie, and Zip. For appearance's sake, the Justice Department lawyers added the names of a few more minor wiseguys, mainly from Whitey's South Boston crew. But they were just filler: How could Martorano testify against hoodlums he'd never even met, let alone committed crimes with? Under the terms his lawyers painstakingly hammered out, Johnny would not have to testify against his brother Jimmy or against his fellow Winter Hill gang leader, Howie Winter. And Johnny Martorano would end up doing twelve years, for twenty murders.

"Did you ever calculate how many months you did per body?" Casabielle asked Martorano.

"No."

"Could it have been about seven months?"

"Could have been."

"That's a pretty good deal, isn't it?"

"I had good lawyers. I made a good deal. I don't deny I made a good deal."

THE JUDGE WAS giving defense lawyer Casabielle a free hand. The prosecutors had gone through the list of killings in a perfunctory manner. But Zip's lawyer, knowing he had the jury's undivided attention, was still trying to pile as many additional gory details onto the record as possible. He wanted the jurors to be disgusted that their government would cut a deal with a killing machine like Johnny Martorano.

Flemmi, Casabielle knew, would not be nearly as effective a witness when he took the stand after Martorano. With his twitches, and his stuttering when challenged, the seventy-four-year-old Flemmi was easier to rattle. And he had trouble keeping his stories straight from one deposition or trial to another.

As Casabielle went over the list of Martorano's twenty victims, Johnny often admitted to killing hoodlums because he thought they might testify against someone he knew, or because they had disrespected one or another of his friends. But Casabielle preferred concentrating on the law-abiding citizens—the civilians—that Johnny Martorano had murdered by mistake. Like Michael Milano, a bartender Martorano machine-gunned at a stoplight in Brighton in 1973. Milano died because his new Mercedes and a long leather coat made him look like his employer—a gangster whose North Station bar the Hill had staked out.

"You killed him by mistake?" Casabielle asked.

"Not by my mistake," Martorano said. "Somebody said that was a certain guy we were looking for."

"Did you know what that person looked like?"

"No," said Martorano.

"So you went out looking for someone you didn't know, that you didn't know what he looked like, and by mistake you shot Mr. Michael Milano?"

"Somebody else said that was him."

"And you took that person's word?" Casabielle said.

"Yes."

"That was enough for you to kill somebody?"

"At the time, yeah."

A COUPLE OF murders later, Casabielle brought up a guy named William O'Brien. The Hill had been looking for a tough ex-con named Ralph DeMasi, and O'Brien was driving him on Morrissey Boulevard in Dorchester. They had just left a meeting at which they'd been trying to buy guns for the gang war in which the bartender had been killed a couple of weeks earlier. They were headed for South Boston to pick up O'Brien's ten-year-old daughter Marie. It was her birthday, and he had a cake for her in the backseat of the car. But O'Brien never made it back to South Boston. A Winter Hill hit car pulled up alongside his and Johnny Martorano opened fire with a machine gun, killing O'Brien and wounding DeMasi.

Casabielle asked Martorano about William O'Brien.

"I didn't know him. I was looking for the other guy that was with him."

"So William O'Brien, again, was a mistake?"

"It could have been."

"We are talking about somebody that was possibly innocent."

"He was possibly guilty, too. They both showed up looking to buy guns to kill someone."

The O'Brien hit was one of at least five murders committed by the Winter Hill Gang in 1973–74, when they were settling a score for the Mafia with a rogue organized-crime crew. Martorano explained how the other gang, which the Hill completely destroyed, had started the war by killing an LCN bookie—"his name was Paulie," Martorano said, "I forget his last name."

After the gang was wiped out, Johnny Martorano and Howie Winter went to the North End, and Jerry Angiulo, the Mafia underboss of Boston, gave them $25,000. But Johnny Martorano steadfastly maintained he never took money for killing people, not even from the Mafia and Jerry Angiulo.

"That was like a donation from him," Martorano said of the $25,000, "for our help."

Then Casabielle mentioned a 1981 murder he did in Oklahoma for John Callahan, whom Johnny would murder in Florida a year later. Callahan gave Martorano $50,000 after he traveled to Oklahoma to murder the owner of Callahan's former company, who had to die because he suspected Callahan had been skimming money from his jai-alai frontons.

When he got the money, Johnny gave half of it— $25,000—to his driver on the hit, fellow Winter Hill fugitive Joe McDonald. Then he split the remaining $25,000 with Stevie and Whitey back in Boston. So Johnny Martorano had banked a little over $8,000 for his nineteenth murder.

"Was that also a donation?" Casabielle asked.

"Positively."

"What charity were they donating to?"

"To Winter Hill."

"Are you seriously telling this group of people that the money . . . was a contribution to Winter Hill, the Winter Hill charity? Is that your testimony?"

"It was a gift from him [Callahan]. He was so happy he didn't get indicted. Better than giving it to a lawyer, I guess."

At that point Casabielle didn't even bother to point out that a year after accepting the $50,000, Martorano killed the guy who had given it to him. Later Johnny would tell the jury he "felt lousy" about having to "kill a guy who I had just killed a guy for."

"It was very distasteful," he elaborated.

Instead, Casabielle stayed with the larger theme of the Winter Hill gang as a charity, returning to the money the Hill accepted for wiping out a small rival gang for the Mafia.

"And what good deeds did Winter Hill do other than kill people and feel good about it?"

"I believe they helped a lot of people over time."

"And they hurt a lot of people as well?"

"Yes."

"Are you saying to this group of people that when Mr. Angiulo gave you $25,000 for those murders, that was also a contribution to the Winter Hill charity?"

"Correct. He was giving us money because we killed a guy who killed his friends."

"And your testimony, sir, is that you don't kill for money?"

"No."

As the lawyer continued this line of questioning, Johnny Martorano was thinking to himself, *Does this guy really believe I'd kill somebody for $8,000? For a million maybe, but eight grand? Nobody risks his life for eight grand—a junkie possibly, but nobody else.* Jerry Angiulo understood that—it was just a nice gesture he'd made, splitting up the fifty large like that. He was cutting up a score with his partners, which is what the Winter Hill Gang was with the Mafia—partners.

IN THE END, though, everything always seemed to come back to Whitey. After all the books and movies and FBI press conferences, after all the "age-enhanced" mug shots and all the dozen-plus segments about him on *America's Most Wanted,* most people still didn't get it. In the Boston underworld, until rather late in his career, Whitey had always been a small-timer, a ham-and-egger. He was from Southie, where a gang war was cowboys biting off one another's noses outside barrooms in the Lower End, driving around and shooting point-blank at each other—and missing.

Now that he had disappeared, though, Whitey had become a legend, a criminal mastermind, when all he really was was a rat. Zip Connolly's lawyer was trying to draw that bitterness out of Martorano, asking him what he thought now of his youngest son's godfather.

Casabielle: "He was dishonest with you for how many years, twenty-five, thirty years?"

Martorano: "From '72."

When Johnny first got to know Whitey Bulger, Whitey was already forty-three, a late bloomer in criminal terms. Whitey had been shipped off to prison for bank robbery at the age of twenty-six in 1956, when Johnny was fifteen. Whitey didn't return to Boston until 1965. Johnny was running bars in Roxbury while Whitey was on the Rock—Alcatraz.

The first time Johnny actually sat down with Whitey, in early 1972, Whitey was up to his eyeballs in one of those slapstick Southie gang wars. He was being hunted all over town by younger, quicker hoods. Which was why he'd shown up at Johnny's bar in the South End, dressed in a suit. Whitey needed a favor—he asked Johnny to introduce him to Howie Winter over in Somerville.

He wanted Howie to use his muscle to settle the war over in Southie, even if it meant that Whitey's boss would have to be killed, not by Whitey of course, but by some of the guys in the other gang, the ones who had been chasing Whitey. No wonder Johnny's pal Joe McDonald had never trusted Whitey as far as he could throw him.

So Johnny and Whitey didn't go way back, the way Martorano did with Stevie Flemmi. Stevie he'd known since he was practically a kid. He'd killed guys for Stevie—well, he'd killed at least one guy in Southie for Whitey, too, but by then it wasn't personal, it was business, a Winter Hill rubout. But after all the favors, when Johnny Martorano went on the lam in 1979, Whitey told him that from now on he should do all his talking on the phone to Stevie. Whitey didn't do phones. Phones could be tapped.

Now Casabielle was again asking about Johnny Martorano's relationship with the two rats in his gang.

"Mr. Flemmi and Mr. Bulger were dishonest with you, correct?"

"Technically," Martorano replied.

"What do you mean, 'technically'?"

"With that [being informants]. But they were honest about a lot of things. You can't be dishonest without showing some honesty."

"That's part of the charade, isn't it?" Casabielle said.

"Yeah," Martorano said, with a slight sigh, "I guess."

BY 1988, JOHNNY Martorano had been on the lam for almost a decade. During that time, he'd killed two more guys for Whitey and Stevie. But his monthly cut from the Winter Hill rackets back in Boston continued to dwindle, and what could Johnny Martorano do about it from Florida? Whitey was the big shot now, and Martorano the supplicant. And Whitey was tiring of his responsibilities to his one-time partner, the guy who had once saved his life.

In 1987, Whitey had been recorded on a DEA bug saying, "Fuck Howie" and "There is no Winter Hill Gang." But even as they were writing off their old Somerville partners, Whitey and Stevie were rolling in drug money. They were making more money than the old gang from Winter Hill had ever dreamed of—$5 million "protection money" from one marijuana dealer alone, Stevie would later brag.

And yet . . . the cops left Whitey and Stevie alone. If any police ever did make a move against them, they were slapped down, transferred, demoted, or forced to retire. The FBI, the Massachusetts State Police, the Boston PD—nobody could ever seem to build a case against "the two guys," as they had become known on the street. After a while, few cops even tried.

Eventually, the inevitable question began to be asked: Was Whitey a rat?

"Did you ever ask Mr. Bulger," Casabielle asked, "whether or not he was a rat?"

"No," Martorano said. "There was one incident, though. There was an article in the *Globe,* 1988, accusing him of being a rat, and I asked him about it. He said, 'They just put that in the paper every time my brother runs for reelection.'"

"So you actually asked him if he was a rat?"

"I asked him what the article meant."

"What was his response?" Casabielle asked.

"He said, 'It was something to cause my brother trouble.'"

"So he denied being a rat, correct?"

"I only asked him because of the article."

"So he was lying to you at that time?"

"Yeah," said Martorano. "I don't blame him."

"Why, sir? If you had found out he was a rat, what would you have done?"

"Well, I wouldn't have stayed friends with him."

"You would have killed him, wouldn't you?" Casabielle asked.

"Maybe."

"Possibly?"

"Possibly."

"Probably?"

"Probably," Martorano said. "You're using my words."

"I guess after a few hours of hearing, you use them," Casabielle conceded. "They kind of stick."

1

"Always Be a Man"

FROM HIS BIRTH at Cambridge City Hospital on December 13, 1940, John Vincent Martorano was an unlikely gangster. He had only one sibling, and he grew up in a stable middle-class household with both parents present. After the age of eleven he lived in the suburbs.

His father owned a profitable business and no one in the family ever lacked for money. In the somnabulent 1950s, young Johnny Martorano served as an altar boy and later went to both parochial and prep schools where his friends included, among others, a future congressman and a future CBS news reporter. Summers he and his brother Jimmy went to camp in the Berkshires. His parents owned a second home on the South Shore. At age sixteen, as soon as he got his driver's license, his father bought him a blue 1949 Plymouth sedan.

And yet somehow, Johnny Martorano was always fascinated by the city. He was always drawn back to the mean streets of Boston, where his father ran a restaurant and after-hours club in what would soon become known as the Combat Zone.

Both his parents came from large immigrant families.

His maternal grandparents were Irish, had met in England, and later immigrated to the United States, where they raised eleven children in the Somerville-Medford area, just north of Boston. His mother's maiden name was Elizabeth Mary Hunt. Everyone called her Bess.

His father was born in Riesi, Sicily, the son of a cobbler, one of thirteen children, only five of whom survived beyond childhood. The Martoranos immigrated to the United States when Angelo Martorano was seven years old, around 1915. They lived in East Boston. His first name was soon Anglicized to "Andy," and for the rest of his life he answered to either Angelo or Andy.

Johnny's father was always a hard worker, and after graduating from high school, he became a cab driver. Soon he owned his own Boston medallion, then two. He supplemented his income by working as a small-time bookie, taking numbers and bets, mostly on horses. In 1939, he met his future wife, who was working for a dry cleaner in Somerville.

After their marriage, Mr. and Mrs. Martorano moved to Bess's hometown of Somerville. They lived on the first floor of a rented two-decker off Ball Square, at 96 Pritchard Avenue. Johnny's cousins lived on the second floor. Eleven months after Johnny's birth, his only sibling, Jimmy, was born. Some of Johnny's earliest memories were of visiting his paternal grandparents, who lived on Neptune Road in East Boston.

In Somerville, just after the end of World War II, Johnny began school at St. Clement's. He was young, five years old, when he started the first grade, and the nuns decided to hold him back. From then on, he and his brother Jimmy would go through school together in the same grade.

I was Sister Patricia's pet—the teacher's pet. I used to wait every morning to carry her bag from the rectory to the school. But I got into trouble, too. I remember one day, I must have been eight or nine. My father had a big black four-door Dodge outside the house; he always had a big bankroll. Anyway, he was sleeping one morning, and I went downstairs. I put on his hat and took one of his cigars. Then I grabbed his bankroll and I went out onto the street and started giving money away. I looked like one of the Little Rascals. Finally my mother got a telephone call from one of the neighbors and she ran out of the house chasing me, trying to get the money back.

Andy Martorano was doing well in the postwar economy. He bought another medallion, and put his brothers, Danny and Louie, to work as drivers, until Louie got a job selling cars. By then, though, Andy had gone into the restaurant business, with Abie Sarkis, a big-time Boston bookmaker who became Andy's lifelong friend. Their place was on the second floor above the Intermission Lounge at 699 Washington Street in the middle of what would someday

Abie Sarkis, major Boston bookie
and longtime business partner of
Andy Martorano.

be the Combat Zone, although in those days the city's red-light district was still a few blocks north, on Tremont Street. It was known as Scollay Square.

Abie and Andy called their restaurant Luigi's, and it did well from the start. But it did better when they opened up what they called the "backroom," an after-hours club. They could charge more for a drink after last call, and they didn't need to keep the kitchen open. The only overhead was the weekly payoff to the cops in District 4. But in the mid-1950s, Abie Sarkis had a bad run in the numbers. He was deeply in debt, and to raise money, he sold out his half of Luigi's to Andy Martorano.

Now owning Luigi's outright, Andy Martorano soon had even more disposable income. He had a friend in Revere, Joe DeAngelis, who was trying to set himself up as a shylock on Shirley Avenue. In those days no one but the wealthy had credit cards, and for the workingman the only line of credit came from the loan shark on the corner. By the 1960s, Joe Dee had $100,000 of Andy's money out on the street, at a point or two (1 or 2 percent) a week. It was a good solid return on investment, and like municipal bonds, it was tax-free.

Soon, Andy and Bess Martorano decided that Milton, just south of the city, would be a better place to raise the boys than rough-and-tumble Somerville. Their first house was at 79 California Avenue. Later, Andy bought a vacant lot around the corner and built a new house, on 64 Lockland Street.

After he got married, my father quit as a bookie, but he still loved to gamble. And Andy liked baseball better than the track; in the summer he was always at the ballgames. This was back before the Braves moved to Milwaukee in '53, so there was a game in Boston almost every day, either at Fenway or at Braves Field, which is now Nickerson Field at BU.

My father used to take me with him to a lot of the games. One time I remember Sam Jethroe, the first black player on the Braves, was playing center field, and he misjudged a fly ball and it hit him on the head.

We used to sit with this group of guys, usually way up in the right-field grandstand, or sometimes in the bleachers—always off by themselves. They knew all the ushers, so they got in for free. There was plenty of room, and plenty of empty seats. Back then, the Red Sox didn't draw like they do now, and the Braves drew nobody. That's why they finally had to move.

My father and his friends didn't care if nobody was there. They were there to gamble. There were maybe fifty to a hundred of them, depending on the game, who the Sox or the Braves were playing. Mostly Italians in the group, but other people, too. The common denominator was betting. That's what these guys did. Some of them had businesses, like my father. There was another guy who owned a baby carriage company. I guess there were some wiseguys there, too. They'd gamble on every pitch, was it going to be a ball, or a strike? They'd bet on whether the batter was going to get a hit, strike out, ground out, or fly out. Anything, just action. Ted Williams comes up, maybe the odds were 20-1 or 30-1 that he'd hit a home run, depending on how good the pitcher was. Longer odds if the batter wasn't that good a hitter, or if the pitcher was better. Everybody kept a pad of paper and a pen on their laps so they could keep track of the bets, because they'd be making so many of them over the course of nine innings. At the end of the game, everybody would settle up.

That's how I learned to gamble, from my father. He taught me how to gamble and how to drink.

Johnny and Jimmy were now enrolled in St. Agatha's parochial school in Milton. They were in the same class as a young Quincy boy named Billy Delahunt, a lefty. Johnny was a good all-around athlete, but his best sport was football. One day on the playground he ran over Mother Superior, and she chased him down the street with her cane. Another time he kicked a football through a window in the school.

Johnny was a popular kid, a natural leader. Years later, Billy Delahunt, by then a congressman, was bragging at a party that he had never lost an election—as state rep, district attorney, or congressman. Someone else at the party, another St. Agatha's alumnus, corrected Delahunt—he had lost at least one election, for the presidency of the seventh-grade class at St. Agatha's. To Johnny Martorano.

> There was a priest there, a young guy, Father Riley. A great athlete. He called me Rocky. One day I went to him, I was in the seventh or eighth grade, and I asked him, Father, can you teach me how to throw and kick a football like you do? And he said, I'll make a deal with you, Rocky, if you become an altar boy, I'll coach you. It was a deal. I think I served Mass maybe once—somewhere there's a photo of me and Billy Delahunt, in our robes, and in the middle is Cardinal Cushing.

Johnny graduated from the eighth grade at St. Agatha's, but he was becoming harder and harder for his parents to handle. Andy decided to ship him off to what was then an all-boys Catholic prep school in Woonsocket, Rhode Island, Mount St. Charles Academy. Jimmy stayed behind in Milton and enrolled in the public junior high school.

As a freshman, Johnny became the starting fullback on the Mount St. Charles football team. His teammates called him "the Milkman."

"That was because he always delivered," his teammate Ed Bradley would explain a half century later.

It was funny how Ed Bradley and I became friends. He was black, I was white, he was on scholarship, I was from a middle-class family paying full tuition. I had a father, he didn't. I know he thought about it a lot later, and so did I: How did he end up what he became, starting with nothing, while I became . . . well, what I became.

He was a quiet guy, I was a quiet guy. One day after practice, we were walking back to the locker room, and he said to me, "You know, Johnny, you're white and I'm black, but one thing we got in common is the same teeth." See, he had a space between his two upper front middle teeth, just like me. We laughed, and that's when our friendship started to develop. I called him Big Ed—that's all I ever knew him as. When he came looking for me at the prison all those years later, at first I had no idea who "Ed Bradley" was. But I remembered Big Ed, just like he remembered "the Milkman."

I've run into a few guys from the old team since I got out. One guy, John McLaughlin, we called him "Clem," I saw him and he reminded me how there was another kid from Boston, a little guy named Johnny August. Johnny's dead now, but Clem told me how one time he was picking on Johnny August, and I grabbed Clem and told him to lay off Johnny August.

I'd forgotten all about it, but he was bullying the kid, and I had to stop it. That's just the way I am, always have been. That's what I was always taught. All my childhood, I was around people who instilled in me the same values. Be loyal to your family and your friends. My father wanted the best for me; he didn't care whether I became a doctor, a lawyer, or if I made a lot of money. He would say, "Always be a man." Take care of the people around you. There's an old Sicilian expression that Andy used—*Sangu du mio sangu*. It means "Blood of my blood."

And that's what I always tried to do—protect the "blood of my blood," not just my families and my brother, but also my friends. I always tried to make my father proud and live up to his expectations.

It's the same lesson I got from Father Riley, and later on from my coaches at Milton High. I learned from Big Ed, too. He taught me that blacks were no different than anybody else. If you're on my team, I'm with you all the way. Later on, that's how I felt about the gang. It was just another team, and we were all on the same team. Although of course I found out later that we weren't—on the same team, that is.

Another thing I always believed, even back then. If a friend asks you to do something, you try your best to do it for them, as long as it's the right thing to do and they deserve help. I always lived by that code. That's a lot of the explanation for what happened later. I was doing what people asked me to do, to help them out. You can say to me, you killed a lot of people, and you're right, I did. But I always had my reasons. I didn't kill for the hell of it, like the other guys. I was always helping somebody out, or I thought I was. When somebody gets hit, it always helps somebody else.

You know, I'm still on good terms with all the different people from the various periods of my life, even my kids' mothers. I don't have any enemies, never did. My problem was that I had a lot of friends who had enemies.

Johnny didn't last long at Mount St. Charles. One weekend he hitchhiked back to Milton, and called up one of the neighborhood girls. They arranged to meet at the old Strand Theater in Quincy. During the course of the date, it occurred to Johnny that Milton and Boston were a lot more fun than an all-male Catholic prep school in Rhode Island. He never went back. The next Monday, he joined his brother Jimmy at Cunningham Junior High School.

I always liked guns. My father had some around, because he carried a lot of cash, from the restaurant. I think the first one I shot was a .22, at an amusement park in Nantasket Beach in Hull.

When I was thirteen, fourteen, fifteen, somewhere in there, my brother and I would go to camp every summer in the Berkshires. I'm pretty sure that's when I bought my first gun, a .22 rifle, to take to camp.

Johnny, Andy, and Jimmy Martorano in the early 1960s.

He was still a wild and crazy kid. By the time he was fourteen, he was occasionally stealing his mother's car, a Ford, to go out joyriding. One afternoon Johnny made the mistake of taking off in the car before his father left for Luigi's. Andy saw him and jumped in his own Pontiac, a coupe, and began chasing Johnny through Milton, honking his horn. Johnny figured he could lose him down by the quarry. So he took a left, onto what he quickly realized was a dead-end street. It was a lesson for the future— always know your getaway route.

> My father was closing in on me, so I slowed the car down to the point where I could jump out. The problem was, the Ford was still in gear, so it kept going, and slammed into a house. I took off running for the quarry, on some little path through the woods. I can hear Andy behind me, screaming, "I'm gonna kill you." He's running after me, and he's so mad he takes off his belt, and he's trying to wave it around. The only problem is, once the belt's off, there's nothing to keep his pants up, and they fall down, and then so does he. Boy, was he pissed at me that day.

In 1956, Johnny got his first driver's license, and he quickly decided that he wanted to check out the family's new summer "cottage" in Scituate. One winter day, Johnny had a date, and they decided to enjoy a little privacy down at the beach house. But when they got there, they quickly realized there was no heat. That wasn't a problem for Johnny. He found an ax, chopped up the living room furniture, threw it into the fireplace, and started a blaze.

Things didn't work out with that girl, at least not then, but more than a decade later, they would have a memorable date in Boston.

Soon Johnny started going out with a "nice" girl from

North Quincy, Nancy O'Neill, whose uncle would some-day become a Boston city councilor—the colorful Albert "Dapper" O'Neil. (Different branches of the family spelled their surnames differently.)

At Milton High, Johnny was a three-sport letterman—football, basketball, and baseball. But he struggled aca-demically. The word was unknown at the time, but thirty years later, Johnny would discover his problem—he was dyslexic. Reading was more than a chore for him, it was torture. There was no "special education," and there was no tutoring for good athletes. Football coach Tom Brennan would simply go to Johnny's teachers and ask them to cut his star two-way player some slack. Andy couldn't under-stand what the problem was. Jimmy, eleven months younger, had no such academic problems, and was al-most as good an athlete as Johnny. He was going to Bos-ton College.

As for Johnny, he began going into Boston with his fa-ther. Andy got him a job as an usher at the Center Theater, across Washington Street from Luigi's. Then he arranged for Johnny to work as a shoeshine boy at the stand down-stairs from Luigi's.

I started at the bottom, and was supposed to work my way up. That was the way my father wanted it. It was like the Greeks with their kids in the restaurants—you start out as a dishwasher, then a busboy, you learn every job going up the ladder, so later you can fill in anywhere you're needed.

But I didn't like working. I liked having fun. I'd rather hang out at the poolroom on Washington Street, just watch the people playing, taking action. I learned all the different games—eight ball, billiards, pocket pool. I bought a short-brimmed hat, I smoked cigars, and started hanging out with black guys. We'd go down into the subway at Essex Street and drink fortified wine—Silver Satin. No cork in Silver Satin, just a screw top.

There was an ex-boxer, Pineapple Stevens, and Johnny Mendez, another black guy. He was all scarred up, razor cuts. You didn't see guys like that in Milton.

One day, me and another guy from Milton went up to Scollay Square and got tattoos. This was before they outlawed tattoos in Massachusetts. Now they're legal again. On my right arm I got Nancy's name and on my left arm, a cross and underneath it the initials IHS. That was a Catholic thing—*In hoc signo*, you know the cross Constantine the Great was supposed to have seen in the sky before he won the big battle and converted to Christianity. *In hoc signo*—"In this sign you will conquer." It was a message from God. I went back to Milton High and told people "IHS" stood for "I hate school."

In the fall of 1958, both Jimmy and Johnny Martorano made the Quincy *Patriot Ledger*'s South Shore All-Scholastic Football Team. Johnny was the only all-star to repeat for a second year. In addition to fullback, he played linebacker on defense for Milton High.

"To top things off," the reporter wrote, "the 5'9", 180-lb. blockbuster is a top-flight punter, and more than once during his school career got off booming punts that carried over 70 yards."

The story continued, "John plans to attend college next year, but has no preference yet as to which one, since he has received several applications from the local colleges and universities who are very eager to have him play for their school."

The two schools that seemed most interested in him as a football prospect were Vanderbilt and Tennessee. Johnny doubted he could survive academically at either place, but that wasn't the kind of thing he could admit to a reporter, especially when he knew that Andy would be reading the story, and that Bess would be cutting it out and pasting it into the boys' scrapbook.

Then the writer mentioned Jimmy's plans to attend Boston College, adding, "No doubt the Heights would be landing a prize catch if they could get their hooks into Jim, and John as well."

Something would soon have its hooks into Johnny Martorano, but it wouldn't be Boston College.

2

Apprentice Gangster

LAWYER: Prior to 1999, you were a businessman of
   sorts, were you not?
MARTORANO: Monkey business.

JOHNNY MARTORANO GRADUATED from Milton
High School in June 1959. His italicized quote in the
high school yearbook was "Courage can be a very difficult neurosis."

"I have no idea what it means," he says now, "or where
it came from."

Immediately after graduation, he went to work full-
time at Luigi's. Despite the football scholarships he could
have had, he had no interest in college, especially any
place far away from Boston. Even the nationally recognized programs, like the University of Tennessee, meant
nothing to Johnny. He wasn't volunteering for the Vols, or
for anybody else.

Andy Martorano wasn't happy with his son's decision
not to go to college, but what could he do? Maybe after
knocking around on the street for a year or so, Johnny
would reconsider. In the meantime, Luigi's beckoned.

The city's old red-light district, Scollay Square, was on its last legs, and most of the action had already moved south. Nearby were clubs like the Palace, and Izzy Ott's Novelty. The Venios family, better known as the Venus brothers, controlled a couple of dives teeming with what were commonly called B-girls. Even in those early days, the Zone was a magnet for servicemen and sailors on shore leave.

At Luigi's, nineteen marble stairs led from Washington Street to the second-floor landing, and anyone who spent time at Luigi's quickly learned never to turn his back to the stairs. If a fight broke out—always a possibility—you didn't want somebody that you couldn't see punching or pulling you from behind . . . not unless you didn't mind tumbling down those nineteen hard stairs.

At the top of the steps were two doors. The one on the right led to the regular, legitimate restaurant and lounge that opened at 11 A.M. and closed at 1. The door on the left was to the after-hours bar, basically a backroom club-house for Boston wiseguys. Every Friday, a bagman from Boston police District 4 would arrive to pick up the pay-off for the local captain and lieutenant; the uniforms got taken care of only once a year, at Christmas, or when they had to answer a call—a squeal— at the club. In return for the weekly envelope, the Martoranos would get a tip when one of the BPD's "flying squads" was planning a raid, usually around election time, and often accompanied by newspaper photographers. Even in the most corrupt departments, there were always one or two cops on the job who loved busting up bookie joints and after-hours barrooms. In Boston in the early 1960s it was Captain John Slattery.

Sometimes, the squads would manage to get into the Zone undetected. The stairs, though, provided an early-warning system for Luigi's. As the cops rushed up, the doorman, usually Johnny, would flash the lights in the

John Harry Williams (real name Gugliemo),
old-time Mafioso who tried to keep Johnny
on the straight and narrow.

after-hours club. Just in case there was a problem, or an
electrical short, the hatcheck girl also had a switch to flash
the lights. In the after-hours joint, everything was served
in plastic cups. The customers all understood that in the
event of a raid they were expected to immediately throw
their cups to the floor, thereby destroying the evidence of
serving after hours.

When the cops would get inside the back room and see
the empty cups scattered on the floor, whoever was running the club that night would shrug and explain, they
were just left over from a party earlier in the evening,
during legal serving hours. If the police complained that
the door was locked in violation of the fire code, Johnny
or whoever would blame it on some drunk.

LUIGI'S WAS THE perfect training-ground for a future
gangster. Working at an after-hours joint, particularly one

that his father owned, meant that Johnny always had plenty of cash. He learned how to size up drunks, gangsters, and cops, as well as their propensity for sudden violence, especially after they'd been drinking. Hanging out in the Combat Zone also meant that he would meet on neutral ground most of the city's top wiseguys, the hoods who had enough cash to actually escape Boston's suffocatingly insular neighborhoods, if only for a few hours.

Before he was even out of his teens, Johnny was mixed up with a bad bunch, even by Combat Zone standards. Andy Martorano knew just how rough Johnny's crowd was—they were, after all, his customers, his clientele. But Andy thought he had just the guy to straighten out his wayward son—John Harry Williams, né Gugliemo, an old-time Mafioso who had spent much of the 1950s as Raymond L. S. Patriarca's man in Havana, Cuba. Now in semiretirement after Castro's revolution, Williams passed his days quietly in a suite at the Bostonian Hotel in the Fenway. He wasn't like the raucous younger hoods Johnny was running with—he wore a suit and a tie and spent his afternoons in the hotel lounge sipping anisette.

"Me and your father go way back," Williams told Martorano. "Look, just behave and good things will happen to you. Stop drinking, stop fighting."

Within a few weeks, Johnny Martorano was arrested for the first time. Despite Williams's admonitions, he had taken to carrying a pistol, like everyone he knew and looked up to in the Zone. He bought it from some local character, and of course Johnny had never inquired about its pedigree, whether it was registered, if it was hot, and if so, how hot? Those were questions for a square, not an aspiring Combat Zone wiseguy.

What could Andy say? He often carried a gun himself, a small automatic at Luigi's, and at home in Milton he had more revolvers. It was a basic precaution for anyone carrying large sums of cash in a rough neighborhood.

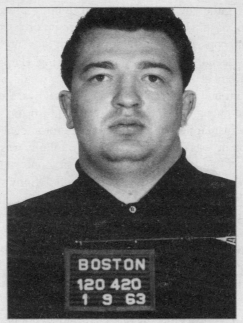

John Vincent Martorano at age 22.

Johnny, on the other hand, had no particular need for a gun, except to impress his fellow wannabe wiseguys. One afternoon he was in an apartment building in the South End, across from the District 4 police station, when a Boston detective barged in, his gun drawn, responding to a call. It was Eddie Walsh, near the beginning of his long career with the BPD, a career that would intersect more than once with Johnny's life of crime. He arrested Johnny for possession of an unregistered firearm, then a state crime, but not a federal offense.

Andy Martorano paid the bail and then he and Johnny went directly to the Bostonian, where Johnny Williams was sitting in the cocktail lounge sipping his liqueur.

"Johnny," he said, "Johnny, Johnny, Johnny . . ."

• • •

NEXT ANDY CALLED his police bagman. This is what he paid the brass for every week, to make aggravations like this go away. When the day for Johnny's next court appearance arrived, the arresting officer Walsh wasn't there, but the bagman was. He did the talking to the judge—"This young man would like to straighten everything out, Your Honor." In Boston courtrooms in those days, that only meant one thing—jail or the military. It worked the same way if you knocked up a girl—marriage or the marines.

Realizing for the first time the peril that he was in, Johnny stood up and asked to address the judge.

"Your Honor," he said, "if possible, I'd ask you to give me tonight to decide which branch of the service I'll be enlisting in."

As soon as he was outside the old courthouse in Pemberton Square, Johnny took off. At age nineteen, he went on the lam for the first time. He got into his old car and drove straight to his uncle's house in Miami. In a dry run for his flight twenty years later, he spent six months in South Florida, hanging out in Miami Beach.

He hooked up with a local boxer/wiseguy known as Johnny Angel, a common moniker in those days. His father's shylocking partner from Revere, Joe DeAngelis, flew down from Boston and handed Johnny a wad of cash at the airport, then turned around and caught the next flight back to Boston. A friend of Johnny's from Brookline stopped by on his way to Cuba, where Johnny had vaguely heard there'd recently been trouble involving some guys with beards who'd come out of the hills wearing military fatigues.

Soon Johnny and his friend were in Havana, checking into the Capri. They knew nothing about its owner, gangster Meyer Lansky, or his front man, George Raft, the former Hollywood actor and pal of old-time New York mobsters like Bugsy Siegel and Owney Madden. But when he saw some of those bearded guys in fatigues swaggering through the streets of Havana brandishing machine guns, Johnny instinctively understood that it was time to get back to Miami.

Six months later, Johnny returned to Boston. In his absence, the police bagman had made the gun charges filed by Eddie Walsh go away. Johnny went back to work at Luigi's, staying out all night, brawling, picking up women. He was driving Andy crazy. He wanted Johnny out of his hair and into the army—it was peacetime and there was no danger. It would be good to get Johnny out of the Combat Zone and into an organization that might instill some discipline in him. Andy called a friend who was a high-ranking military officer, and within days, Johnny got a notice from his Selective Service board in Milton to re-

Benedetto "Chubby" Oddo, who took
Johnny's army physical for him—and got
Johnny the 4-F classification he wanted.

port for his preinduction physical at the army recruiting center in South Boston.

Johnny, though, had figured out a scheme. He would have someone else take his physical for him.

I know a guy from the West End, Chubby Oddo—my father and his father came over from Sicily together. He kinda looked like me, only a little older, and physically he was a wreck, flat feet, bad eyes, his insides all messed up—I think he had some shrapnel or something in him, too, from what I have no idea. The night before I had to go in for my physical, I kept him up all night, drinking, making sure he memorized my Social Security number, my D-O-B, all the stuff he'd have to know by heart. Then in the morning I had him shave real close, so he'd look younger.

In the morning, Johnny dropped Oddo off in South Boston. All morning, and into the afternoon, Johnny waited nervously by the telephone for Chubby's call. Finally Chubby phoned to say that he'd completed the physical and that he thought it had gone okay. He hadn't passed a single test, so he assumed that Johnny would probably be getting his 4-F notice soon.

Johnny went crazy. He couldn't endure a week or two of tension before finding out whether or not he was going to be drafted. He ordered Chubby to go back inside and find out immediately. Chubby shuffled back up the stairs of the recruiting station to seek out the physician who'd examined him.

"Am I in?" Chubby asked.

"Kid," said the physician, "you couldn't get in the Boy Scouts."

I've always regretted never serving in the military.
In the army, if you shoot the enemy, you get a medal.

Out on the street, all that happens is you either get shot yourself or if you're lucky you get arrested. I went the wrong way, no doubt about it.

The Boston gangsters who hung out in the Combat Zone were a more diverse lot than in many other large American cities. In the years following Prohibition, the Mafia had gradually become the dominant force in urban organized crime. But in Boston, there were just too many Irish, and not enough Italians, for the Mafia to take over completely.

As far back as the 1920s, Irish and Italian gangs had been battling one another for control of the city's rackets. During Prohibition, South Boston had been ruled by the Gustin Gang, who made their living hijacking other mobs' booze trucks. In 1931, the Italians arranged a sit-down in the North End, then ambushed the Irish gang leader, Frankie Wallace, killing him and another Irish hood named Dodo Walsh. After that, the remaining Wallaces sank into drunken street crime, and the South Boston underworld was taken over by Dan Carroll. He was an ex–Boston cop who kept a framed photograph of President Calvin Coolidge in his office. It was a reminder of the favor the then governor Coolidge had done Carroll by firing him—as well as hundreds of other Boston cops—for taking part in the Boston police strike of 1919. The papers invariably referred to Carroll as a "sportsman," and it didn't hurt his underworld prospects when his brother Ed was elected to the state senate, the same body Coolidge had once been president of.

IN 1960, ORGANIZED crime in Boston was in your face. The city was teeming with wiseguys of every ethnic group. As Stevie Flemmi testified in 1998, "In them days it was open. It was just a way of doing, a way of life in them days."

The Hearst tabloid the *American* survived in large part because it ran the winning daily number in the city's underworld lottery, which even the more respectable Boston newspapers openly called "nigger pool."

Following Prohibition, the city's various mobs had settled into a relatively peaceful coexistence. When violence did erupt, it was mostly Italians shooting Italians, Irish killing Irish. Compared with what most workingmen in the city were making, the money was good enough for most gangsters not to rock the boat. In 1946, when Dan Carroll died at age sixty-three, the papers ran a routine list of dignitaries who attended his funeral. In addition to Mayor James Michael Curley, a congressman, and more than a dozen local politicians and police captains, the papers listed one "manager Phil Buccola"—the boss of Boston's local Mafia. Buccola was just paying his respects to a fellow "prominent sportsman."

Buccola had been among the Italians who'd ambushed the Gustins back in 1931, and he remained on top in the North End until 1950, when an ambitious Tennessee senator named Estes Kefauver decided to hold televised hearings in major cities around the country on the threat of organized crime.

By then, Buccola and his generation of local Mafia chieftains had accumulated enough money to retire in style, either in Boston or back in the old country. So rather than take the heat, many of them stepped aside. That opened the way for an ambitious thirty-one-year-old World War II navy veteran named Gennaro "Jerry" Angiulo and his five brothers.

Jerry Angiulo was less a muscle guy than a businessman, and his genius was in setting up what amounted to a profit-sharing plan in the numbers. For every four numbers his runners turned in, they got a free one. It was trickle-down economics, and it worked. The Boston numbers racket—nigger pool—took off. Kefauver's hearings turned out to be a flash in the pan, but when the dust cleared, Jerry Angiulo was the richest gangster in Boston.

Not having any direct protection from the Mafia, Jerry

Ilario Zannino, aka Larry Baione,
Jerry Angiulo's top enforcer.

was soon being shaken down by tougher Italian hoods, especially Larry Zannino, a vicious South End gangster also known as Larry Baione. Finally, Jerry decided he needed to hook up with "the Man," Raymond L. S. Patriarca, the godfather of the New England Mafia. Angiulo drove to the Man's headquarters on Federal Hill in Providence, Rhode Island, and handed Patriarca a brown paper bag full of cash. The loot, later estimated at as much as $100,000, was Angiulo's ticket into the Mafia. Jerry never personally killed anyone—never made his bones, as the old-timers said. He had Larry Baione to make them for him, and now Larry worked for him. So did Angiulo's four brothers.

Nobody in Boston ever referred to Angiulo's organization as the Mafia, or La Cosa Nostra, a name that would not come into common usage until years later when New York Mafioso Joe Valachi testified before Congress. In

Raymond L. S. Patriarca, the boss of the
New England Mafia, never liked
having his picture taken.

Chicago it was "the Outfit" and in Providence "the Office."
In Boston, the Mafia was known simply as "In Town." The
reason was simple: to visit Angiulo, you had to go to his
headquarters in the North End—In Town.

But "In Town" was far from the only game in town. The
North End often farmed out its heavier enforcement
work—up to and including murder—to other gangs. One
of In Town's favorite subcontractors was the McLaughlin
Gang of Charlestown. Loan sharks to the longshoremen,
the McLaughlin brothers and their gunsels dominated
crime along the docks and at the Charlestown Navy Yard.

The Angiulo brothers before a grand jury appearance in Boston, 1964. Jerry is second from right.

Their top enforcers included the Hughes brothers, Steve and Connie.

Next door to the McLaughlins in Somerville was the crew run by Buddy McLean, a cherubic-faced blond hoodlum from the Winter Hill neighborhood. The Somerville guys were all Teamsters, members of Local 25, a totally mobbed-up union. Naturally, one of Winter Hill's most profitable criminal enterprises was truck hijackings—most of which were inside jobs.

In Italian East Boston, where the Martoranos had first settled when they arrived from Sicily, In Town called the shots. But a young Portuguese-American psychopath from New Bedford named Joe Barboza had also established a beachhead. Like the McLaughlins, the New Bedford native handled the occasional murder contract for In Town, but he had a dream: to become the first non-Italian member of La Cosa Nostra. He didn't know that behind his back, the Italians in the North End and Providence referred to him as "the nigger." His better-known nickname was "the Animal."

Buddy McLean, the first boss of
what became the Winter Hill Gang.

Roxbury and the South End were controlled by Edward
"Wimpy" Bennett, a treacherous old-time Irish thug who
had been a B-29 tailgunner during World War II. His
nickname came from the hamburgers that he was always
munching on at the White Castle on Tremont Street. All
through the fifties, he had been linked to the famous
Brinks robbery of 1950. Bennett's only vanity was a wig;
whenever he appeared in court or had to have his mug
shot taken, he tried to make sure he didn't have to remove
his fedora—or his rug.

Wimpy Bennett was amazing. Behind his back, everyone called him "the fox." He always talked with
his hand to his mouth, even when he was inside, so

Edward "Wimpy" Bennett, the Roxbury gangster,
who brought the Flemmi brothers
into the rackets.

that nobody could read his lips. He said he learned it
in prison. Then he would hire lip readers to hang
around other wiseguys he was lining up, so he'd know
what they were talking about. He was continually
looking for an edge. I always wanted to stay on
Wimpy's good side, so he wouldn't be talking behind
my back. That's probably how Stevie learned how to
be so devious, from working for Wimpy. Wimpy got
along great with Patriarca, always called him "George"
for some reason I never found out. Everybody figured
he was the spy for "George" in Boston, which was one
reason In Town hated him so much.

After Jerry Angiulo, Wimpy the Fox probably
had more money than anybody else in Boston—he

had a piece of everything in Roxbury. But he always dressed like a laborer off Dudley Street, which is what he'd been before he got into the rackets. He smoked these really cheap cigars—White Owls or something. And he was a compulsive thief; he wouldn't pay for anything. He had overalls specially made—"booster clothes"—so he could go into a store and shoplift. Sometimes I'd be there in his garage when he'd be changing into his booster clothes, and he would literally take a roll of maybe 10,000 bucks out of his pocket before he went shoplifting. He'd look at me like he knew what I was thinking, which was how crazy is this, a guy with that kind of dough shop-lifting, a kleptomaniac basically. And he'd say to me, "No way am I ever gonna pay for hamburger, or razor

Vincent "Jimmy the Bear" Flemmi at age 24.

Stevie Flemmi at age 23, about to be booked, 1957.

blades, or whatever." That was Wimpy.

In the late 1950s, Wimpy recruited a couple of young brothers from Roxbury. Vincent Flemmi, born in 1932, was better known as Jimmy the Bear. His brother Stevie, born in 1934, had drifted into the underworld after returning from two tours of duty in the Korean War. On his first eight-man combat patrol, his unit ran into a company of Chinese regulars, and Stevie had killed five of the enemy, hence his subsequent nickname, the Rifleman. In the early 1960s, one of the Mafia guys from Revere was quoted in an FBI report as describing the Flemmis as "a couple of bad kids"—an understatement, as it turned out.

Johnny Martorano got to know the Bear in the early

'60s, before he ran into Stevie. Jimmy had just finished a stretch in prison for the 1957 robbery of a credit union at South Station. The Bear's life was always tumultuous, even when he was in prison, where he ended up spending more than half his adult life. While doing time at MCI-Walpole prison in 1961, the Bear was charged with stabbing another inmate to death. But the Bear beat that charge when several potential witnesses—his fellow prisoners—refused to testify against him. That would be a recurring pattern for the rest of his life.

Meeting Jimmy Flemmi was my downfall. I never had done anything really serious until I met the Bear. I mean, I killed people later on, but I always needed a reason, unlike those other guys I was hooked up with. Jimmy chopped people's heads off. Then there was Barboza—they didn't call him "the Animal" for nothing. As for Stevie—I never killed any of my girlfriends, or my daughter. And Whitey, well, this was a guy who killed Stevie's girlfriend and daughter—for kicks. I know I was with them, but please, don't ever put me in the same category with any of those guys.

South Boston was a bit off the gangland radar screen, with its "organized" crime being more than somewhat disorganized. When they weren't getting picked up for "DK"—public drunkenness—Southie hoods often made their living "tailgating": stealing cargo off the backs of trucks, with an occasional hijacking thrown in. The top guys in "the Town," as Southie was known, were the Killeen brothers. They ran their small-time numbers and loansharking rackets out of a barroom in the Lower End, the Transit Café.

There were smaller crews in Boston as well. Harry "Doc Jasper" Sagansky was a Tufts-educated dentist born

Charles "King" Solomon, a major
Prohibition-era gangster, relaxing at
the Cotton Club in 1932.

in 1898. He handled layoff bets for all the city's numbers
operations, from Angiulo on down. During a police raid
in Charlestown in 1943, "Doc Jasper" was found in possession of a life insurance policy he'd taken out on Mayor
Curley—the only way Doc could be sure of being repaid
what the "Purple Shamrock" had borrowed from him.
Sagansky still backed various gambling rackets, paying
short money to the Angiulos for protection.

Until his fatal heart attack in 1963, an old-time Jewish
mobster named Louis Fox—LF—controlled Revere, a
notoriously corrupt city north of Boston. Revere was the
home of Arthur's Farm, a sprawling warehouse-type store
where stolen merchandise was openly fenced to anyone
with cash, including some of Boston's top professional athletes. The owner of Arthur's Farm was Arthur Ventola, and
he eventually became so notorious that he and his well-

heeled clientele were written up in a *Life* magazine cover story. As for LF, he'd been around since Prohibition, when he was a lieutenant to the famous bootlegger Charles "King" Solomon. In the early '60s, LF controlled the illegal slot machines along Revere Beach and Shirley Avenue. Like Dan Carroll and Phil Buccola before him, LF was always respectfully referred to in the Boston papers as a "prominent local sportsman."

IN 1961, BOSTON was running wide-open. But on Labor Day weekend that year in Salisbury Beach, everything changed. Georgie McLaughlin, the youngest of the three Charlestown brothers, was drunk as usual, so loaded that he tried to pick up the girlfriend of a Somerville guy connected to Buddy McLean. Georgie wouldn't take no for

Georgie McLaughlin, the youngest of the
Charlestown brothers, in police custody
in the 1950s.

an answer, so the Somerville guys finally beat him sense-less, dumping him unconscious on the lawn in front of a local hospital.

Bernie McLaughlin, the Charlestown boss, demanded that Buddy hand over the men who'd beaten his brother. McLean refused, saying Georgie had been way out of line. In retaliation, the McLaughlins tried to wire explo-sives under one of McLean's cars, the one that his wife used to drive the family's young children to school. McLean was irate at such a breach of gangland protocol. A few days later, as Bernie McLaughlin was making his daily collec-tions at high noon in City Square in Charlestown, Buddy McLean calmly walked up behind him on the sidewalk outside the Morning Glory Cafe. Buddy McLean shot Bernie McLaughlin at point-blank range in the back of the head, in front of dozens of witnesses, none of whom saw a thing.

An off-duty Metropolitan District Commission (MDC) police officer drove the getaway car for Buddy. The war was on.

AT FIRST, IN Town loved the bloodshed. For one thing, it was the Irish, and their non-LCN allies, many of whom happened to be Italians, killing each other. The ongoing mayhem also gave the Mafia carte blanche to handle their own internal problems, knowing that every organized-crime hit would now be written off in the newspapers as part of the so-called Irish Gang War.

But in that same year, 1961, something else changed in organized crime. On orders of the new attorney general, Robert F. Kennedy, the FBI started picking sides. The target was what would soon be called La Cosa Nostra. Under pressure from the new Kennedy administration, on March 14, 1961, FBI director J. Edgar Hoover issued the following order to all of his field offices: "Infiltrate orga-nized crime groups to the same degree that we have been

Bernie McLaughlin, the top hoodlum in
Charlestown, shot to death by
Buddy McLean in 1961.

able to penetrate the Communist Party and other subver-
sive organizations."

Bobby Kennedy loathed the Mafia. As a young Senate staffer, he had pursued Jimmy Hoffa, the Teamsters'
Mafia-connected president. Bobby Kennedy knew full
well the rumors about his father's liquor smuggling with
organized crime during Prohibition. As his brother's 1960
campaign manager, he certainly understood the role of
the Chicago Outfit in John F. Kennedy's razor-thin vic-
tory over Richard Nixon in Illinois, and the fact that his
brother the president was now sharing a girlfriend with
Chicago boss Sam "Momo" Giancana. Whatever his reasons, or ulterior motives, Bobby Kennedy was determined
to destroy the Mafia. And as attorney general, he could

Corrupt ex–FBI agent H. Paul Rico,
testifying before Congress in 2002.

command the FBI to enforce his directives.

What Hoover's order meant, in effect, was that Italian organized crime—the Mafia—would now be the primary target of the Bureau. Anyone who could inform on the Mafia—even if they themselves were gangsters—would get a pass, but only if they could provide usable information against La Cosa Nostra.

In the Boston FBI office, the new anti-Mafia assignment fell primarily to two Boston natives, H. Paul Rico, who despite his last name was of Spanish rather than Italian extraction, and Dennis Condon of Charlestown. Both had joined the Bureau within a month of each other in 1951. People who knew Rico still recall him as a cop who dressed and talked like a gangster. Only much later would it become clear that it was not an act.

BACK AT LUIGI'S, it was business as usual—sailors

until 1 A.M., wiseguys until 4. Andy Martorano wouldn't give up his dream of a better, squarer life for his firstborn son, his golden boy. He wanted Johnny on the straight and narrow. Still perplexed at his son's 4-F—"he's as strong as a horse," he would tell his friends—Andy was always happiest when Johnny spent a rare evening out of the Zone, on a date with his high-school sweetheart, Nancy O'Neill.

It was the end of the 1950s, and "shacking up" was not an option, especially with an Irish-Catholic girl from North Quincy. So Johnny and Nancy decided to get married. Andy was ecstatic. Finally, he thought, Johnny might settle down. Maybe Nancy could accomplish what Johnny Williams had never been able to do: convince him to get a real job, or go to college, or perhaps even both. The wedding, in 1961, was big, and everyone from the Zone showed up to pay their respects, bearing envelopes bulging with cash. The honeymooners flew off to Miami Beach, and quickly checked into the bridal suite at one of Johnny's old Collins Avenue hangouts, the Deauville Hotel.

The fact that at least one of Johnny's old buddies, a wiseguy named Skinny, immediately began calling the bridal suite from the hotel bar downstairs was not a propitious omen for the marriage.

On their return to Boston, the newlyweds settled in Squantum, a middle-class section of Quincy. Nancy was soon pregnant with their first child, Jeannie. But Johnny had other things on his mind. His father had taken over the lease on a new club on the South End–Roxbury line.

They were going to call it Basin Street South.

LAWYER: Did you hire prostitutes to work at your restaurants for people?

MARTORANO: No. . . . Socialized with prostitutes, I've gone with prostitutes. In my life, you were either a prostitute or singer or dancer, waitress or barmaid. That's all the people I knew.

LAWYER: And when you socialized with prostitutes, you paid them, didn't you?

MARTORANO: I might help them. I might give them money but not for sex.

LAWYER: They were just gifts? Is that right?

MARTORANO: Sure. I received plenty of gifts from prostitutes and I gave them plenty of gifts.

The way Johnny Martorano would describe it decades later, Basin Street South was Boston's version of the Cotton Club, the famous gangster-owned Harlem nightspot of Prohibition days. Basin Street attracted a mixed crowd—"black and tan," as the phrase went. It featured a scantily clad chorus line and top-of-the-line black musical acts. Basin Street tended to showcase black acts either on the way up—Aretha Franklin, the Supremes, Lou Rawls, comedian Redd Foxx—or on the way down, like Count Basie.

Basin Street South was at 1844 Washington Street. The building that housed Basin Street South, and the liquor license that went with it, were owned by an In Town wiseguy named Rocco Lamattina. Next door on Massachusetts Avenue (called Mass Ave by the locals) was Jules' Pool Room, where upstairs the crap games never ended. As one of Jules's few white patrons, Johnny quickly met another white guy, an ex-con stick-up artist named Bobby Palladino.

The next building down Mass Ave served as a rooming house for the dancers and some of the acts. There were efficiency apartments upstairs, which were often rented out to the women who worked at the club. Soon Johnny was spending fewer nights at home in Squantum, and by 1962, he was never coming home. He had a year-old baby, and Nancy was seven months pregnant with his second

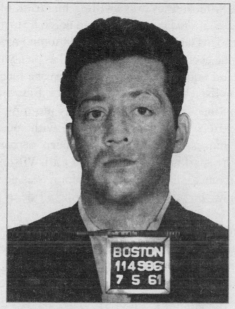

Bobby Palladino, the first man Johnny Martorano
would murder.

daughter, Lisa. But Johnny's first marriage was over.

Irreconcilable differences—which was another way of
saying, Basin Street South.

· · ·

BY 1962, EVEN the Boston Red Sox had integrated.
They had two black players—infielder Pumpsie Green
and a promising young pitcher named Earl Wilson, who
roomed together in an apartment in the Back Bay. Like
most of their white Red Sox teammates, they liked to
drink. Wilson especially enjoyed the nightlife, which, for
black high-rollers in Boston in 1962, was largely centered
at Basin Street South.

One Saturday night—June 25, 1962—Earl Wilson
rolled into Basin Street, looking for a party. Separated

from his wife, Johnny was swilling his drink of choice, champagne. He had nothing better to do, so he invited Wilson over to his table. After closing, Martorano rounded up some of the chorus-line dancers, as well as plenty of champagne, hard liquor, and marijuana. Everyone then headed over to Wilson's apartment in the Back Bay, where the party continued all night, into Sunday morning.

Around eleven the next morning, with most of the women and assorted hangers-on asleep or passed out around the apartment, a bleary-eyed Earl Wilson walked unsteadily up to the couch where Johnny was dozing off.

"Johnny," he said, "can you give me a ride to the ball-park?"

"What?" Johnny said.

"I gotta get to the park," Wilson said. "I'm pitching the first game of the doubleheader."

"You're kidding, right?"

"No, man, I gotta go."

Johnny and Wilson made their way unsteadily down-stairs, into Johnny's car. During the short drive to Kenmore Square, Wilson nodded off a couple of times, but awoke long enough to give Johnny directions to the green door in Fenway's center-field wall that served as the players' entrance. With the street still deserted, Johnny stopped the car. Earl Wilson opened the door, tried to get out, and tumbled face first into the gutter. Johnny helped him to his feet, leaned him up against the green door, and rang the bell. Then he ran back to his car. He didn't want to have to answer any questions about the condition of the Sox's starting pitcher for the first game. He stepped on the gas, keeping his eye on the rearview mirror as the door opened and Earl Wilson fell inside.

Was it a crime in Boston to get a starting pitcher for the Red Sox drunk the night before his next turn in the rotation?

Johnny drove back to his own apartment, slowly sobering up during the ride, and realizing his opportunity. This was exactly the kind of "inside information" he'd always heard so much about in the stands at Braves Field and Fenway Park with his father. Now, if only he could take advantage of it. Back at his own apartment, he began calling every bookie he knew, getting as much money down on the Los Angeles Angels as he could. The Angels' starter was Bo Belinsky, another party animal who'd already thrown a no-hitter earlier in the year.

"I was in for everything," Martorano said. "When you're twenty-one, twenty-two, you can't get that much money up, but I put everything down I could against Wilson. I figured it was guaranteed."

But Wilson threw a no-hitter. He was the first black pitcher ever to throw a no-hitter, and he also hit a home run—only the third pitcher ever to do that while tossing a no-hitter. Wilson outpitched Belinsky, 2-0.

> That night I'm sitting in the club, wondering what I'm going to do to come up with all the money I owe every bookie in town. I had already told everybody in the club they're not getting paid this week. And in walks Earl Wilson. He says to me, "This is the best day of my life, and it started right here, last night. Johnny, I owe it all to you!" Then he ordered champagne for the house.

Johnny said nothing to him that night, but a year or so later, on another late evening at the club, Martorano finally confessed to Wilson what he'd done, betting against him on the day he pitched his no-hitter.

"Why didn't you tell me, Johnny?" Wilson said, smiling broadly. "I'd have thrown the game for you."

THE GANG WAR was spiraling out of control. All the old scores were getting settled, whether they had anything to do with Charlestown and Somerville or not. A Rhode Island con wrote a letter from his prison cell to Patriarca, comparing "the Man" to Fagan in *Oliver Twist,* the boss of a gang of thieves. When the Dickens-reading con was released from prison, a Mafia hit squad tracked him to Quincy, murdered him and a friend, and stuffed their bodies in the trunk of a car at a motel. Both victims were Italians, as were their killers. The next day the papers listed them as two more victims of the "Irish Gang War."

Another alleged victim of the war was a Roxbury loan shark named Henry Reddington. Wimpy Bennett borrowed $25,000 from Reddington, then figured out a way he wouldn't have to pay. He called one of the local McLaughlins, a guy named Spike O'Toole, and told him that Reddington had been sleeping with his girlfriend. O'Toole immediately drove to Reddington's suburban office and murdered him. The papers had another "victim" to write about, and Wimpy was off the hook for $25,000.

The police wanted to at least appear to be cracking down on the mayhem, so they started clamping down on known hoodlums, pulling their cars over, searching them for weapons, taking them in for "questioning." Deprived of their usual sources of income, hard-up mobsters began committing crimes that would have been unthinkable in better times—robbing bookmakers, doing home invasions. Such crimes invariably led to retaliations, and yet more bodies, which meant yet heavier police crackdowns, with hoods rousted and rounded up no matter how much they'd paid off the cops in the past.

Since everyone now carried guns, and since most hoods already had criminal records, it was easy for the cops to bag anyone they wanted for being a felon in possession of an unregistered firearm. It wasn't a major crime, but it could be used to get somebody hot off the street and into

Joe "the Animal" Barboza, the first gangster
in the Witness Protection Program.

the House of Correction for a few months.

Soon two of Johnny's friends—Jimmy Flemmi and Joe "the Animal" Barboza—were doing state time. And that led to more problems: they quickly discovered that every morning, there was a "pill line," where prisoners diagnosed with psychiatric problems would be given their daily doses of antidepressants or barbiturates. The Bear and the Animal began robbing everyone as they left the line, gobbling whatever they could. Their already erratic behavior quickly deteriorated even further. Plus, they had a lot more enemies: everyone they had crossed while in prison.

Within months after his release from prison in 1963, Jimmy Flemmi had murdered two of his fellow ex-cons,

Walpole warriors, as they were known on the street. One he shot to death; he then drove the body to Pembroke but ran out of gas and ended up on the side of the road after dumping the corpse in the woods. The other he shot in the head in a Dorchester bar owned by the Bennetts, using a gun Wimpy had gotten from a Boston policeman on his payroll. Not knowing whether the cop's gun could be traced, the Bear chopped off the ex-con's head with the bullet in it, put it in his car, and then torched the bar. That was one way to beat a ballistics test.

Barboza, meanwhile, got married, and less than a week later murdered one of the hoods who had been in the wedding party. Another time he severely beat a teenager who he thought had refused to let him and a girlfriend cut in line

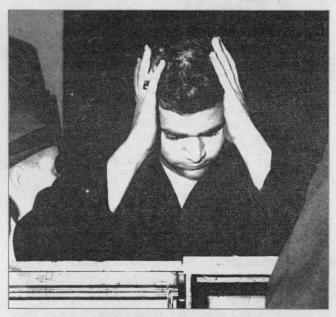

Bobo Petricone of Somerville, under arrest in 1961, before he went to Hollywood and became the actor Alex Rocco, who specialized in gangster roles.

for a ride at the amusement park in Revere Beach. The problem was, he beat up the wrong guy, but that didn't matter to Barboza. He'd delivered a message to those punks at the amusement park—don't fuck with Joe Barboza when he wants to cut in line. One day he used a baseball bat to knock out the windows of a car in East Boston whose driver had the temerity to honk at him. Oddly, though, Barboza would not tolerate anyone swearing in front of a woman. Violation of his "code" was good for a beating, at the very least.

Jimmy the Bear was also busy. High on Seconal one night, Jimmy Flemmi stabbed a twenty-two-year-old man who had the misfortune to bump into him at a Hayes & Bickford cafeteria downtown one night after the bars closed.

Even hoodlums began clearing out of Boston. It was safer that way. A guy from the North End became a courier for Meyer Lansky. One of Buddy McLean's friends moved to Hollywood, lost fifty pounds, took acting lessons, and changed his name from Bobo Petricone to Alex Rocco. His agent told him he might have a future in gangster movies. Years later in *The Godfather,* playing the Jewish gangster based on Bugsy Siegel, Alex Rocco would tell Al Pacino: "I made my bones while you were fucking cheerleaders."

Everyone in Somerville agreed Bobo delivered his line very convincingly.

AS THE BODIES piled up, Johnny continued to split his time between Basin Street South and Luigi's. He was also handling stolen furs. The Bear, in one of his increasingly rare sober moments, had introduced Martorano to a bold booster, who made his living climbing up the side of the old Furriers Building on Washington Street and also hitting the high-end fur shops on Newbury Street. Johnny would stash the stolen furs at Luigi's until he could move them out of town. The clubs were doing well, but he could always use extra money. He still had his ex-wife Nancy and the two girls to support.

But one night in November 1964, Martorano got a telephone call that changed his life. The Boston cops were swarming into Luigi's, searching the upstairs floors where the stolen furs were kept. They had a search warrant, based on a "tip" from the same cop whose gun the Bear had used to kill his fellow Walpole warrior a few months earlier. Supposedly the cops were looking for furs, but they quickly discovered a body wrapped up in a rug, "like it was ready for the river," as one cop put it.

It was Margaret "Margie" Sylvester, age thirty-five, a blond divorcée from Dorchester, a longtime friend of Andy Martorano, who had been a waitress at Luigi's for years. She had been stabbed to death.

Johnny was not a suspect; the night Margie vanished, he'd spent one of his rare nights at home. But his brother Jimmy had a problem. The morning after Margie's slaying, he'd replaced a rug at Luigi's. He told police that his

POLICE DEPT.
BOSTON, MASS.
1·8·2·4·3·4· 4-08-75

Jimmy Martorano mug shots from the 1960s and 1970s.

mother, who did the books for Luigi's, had noticed a section of the rug in the back room missing and had asked him to put in a new section. The cops weren't buying his story, but they couldn't prove anything to the contrary. Jimmy swore to Johnny he knew nothing about Margie's murder, although he admitted to Johnny that he had noticed blood stains on the edges of the rug that remained after he had replaced the missing section.

Johnny began his own investigation. He learned it had been a slow night at Luigi's. Bobby Palladino, the ex-con and a friend, had been hanging out in the back room. So had John Jackson, a middle-aged black ex-prizefighter who worked occasionally as a bartender at Luigi's. Johnny quickly found a third guy who'd been there—a former Boston cop who'd been fired for loansharking. The ex-cop was able to remember one more guy who Palladino and Jackson had apparently been afraid to mention: Jimmy the Bear.

"They were petrified of him," Johnny said. "For obvious reasons."

THE SYLVESTER MURDER investigation dragged on for months. Jimmy Martorano was finally indicted—but only as an accessory after the fact, for replacing the rug in the back room. Luigi's, of course, was finished. The Boston Licensing Board had no choice but to pull its liquor license after fourteen years in business.

Life went on for Johnny. The gang war was dragging on, but that didn't directly concern him. He wasn't involved, although he was "rooting for" Buddy McLean and the Flemmis to prevail, as he put it in court almost forty years later. The Roxbury crew had started out on the side of the McLaughlins—they had handled some of the hits Wimpy farmed out. In 1962, when George McLaughlin blew up a car belonging to Buddy McLean's top hand, Howie Winter, it was Stevie Flemmi and Wimpy who drove McLaughlin over to Somerville to plant the bomb.

But after a while, Wimpy the Fox realized that Somerville was gaining the upper hand. A peace meeting was brokered by a Boston police detective on the Roxbury payroll, and Buddy McLean sat down with Stevie and Wimpy at the Holiday Inn in Somerville to hash out their differences.

Through it all, Johnny remained tight with the Bear, who was turning into the main target of the McLaughlins after Buddy McLean. In 1964, Flemmi was shot and wounded by a Charlestown hit squad in Dorchester. In May 1965, he was ambushed by two McLaughlin gunmen as he left his apartment in Dorchester. The Bear was struck by nine bullets, and the shooters were walking toward him to administer the coup de grâce when the wounded Bear managed to pull his .38 out of his coat and begin wildly firing in the direction of his would-be killers. They fled, and Flemmi was taken to Boston City Hospital (BCH).

A couple of days later, against his doctors' orders, the Bear checked himself out of BCH. Johnny Martorano was waiting for him in a car. They would drive to Vermont, where an undertaker friend of Johnny's would rent them a cabin in which the Bear could recuperate in peace and quiet—and safety.

In addition to guns, Martorano had stocked the car with booze, which they got into as soon as they hit the road. Once they were drunk Johnny and the Bear began talking about how much fun it would be to pull into their campground with a dead deer strapped to the hood, as they'd seen so often during hunting season in northern New England. It was dark by the time they crossed into Vermont. Suddenly the Bear screamed—he had seen glowing eyes in a field by the side of the road.

"Turn around, Johnny," he yelled. "It's a fucking deer!"

Martorano put the car in reverse and backed up until he, too, saw the eyes, peering over a fence. The deer seemed remarkably serene, but they were too drunk to notice. They stumbled out of the car, Martorano brandishing a carbine, the Bear a revolver. Both emptied their guns in the direction of the eyes, yelled in exultation, then climbed over the fence. Johnny had a flashlight, which he shined down on the carcass . . . of a dead cow.

"Shit," Johnny said, shaking his head. "I'm not putting a cow on the hood of my car."

At the campground, their host was not impressed by their story.

"Don't tell anybody else here about that," he warned them. "You'll get more time in Vermont for shooting a cow than for shooting a human."

AS THE SUMMER of 1965 wore on, Johnny was hanging out more and more with the Bear's younger brother, Stevie—the Rifleman. As for the Bear, he had totally lost it—in September, he defaulted on a $25,000 bond in the Hayes & Bickford stabbing. A fugitive warrant was issued. His own lawyer said he didn't know if the Bear was alive or dead.

Stevie Flemmi was running a grocery store at Dearborn and Dudley streets in Roxbury, and that was where Wimpy Bennett and his gang were spending more of their time when they weren't at the garage. Almost a year after the murder of Margie Sylvester, one afternoon Stevie and Wimpy pulled Johnny aside and took him to the back of the store. Wimpy was known to have excellent police sources, and Stevie likewise seemed to have a sixth sense about what the cops were up to.

"Palladino and Jackson," Wimpy said.

"They're saying bad things," Stevie added. "They're talking about what happened."

Johnny Martorano, age twenty-four, was hours away from committing his first murder.

I still don't know who killed Margie. But what I do know now is that the Bear was there in Luigi's the night she was murdered, and that the tip to search the loft came from one of Stevie's cops. So I have to believe that when Stevie was basically telling me I had to kill this guy, Palladino, to protect my family, the reality was, I was killing to protect his family, his brother, the Bear. But after that day, for thirty years I believed I was indebted to Stevie. That "debt"—that's what started my killing spree.

LAWYER: Mr. Palladino was killed because he could have been a witness?
MARTORANO: I went to kill—went there with the intention if I had to kill him, I would, but not with the intention until I found out what he had to say.
LAWYER: So you found out what he had to say, and then you killed him?
MARTORANO: No. Before I found out what he had to say, he pulled a gun, and my [friend] grabbed his hand, and he shot and then I shot him.
LAWYER: So your testimony is that was in self-defense? Is that right?
MARTORANO: Indirectly. He might have got shot anyway, but it happened that way.

As soon as he got the tip, Johnny Martorano picked up a friend, and a gun, and started looking for Bobby Palladino. For once, Palladino was flush—he'd just made a big score, on a home invasion. He was part of a crew that had robbed Abie Sarkis, Andy's old partner in Luigi's. Palladino had gotten them into Sarkis's suburban house by dressing as a priest and talking his way inside. Once inside the Sarkis house, Palladino's crew had threatened to use hot irons on the family's faces if the Sarkises didn't come up with the cash the gang had been told Abie Sarkis kept in his house. In those days, a lot of the big-time gamblers had "traps" built into the walls or floors of their houses where they would hide cash. There was a shadowy guy around Boston who made a decent living installing such hidden drops—Frank the Trapper, he was called.

Somehow Abie Sarkis got upstairs and escaped by jumping out a window. According to the story later told in Boston underworld circles, Mrs. Sarkis then told Palladino and his friends, "You might as well just burn us now, because Abie's never giving you any money now that he's escaped."

The crew fled, not quite empty-handed, but with a lot less cash than they'd envisioned when they were planning the score. Frank the Trapper had done his work well.

FOR A WELL-PLANNED hit, Johnny would have stolen a car. But it seemed imperative to find Palladino immediately, before he could talk, if indeed he was talking. So that night Johnny was hunting Palladino in his own brand-new car, a 1966 emerald green Cadillac El Dorado convertible with white leather upholstery.

> I know this makes me look like a pimp, which I really wasn't, but a working girl gave me that car. She liked me. Back in those days, the higher-class hookers all had this circuit that they worked, and she'd gone off to work at a bordello in Gary, Indiana. While she was gone, she gave me the keys to her apartment in Brookline and to the Cadillac.

Johnny and his friend went from downtown bar to bar—the Attic, the Carribe, the 1-2-3, the 4 Corners. Around 2:30 A.M., they found Palladino in a blackjack game at Footsie Pucino's club, which he operated above a deli on Blue Hill Avenue. They asked Palladino to step outside, and he shrugged and walked out onto the sidewalk. Palladino had been drinking, but was cooperative until Johnny told him he'd been "hearing stories." Finally, though, they reached the street and got into the Cadillac, Palladino very warily. Johnny's friend was driving, and Palladino sat next to him in the front seat, with Johnny in the back—the first of many times over the next seventeen years that Johnny would end up in the hitman's seat.

"Let's go for a ride," Johnny said. As his friend pulled the Caddy out into traffic, heading back downtown, Palladino panicked and pulled out a revolver and fired at Johnny's friend. He missed, instead blasting out the front window on the driver's side. Johnny drew his revolver and fired at Palladino's head from point-blank range. One shot was all it took.

Johnny Martorano, age twenty-four, was a murderer.

At first it didn't sink in what he'd done. The body of a guy he knew well was slumped in the front seat, dead, and Johnny had killed him. Now he had to get rid of the gun, figure out what to do with the blood-soaked Cadillac, and, most important, get rid of Palladino's corpse. He had neither the time nor the inclination to ruminate over what he had done. All Johnny and his friend could think about was how to avoid getting caught and sent to prison for the rest of their lives. Johnny's friend kept driving north on Blue Hill Avenue toward downtown, and they began a calm discussion of where they should dump Palladino's body.

They quickly decided the best place would be down by the North Station. Nobody was ever around down there at this time of night.

THEY DRAGGED PALLADINO'S body out of the car and propped it up against one of the stanchions under the Central Artery, but the corpse fell over onto the pavement. Early that morning a *Herald* photographer got a grainy

Bobby Palladino's body was dumped
at North Station.

shot of the corpse from up above on the highway, with a
Boston police car and a detective nearby. It was a perfect
picture that *Life* magazine used in 1967 as the lead illus-
tration of its four-page spread about the carnage in the
Boston underworld.

It was almost dawn when Johnny got the Cadillac to
the Inter-City Garage on Mass Ave in the South End. Waiting for him was another of his new friends—George
Kaufman, a skilled mechanic and gang associate. Kaufman
chopped up the Caddy, the first of many favors he would do
for Johnny over the years.

The murder itself led the Boston papers' evening edi-
tions, but Palladino's death was quickly relegated to the
back pages a few hours later when Joe Barboza and Jimmy
the Bear committed one of their most atrocious crimes.

George Kaufman chopped up
the Cadillac that had been used
in the Palladino hit.

They'd been looking for one of the McLaughlin Gang's few Italian members, and had decided to take him out on a slow weeknight at the Revere Beach club where he tended bar—the Mickey Mouse Lounge. But when Barboza and Flemmi walked in, a construction worker was buying cigarettes at the bar. He was a young father of four from New Hampshire who'd been planning to move back to the White Mountains. Barboza and the Bear didn't care—they shot the McLaughlin gangster first, then the construction worker as he begged for his life.

For the next few days, the papers were full of pictures of the construction worker's attractive young widow and her four adorable children. As angry editorials were written demanding an end to the underworld carnage, everybody forgot about Bobby Palladino. Everybody except In Town—specifically Jerry Angiulo. The murder might have left the police "baffled," as the papers always put it, but Angiulo wasn't. The next day, Johnny got the message that he and his friend were expected at Angiulo's headquarters, the Dog House—immediately. It was an invitation they couldn't turn down.

Once they sat down, Jerry Angiulo got right to the point. They'd dumped the body too close to 98 Prince Street, maybe five blocks away.

"The fuck is it with youse guys!" he yelled. "Ya leave a fuckin' stiff in my fuckin' backyard! What the fuck was ya thinking?"

"Jerry," said Johnny, "I have no idea what you're talking about."

Gang War

LAWYER: Were you ever known as Bwana Johnny?
MARTORANO: No.
LAWYER: Machine Gun Johnny?
MARTORANO: No.
LAWYER: You don't recall that being your nickname when you were running with Barboza?
MARTORANO: No. I never had a machine gun when I knew Barboza.
LAWYER: You just got those later?
MARTORANO: Wasn't when I was with Barboza.

FBI AGENT H. PAUL Rico's assigned task was to destroy the Mafia in Boston. His hobby—his obsession—was wiping out the McLaughlin Gang. With La Cosa Nostra, it was just business, another assignment from "the Director," J. Edgar Hoover. With the McLaughlins, it was personal. They were barroom brawlers, up from the docks. Two of their brothers had been killed in World War II. They were old-line shanty Irish. When somebody died, they didn't have the wake at a funeral home. They'd put the casket in the front parlor, passing beers back and forth across the bier. They didn't like cops, and they hated homosexuals, which they assumed Rico was.

Rico knew this because Hoover had instructed his agents to install "gypsy" wires—illegal taps on phones as well as hidden recording devices, known as bugs—anywhere hoodlums did business. Having no warrant, the FBI couldn't directly use any of the information they obtained from the gypsy bugs as evidence in court, but that did not prove to be an insurmountable problem. All the G-men had to do was attribute the information to an anonymous "source," and then they could go to a judge and obtain a legal search warrant.

The feds put a gypsy wire on a phone in some McLaughlin hangout, right around the time Rico made his occasional pilgrimage to D.C. to pick up a crime-fighting award and token cash bonus from the Director. Every year, the *Record-American* would dutifully run the photo of Rico

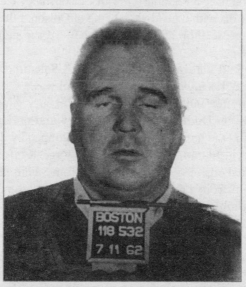

Punchy McLaughlin, murdered by
Stevie Flemmi and Frank Salemme in 1965.

at FBI headquarters, shaking hands with J. Edgar as Hoover's top deputy, while another confirmed bachelor named Clyde Tolson looked on.

On the day the *Record* was carrying its annual story about Rico's visit to Hoover to pick up his latest commendation, the agents were listening. And they heard Punchy McLaughlin sneering to another gangster about the Boston FBI office.

In his 2003 testimony, the mobster Frank Salemme recounted for a congressional committee what Rico had once told him about this one bugged conversation between the McLaughlins.

"They were always on the phone, according to him, and . . . the feds would pick up the McLaughlins and the Hugheses casting aspersions on Paul's manhood and his relationship with J. Edgar Hoover, and J. Edgar Hoover was, excuse me again, a fag, and that Paul used to go down there and have a relationship with Colson. They had a ménage à trois with a guy by the name of Colson, I think—"

The prosecutor interrupted: "I believe the name was Tolson."

"So Paul naturally didn't like that," Salemme continued. "He was always on their case, Paul was."

Rico often hung out down at the Roxbury gang's two garages, on Dudley Street in Roxbury and on Hancock Street in Dorchester. Wimpy Bennett stopped by daily, as did Stevie Flemmi and Salemme. George Kaufman ran the actual business, with some help from Salemme, a tall hoodlum from Jamaica Plain who had had some vocational training as both an auto mechanic and an electrician. Despite the fact that Salemme was half-Irish—his middle name was Patrick—like Barboza he dreamed of someday being inducted into La Cosa Nostra. Because of his taste in automobiles, everyone called Salemme "Cadillac Frank."

When Rico declared war on the McLaughlins, he

swore that if he ever got the right opportunity—that is, no witnesses—he would shoot Punchy or anyone else from Charlestown in cold blood. He regarded them all as his "archenemies," as Salemme put it. They had called him a fag.

Rico often spent his weekday afternoons at Suffolk Downs in East Boston. One day his official FBI vehicle was sideswiped in the horse track's parking lot. There was no way Rico could explain such an accident to his superiors. So he called Salemme, and Kaufman sent over a tow truck. They brought the fed's car back to the garage, where they worked all night completing the repair job so that Rico could drive the car to work in the morning as if nothing had happened.

The Roxbury gang's charge to its FBI friend: nothing.

Rico, of course, returned whatever favors he could. Back in the 1950s, as a young agent, he'd been involved

An early mug shot of Francis Patrick Salemme,
aka Cadillac Frank.

in breaking up an interstate bank-robbing gang that had included a young career criminal from Southie named Jimmy Bulger, as well as Ronnie Dermody, a hard-luck Cambridge hood whose father had died in prison, and whose brother soon would.

By 1964, everyone in Whitey Bulger's old gang was finishing their federal sentences, and Dermody got out first. He quickly fell for the wife of yet another member of the old gang. During her husband's prison sentence, this woman had taken up with another local hoodlum.

Head over heels in love, Dermody bumped into some of the McLaughlins. He told them how much he'd like to be rid of his new girlfriend's ex-beau, who was now him-

Ronnie Dermody made a fatal mistake—he trusted H. Paul Rico.

self serving a state prison sentence. The McLaughlins quickly suggested a deal: if Dermody, who wasn't known on Winter Hill, could get close enough to Buddy McLean to shoot him, then one of the several McLaughlin Gang members serving state time would eliminate Dermody's rival for the affections of the well-traveled moll.

Dermody instantly accepted the offer, but the problem was that he had no idea what Buddy looked like. Still, Dermody gamely drove over to Winter Hill, quickly spotted a wiry blond guy walking down Broadway, and opened fire. It wasn't Buddy, and Dermody only wounded his mistaken target. Worse, as he fled, Dermody was identified, not by cops but by people connected to Buddy McLean, which in Somerville was almost everyone. Soon Winter Hill gunmen were tracking Dermody in Cambridge.

Dermody was frantic. He didn't know who to call for help, so he finally turned to the one cop he figured had to be straight, the guy who had once arrested him—Rico of the FBI. Rico, who lived in Belmont, gave Dermody directions to a secluded street on the Watertown-Belmont line. He told Dermody he'd meet him there, just after dark. Rico's final instructions to him: Come alone, unarmed. And don't tell anyone where you're going.

Then Rico called McLean. He told him that the guy who'd just tried to shoot him would be waiting there, by himself, in a car. Then he asked Buddy if he needed a lift to Watertown. An hour or so later, Dermody was shot to death in his car. Nobody in the neighborhood could identify the shooter, or the car he'd been in. It had been too dark.

The next morning, all the newspapers carried ominous front-page headlines. The gang war, confined so long to the city and its grittier neighborhoods, had finally spread to the suburbs. Yet Rico did not file a report. Buddy McLean, meanwhile, vanished until the heat died down. His hideout was the Belmont basement of his getaway driver, H. Paul Rico.

. . .

JIMMY FLEMMI AND Joe Barboza were still killing anyone who got in their way. In the fall of 1964, Barboza was reined in by the Office in Providence. He was told that from now on, whenever he wanted to kill somebody, he would have to get a personal sign-off from "the Man."

One FBI informant was listening in Patriarca's Federal Hill headquarters in 1965 as Barboza tried to convince "the Man" to let him kill a guy who lived in a three-decker with his mother. Barboza planned to start a fire in the basement and then shoot the guy as he fled the burning building. He was going to bring with him three other shooters, to cover every side of the building. Barboza would cut all the phone lines to the neighbors' homes so that they couldn't call in a fire alarm. Just in case, Barboza also planned to phone in false alarms around the city to tie up all the fire companies. Patriarca listened in silence before he finally spoke. He'd been thinking about the would-be victim's mother.

"What happens when his mother runs out?" Patriarca asked. "You're going to kill his mother, too?"

"It ain't my fault she lives there."

Patriarca vetoed the hit.

SINCE THE BEAR was from Boston, Jerry Angiulo was told to handle him. The feds had put another one of their illegal bugs in Angiulo's Tremont Street bar, Jay's Lounge. One night the FBI agents were listening as Jerry personally delivered the news to Jimmy that from now on he was under the same rules as Barboza: Patriarca had to personally okay every hit.

"The Man says that you don't use common sense when it comes to killing people," Angiulo said quietly. "Jimmy, you don't kill somebody just because you have an argument with him."

But in fact that was exactly what the Bear did. Soon he

was bragging that he was through robbing banks, that being a hitman was a much better job. Meanwhile, he and Johnny Martorano were still hanging out together.

One morning at dawn, as they stumbled out of an after-hours joint in Roxbury, Jimmy looked up and noticed that the streetlights were still on.

He pulled out his gun and started shooting at the lights. Then Johnny joined him in the fun. They only stopped shooting to reload. It wasn't long before a Boston police car pulled up, and the two cops inside prepared to confront the shooters. But when they saw who was doing the shooting, they looked at one another, shook their heads, and drove off.

Another night, Jimmy and Johnny were sitting at the bar at the 4 Corners, the club downstairs from the Attic. The Bear was in the throes of one of his periodic crushes, this one on the manager of the 4 Corners, a good-looking blonde named Elaine. This night Elaine was tending bar and the Bear just kept staring at her, stupefied on booze and Seconals. Sitting next to them at the bar were two big, tough-looking black guys.

One of the black guys leaned over the bar, trying to get Elaine's attention. This deeply offended the Bear. He turned to Johnny.

"You got a knife on ya?"

Johnny nodded, reached into his coat, and pulled out a blade, which he handed to Flemmi. In a single motion, Flemmi grabbed the knife and then turned on his barstool toward the black guy, who had his back turned to the Bear as he continued trying to catch Elaine's eye. Without a word, the Bear stabbed him in the ass.

The black guy turned, in horror, looking down at the blood gushing out of his wound. He and his friend immediately took off running, as Flemmi yelled after them.

"You got what you deserved, motherfucker! You had it coming!"

Then he turned back around, handed the knife back to Johnny, picked up his glass, and shook the ice cubes to get Elaine's attention. The Bear needed a refill.

RICO WAS TRYING to recruit informants. In December 1964, he signed up a forty-one-year-old ex-con from Somerville named George Ash. He had a criminal record dating back to World War II, had just gotten out of prison, knew every wiseguy in the city, and he wasn't Mafia. He was just what the FBI was looking for.

But on the night he was officially approved by Washington and given his own informant's identification number, Ash decided to go out for a few drinks. He ran into the Bear. A few hours later, they were both sitting in the South End in a Corvair that belonged to Ash's sister. Suddenly the Bear decided to stab and shoot his old friend. After finishing Ash off, the Bear climbed unsteadily out of the car and wandered off, unaware that two uniformed Boston cops were watching him from across the street.

The cops knew what to do. They immediately drove to Stevie's store, told him what had happened, and demanded $1,000 to keep their mouths shut. Stevie paid them off and, according to a later federal report that named the two officers, "then chastised his brother Jimmy the Bear and reminded Jimmy how lucky he was that he ran into two police officers who were his friends."

Ash's murder was a tough break for Rico, but a few months later, Rico decided to reel in Jimmy the Bear. Guys like George Ash were useful, up to a point, but Jimmy the Bear would be a spectacular catch—he did hits for In Town. In fact, even as Rico recruited him, the Bear was planning a murder in Chelsea. A burglar named Teddy Deegan had been breaking into houses that belonged to Mafia bookies. And he was tight with the McLaughlins. Either fact alone would have been enough to put Deegan at the top of what the hoods called the Hit Parade, after

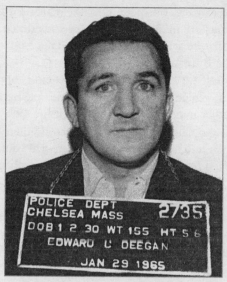

POLICE DEPT
CHELSEA MASS 2735
DOB 1 2 30 WT 155 HT 5 6
EDWARD L DEEGAN
JAN 29 1965

Teddy Deegan a few weeks before he was shot to death in 1965.

the old Saturday-night network radio show. Later, other reports surfaced that Deegan's death may have had nothing to do with the Mafia, that the Bear had just been drunkenly ranting about him as a "treacherous sneak." Whatever the real reasons, Deegan was on his way out.

An elaborate plot was hatched at the Ebb Tide, a new bar at the end of Revere Beach where Joe Barboza had set up shop. It was run by a local wiseguy named Richie Castucci, the nephew of Revere's top fence, Arthur Ventola. Deegan was told that a finance company in downtown Chelsea would be a soft touch after hours. Deegan immediately declared that he was in.

Two days before Deegan's murder, on March 10, 1965, Rico sent a report to Washington stating flatly that the Bear was about to kill Deegan—"a dry run has already been made and a close associate of Deegan's has agreed to set him up."

Apparently no one in either the Boston FBI office or headquarters in Washington ever considered warning Deegan that he was in mortal peril. That might have irritated the Bureau's new star snitch.

On March 12, 1965, the Bear was officially approved as an FBI informant. That evening he and Joe Barboza and several other gangsters met Deegan at the Ebb Tide and then drove to Chelsea in one car to burgle the safe. They got Deegan into an alley behind the finance company and then opened fire. The driver, correctly suspecting that he, too, was on the Hit Parade, took off. Within an hour, the shooters were back at the Ebb Tide, celebrating.

The next day, Rico sent a memo to J. Edgar Hoover correctly identifying by name the "prominent local hoodlums" who had murdered Teddy Deegan. Stevie asked his brother if he knew who had helped rob the Deegan book-

Whitey Bulger, age 23, under arrest shortly
after his discharge from the air force.

ies. *It was me,* Jimmy told him. *What if they'd given you the contract to hit me?* Stevie asked his brother. Jimmy just shrugged.

A day or so later, Barboza bragged to Johnny Martorano that he and the Bear had murdered Deegan. He told the same story to at least one other member of his East Boston crew, a young bookie named Dido Vaccari. Barboza named all the shooters—the real killers, the same ones whose names Rico had put into his report, not the four innocent men his false testimony a few years later would send to prison for thirty years, as the FBI agents who knew the truth sat silently in the courtroom.

More than three decades later, it would be Deegan's murder, and the subsequent framing of the four innocent men, that would bring down the entire corrupt conspiracy between the Boston FBI office and its underworld allies. But no one could have foreseen that in 1965.

In fact, on the night Deegan was murdered, the gangster who came to eventually symbolize the two generations of collusion between the FBI and the Boston underworld was still in prison, only days from being released from Leavenworth after serving nine years for bank robbery.

His name was James J. "Whitey" Bulger.

GROWING UP IN the public-housing projects of South Boston, Whitey Bulger had always been a bad kid. In his teens, after dropping out of high school, he turned tricks as a male prostitute in the bars of the neighborhood later known as Bay Village. Until he disappeared after his 1994 indictment, virtually no one in his future life would ever know this side of Whitey. "If all that was true—and I'm still saying if—it was a well-kept secret," Martorano says, "just like his being a rat."

Whitey rolled drunks, and committed various other petty crimes before enlisting in the air force in 1949. In 1950, he was charged with raping a woman in Montana.

That charge was dropped, but he continued to be a disciplinary problem. One of Bulger's superior officers eventually warned him that if he got a dishonorable discharge he wouldn't be able to find a job in civilian life. Whitey just laughed and, according to his military records, replied, "I could go back to the work I used to do, no matter what kind of discharge I get."

In 1952, Whitey Bulger was honorably discharged from the air force. He returned to Boston and quickly went back to hustling in the gay clubs. There he met a young FBI agent named H. Paul Rico, who trolled the bars at night claiming he was cultivating "sources." Even then, as he turned tricks, Whitey was determined that someday he would be a big shot. Shortly after being arrested for trying to steal a beer truck in the Back Bay, Whitey fell in with an older crew that was planning to rob some banks.

In May 1955, Whitey's new gang stuck up a bank in Pawtucket, Rhode Island, taking $42,000. Whitey's one-third cut financed a long vacation to Florida with his new girlfriend—his evenings of rolling gays outside the Punch Bowl and the Sail Aweigh were finally behind him. In October 1955, the gang hit a bank in Hammond, Indiana, but this time the take was less than $13,000.

On January 4, 1956, a federal warrant was issued for Whitey's arrest. He fled to California, then returned to Delaware to pick up his girlfriend, after which he took off again, driving across the country. Eventually the woman became homesick, and after less than two months on the lam, Whitey returned to Boston.

"To avoid apprehension," his FBI presentencing report later stated, "BULGER dyed his hair black, adopted the wearing of horn-rimmed glasses, changed the style and color of his clothing, and assumed the practice of carrying a cigar in his mouth to distort his facial features."

None of Whitey's ruses did him any good. In March 1956, Rico got a tip that his old acquaintance had been hanging out at a nightclub in Revere with an ex-con named DeFeo. Rico volunteered to handle the stakeout, and a couple of nights later, after a brief scuffle, Rico arrested Whitey as he left the club. It was a typical Hoover-era FBI public-relations extravaganza: newspaper photographers had been invited along to record the pinch of the black-haired Whitey.

The next morning, in federal court, the prosecutor asked for high bail, describing Whitey as "a vicious person, known to carry guns, and [who] by his own admission has an intense dislike for police and law enforcement officers."

Bail was set at $50,000, and, after a brief trial in June 1956, Whitey was convicted. In his presentencing report,

Whitey Bulger, his hair dyed black,
resisting arrest by the FBI in Revere, 1956.

Rico wrote that the Boston FBI office knew Whitey well "because of his suspected implication in tailgate thefts. We knew of his extremely dangerous character, his remarkable agility, his reckless daring in driving vehicles, and his unstable, vicious characteristics."

The judge sentenced him to twenty years. Whitey Bulger would not set foot in Boston again for nine years—until March 1965, a few days after Teddy Deegan's murder in Chelsea.

THE GANG WAR was not going well for the McLaughlins. Unlike Buddy McLean's crew in Somerville, the Charlestown outfit was not a diversified criminal organization. They were no longer getting paid for murder contracts, since in the ongoing anarchy every mob was handling its own work. It was likewise tough for the McLaughlins to make their loan-shark collections, since any barroom or dock where they were known was now likely to be staked out by hit squads from Winter Hill. The longshoremen had no loyalty to the McLaughlins for many reasons, not the least of which was that in the underworld, death almost always cancels a debt.

Hard up for cash, the McLaughlins began robbing bookies, many of whom were protected by Jerry Angiulo or other mobs. Then they started doing home invasions like the one that possibly cost Teddy Deegan his life. The McLaughlins' enemies multiplied.

Their other problem was a familiar one—alcohol. In March 1964, Georgie McLaughlin turned up drunk again, this time at a christening in a Roxbury housing project. For no apparent reason he shot and killed a twenty-one-year-old bank teller as he left the party.

Georgie took it on the lam. Suddenly, at the age of forty-eight, Punchy McLaughlin was the head of the gang. And it was a mob ever more desperate for cash, as Georgie learned what Johnny Martorano would one day discover: that everything costs at least twice as much when you're a fugitive. It's hard to haggle over price when there's a bounty on your head.

In the summer of 1964, the Hill got a tip that two McLaughlins were holed up in an apartment in Bowdoin Street in Dorchester, way outside their territory. So a five-man Hill squad broke into the apartment and awaited the return of the McLaughlins. Once captured, the two hoods, a fifty-four-year-old hitman and a twenty-seven-year-old rapist from South Boston, were driven back to Somerville. One of them was stripped, and then the Hill executioners took an acetylene torch to his testicles. No quarter was given, or expected. Finally the Somerville crew strangled the McLaughlins and threw their bodies into the harbor.

A couple of months later, in November 1964, an old-time Roxbury hoodlum named Earl Smith arranged to meet Punchy in a parking lot at Beth Israel Hospital. A future score had been mentioned, an easy payday to relieve some of the pressure of Georgie's enormous on-the-lam overhead.

Punchy trusted Smith. They'd done at least one hit together, back in 1962, clipping yet another shylock who'd made the mistake of loaning Wimpy Bennett $25,000. For the price of $5,000 to Smith and McLaughlin, Wimpy permanently erased another debt—and another loan shark.

Two years later, Punchy was waiting in his car for Smith when suddenly he saw two men dressed as Hasidic rabbis walking rapidly toward him. It was Stevie Flemmi and Frank Salemme, one armed with a revolver, the other with a shotgun. A blast from the shotgun shattered Punchy's jaw, but they couldn't finish the job. There were too many people around. The rabbis were last seen fleeing in a car with Rhode Island plates. After Punchy was brought into

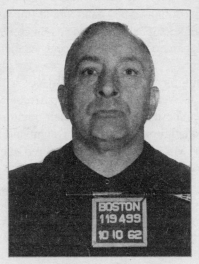

Earl Smith set up his old pal
Punchy McLaughlin in 1964.

the hospital, police searched his car. In the backseat they
found a paperback book: *Mafia*.

BY EARLY 1965, In Town had had enough. The war had
gone on too long. Nobody was making any money. A
summit was called for the Ebb Tide in Revere Beach,
where the Deegan hit would soon be planned. Both the
McLeans and the McLaughlins were expected for a sit-
down, at which Henry Tameleo, Patriarca's personal rep-
resentative in Boston, would mediate the dispute. There
was only one precondition: no guns. Speaking for the Office, Tameleo guaranteed everyone's safety. The Somerville crew arrived first—unarmed. A few minutes later, the
McLaughlins arrived, carrying paper bags. They didn't
trust In Town, or the Office. Tameleo started screaming
and threw them out. From that moment on it was the
McLaughlins against the entire Boston underworld.

By March 1965, the FBI was closing in on Georgie

The Hughes brothers of Charlestown, Connie and Steve.

McLaughlin. Rico showed up at the garage and said he needed a throwdown—an untraceable handgun. Stevie asked why. Rico smiled and said, "Because we know where Georgie is, and when we bust in, we're going to shoot him, but we need a throwdown that we can say he drew on us first." Stevie nodded, and an hour or so later, Rico picked up his gun.

The next day, Georgie McLaughlin was finally captured, alive, hiding in a Mattapan apartment with another gang member, Spike O'Toole, the guy who'd killed Henry Reddington after believing a false rumor from Wimpy Bennett. The *Record-American* reported that Georgie had been traveling the country as a woman, in drag, "with tight slacks, kerchiefs and the ever present lipstick and makeup." But the shootout Rico had envisioned never occurred.

A day or so later, Stevie asked Rico why his G-man raiding party hadn't shot McLaughlin. Rico shook his head sadly and explained that of the five agents, four had been on board with the plan, but that they hadn't been sure about the fifth fed, so they decided not to take the chance. Georgie was quickly indicted for murder, and the McLaughlins were down to three capable men: Punchy and the two Hughes brothers, Steve and Connie.

By now even his home base of Charlestown was too hot for Punchy. He fled to Canton, where he shacked up with his girlfriend. The various hit squads from Winter Hill, Roxbury, and In Town continued searching for him, but could never quite nail down his girlfriend's address. Finally, in August 1965, Flemmi and Salemme decided to ambush him in Westwood as he drove along what was then a rural road. Flemmi was perched in a tree when he opened fire on Punchy's car with his trademark rifle. Many of the bullets from Flemmi's high-powered rifle ricocheted, hitting a couple of nearby farmhouses. Punchy again survived the assassination attempt, but this time he was shot in the right hand, which doctors in the emergency room were forced to amputate.

The next morning, FBI agent H. Paul Rico showed up at the garage in Roxbury and struck up a conversation with Salemme. In his testimony before congressional investigators in 2003, Salemme recalled how Rico brought up the botched hit: "Paul was a very shrewd individual . . . he'd have the papers and say, 'Boy, what a sloppy piece of work that was, other people could have got hurt.'"

After some small talk, Salemme came clean with Rico about why they couldn't seem to finish Punchy off: "The bottom line is, Paul, I don't have his address, he's a tough guy to pin down, but I don't know where his starting point is."

Rico nodded and left. A couple of days later, Rico returned to the garage.

"He'd just be patting my shoulder like he usually does, and he hit my hand . . . he kept walking, and [I saw] there was a piece of paper with an address, and I didn't have to ask anymore. I knew who it was. It was Helen Kronis,

Punchy's girlfriend or common-law wife or whatever. So I went out and started to work on that."

Georgie McLaughlin's trial for the murder of the bank teller in Roxbury got underway in Pemberton Square in October 1965. No longer able to drive, the one-handed Punchy would get a ride every morning from his girlfriend to the Spring Street bus turnaround in West Roxbury. There he would catch a bus to the Orange Line station in Forest Hills, where he'd board the subway that would take him downtown to the courthouse. In his one remaining hand, he carried a plain, brown lunch bag with a loaded revolver inside.

In his final days, Punchy was depressed. He couldn't believe what had happened, how many of his friends, not to mention his brother, had been killed.

"All this," he told one fellow hoodlum, "over a broad."

On October 20, 1965, Punchy was boarding the bus in West Roxbury for Georgie's trial downtown when two men in suits suddenly approached on foot, drew guns, and began firing at him. Stevie was wearing a wig and makeup applied by one of his second-string girlfriends; he was carrying a .38-caliber, long-barrelled Webbley handgun. Punchy had no time to remove his own weapon from the bag, so he began running, pausing only long enough to hand his paper bag to a mother of five. The two men continued firing at Punchy until he fell. Witnesses later described them as having "olive complexions"—newspaper code for Italian. For Stevie and Frankie, the third time was indeed the charm. Punchy was pronounced dead at the Faulkner Hospital in Dorchester at 8:34 A.M. The cause of death was "multiple gunshot wounds of the heart, lungs, spleen, liver and intestines," as the coroner put it.

The housewife to whom Punchy handed the bag took it home where she opened it, saw the gun, and promptly fainted.

Rico had conveniently taken that day off to play a round of golf. But the next morning he showed up back at the garage. "Nice shooting," he told Flemmi and Salemme.

TEN DAYS LATER, Buddy McLean and two bodyguards were leaving the Peppermint Lounge on Winter Hill at midnight. Suddenly, on the sidewalk just outside the shuttered Capitol Theater across Broadway, Steve Hughes stepped from the shadows, raised an automatic rifle, and fired at Buddy, hitting him in the head. McLean died a few hours later. Both his bodyguards survived their wounds, but were returned to prison for parole violations.

The gang war continued.

JIMMY THE BEAR was still on the lam. And just as Punchy McLaughlin had struggled to support Georgie, Stevie was likewise hard-pressed to keep his fugitive brother in money. Stevie also needed cash for his estranged wife, and their two daughters. And now Stevie was living with another woman, the hot-tempered Marion Hussey, who had already borne him two illegitimate children. Stevie was paying all the bills for the Hussey household, which also included Marion's three children by her former husband. Stevie always had to be hustling, looking for new customers for his shylocking racket. He was continually starting up new businesses—a grocery store, a funeral home, a barroom. If they didn't pan out, Flemmi would just torch them for the insurance money. For Stevie, every day was a financial struggle.

Johnny Martorano wanted to help out the Flemmis, and he thought he hàd just the right place for the Bear to hide out in—the Brookline apartment that had been left to him by the working girl who'd also given him the Cadillac in which he'd murdered Bobby Palladino. Johnny had been staying there off and on for months, depending on how he was getting along with his various women.

One day in November 1965, Jimmy Martorano called the Brookline apartment looking for his brother. Jimmy the Bear picked up the phone, and after overcoming his surprise, Jimmy Martorano asked the Bear if he needed anything.

"Can you bring me a sandwich?" Flemmi said.

A couple of hours later, Jimmy Martorano arrived at his brother's apartment. A few seconds after he got inside, a posse of state and Brookline police burst through the door, accompanied by reporters and photographers from every paper in town. The cops claimed they had the apartment staked out and had seen someone raise a blind.

> I never believed that. There were only two people who knew the Bear was there—me and his brother, Stevie. I know I didn't tell the cops. The Bear had become a pain in the ass for everybody, but especially for his brother. I think Stevie tipped the cops to save himself some money.

Johnny Martorano was spending more time with Joe Barboza and his East Boston crew. At nights they could be found at the Ebb Tide, and they usually spent their days at Champi's Bar at the corner of Brooks and Bennington streets. They also rented the rooms upstairs, where they stored their guns and ammunition in a refrigerator, and generally terrorized the owner of the bar and everyone else in the neighborhood.

Like the Bear, the Animal was certifiably insane. But he liked a good time, and with his East Boston roots Johnny fit in well with the Barboza gang. The crew included Chico Amico, a former short-order cook in Malden whom Barboza treated like a younger brother, and Nicky Femia, a hulking thug who likewise never strayed far from Barboza's side. He'd been the driver on the Mickey Mouse Lounge hit. There was Dido Vaccari, to whom Barboza

Nicky Femia, one of Joe Barboza's top hands,
later worked for Whitey.

had confessed his role in the Deegan hit. Barboza also
had a younger guy named Patsy Fabiano, who was a sort
of mascot, comic relief, for the rest of the gang.

The crew also included Jimmy Kearns, Tommy De-
Prisco, and Arthur "Tash" Bratsos. Like so many Boston
hoods of the era, including Stevie Flemmi, Bratsos had a
brother in the Boston Police Department. Tash also had an
older brother, who had been a gangster in the South End,
and who, back in 1954, had gotten into a beef with Larry
Baione. Shortly thereafter, the older Bratsos brother disappeared. He had "gone to California," as they said in the
underworld. Baione had murdered the older Bratsos and
then disposed of his body.

Whenever Tash got drunk, which was often, he would
loudly proclaim his intention to kill Baione. Word had
long since gotten back to Larry, and he looked askance
not only at Tash, but at everyone who hung with him, and
that now meant Johnny Martorano.

• • •

LAST CALL AT Basin Street South was usually only the beginning of Johnny's nightly prowls through the city. There were always women, either working girls or girlfriends or both. One night, he was in bed with a married woman when her estranged husband burst into the bedroom, brandishing a pistol. He pulled the trigger, but the gun misfired. Johnny picked up a bottle and hurled it at the husband. The husband threw down the misfiring gun and ran out of the apartment.

One night at Basin Street Johnny met a girl named Barbara who'd just gotten into town from Florida. Somehow she'd hooked up with a wiseguy from the North End, a guy who years later would set up another girlfriend for a gangland hit by telling her to wear a cowboy hat to a bar. He told her the hat turned him on. That night, as she waited for her gangster boyfriend in the bar, two guys she'd never seen before walked in, looked for the woman wearing a cowboy hat, then headed straight for her and shot her in the head.

Johnny and Barbara hit it off immediately, and soon the hood from In Town was history. And Barbara was pregnant with Johnny's first son, John. He was born in 1965. Jimmy the Bear sobered up long enough to appear at his godson's christening.

Despite his increasing familial responsibilities, Johnny never let it affect his social life. Another night he and Jimmy Kearns were drinking at the Attic when they noticed a new working girl, a teenager, sitting alone at a table, weeping.

I went over and asked her what the problem was. She said she couldn't go home without at least a couple of hundred dollars for her pimp. She'd just had a baby and she'd fallen in with the pimp, and now she was living in his apartment in the Back Bay and he'd

Jimmy Kearns, a friend of Johnny's,
died in federal prison.

put her out on the street. She said that he just sat around the apartment, smoking pot, and blowing the smoke in the baby's face to keep him quiet. I was furious when I heard that.

I asked her if she wanted to get out and she said yes. I went back to our table and asked Jimmy Kearns if he was doing anything and he said no. Then I said, "Jimmy, let's go take a ride."

We drove over to the apartment with the girl and went in. I told the pimp the girl and the baby were going with us, and when he objected, I pistol-whipped him. I was hitting him so hard that somehow the trigger cut my middle finger at the bottom joint. To this day I still can't move it. Anyway, I ended up throwing the pimp out the window—his place was on the second floor.

We got the girl and her baby into the car and start driving away and Jimmy asked me, "Where are we going now?" And I said I have no idea. Jimmy smiled and said, "I see you have not thought this thing through." So we considered where we could take her, especially with a baby and all. Finally we remembered this pharmacist in East Boston, on Pembroke Street, near where Barboza and Jimmy and the rest of them hung out. This guy's wife had just died recently, so we knew he had room, and we figured maybe he'd take her and the baby in as a favor to us.

And he did, and shortly afterward, they were married. She was supposed to stay there for a couple of weeks and she ended up living with the guy 'til he died. I bring this up only because sometimes I really did help people back in those days.

A lot of nights in the mid-sixties, Johnny would eventually drift into Roxbury and its flourishing after-hours clubs. Roxbury was changing. Blacks had been moving into the neighborhood since the 1950s, but now the pace of migration was quickening. So was white flight, and the resentment of the departing white working classes was growing.

The increasing crime in the neighborhood bothered even the white gangsters from Roxbury, like the Flemmis. Soon the FBI's informants were reporting that the Flemmis' mother had been mugged near Boston City Hospital "by a couple of colored fellows." The Flemmis quickly moved out of Roxbury, to Mattapan, a predominantly Jewish neighborhood that, like Roxbury, would soon be devastated by a white exodus.

Johnny Martorano had no such worries. His Basin Street South was one of the few integrated nightspots in the city. But as time went on, the white presence in Roxbury began to fade, especially after midnight. In the after-hours joints in Roxbury, often Johnny would find only one other white man—a fellow gangster named Billy O'Sullivan. Billy O, as he was called, was a hard-nosed loan shark from Southie who had moved to Savin Hill in Dorchester. With six kids, he needed health insurance, so he'd finagled himself a no-show state job. He was a heavy drinker—at least six arrests for public drunkenness, and one for driving under. When Billy O drank, he'd sometimes start muttering about "the niggers." More than once, Johnny had to sidle up to Billy O in some crowded after-hours barroom in Roxbury to whisper, "I don't know how many guns you got on you, Billy, but you and me are gonna need 'em all to shoot our way out of here if you don't calm down and shut the fuck up."

At which point Billy O would laugh and then shut the fuck up.

One night in April 1966, Johnny bumped into Billy O. O'Sullivan told him he was opening a new after-hours club above the TV store on Dudley Street in Roxbury that was owned by Wimpy Bennett's older brother Walter. Directly across the street from Walter's Lounge, it was a good location for an after-hours spot, and Billy O invited Johnny to stop by on opening night. Martorano, always looking for a new place to party, said he'd be there.

The night before the opening, Barboza gang member

Billy O'Sullivan, a friend of Johnny's—and Whitey's.

Tommy DePrisco had stopped by a bar in South Boston with another friend of Johnny's. DePrisco had been trying to collect a loansharking debt from Tony Veranis, a twenty-seven-year-old ex-boxer who had been undefeated in twenty-six bouts until a head injury prematurely ended his pugilistic career in 1958. After that Veranis had drifted into petty crime, and since completing a stretch in state prison he'd been working construction. Looking for money Veranis owed him, DePrisco made a foolhardy move—walking into a strange bar in somebody else's neighborhood.

"There were twenty or thirty guys in the bar," Martorano recalled, "and they forced him to leave. He probably got a couple of whacks, and he got embarrassed."

After being roughly thrown out of the bar, DePrisco and the other guy waited around outside the barroom for Veranis to leave, but they never saw him. So they gave up and drove back across the bridge. Guys like Veranis, they knew, you always run into again.

The next night Johnny and Tash and their dates showed up at Billy O's new place around 3 A.M. The joint was packed. Everyone was standing around when a short, wiry young guy suddenly got in Johnny's face and began yelling at him. He was loaded, blind drunk.

"I'm Tony Veranis," he began, slurring his words. "You know who I am. I just had a beef with your friend. I kicked him outta Southie with his tail between his legs. Fuck him and fuck you, too."

He reached for his gun but Johnny beat him to it with his .38. Taller than Veranis, he fired down, into the ex-boxer's skull. Dozens of after-hours partygoers instantly vanished. Within seconds, the only ones left in the room were Johnny, Tash, their dates, and the proprietor, Billy O. Johnny handed some bills to the girls and told them to grab a cab home and keep their mouths shut. Then the three gangsters looked down at Tony Veranis's body. He

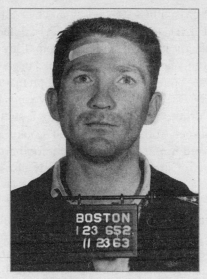

Tony Veranis, shot to death by
Johnny Martorano in 1966.

was lying on his back, mouth open, arms outstretched, his dead eyes wide open, an ever-larger pool of blood seeping out of his gaping head wound.

Billy O shook his head sadly. Opening night was going to be closing night. He glanced over at Johnny Martorano.

"Thanks, pal," he said.

Tash went down the stairs to get the car, while Billy O started cleaning up Tony Veranis's blood and brains. Johnny knew that after this, he owed Billy O—big time. When Tash came back, he and Johnny dragged the body downstairs, leaving Billy O to finish cleaning up. They put Veranis's body in the trunk of Tash's black Cadillac.

Johnny decided to dispose of the body in the woods, in Norfolk County. They drove through Milton into the Blue Hills, eventually dumping the corpse down a twenty-five-foot embankment. Then Tash noticed he needed gas, so they headed to an all-night service station on Route 128. It

Arthur "Tash" Bratsos, one of
two brothers murdered by Larry Baione.

was almost dawn when Tash reached into his coat pocket
and realized his wallet was gone.

They hurriedly drove back to where they had dumped
the body. After parking the car, they scrambled down
the embankment and saw Tash's wallet next to Veranis's
corpse. Less than half an hour later, the body would be
discovered by an early-morning jogger. The cops sur-
veyed his pockets, finding $2.83 in change and two keys.
On Veranis's fingers were tattooed the letters "l-u-c-k"
and "T-o-n-y."

The *Record-American* reported, accurately, that the
dead man was "in the toils of loan sharks." The *Globe* ran
a sob story by sports columnist Bud Collins, who had
known Veranis a decade earlier as a teenage welterweight.

"Nothing Tony Veranis ever did warranted his vicious
killing," Collins wrote. "He was a good kid, as nice as
I've met in sports. Confused, I guess, but trying to find
the right way. But he did something to offend the animals
that killed him. . . ."

So the cops couldn't totally write off Veranis's murder. A year later, one of the witnesses, a small-time hood himself, was asked by a Suffolk County grand jury if he had witnessed the killing. He refused to answer, was found guilty of contempt, and was sent to prison for several months.

Meanwhile, a South Boston man in jail awaiting trial for another killing bragged to his fellow inmates that he had killed Veranis. That was enough for the prosecutors—they indicted him, although he was acquitted after a trial.

A couple of days after killing Veranis, Johnny was leaving a joint in the Combat Zone when one of the guys from In Town asked him for a ride home. Johnny said sure, and as they were driving to the Mafia soldier's home, the made man lowered his voice.

"We heard your crew had some problems with that kid Veranis," the Mafia guy said. "So we took care of him for you."

"You did?" Johnny said. "Good work. Thank you."

IN 2002, IN Boston, Zip Connolly's lawyer asked Martorano about killing Veranis.

"He's another one reaching for a gun now," she asked. "Is that right?"

"Right, and another time I was faster than the other guy."

4

The Animal Flips

LAWYER: People can be killed for so much as talking to another associate in a bar, isn't that right?

MARTORANO: It happens.

LAWYER: Happened a lot, didn't it?

MARTORANO: The seventies and sixties were tough times.

BY 1966, THE FBI was keeping tabs on Johnny Martorano. The source of their information was his good pal, Stevie "the Rifleman" Flemmi. FBI agent H. Paul Rico had hoped to make Stevie's older brother, Jimmy, his informant, but that just hadn't worked out, what with Jimmy's drug habit, his indiscriminate murders, and his increasingly frequent trips to jail.

But Stevie, from the earliest days of his twenty-five-year career as a "Top Echelon" informant, was an endless font of information about the Boston underworld. The Bear's younger brother tried to keep his hand in every racket in the city. The more wiseguys he talked to, the more gangland gossip he could pass on to Rico, and the more protection Rico could provide for him. Plus there was the occasional $20 or $25 in cash Stevie would collect as an informant's fee, although decades later he would claim Rico had been pocketing the government money for himself.

Stevie Flemmi officially became an FBI informant, complete with identification number, in November 1965. In the first report on his latest catch, Rico conceded that Stevie "probably is the individual" who murdered Punchy McLaughlin, which in fact he was. That justified Rico's description of Stevie as "a very capable individual," if capable meant the ability to murder someone in broad daylight in front of dozens of witnesses at a busy bus station and get away with it.

Still, Rico pointed out that even very capable individuals have problems, which was why Flemmi "has no permanent residence at this time due to the fact that he realizes that if he established a permanent residence and the residence becomes known, an attempt would probably be made on his life."

STEVIE FLEMMI QUICKLY became one of the FBI's main sources of information about the Boston underworld—a hoodlum, as Rico pointed out, "known to have contacts in the criminal elements in Somerville, East Boston, South Boston and Roxbury, Mass."

The only missing link was In Town. Stevie never really got along that well with Jerry Angiulo and Larry Baione. He later claimed that when he was a young gangster back in the 1950s, In Town had declined to pay off on a $3,000 numbers hit, leaving him holding the bag. As he later explained it in court, "The only common denominator with them was crime. I certainly didn't play whist with them."

JOHNNY MARTORANO HAD already killed at least one person for Stevie Flemmi: Bobby Palladino. But Stevie had much greater plans in store for Johnny Martorano.

In June 1966, Flemmi discussed with Rico his plans to do away with Larry Baione. Johnny Martorano had been assigned an important role in the plot—as the fall guy. The first part of the plan was to invent a false story that would give Johnny a reason for wanting to murder Baione. Stevie concocted a story to involve the Martoranos in the murder he was planning, and then fed it to Rico, who dutifully put it into his next report:

> Informant advised that BAIONE definitely has "got to go." The only thing is that suspicion has to be thrown on to some other group. Informant advised that it is for this reason there was a story being manufactured now that indicates it is partially based on fact that the MARTORANO brothers are very disturbed over LARRY BAIONE and over the way one of BAIONE's associates slapped their [MARTORANOS] father around in Basin Street South.
>
> Informant advised that he is hopeful that if BAIONE is killed that suspicion will go to one of the MARTORANOS.

Johnny Martorano was, as usual, hustling. Basin Street South was a nice place to own, to hang out in, but profits were spotty. Overhead—with musical acts, a chorus line, and rent, among other expenses—was high. Bad weather, or a weak act, and the club could lose thousands in a weekend.

Johnny didn't spend all his time at Basin Street. Sometimes he would head into the North End. One of his regular after-hours haunts was Bobby the Greaser's joint on Commercial Street. Bobby the Greaser's real name was Bobby LaBella. He was a friend of Wimpy Bennett's, and he and Johnny hit it off well.

"If you ever need me to drive on a hit, I'm glad to help out," Bobby the Greaser would tell him. "Just don't ever ask me to lend you money. That is the one thing I will never do. That's bad business between friends."

Most often, though, if Johnny wasn't hanging at Basin Street, he could now be found at Enrico's, a little Italian dive on LaGrange Street, on the edge of the Combat Zone. It was owned by an in-law of Ralphie Chong, whose real name was Lamattina. Ralphie Chong was In Town through-and-through, on Larry Baione's crew, and a member of the mobbed-up family that rented Basin Street South to Johnny. Enrico's was a popular hangout for working girls between tricks, and that naturally attracted a certain male clientele that Johnny was all too happy to get acquainted with.

The state attorney general had his investigative offices nearby, and soon Johnny was hobnobbing with various plainclothes state police, among them Dick Schneiderhan. One night in Enrico's, when Schneiderhan was jumped by bikers, Martorano came to his defense, and a fast friendship formed. It was cemented when Johnny began wordlessly leaving him envelopes of cash in return for, say, the telephone numbers of bookie parlors that the staties or Boston police were tapping in preparation for raids. Even though Johnny didn't yet have any bookmaking operations of his own, having lists of targeted phone numbers made him a very valuable person for other wiseguys to know, and guys with access to that kind of inside police information were a lot less likely to get knocked off.

Another valuable acquaintance that Johnny made in Enrico's was a banker from Mission Hill named Donald B. Wallace. He'd stroll into Enrico's for the same reason most of the customers did.

He'd look around and say to me, "Say, Johnny, do you see that girl that was in here last week? You know, the blonde." So I'd look around, and if she was there, I'd

Massachusetts State Trooper Richard Schneiderhan,
one of Johnny's police sources.

pull her aside and get her a "date" with Wallace. I
mean, I wouldn't pay her off right there in front of
him. That would have been crass. But if the girl he
wanted wasn't there, there was always somebody else
I could send him out with. He wasn't exactly particular when he was out on the prowl after a few drinks.
Do you follow me?

As far back as Luigi's, Johnny had always dealt in stolen
goods he bought from "boosters"—burglars, most of
whom took out stores downtown. Now Johnny was

expanding his roster of burglars to include the more numerous gangs that specialized in robbing homes. Well into the sixties, millions of Americans still retained their old World War II–era habit of buying low-interest U.S. savings bonds, and then stashing them at home under a mattress, or in an antique strongbox.

"I used to have guys bringing me huge stacks of those E bonds, so thick they'd choke a horse. I wouldn't even bother to count 'em there'd be so many, I'd just throw the guy a few hundred. Pennies on the dollar. Take it or leave it. Nobody wanted those kinds of bonds."

But then of course Johnny had to unload them, at not that much of a markup. It was a minor racket, a low-return business. Until Johnny met Donald B. Wallace of the Lincoln Savings Bank, Roxbury, Massachusetts.

"He would pay me off on the face value—never saw anything like it, before or since. I still have no idea how he unloaded all those stolen bonds, but he did."

Wallace soon introduced Johnny to another scam: $1,000 no-collateral cash loans.

"Don was a good guy, always trying to help. All I had to do was come up with a real name, I guess so they could check the credit ratings. Not somebody famous—not Bobby Orr or Carl Yastrzemski. Just somebody real. He told me, as long as I made one payment on the loan—say, twenty bucks—then it was legal, and he could keep it on the books forever."

Pretty soon a lot of Johnny's friends were getting their car loans from Lincoln Savings. A notation in one of Rico's FBI reports from Stevie Flemmi noted that the mob had "married" him.

There were other ways for wiseguys to make money off their cars. Especially since one of Johnny's good friends, George Kaufman, always owned a garage. Whenever Martorano figured he'd waited long enough since his last "accident," he'd drive his car in to wherever Kaufman was

The Hughes brothers are taken into Boston police headquarters, 1965.

operating his garage that year. (Kaufman tended to change locations fairly often, because when his regular customers noticed the type of people who had taken to hanging out in his waiting room, business had a way of dropping off.)

Kaufman would put a dent in Johnny's car, then call one of his claims adjusters. Sometimes it took a small bribe to get the guy to inflate the value of the dent enough to make insurance fraud worth everyone's while. Other times, the adjuster would do it on the arm, especially if he owed money to one or another of the shylocks loitering in Georgie's waiting room.

• • •

TIME WAS RUNNING out for the Hughes brothers of Charlestown. In March 1966, they drove into an ambush outside Connie Hughes's little bungalow-style home in Malden. Just before shots rang out, neighbors heard a male voice scream: "How do you like that, you mother-fuckers?" Connie ran, but Steve was hit, and spent a month recuperating in Malden Hospital.

"They shot me like a dog," Steve Hughes told a relative. Connie, meanwhile, disappeared for a week before resurfacing at police headquarters in Malden with a lawyer.

On May 24, 1966, Connie and another of the lesser McLaughlins were hunting Howie Winter, who had taken over the Winter Hill gang since Buddy McLean's murder the previous fall. Connie Hughes took his investigation to a barroom on the Charlestown-Somerville line known as the Stork Club. Thirsty as usual, Connie lingered a bit too long in the shebeen. He was spotted by a young kid named Brian Halloran, who quickly called the Hill. By the time Hughes stumbled out of the bar long after last call, a dark sedan was ready to pick up his trail as he drove home to Malden.

Inebriated as he was, Connie still caught the play, and tried to escape on the Northeast Expressway near the Chelsea-Revere line. But his Nova was no match for the hit car, and when it pulled alongside, a gunner opened up with an M-1 army rifle. Between six and eight armor-piercing slugs struck the car. Two of them hit Connie in the head, killing him instantly. A few hours later, Steve Hughes identified his brother's body at the Northern Mortuary.

Steve Hughes was now the only "capable" McLaughlin still breathing, and on the street.

A week later, Stevie Flemmi reported in to Rico of the FBI. Flemmi, whom Rico identified interchangeably either by his own name or as "informant," reported that

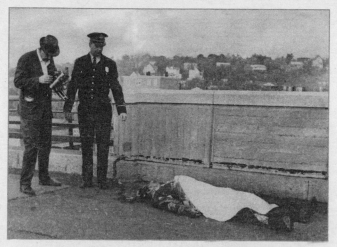

The end of the road for Connie Hughes, 1966.

Connie "had previously been around Dearborn Square, Roxbury, Mass., obviously in an effort to set him up for a 'hit.' The fact that CONNIE is now deceased is not displeasing to him. Informant was asked if he had an idea who committed the murder, and he advised that 'he had an excellent idea who committed the murder' but it would be better if he did not say anything about the murder."

BY THE FALL of 1966, both Johnny Martorano and Stevie Flemmi were lining up their next hits. Johnny was concerned about John Jackson, the black bartender who had been at Luigi's the night Margie Sylvester was murdered in 1964. After Palladino's killing the previous year, Jackson had wisely disappeared, but months later he reappeared in Boston as if everything had blown over. It hadn't.

Meanwhile, Stevie Flemmi and Frankie Salemme were setting up Steve Hughes. Hughes had gotten tight with Sammy Lindenbaum, a mob jack-of-all-trades from Revere; he was an abortionist and a shylock, among other

Sammy Lindenbaum, murdered with
Steve Hughes in Middleton in 1966.

things. The ex-con Lindenbaum had been born in Russia
in 1899, and as a youth had boxed under the name of
"Young Leonard." Every Friday he made collections from
his agents in the Lawrence area, and Steve Hughes started
accompanying him every week.

Lindenbaum was repeatedly warned by the Office to
stay away from Hughes, but he didn't take the hint. Down
in Providence, the Man finally shrugged and okayed the
hit. On the last day of his life, September 23, 1966, Lindenbaum seemed remarkably serene, considering how hot
Steve Hughes was. They enjoyed a long, leisurely lunch at
Blinn's Clam Stand in Bradford Hills, where the paunchy
Lindenbaum ordered his usual Friday feast: two lobster
rolls, french fries, and a side of fried clams. Then they
headed east on 125 to pick up 114. Lindenbaum's two Chihuahuas scampered around the backseat of his Pontiac
Tempest.

Suddenly a car described as a black Lincoln or Mercury with four occupants approached Lindenbaum's vehicle at high speed, pulling alongside.

"What appeared to be a pole protruded from the right passenger side of the front seat," the state police report said. "A series of sounds like the backfiring of a car was heard. The Pontiac car went out of control and tore away nine cement guardrail posts and came to rest about fifteen feet off the right shoulder of the highway in a swamp area."

No one got the license number of the black sedan. On Lindenbaum's body police found $1,060 in cash. Hughes was carrying $55. The cops also found a large number of betting slips. Inside Hughes's coat pocket was a fully loaded .38-caliber Smith & Wesson revolver with the serial number filed off.

Outside the wrecked, bullet-riddled car, in the tall swamp grass, Lindenbaum's two Chihuahuas were playfully scampering around. They had apparently climbed out of the shattered backseat window after the crash.

During the autopsy, in addition to the four bullets that had killed Hughes, the coroner discovered in his body another older bullet, left over from the shooting earlier that year in Malden.

Stevie Flemmi provided the underworld take on Hughes's death to Rico.

"On 10/10/66, informant advised that since STEVE HUGHES was murdered that the entire city is much more at ease."

NOT JOHNNY MARTORANO, though. By late September 1966, another grand jury was looking into the Margie Sylvester murder. Since John Jackson's return to Boston, he had been tending bar at a waterfront saloon called the Yankee Fisherman. Johnny started hunting for Jackson, prowling through the city at night, looking for his car—an easy-to-spot red convertible.

Jackson had moved back into his girlfriend's apartment at 102 Queensberry Street in the Fenway. That was where Johnny decided to take him, using a few of Barboza's guys as backup. In the early morning of September 28, 1966, they drove to the Fenway in Tash's black Cadillac, which had been used a few months earlier to dispose of Tony Veranis's body.

Tash and Jimmy Kearns would remain in the car, while Johnny and Tommy DePrisco would handle the hit.

Just after 3 A.M. they watched as his red convertible pulled into the parking lot of the apartment building. Armed with a shotgun, Martorano waited with DePrisco on the other side of the chain-link fence that enclosed the lot. Jackson got out of his car, and Martorano immediately fired, dropping the bartender. Tommy DePrisco's job was to get over the chain-link fence and, if necessary, finish off Jackson with a head shot. Revolver in hand, DePrisco climbed onto a wooden barrel next to the fence, figuring to use it to jump over the fence. But when he put all his weight on top of the barrel, it gave way, and he fell through the rotting wood into the barrel, which was full of fetid water.

John W. Jackson, potential grand-jury witness, murdered, by Johnny, 1966.

DePrisco began swearing loudly, which witnesses remembered when they were interviewed by the police later that morning. The newspapers reported that Jackson had recognized his killer, and had cursed him as he bled to death. Actually, Jackson had died instantly, without saying a word. The only guy screaming "Motherfucker!" that night was Tommy DePrisco.

A DAY LATER, the *Record-American* reported that Jackson "had a hunch that his days were running out." The reporters tracked down his mother in Cambridge, who told them, "My son wasn't a gangster." The cops found the shotgun, with two shells still in it, on the lawn outside the Russian Orthodox Church on Park Drive. It was a 12-gauge Remington, and it was quickly traced back to the Sears Roebuck in Cambridge, where the trail went cold. Someone had bought the weapon under an assumed name.

As always when he spoke to Rico, Stevie Flemmi dropped broad hints:

> Informant advised that JOHNNY MARTORANO has been hanging around with JIMMY KEARNS and TOMMY DE PRISCO and that these individuals were the type that could have murdered Jackson.
>
> The information regarding JACKSON was disseminated to Lt. SHERRY of the Boston PD on 9/28/66, and Lt. SHERRY advised that they do suspect MARTORANO as being responsible for this shotgun killing.

MARTORANO: I tried to talk to Bobby Palladino to find out the truth, but I never got to the truth. Jackson I killed because I didn't want to take a chance.

LAWYER: Did you ask Mr. Barboza to help you kill him?

> MARTORANO: I don't recall that. It's possible,
> though, because we were all hanging around to-
> gether at this time.
> LAWYER: And he would have helped you, right?
> MARTORANO: If I asked him.
> LAWYER: There were no discussions with Mr. Jack-
> son, right? It was purely a preventative measure?
> MARTORANO: Purely preventative.

Wimpy Bennett and Joe Barboza seemed well positioned to cash in big in the new post-gang-war order in the Boston underworld. They'd both been closely allied with the winning side, doing yeoman's work in tracking down the McLaughlins. Like the Mafia, Wimpy had also taken advantage of the cover provided by the gang war to rid himself of several longstanding rivals in the South End. Barboza had done likewise in East Boston. Both had handled contracts for In Town as well.

But neither Barboza nor Bennett really got along with the Mafia. At age forty-six, Wimpy was a throwback to the days when the Irish ran everything in Boston crime.

Wimpy's older brother, Walter, was more of a businessman. He owned at least two barrooms, and had been partners in various rackets with Larry Baione's brother, Petey. The oldest Bennett brother, Billy, was a bartender at Walter's Lounge in Uphams Corner. Wimpy got a cut of everything in Roxbury, including numbers, but his big racket was shylocking. Wimpy would loan, say, Stevie Flemmi cash at 1.5 percent a week, and Stevie would then put it out on the street at 5 percent.

After Steve Hughes's murder, it was easier for everyone to move around the city again at night. They didn't have to worry about being ambushed from the shadows, the way Buddy McLean and Jimmy Flemmi had been. Soon Stevie Flemmi and Frank Salemme were hanging out nightly with the North End crowd at the Bat Cove,

Peter Limone's club on Friend Street, where Larry Baione was a fixture.

Flemmi reported to Rico that he never drank heavily at the Bat Cove, because he didn't trust anyone from In Town. But Salemme lapped up the Mafia talk, and soon his friends were noticing that he was even starting to mimic Baione's vocal mannerisms. That did not bode well for Wimpy Bennett.

BOTH IN TOWN and the police wanted to rid themselves of Joe Barboza. A killing machine, he was useful in wartime, but now the war was over. The Mafia's own soldiers could handle the occasional housekeeping hit—the freelancer sticking up protected card games, the numbers runner skimming the week's football-card receipts. Anyone could handle such routine rubouts—that was how Jerry Angiulo saw it.

At the end of his life, in his 1976 ghostwritten autobiography, Barboza would brag that he was extorting vast sums of money from clubs in Boston. In reality, he was broke. He paid his top two guys, Chico Amico and Nicky Femia, $100 a week. Everyone else got $75.

Larry Baione was still concerned about Tash Bratsos trying to avenge his brother's murder. Night after night, Tash would sit at Enrico's in the Combat Zone, spinning out his fantasies about what he was going to do to Larry. Tash didn't seem to care about the owner's familial ties to In Town.

"I used to tell Tash," Martorano recalled, "if you're gonna kill somebody, either do it or shut the fuck up about it. Because the walls have ears, especially the walls in Enrico's."

The cops nurtured any number of grudges against Barboza. They didn't like his "James Bond car"—a 1965 gold Oldsmobile, a 360-horsepower whitewalled fuck-you to the police. Unbeknownst to the cops, Barboza had

had a specially built panel installed in the front door on the driver's side. It held three revolvers. The cops hated that car so much that when Barboza finally passed it on to gang associate Dido Vaccari, the cops quickly pulled Dido over. Unable to find any guns in the car—they never did discover the panel—they came up with an archaic statute to use against Vaccari. They charged him with "being abroad in the night." Later the police added a second charge of possession of a dangerous weapon, a bowling pin they'd found in the backseat.

Barboza had a big mouth, and when he was pulled over—which happened most nights—he would invariably start popping off and acting like he was the one with the badge. Despite his professed aversion to swearing around women, he had an off-putting habit of telling anyone who pissed him off that "you fuck your dead mother in the mouth!"

But somehow nothing ever stuck to Barboza. In July 1966, the cops thought they had him cold when he was arrested in the parking lot of the Tiger Tail nightclub on Revere Beach along with Nicky Femia and Chico Amico. They were all charged with stabbing a twenty-three-year-old ex-con named Arthur Pearson in the stomach. In the hospital emergency room, Pearson identified mug shots of all three gangsters. But after a visit from his two connected friends, Pearson recanted, saying he was "in a fog" when he fingered the three killers.

Brought before a judge, Pearson first took the Fifth Amendment—and then threw in the First, Fourth, and Sixth amendments for good measure. The judge found Pearson guilty of contempt and sentenced him to a year in jail. Pearson kept his mouth tightly shut until his release twelve months later.

"I knew if I talked I would be killed," he said later. "And my family would be killed."

•   •   •

EVENTUALLY, LAW ENFORCEMENT made a collective decision that the best way to get Barboza off the street once and for all would be to catch him with an unregistered handgun. Then the cops could lock him up for violating his parole, after which they would hang the habitual-offender tag on him. Barboza was already a convicted felon, and if they could make the habitual-offender tag stick, they could pack him off to Walpole more or less permanently.

Both the Boston and state police took runs at rousting Barboza with a gun, but his luck held until November 5, 1966. Barboza and the boys were driving around the Combat Zone in Tash Bratsos's black Cadillac when the cops pulled them over. They were laughing until Tash suddenly remembered: he'd left an unregistered .45 in the glove compartment.

Finally, they had Barboza. His bail was set at $100,000, and $50,000 for Nicky Femia. Tash got out on a lower bond and went to work with DePrisco, shaking down whoever they could to raise the bail money for their boss.

The Mafia sensed an opening. Tash was approached, and was told that after he and DePrisco raised whatever cash they could, In Town would make up the difference to get them to $100,000—the amount Barboza needed to make bail. It was explained to Tash as a goodwill gesture of sorts, for services rendered in the recent conflict.

"One night Tash came into Enrico's," Martorano said, "and all of a sudden he's talking about how the North End's not so bad after all. I thought to myself, *Uh-oh. They're lulling him to sleep.*"

On the last afternoon of his life, Tash was showing off at Champi's in East Boston, counting out seventy $1,000 bills onto the bar. He and DePrisco had $82,000 cash that evening by the time they arrived at the Nite Lite, a Mafia after-hours joint just down Commercial Street from Bobby the Greaser's. Larry Baione had told them to bring all the

Detective looks at the body of Tash Bratsos in the backseat of his Cadillac, which was used in four murders in 1966, the last of which was Tash's own.

cash they'd collected, so that In Town would know that their money was really going to pay Barboza's bail, and not for some scam. Patsy Fabiano was supposed to come in with them, but he begged off at the last moment, which saved his life. More than a dozen hoods from In Town were waiting for Tash and DePrisco. Barboza's two guys were beaten, shot, and stabbed to death. His bail money was whacked up among the killers.

The Mafia crew then dumped the bodies into the backseat of Tash's black Cadillac, which in the past seven months had also been used in the murders of Tony Veranis and John Jackson. The jinxed Cadillac was driven into Southie and left in the Lower End—a feeble attempt to make the cops think the murders had been committed by gangsters from Southie.

Wimpy Bennett was driving home from Bobby the Greaser's when he spotted Tash's Cadillac. He quickly put two and two together and tipped the Boston police. Just after dawn, when the cops arrived at the Nite Lite, they found John Cincotti, one of the sometime-owners of Basin Street South, trying to scrub the blood off the floor. Ralphie Chong, the owner of record, ended up getting a four- to five-year sentence as an accessory after the fact— the same charge that had landed Jimmy Martorano his first prison sentence.

In the Charles Street jail, Barboza went wild and ordered revenge.

WIMPY BENNETT WAS on the phone to Johnny Martorano.

"I just got a call from George," he said, using his code name for Raymond Patriarca. "He wants to see all of us."

Patriarca was trying to head off a new gang war in Boston before it could start. So he'd told Wimpy to round up the Martorano brothers and Frank Salemme. Wimpy was

Joseph "Chico" Amico,
Joe Barboza's best friend . . .

to bring everyone down to the Office, Patriarca's head-
quarters in the back of a vending-machine company on
Atwells Avenue in the Italian neighborhood of Federal
Hill in Providence.

"First and only time I ever went down there," Martorano recalled, "he just wanted to know our intentions,
where we stood. I talked more than the other guys. I said
I liked Tash and Tommy a lot. Tommy was just a kid from
Hyde Park, an ironworker. Tash bought him a suit and
made him a shy. But I told Raymond, it was really stupid
what Tash had been doing, threatening Larry like that all
the time. I said you really can't blame Larry for finally
killing him, and I'm not going to pick up the gun to
avenge that. I guess he heard what he wanted to hear, because that was the end of it."

But not for Joe Barboza.

HE WAS LOCKED up, but Barboza still had a few guys
out on the street—including Chico Amico and Jimmy
Kearns. Despite everything, Amico and Kearns were still
hanging out at Enrico's. One night Amico spotted a Mafia
soldier there and slapped him around, saying, "That's for
Larry." Then he mentioned that he and Kearns were going up to Alphonse's Broken-Hearts Lounge in Revere,
another Mafia hangout.

They got there, had a couple of drinks, and then stood
up to leave. One of the guys they'd been drinking with
walked over to the window and rapped on it, loud enough
to be heard by several guys with rifles in a car with stolen
Wisconsin license plates. The Wisconsin car followed
Chico Amico's car out of Alphonse's parking lot. Kearns
was driving. They hadn't gotten far when J. R. "Joe" Russo,
a young East Boston Mafioso, opened fire with a carbine.

The first shot went through the back window and into
the back of Amico's head, killing him instantly. They
kept firing, but even though he was shot in the back,

. . . and the East Boston Mafioso who
killed him, J. R. "Joe" Russo.

Kearns was able to continue swerving until he finally ran off the road, down an embankment, and into a ditch. He survived. A few hours later, just before Kearns was brought into the Charles Street jail, all bandaged up, detectives arrived at Barboza's cell to break the news to him about Chico.

"I just sat stunned," the Animal recalled in his 1976 book. "No matter who died it affected me, but Chico's death affected me the worst. He was like my son, my brother, my partner."

Joe Barboza would have his revenge, but now it wouldn't be on the street, it would be in a courtroom.

WIMPY BENNETT NEVER saw it coming. He got it in the garage in January 1967. Stevie Flemmi had accused Peter Poulos, the gang's bookkeeper, of stealing money from their numbers racket. He pulled a gun and put it to Poulos's head. Poulos denied stealing the money, and said

Peter Poulos, taken for a ride in the
Nevada desert by Stevie Flemmi.

he'd given it to Wimpy. According to Salemme's sworn
testimony in 2003, he stepped in and told Stevie that he
needed to ask Wimpy directly.

So we got Wimpy up there either that night or the
next night at six o'clock. There was a meeting with
everyone there. And the next thing you know, Peter
put it right on him, I gave the money to you, and you
did it before. Bennett couldn't even explain himself,
and so Flemmi took the pistol out and shot him in
the head.

They buried Wimpy out in Hopkinton, at a shooting
range they'd used for target practice during the recent
gang war. The next morning, George Kaufman sold
Wimpy's car to someone for $6,000—or so Stevie later
told the feds. But there was more to Wimpy's murder than

just money, as important as money was to Stevie. As Johnny Martorano saw it, there was also underworld status involved.

"They wanted to impress Larry. Killing Wimpy makes 'em big shots down at the Bat Cove. It was a two-birds-with-one-stone thing. Same with Larry. He had two reasons for wanting Wimpy dead. Number one, Wimpy was Irish, which he didn't like, and number two, Wimpy was too sneaky for Larry."

Soon the newspapers were reporting that Wimpy the Fox had vanished—"missing from usual haunts . . . foul play suspected . . ." "rubout victim?" Flemmi assured the FBI that there was "absolutely no hope of finding BENNETT alive," as if Rico didn't know.

Walter was the next Bennett brother to go, in April. He'd been noticed lurking around Larry Baione's neighborhood in Jamaica Plain. Bennett had figured out the Mafia angle, Salemme said.

"The word got out that Stevie Flemmi did it for the Italians, for lack of a better—the guineas is what he [Walter] said."

Walter, however, still trusted Salemme and Poulos. As Salemme explained, that was Walter Bennett's fatal mistake.

We lured Walter to the garage to a meeting with me at six o'clock one night. Peter Poulos drove him to the garage, and I had a big door that you press a button to open. It was a huge garage, and he drove in and walked up the stairs to the office. Stevie was waiting at the end of the stairs, shot him, and he took him out to the car.

They buried him next to Wimpy in Hopkinton. Two Bennetts down, one to go.

•   •   •

BARBOZA WAS SHIPPED off to MCI-Walpole in January 1967. He was doing four-to-five. The Bear had also ended up there, on a parole violation, and Nicky Femia was also doing time at Walpole, on the same gun charge they'd used to take Barboza off the street. It looked like they'd all be gone for a good long time. The owner of Champi's even screwed up his courage long enough to appear at a Boston Licensing Board hearing to beg the city not to revoke his liquor license. The man had been living in abject fear, an East Boston detective testified on his behalf. Why, Nicky Femia, the tenant of record, hadn't even been paying rent on the upstairs apartment where they stashed their arsenal in an old Frigidaire.

"I'm a victim of circumstance," the owner of Champi's told the board. "That's all I can say."

MEANWHILE, STEVIE STARTED driving down to visit his brother more often after murdering Wimpy. Johnny Martorano would often go along for the ride. Johnny would talk with Barboza while Jimmy Flemmi would huddle with his brother. A couple of times the Flemmis got into fistfights in the visiting room. After the brothers finished their private conversations, they'd switch off—Stevie would sit down with Barboza and Johnny with the Bear.

The FBI, in the persons of H. Paul Rico and Dennis Condon, would soon be paying Barboza a recruiting visit, and Martorano thinks he knows now what Stevie was discussing in hushed tones with Barboza and his brother.

If one of them was going to flip, which one would be the better witness, Barboza or the Bear? Barboza was looking at serious time, while Jimmy was about to get out. Plus, if Jimmy flips, it's all over for Stevie too. So you'd want Barboza to do it, but then you've got the Deegan problem. The Bear was in on that hit, you've got witnesses in Chelsea who remember seeing a bald guy in the front seat. Who else can that be but the Bear? They had to get that whole Deegan thing straightened out, one way or the other.

More than thirty years later, as they all sat in the Plymouth House of Correction, awaiting their trial on federal racketeering charges, Salemme put it directly to Flemmi. He asked his old partner if he had gone down to Walpole to broker the deal for the FBI, arranging to turn Barboza into a rat, in order to protect his brother the Bear.

"He didn't deny it," Salemme told the prosecutors in 2003. "He said, what could I do? You know, he's my brother. . . . He said, I had to protect my brother. I accused him right out, you went up there for this guy, Rico. He just put his head down and was nodding his head yes."

It didn't take long for Barboza to agree to all of the FBI's demands—that he put the finger on everyone in the top hierarchy of the New England Mafia. He tied Patriarca to a contract hit on two brothers in Providence who had started a card game on Federal Hill that was not "protected." He fingered Jerry Angiulo for setting up the murder of an ex-boxer who'd been sticking up Mafia-protected dice games known as barbooth. As an added personal bonus on that one, Barboza named as the shooters several of the same hoodlums who had killed Chico Amico.

Finally, Barboza accused three made LCN members—Henry Tameleo, Peter Limone, and Louie Grieco—of having taken part in the 1965 Deegan slaying.

To explain away the bald man in the front seat the night Deegan was murdered, Barboza replaced his bald friend the Bear with the doorman at the Colosseum nightclub, Joe "the Horse" Salvati. Barboza swore that Salvati had donned a "bald wig" before going into the alley to shoot Deegan.

Three of the men framed by the FBI for the
murder of Teddy Deegan: (top left) Peter Limone,
(top right) Henry Tameleo, and Joe "the Horse" Salvati.

The Federal Witness Protection Program had just been
started. Barboza was a one-man pilot program, an experi-
ment of sorts. Now the feds would find out if they could
protect a witness from Mafia retribution. They moved
Barboza from safehouse to safehouse, including jails and
islands owned by the Coast Guard, as well as gated com-

pounds they rented north of Boston in Essex County along the coast.

One day in early 1968, Johnny Martorano got a call from his old pal Barboza, whom the newspapers had taken to calling "the Canary" or "the Turncoat."

"I was living in Lynn with some girl, and he tracks me down somehow. I don't know where they had him stashed at the time. He says to me, listen, I consider you a friend, I'm not going to bother you. But I gotta do this and I'm not concerned with who's guilty or innocent. I just don't want you coming in and calling me a liar."

Johnny had of course followed Barboza's story as it unfolded in the papers. But to actually hear Barboza calmly explain how he planned to lie, under oath, in a capital murder case, was still a shock. Barboza obviously remembered that he'd told Johnny who had really killed Deegan.

"I think you're wrong, Joe," Martorano told him. "I don't think this is the right thing to do."

"That's it," Barboza said. "This is what I'm gonna do." Then he hung up. They never spoke again.

JOHNNY STILL DIDN'T care much for Jerry Angiulo or Larry Baione. But he couldn't stand by as Barboza railroaded guys who'd had nothing to do with the murder of Teddy Deegan. He called the Dog House, and asked for a sit-down with Jerry Angiulo.

Dido Vaccari had already stopped by 98 Prince Street to tell Jerry's brother Danny Angiulo what Barboza had told him about the Deegan hit. If necessary, Dido was ready to take the witness stand to impeach Barboza's testimony. Now it was Johnny's turn to lay it all out to the underboss. Johnny said he was also willing to testify if it came to that, to recount under oath what Barboza had told him about the murder itself, and his plans to commit perjury.

For once, Jerry Angiulo was polite, gracious. It's a generous offer, he told Johnny, but it's not necessary. It's all bullshit. Everybody knows it's bullshit. Why, Louie Grieco was in Florida when Deegan got hit, and he can prove it. Plus he's a World War II hero—decorated veteran, combat, European theater. As for Joe the Horse, he owed Barboza a couple of hundred bucks, and when Barboza was in the can and sent somebody over to get the dough, the Horse told Barboza's guy to go fuck himself. If the Horse had just ponied up fifty bucks, Jerry went on, he wouldn't be in this jam, but what are you gonna do now? Plus, Barboza's admitted killing like twenty-six people. Who's gonna believe him?

As he left 98 Prince Street, Johnny was reassured. No way a jury would ever believe Barboza, right?

THE MAFIA, THOUGH, was a lot more worried than Jerry Angiulo was letting on. They put out a $300,000 contract on Barboza. And then they decided to whack Barboza's new lawyer, John Fitzgerald.

He was the son of a minister, with five children, but despite the squeaky-clean image he acquired later, Fitzgerald was in fact a rather shady character, even by the standards of mob lawyers. He was running around with a gangland groupie, and he had taken over the payments on Joe Barboza's gold Oldsmobile. Earlier he had represented Georgie McLaughlin—enough in itself to make him persona non grata with much of Boston's underworld. Now he was Joe Barboza's mouthpiece.

Stevie Flemmi and Frank Salemme drew the assignment from their new Mafia friends at the Bat Cove: hit Fitzgerald. But first Stevie needed to handle one more pressing piece of personal business in Roxbury: clipping the last of the Bennett brothers, Billy.

On December 22, 1967, after speaking to Flemmi, Rico filed this report:

STEVIE FLEMMI indicated that they are going to have to do something about Wimpy Bennett's brother . . . as he has accused them of being responsible for the murder of his brothers and he has indicated that he is going to kill him.

As he sometimes did when writing about Flemmi, Rico quoted Stevie as "informant" as he described his own plans.

Informant advised that FLEMMI and SALEMME will probably take out Bennett because they have much better connections and information on Billy's activities than he has on their activities.

Stevie and Frankie had an ace in the hole. After the murders of his two brothers, Billy trusted almost no one in the underworld, but he remained close to two hoods named Richard Grasso and Hugh "Sonny" Shields, whom he recruited for his mission of revenge. In a section of an FBI report that was later heavily redacted, Rico wrote that one of them, probably Grasso, "has made a mistake and is out to 'clear himself.' "

Namely, by setting up Billy Bennett. Which Grasso did on the day after Rico filed his report about Billy Bennett's imminent murder. It was almost Christmas, and Billy was seldom venturing outside his modest Mattapan home, but this snowy evening, Grasso picked him up in his car. Wearing a shoulder holster with a loaded .38, Billy hopped in the front seat. Sonny Shields sat in the back. Following behind at a discreet distance was another car, with Flemmi and Salemme. They had a plan—they would let Grasso and Shields shoot Bennett and then they'd all head out to Hopkinton for yet another unceremonious burial. That way, they used to joke, the Bennetts could all play bid whist together.

Hugh "Sonny" Shields did not age well during the
gang wars of the 1960s.

They were also planning to kill Grasso and Shields.
What better way than for Grasso to "clear himself" of
whatever he'd done than by being shot to death?

According to testimony in a later murder trial, the
plan went awry as Grasso was driving Billy Bennett
through Mattapan. Bennett spotted Shields pulling a
gun out of his coat, and tried to jump out of the car. According to prosecutors, as Bennett opened the door,
Shields fired, killing him. The force of the bullet pushed
Bennett's body out of the car, into the street, and up
against a snowbank. A cab was coming in the other direction, which left Grasso no choice but to drive off,
leaving Bennett's body in the street. There would be no
third Bennett brother for that ghostly bid-whist game
out in Hopkinton.

In that same state murder trial, a witness would testify
that while Bennett's body was still lying in the street,
Stevie Flemmi called a Boston cop, the same one who
five years earlier had gotten the warrant to go into the at-

tic at Luigi's to find Margie Sylvester's body. The witness said Stevie wanted the cop to confirm for them that Billy Bennett was dead.

But the cop would later be acquitted, as would Sonny Shields. Grasso didn't live long enough to stand trial. Grasso ended up shot twice in the head, his body then thrown into the trunk of his car—the Billy Bennett death car. Grasso's car was then dropped off in Brookline, in Norfolk County—a clever ploy designed to ensure minimum police interest in the murder.

From experience, the gangsters understood that if possible, it was always a good idea to dump any corpse in a different police district in Boston than where the murder had actually been committed. It was even better to unload the stiff in a different city or town, and best of all to leave the body in a different county—that really created a jurisdictional nightmare for law enforcement, trying to figure out where the murder had been committed, which determined who would be stuck handling the dead-end investigation. It could get messy, and the last thing cops and prosecutors want is a mess, especially in an organized-crime murder case.

Once Grasso's body was found in Brookline, the Boston cops pretty much washed their hands of the murder. Stevie Flemmi had expected nothing less. This was what he paid them for.

WITH BILLY BENNETT dead, only one piece of unfinished business remained with the Bennetts. Stevie Flemmi wanted the brothers' shylocking records. If Stevie had the ledger books, that would prove that he, and not the Bennetts, was the loan shark of record. He could continue collecting in Wimpy's name. It would be a score worth hundreds of thousands of dollars. Stevie knew that Billy had gotten the books from Walter before either of them had been murdered, but the question now was, how could Stevie spirit them out of Billy's house?

Billy's wife, Louise, stricken with multiple sclerosis, would never open the door to Stevie, or Frankie. It would take someone above reproach to get inside to grab the ledgers.

It would take H. Paul Rico of the FBI.

Rico showed up on Louise Bennett's doorstep in Mattapan, immaculately dressed as always, offering his condolences to the grieving widow. It was imperative, he told her, that she immediately hand over any records that could be used to implicate her in the nefarious criminal enterprises of her late brothers-in-law, not to mention the fact that it just wasn't safe to keep such records around with the likes of such a notorious killer as Stevie Flemmi still at large.

But Billy had carefully instructed his wife: trust no one, especially cops, even the FBI. Especially the FBI. So she told Rico that she had nothing to turn over, that she had no idea what he was talking about. Rico worked it from every possible angle, until he finally gave up and left, without leaving behind a business card. No paper trails for Rico.

It was one of the few times Rico ever failed his friends in the underworld. But by now he had more pressing matters to attend to. His new star witness, Joe Barboza, was about to begin his career as a mob canary. First he could testify against Raymond Patriarca down in Providence, then against Jerry Angiulo in Boston, and finally, in the Teddy Deegan murder case.

But before the Deegan trial could even start, Stevie Flemmi got himself beaten up at Basin Street South.

5

Bwana Johnny

LAWYER: When you met [Hubert] Smith and killed him, you got into a car with him. Is that right?

MARTORANO: Yes, I did.

LAWYER: There were two teenagers with him, isn't that right?

MARTORANO: When I met him in Roxbury, there was three people in the car, and I took it to be three guys. It was the middle of a snowstorm at two in the morning.

LAWYER: How far away were you from Mr. Smith when you shot him?

MARTORANO: A foot.

LAWYER: And people in the car were right next to him, isn't that right?

MARTORANO: Was the middle of winter. They were dressed in winter clothes, and I just got in the car and started shooting. . . . He was supposed to be alone. I saw three—what I took—what I believed was three men, and I said to myself I better shoot fast because they may have the same thing on their mind for me as I have for them.

LAWYER: And you didn't look to see if the people—
MARTORANO: I just shot three times. After the first
flash, it was just shadows.

WHEN STEVIE FLEMMI got excited, he would stutter. His speech would dissolve into sentence fragments, as if he were too angry to put together a coherent thought. On the morning of January 6, 1968—early in the day for Stevie to be up—he was stuttering and spitting out his words.

He was talking on the phone to Johnny Martorano, and he was in a rage.

"Basin Street . . . down there looking for you . . . got a beating . . . that big nigger Smith . . . motherfucking nigger . . . your fuckin' place, Johnny . . . they held me down . . . what the fuck. . . ."

At first Johnny couldn't believe such a thing could happen at Basin Street. All through the '60s, the club kept changing hands, going back and forth between the Martoranos and the Lamattinas. In early 1968, it was the Lamattinas' club. But as far as everybody in the city was concerned, Basin Street would always be Johnny Martorano's place. He still hung there, it was where you went first if you were looking for him. And Johnny still owed Stevie—at least that was the way Johnny figured it, and that was how Stevie saw it, too. Stevie had tipped Johnny that Palladino and Jackson were going to testify against his brother Jimmy. Of course it wasn't true, but Johnny Martorano wouldn't know that for another thirty years.

"Motherfucker held me from behind, Johnny . . . give me a beating . . . sapped on the head . . . Johnny, your place."

Johnny told Stevie he would take care of it. All day, he could think of nothing else. He didn't really know this Smith. Smitty, everybody at Basin Street called him. Lived in Dorchester, about forty-seven years old. Johnny would have to figure out what had happened, and there was only one way to do that. He would seek out Smitty and ask him directly. That night, a Friday, Johnny met up with another of his buddies, Steve Brucias—Steve the Greek. The Greek lived on Dudley Street with his two teenaged kids, whom he was raising alone. He owned a piece of a bar out in Hyde Park. Johnny filled him in on what had happened the previous night.

The next day, a detective from the BPD vice squad would file a report about the scene at Basin Street South a few hours before the murders: "I see Smitty in Basin Street every night. I get there between 1:15 and 1:30 A.M. He was drinking Friday night which is very unusual. He is usually on the door but Friday night two young colored kids were on the door, dressed in sport jackets like the band."

The detective saw Johnny Martorano there, too— "dressed in a black cloth coat, white shirt and a tie. I have seen Martorano in a 1967 or 1968 black Pontiac two-door H.T. [hardtop]."

Even though snow was forecast for after midnight, Basin Street was hopping. When Johnny arrived, he spotted Smitty sitting by himself at the bar, sipping a drink. Johnny told Brucias he needed to talk to Smitty alone, so Brucias went down to the other end of the bar while Johnny parked himself on the stool next to Smitty and bought him a drink, then another, and another.

"I said to him, 'I heard Stevie was in here last night and he got a beating.' And he says, 'Yeah, yeah.' I says, 'What happened?' And he says, 'Stevie was way outta line.' That's all he said, 'Way outta line.' I says to him, 'This is a friend of mine, Stevie, he comes down here and you give him a beating?' "

What Johnny didn't know, what Stevie hadn't told him, was that the reason it wasn't such a big deal to Smith was because he'd just been following orders—from Rocco

Lamattina and John Cincotti, the two Mafia soldiers who at that moment ran Basin Street. When he pinned Stevie's arms back, Smitty had just been doing what he was told to do.

> What I find out later is, Stevie's been shylocking to Rocco's son. Now, Rocco is a loan shark himself. Stevie shouldn't be doing this. And now he's down in Rocco's own place—which is what Basin Street was at that point—looking for Rocco's kid, over 300 bucks. I didn't know this, but it was actually Stevie who was out of line, not Smith. Smith was a big guy, so he grabbed Stevie's arms while Rocco and Cincotti worked him over. And of course Stevie is humiliated, but he can't do nothing about the two Mafia guys, so he blames it all on the black guy. That's when he calls me.

An FBI informant later recounted the incident in vague terms, perhaps not realizing the connection to the three murders:

> Informant stated that recently STEVIE FLEMMI had been beaten up over $300. FLEMMI had tried to collect and met some fast talk. FLEMMI later went back to a bar where he was beaten up by a Negro bartender . . . Informant stated that STEVIE FLEMMI was in pretty bad shape; however, stated that he would take care of the matter himself.

By calling Johnny Martorano again.

At Basin Street that cold Friday night in January, Johnny Martorano continued pumping Smith for information, asking him the same questions over and over again. Smith either didn't think it was that big a deal, or he believed that he shouldn't be talking about the Lamattinas' family business. He was observing the underworld code, and it was about to cost him his life.

"He kept giving me all the wrong answers," Johnny Martorano said. "He didn't give me any respect. All he had to do was say, 'I didn't know he was your friend. I'm sorry.' That's all he needed to say. It would have been a whole different ballgame."

Finally Johnny drifted away, back to the other end of the bar, where the Greek had been watching them silently, drinking steadily. Over the din of the band and the drunken conversation, Johnny recounted to the Greek what Smitty had told him.

The Greek was drunk, so his instant recommendation was to kill Smith. Johnny agreed. Now he had to figure out a way to get Smith alone so that he could kill him. A new after-hours card game had just started in Roxbury, so Johnny went back to Smith and asked him if he was going over there after last call.

Smith nodded, sure. Johnny said he'd never been there, wasn't sure exactly where it was. Why don't I meet you somewhere, he said to Smith, and then we can go over together. Smith agreed, so Johnny told him he'd catch up with him on Normandy Street, but first he had to pick up some money for the game.

Smith was okay with that, so Johnny left. But he wasn't going to pick up some money; he was going out to get a gun.

JOHNNY AND BRUCIAS drove to the Greek's place on Dudley Street. The Greek ran upstairs and returned with an untraceable .38-caliber snub nose, five or six shots. Then they drove to Normandy Street, where they saw Smith's 1967 Mercury station wagon. By now it was snowing heavily; there were already several inches on the ground. It was a little after 3 A.M. on the morning of January 7, 1968.

• • •

SMITH HAD THE Mercury idling, and Johnny could see the exhaust. At the corner, he told the Greek to circle the block and come back and pick him up. Johnny got out and trudged through the snow toward the Mercury. He immediately noticed that there were three people inside, and he thought to himself, he'd better shoot fast. He had his hand on the gun as he got into the car. The first one he shot was Smith, in the driver's seat. The other two Johnny could barely see because he'd been practically blinded by the flash of the first shot. He later told cops all of the shooting had taken no more than three seconds. He had shot all of them behind the ear.

LAWYER: It's not your testimony that if you saw it was a woman, you would have stopped it, is it?
MARTORANO: If I knew it was a woman, I wouldn't have done it. But I couldn't stop and leave people behind.
LAWYER: Because is it your testimony that you don't kill women?
MARTORANO: Positively not.

The Mercury was full of smoke from the gunshots. There was no sound in the car, no moans. They were all dead. Johnny reached into the front seat, turned off the ignition, grabbed the keys, but left the headlights on. Then he got out of the car and started walking slowly down Normandy Street, toward Blue Hill Avenue, expecting Steve Brucias to pull up at any moment. But the Greek never returned.

IT WAS 3:30 in the morning. Johnny's prospects looked bleak. He was a white guy, in Roxbury, in a snowstorm, covered with blood. He had to get away from the scene, but first he had to get rid of the gun. There was an alley just before Blue Hill Avenue, so he dumped the gun and the shells under a pile of trash and snow. He threw the car keys as far as he could, into the snow, then walked out to Blue Hill Avenue and got lucky. He hailed down a cab. He told the cabbie, stop at the first pay phone you see, and then wait. Johnny called Stevie at Marion Hussey's house and told him he was coming over, and that it was important.

Then he had to get directions to Marion's place because he'd never been there. It was in Dorchester. When Johnny finally got there, he paid the cabbie and sent him away. He explained to Stevie what had happened, and Stevie gave him one of his coats, which was a little small on Martorano. Johnny handed his own bloody coat to Stevie, and he never saw it again. Then Johnny told Stevie, let's go back and find the Greek; he's still out there somewhere looking for me.

They drove back to Roxbury, not getting too close to Normandy Street, but they couldn't find the Greek anywhere. As they started making the rounds of the after-hours joints, they could hear sirens in the distance, but that was nothing out of the ordinary in Roxbury. Finally they spotted the Greek's car outside one of the clubs, so Johnny walked in and saw Brucias sitting there, playing cards.

Johnny asked him, what happened to you?

"I got stuck around the corner," the Greek said. "We'll do it tomorrow."

Johnny shook his head. There is no tomorrow, he told Steve the Greek. It's over. Now get outta here and go home.

THE THREE BODIES were taken to the Southern Mortuary, where they were identified. The victim in the back-seat was Douglas Barrett, age seventeen. In his pockets, police found one quarter and "a package of Tip-Top cigarette papers." It has never been established what he was doing in the station wagon with Smith.

In the front seat was the body of a teenaged girl who would have turned twenty on February 4—Elizabeth Frances Dixon, better known as Liz. She was unemployed, a graduate of St. Joseph's, a parochial girls' high school in Roxbury. She had taken up in recent weeks with Smith, despite the age difference. The papers would describe her as a "go-go dancer."

"She thought Smith was real nice," a neighbor told police. "Sometimes I ask her where she is going and she would say Basin Street and I would say, 'Do you think that is a nice place to go to?' And she said, 'Mother said I will be all right.'"

Another neighbor told the cops: "She talked about Smitty as if he was a friend. She smoked as much as I do. I think her brand was Kools."

According to the homicide report, Dixon's head "was resting against the driver's right knee. There was a cigarette case in her hand. This case fell to the floor of the car when her body was removed."

IN ADDITION TO his topcoat, Smith was wearing a brown tie and a white shirt when he died. The inventory of his personal effects turned up a black onyx ring on his right ring finger, two wallets that contained a total of $64 cash, and a slip of paper that said, "Smitty, Tina was in here to see you."

The police also recorded that he was wearing a "Timex watch, still running, indicating correct time."

AFTER LEAVING THE Greek, Stevie Flemmi drove Johnny to his girlfriend Barbara's place in Quincy. On the way, neither one of them said much. It was almost dawn. Johnny slept fitfully for a couple of hours, then borrowed

Barbara's car to drive back to Boston to have breakfast in a diner on Mass Ave with Stevie and Frankie Salemme.

By this time, I'd heard on the radio that there was a woman in the car. I was very upset with myself. Then, at the diner, Stevie and Frankie asked me, do you want us to kill the Greek for you? I said no. If they clipped him his two kids, I don't know what would have happened to them. Their mother wasn't around. I told them, just tell him to go to the Cape, go away, I never want to see the guy again.

THE POLICE INVESTIGATION reached a dead end very quickly. It wasn't until later that Johnny learned what had happened at Basin Street the night before he killed three people in the snow on Normandy Street. He never discussed the murders again with Stevie, and certainly not with the two guys from In Town who had worked over Stevie as the late Hubert Smith pinned Flemmi's arms behind him.

"What could they say? If they indicate to me that they know what happened, then they'll have a problem. What are they gonna say anyway? They're just glad they weren't there that night, or the same thing might have happened to them."

THE NEWSPAPERS' FRONT pages were full of Joe Barboza stories, each one more fantastic than the last. He was holed up on Thatcher's Island in Rockport, and the feds were guarding him, the Sunday *Globe* reported, "against a possible intrusion by torpedoes, machine guns or aerial bombs."

The *Record-American* reported that a Chicago hitman had gotten himself arrested for public drunkenness, then used his court appearance to scout out the security measures in the Pemberton Square courthouse. His verdict on the odds of successfully killing Barboza there: "Mission: Impossible."

After the district attorney received death threats, the Boston police assigned their best man to the job of guarding his office—a Medal of Honor recipient from World War II. Barboza was whisked about the Boston area in helicopters and police motorcades. Newspaper readers learned the name of his dog (Zero), as well as his preference in cigarettes (English Ovals, a pack and a half a day). When he was scheduled to appear before a Suffolk County grand jury, police dogs were reportedly released the night before, to roam the darkened corridors of the sixth floor, where the grand jury met, to guard against any possible assassins from La Cosa Nostra.

Barboza's first court appearance came in January 1968, when he testified against Jerry Angiulo and the three hoodlums he'd allegedly convinced to murder Rocco DiSeglio, an ex-boxer with whom the other three had been sticking up Mafia-protected card games.

On January 18, 1968, Jerry and his codefendants were all acquitted. Outside, on the courthouse steps, the Mafia underboss of Boston talked to the press, saying, "I was in the navy during World War II. Now I know what I was fighting for. I want to go home to my poor old mother."

Twelve days later, as Barboza's lawyer, John Fitzgerald, was climbing into Barboza's gold Oldsmobile in Everett, he was almost killed by a bomb that had been planted under the hood by Stevie Flemmi and Frankie Salemme.

THIS TIME THEY had gone too far. They could kill one another as much as they pleased, but Fitzgerald had a reputation, however undeserved, as a straight arrow. They'd tried to shoot him two nights earlier, driving around his neighborhood, looking for the James Bond car. They had ended up killing the wrong guy, a civilian who had the misfortune to be driving a similar Olds.

The day his car was bombed, Fitzgerald had left his law office late in the afternoon. He was carrying two guns. Suspecting that his office phone had been tapped by the Mafia, Fitzgerald walked across the street to a drugstore and used the pay phone to make a few calls. His last one was to H. Paul Rico of the FBI. It was a rainy day and Fitzgerald hadn't bothered to set the car alarm. As he always did, Fitzgerald kept the door open and his left leg outside the Olds while he turned the ignition and put his foot to the accelerator. When he did, two sticks of dynamite exploded.

"The windshield began breaking into a thousand pieces," he wrote later, "as if someone had hit it with a sledge hammer. Fragments were coming at me and there was a grinding effect. It felt like my teeth were tearing my jaw apart."

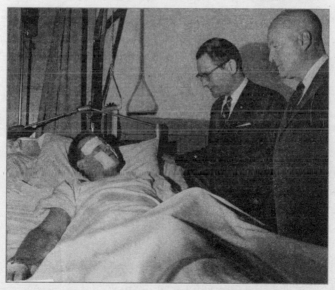

Maimed mob attorney John Fitzgerald is visited in the hospital by State Attorney General Elliot Richardson and Middlesex District Attorney John Droney.

Windows in houses across the street were blown out. A cop on traffic detail a block away ran to Fitzgerald, who was lying on his back in a widening pool of blood. The cop bent over to listen to what might have been the lawyer's last words.

"Call Rico of the FBI," he rasped, before losing consciousness.

Rico and his partner Dennis Condon immediately canceled their plans for the evening—to interview a young prospect for the Bureau, a high-school teacher from South Boston named John J. Connolly. Connolly's father was a longtime friend of U.S. House Speaker John McCormack, who was close to J. Edgar Hoover. Rico and Condon knew they would have plenty of other chances to get to know young Connolly in the years ahead.

They drove instead to Whidden Hospital, where surgeons operated on Fitzgerald for five hours. He lost his right leg just above the knee. Politicians visited him in the hospital. As Barboza sardonically noted in his autobiography, "They had pretty much ignored the gang war all those years with the excuse it was just punks killing off punks and good riddance, but now that a lawyer had been maimed and crippled they rose up in wrath and tried to outdo each other in pious indignation."

It didn't take Johnny long to figure out who had done it, or why.

It was a favor Stevie and Frankie did for the Mafia. But there was more to it that that, at least for Stevie. Fitzgerald was Barboza's lawyer, so he may have known how much of a role Stevie played in inventing Barboza's lies about the Deegan hit, putting Mafia guys in the car to protect his brother Jimmy. So Stevie had a reason for wanting to get rid of Fitzgerald other than impressing Larry, which was all Frankie cared about at the time. See, once Stevie hit

Fitzgerald, how could anyone ever suspect him of being in on the deal to flip Barboza, if he blew up the guy's lawyer?

Barboza's next trial was in federal court in Providence. Patriarca and a couple of his henchmen were charged with conspiracy in the murder of two brothers who'd been running an unauthorized card game on Federal Hill. The Man had been urged to flee to Haiti until a deal could be worked out, but Angiulo's acquittal had emboldened him. He would stay in Rhode Island and fight the charges. At one pretrial hearing in Providence, as Barboza left the courtroom, Patriarca looked him in the eye and silently mouthed two words: "You rat."

Barboza lunged for him, screaming the usual: "You fuck your dead mother in the mouth!" The marshals got to Barboza before he reached Patriarca, but nothing could save Patriarca from the Rhode Island jury. He was convicted, sentenced to five years, and shipped off to Atlanta.

That left the Deegan murder trial. It started in Boston in July 1968. Barboza was on the witness stand for nine days. On cross-examination, the defense lawyers punched one hole after another in his perjurious testimony. At one point Barboza was reduced to snarling at a defense attorney: "All I know is I was there and you wasn't."

Sometimes it was almost as if Barboza was retelling an inside joke. He said In Town wanted Deegan dead because he'd broken into a Mafia bookie's house and stolen $82,000 in cash—the exact figure Tash Bratsos and Tommy DePrisco supposedly had on them when they were murdered in the North End in 1966.

On July 31, the jury brought back guilty verdicts against all six defendants, four of whom had nothing to do with Deegan's murder. Two ended up on Death Row at MCI-Walpole. It would be another thirty years before Johnny Martorano would be able to follow through on his offer to testify on behalf of the men whom Joe Barboza and the FBI had framed.

A COUPLE OF days after the trial ended, FBI agents Rico and Condon stopped by Wimpy Bennett's old garage in Roxbury, which was now run by Cadillac Frank Salemme. The two G-men were elated, especially Condon. In his testimony to congressional investigators in 2003, Salemme recalled his conversation with FBI agent Condon.

"He made the statement, I wonder how Louie Grieco likes it on death row, and he wasn't even there. I was thinking, why was he saying that? I said, you're a Knight of Columbus, you're Holy Name Society."

Condon shrugged. "If you're so smart, why don't you get up on the stand and testify?"

"Dennis, who's going to believe me? But you won't get by St. Peter at the gate, you can't. You broke one of the Ten Commandments, thou shalt not bear false witness, Dennis. You can't get by him, Dennis."

Dennis Condon was irate at such insolence. Frank Salemme wouldn't be on the street much longer.

THE OLD NITE Lite Café on Commercial Street, where Tash Bratsos and Tommy DePrisco were murdered by the Mafia in 1966, had reopened under new management, sort of, as the 416 Lounge. In October 1968, just outside the 416, police responding to a call of men fighting found a young man bleeding, clutching his stomach.

It was Arthur Pearson, the Everett ex-con who had gone to jail two years earlier rather than testify against Barboza. He had been stabbed seventeen times, and was pronounced dead on arrival at Mass. General Hospital.

Witnesses reported seeing two men in "navy uniforms" running toward the coast guard base farther up Commercial Street, but no arrests were ever made in Pearson's murder.

• • •

ZIP CONNOLLY STILL wanted to join the FBI. At age twenty-seven, he was tired of teaching high school in Dorchester. Rico and Condon hadn't been able to meet him the night Fitzgerald's car was bombed, but it didn't hurt Zip's prospects. He still had those Southie connections to John W. McCormack, the Speaker of the U.S. House of Representatives. His father was known in South Boston as "Galway John." How much more did the Speaker need to know about anyone?

In August 1968, Speaker McCormack, second in line to the U.S. presidency after Vice President Hubert H. Humphrey, wrote a letter to his friend J. Edgar Hoover.

"Dear Edgar," it began. "It has come to my attention that the son of a lifelong personal friend has applied to become a special agent of the Federal Bureau of Investigation. . . ."

John J. "Zip" Connolly Jr. was appointed to the FBI in October 1968.

LAWYER: Now, Mr. Hicks, Ronald Hicks, who I believe you testified you murdered, was going to be a witness against friends of yours, isn't that right?

MARTORANO: Against people that I hadn't met yet. They weren't friends until after.

LAWYER: Well, at some point they came to you to ask for your help with an attorney for their defense?

MARTORANO: Nope. That's . . . at one point his wife came to me and asked for some help with an attorney for their defense.

LAWYER: And at some point, you went to see Mr. Hicks to dissuade him from testifying against the woman's—

MARTORANO: No. I met with him. I had a few drinks with him, socialized a couple of times, and I didn't like the guy, and I decided to take him out . . . I didn't go looking for Hicks. He came to my restaurant.

Abie Sarkis, Andy Martorano's old business partner in Luigi's, had a club on Columbus Avenue, the 411. It had a long bar, with bookies hanging out near the door, waiting for the daily number to come in the late afternoon, after which they'd start making their collections and payoffs. Farther back were the working girls. Johnny Martorano knew the place well, and one night a girl from the 411 came into Basin Street looking for Johnny.

Her name was Roberta Campbell—Bert, for short. She needed a favor. She was crying. He told Bert to sit down and the waiter brought her a drink. He asked her what she needed.

"Have you ever heard of the Campbell brothers?" she began, and Johnny's answer was yes. Alvin and Arnold Campbell weren't exactly household names like Joe Barboza, but they were well known enough in Roxbury. Bert was Alvin's wife. The Campbells' father was from the islands, but his sons had been brought up in Boston. He'd taught the boys his trade, which was robbing banks. They'd been arrested in 1957 for a $32,000 bank stickup in Canton. When the judge sentenced them, Alvin was twenty-three and Arnold twenty-five.

Despite their race, up until the bank robbery in Canton, the brothers had somehow led a charmed existence with the law in Boston. At their sentencing, the judge angrily read their rap sheets aloud in court, describing what he called "fix after fix after fix."

"This is a sordid picture," the judge said. "Never in my life have I seen such records."

They were good guys, the Campbells. Even Whitey liked them. He told me later he'd been working out one day in the weight room in Leavenworth, and he heard some guys talking behind him. It was pretty obvious from their accents that they were from Boston, and when Whitey turned around he couldn't believe they were black. It was the Campbells. They used to all walk the track together at Leavenworth, around and around and around, just talking about Boston.

Abie Sarkis liked them, too. He was always helping them out whenever they were in a jam. They were just good people.

By the time the Campbells were paroled, Roxbury was awash in federal money. The War on Poverty was in full swing. The Campbells were looking to get a foothold in the rackets, but the money from Uncle Sam was just as

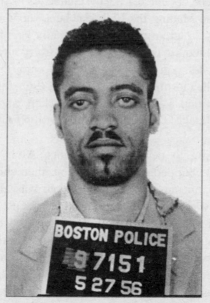

Guido St. Laurent, the founder of NEGRO.

tempting. Other local hustlers had gotten there first, though, especially another black ex-con named Guido St. Laurent. St. Laurent had lost his eyesight in an accident at Walpole, but his blindness didn't stop him from quickly figuring out how to prime Uncle Sam's pump. By 1968, he had set up a sardonically named antipoverty agency of his own—NEGRO, which stood for New England Grass Roots Organization. Its offices were above a sub shop on Blue Hill Avenue.

At NEGRO, St. Laurent surrounded himself with thugs, mostly ex-cons like himself. Some of them weren't from Boston, which seemed to bother the Campbells. In November 1968, NEGRO was on the verge of its biggest score yet, a $1.9-million federal grant to run a "manpower program" that was supposed to train 500 hard-core unemployed Roxbury residents as auto mechanics. Even the Campbells had been promised jobs—in the program management, of course. Like the characters in Tom Wolfe's essay "Mau-Mauing the Flak Catchers," none of the parties involved had any interest in actually learning a trade that would require them to go to work every morning.

But St. Laurent would not live to enjoy his payday. Early on the morning of November 13, 1968, three men— later identified as the Campbell brothers and their top enforcer, Deke Chandler—burst into NEGRO headquarters.

According to newspaper accounts, Alvin Campbell first pistol-whipped the blind ex-con, then shot him. St. Laurent's top muscle, another ex-con, was also shot to death, as was a third man. Two other NEGRO members were wounded. The Campbells and Chandler were quickly arrested and were being held without bail at the Charles Street jail awaiting trial when Alvin's wife showed up at Basin Street to seek Johnny Martorano's assistance.

The Boston police offered protection to the two survivors from NEGRO but both turned down the offer. One of them, Ronald Hicks, a thirty-one-year-old armed robber on parole, went on television and said the shooting was a result of a turf struggle between militant groups over the federal funds. It looked bleak for the Campbells.

Bert Campbell was just looking for any kind of help she could get—money, lawyers, talking the other militant black groups in the city into supporting her husband. Johnny liked her. He wasn't thinking about killing anyone, not until he met the main witness against the Campbells, Ronald Hicks. He was a regular at Basin Street, and after Bert's visit, Johnny made a point of getting to know him. Johnny wanted Hicks to relax around him. He was pleased when Hicks started going out with one of the barmaids—that way he'd be around Basin Street even more often.

What Johnny quickly learned was that Hicks was a drug dealer and a pimp. One night he casually asked Hicks about the Campbells' trial.

"I'm gonna get even with them motherfuckers," Hicks said.

Johnny began thinking about the Campbells, locked up in the Charles Street jail, awaiting trial and possibly facing the death penalty because of this guy. Even though he'd never even met the Campbells, Johnny made a decision to murder Hicks.

He thought it was the right thing to do.

He had just seen Peter Limone and the other three guys from In Town get railroaded onto Death Row because of Joe Barboza. Now it was happening again. It didn't matter to Johnny if they had killed those guys at NEGRO. Johnny's mind was made up. This Hicks was no damn good—he was a lying piece of shit.

It was personal, too. Now Johnny was thinking, *This could be me; I could be in this exact same situation.* First Peter Limone, now Alvin Campbell—who would be next? And if he didn't help, it would be his fault if the

Deke Chandler, Roxbury gangster, a friend of Johnny's.

Campbells were put to death, because who else could step up for them?

Johnny came to a conclusion. It was the right thing to do to kill Hicks. His conscience was telling him he had to do it.

ON THE EVENING of March 19, 1969, Johnny Martorano and another guy went looking for Ronald Hicks. They checked out the new hot spot in town, the Sugar Shack, where Hicks was a regular. The Boston police already had reports of "Hicks pushing H & C (heroin and cocaine) with a big fat negro male at the Sugar Shack; Hicks also recently seen in the company of a white blonde."

As always, Johnny knew the car his prey was driving—a 1967 Cadillac coupe, brown, with a rose-colored top. In other words, a pimpmobile. Around 1 A.M., the other guy with Martorano decided to call it a night and go home. But Johnny continued searching for Hicks by himself in the South End.

Around 1:50 A.M., Hicks drifted into Slade's, the joint on Tremont Street near the Taylor brothers' old Pioneer Club. At Slade's, Hicks ran into a woman he'd once dated. He seemed pleased to see her, she later told the police, and the two decided to go across the street to Birley's to get a hamburger. Afterward, the BPD report continued, "He drove her home. He told her he had business and would like to come back and see her about getting together again. He said he would be back about 4 A.M. . . . . Hicks did not appear to be worried or frightened when he was with her."

After dropping her off at her place, she watched as Hicks made a U-turn in his Cadillac on Huntington Avenue. That was the last she saw of Ronald Hicks.

JOHNNY SPOTTED HIM in the Fenway. He honked and waved and Hicks pulled over into Forsythe Park, near the Museum of Fine Arts. Johnny parked and came over and got in the passenger's side. Hicks seemed glad to see him. He may have been planning to pull over anyway because he had a bag of cocaine that he got out of his pocket as soon as Johnny got in the car. Hicks cut two lines of coke right there on the car seat. Johnny was sitting next to him on the front seat when Hicks leaned over and snorted one of the lines. He still had his head down when he asked Johnny, "You want a line?"

Those were the last words Ronald Hicks ever spoke because at that moment Johnny Martorano shot him in the head. His head snapped back against the horn on the steering wheel and it started blaring, just like in a movie.

Johnny grabbed the keys but left the headlights on, just as he had at Normandy Street a year earlier. The cops made note of the similarities in the MO, but it wasn't nearly enough evidence to pull anyone in on.

HEARING THE HORN, a security guard at the Forsythe Dental Center ran outside and saw the car, pointed toward Mass Ave. Hicks was declared dead at 3:05 A.M. at Boston City Hospital. The district attorney, Garrett Byrne, immediately ordered the sole surviving witness of the NEGRO massacre picked up and placed in protective custody.

"A very vital witness has been assassinated," said the somber prosecutor. "The witness had refused protection."

But the police had to admit that a lot of people had wanted Hicks dead. They had no suspects, although the police report did mention that Hicks's girlfriend who had been with him at Slade's "stated that she [was] a waitress at the Basin Street South and that John Martorano was there all the time."

JOE BARBOZA WAS paroled in March 1969 on one condition—that "he leave Massachusetts and never return." After the parole board cut him loose, he was immediately driven to Logan Airport, where he caught a plane out of the state. A couple of days later Jimmy Flemmi got out of Walpole, crazier than ever.

"He wasn't getting into trouble daily," Martorano recalled. "He was getting into trouble hourly."

By then, the FBI was tightening the screws on Stevie Flemmi and Frank Salemme, or at least appearing to. They had to collar someone for the Fitzgerald bombing. Like baseball scouts, Rico and Condon had gone back into the state prison system and recruited a new snitching prospect—a Roxbury hood named Bobby Daddieco. He hated Larry Baione and he was looking at serious time for a botched bank robbery in Somerville. Daddieco had been in the crash car on the Billy Bennett hit and was now ready to give up Salemme and Flemmi on both the Billy Bennett murder and the Fitzgerald bombing—a twofer.

High as usual on Seconal and Scotch, Jimmy Flemmi started talking about killing Daddieco or anyone else who would testify against his brother. But the Bear was also open to killing just about anyone if the price was right—even his best friends.

One night I'm up at the Bat Cove with the Bear and as I'm leaving he asks for a ride back to his car, which he'd left downtown around the corner from Jay's Lounge, Jerry Angiulo's place. So I'm driving him down there when all of a sudden, he drops his gun onto the floorboard of my car. I picked it up and shoved it in his pocket. I asked him, Jimmy, can you drive or do you want me to take you home? He said he'd be okay. I didn't think anything more of it. But then thirty years later, we're all locked up down in Plymouth, and as part of discovery for our case, they're playing these old FBI tapes for us. They had one bug in the car of Larry Baione's driver, Richie Gambale. And on the tape I hear Larry call Stevie over to the car and Larry says, "Your brother was supposed to kill Johnny last night but he got yellow." You don't hear Stevie say anything back—he probably knew the car was wired. But that was my good friend Jimmy Flemmi.

Stevie Flemmi, meanwhile, was still keeping the FBI up-to-date on both his own brother and Johnny Martorano. "On April 14, 1969, informant advised that Jimmy Flemmi is running with Johnny Martorano and that Johnny Martorano is still 'hustling girls' out of Enrico's. Informant advised Martorano has in the past purchased some stolen

The Bear, about the time he tried to kill Johnny for In Town.

merchandise and he suspects that Martorano is dealing in some kind of drugs. Informant advised that Martorano can usually be reached telephonically at either 716-2091 or VI 6-1529."

I couldn't believe it when I saw that second number—it belonged to a girlfriend of mine in Winthrop who just died. Until 2009, I hadn't thought of that phone number in close to thirty years. You know I didn't get a chance to see a lot of the later FBI 209s as they came in because I was gone from Plymouth in 1998. Until last year, I never realized Stevie had given the feds that phone number. Nobody had that number, nobody but Stevie—my best friend. But I do remember that after I went on the lam I used to call my old girlfriend at that number every six months or so. One time she told me, the feds had started lurking around outside her house. I couldn't figure it out— how could they possibly know she was connected to me? Now I know.

As for that other number Stevie gave them—I have no idea now who it belonged to. Maybe you should ask Stevie.

The feds may have been closing in on them, but Stevie and Frankie were still scheming. They were looking to take over South Boston. Donald Killeen, a regular at the old Luigi's, was still on top of the Southie rackets, but his grip was growing shakier.

Young Southie guys were coming back from Vietnam, and after combat in the DMZ, the Killeens didn't seem so tough. The younger hoods called themselves the Mullens, after the square where they hung out. Donald Killeen realized he needed some new muscle, so he brought in an ex-con bank robber named Whitey Bulger, as well as Johnny's old pal, Billy O'Sullivan. Flemmi and Salemme figured to let the two Southie mobs decimate each other, another Irish gang war in miniature. Then they would move in to pick up the pieces.

But in September 1969, Rico called Flemmi. He told Stevie he had to speak to him and Salemme immediately. They met before dawn on Revere Beach. Rico informed them that they were about to be indicted in state court for both the Fitzgerald bombing and the Billy Bennett murder. Rico told them about Daddieco's testimony, but added that if they got out of town before they were indicted, they could probably ride it out. "Take Poulos with you," Rico added. "He's the weak link." Flemmi and Salemme knew immediately that they would have to flee. The only question was how long they would have to remain on the lam. That depended on the evidence against them, specifically, the witness Bobby Daddieco.

"How good is Daddieco?" Stevie asked Rico.

"He's no Barboza," replied Rico.

DESPITE HICKS'S MURDER, the district attorney went ahead with the Campbell brothers' murder trial. But they all had alibis, and with Ronald Hicks dead there was only one witness to put them at NEGRO headquarters. The all-white jury quickly acquitted the three black hoods, and after the verdicts, they made a pilgrimage to Basin Street South to see Johnny.

"We're here to thank you," Alvin Campbell told him.

"I don't know what you're talking about," Johnny said. "There's nothing to thank me for."

"We're here to thank you anyway," Campbell replied.

The Campbells hadn't been in Vietnam, but they were as hungry as the Mullens across the bridge in Southie. They wanted to take over drugs in the black neighborhoods, by throwing out all the "outsiders"—not so much the whites, because they had mostly abandoned Roxbury by then. The Campbells' ire was directed at the Superfly-style black gangsters who'd been moving into the city in recent years and now dominated the Roxbury rackets. Johnny Martorano was skeptical of the Campbells' strategy.

They were bank robbers, not drug dealers. You don't get rid of people if you don't know how to take over and operate their rackets yourself. It didn't make sense. I know what people believe, but I never took any money from the Campbells. Maybe they gave me a hundred bucks once, but I told them no. They never really made much money anyway.

What was more valuable to me personally about the Campbells was that if anybody ever tried to make a move on me, they'd have to worry about them. On the street you need somebody behind you like that. The more the better. Stevie first had his brother, then Frankie, and then even later Whitey. Every time somebody who doesn't like me sees a black guy walking toward him on the street, he's thinking, is this one of Johnny's guys? I had a lot of black friends, still do.

What I advised the Campbells to do was to go after the barrooms and the numbers in Roxbury. Then I would have been with them. Drugs are too hot. Numbers are slower but cleaner, safer, longer-lasting. I know the state lottery was coming in, but remember, at the start it was only once a week, and then only twice a week for years after that. People in the poor neighborhoods like Roxbury have to play every day. But Alvin didn't have the patience for that—he was an old-fashioned Black Panther–type guy.

Once they beat the NEGRO murder rap, the Campbells moved fast. In September 1969, the FBI sent the following report to the Boston Police Department:

S/A Matthew Seifer received information that the Campbell Bros. had approached all the cocaine dealers in Boston making it very clear that only their "stuff" would be handled. The terms were that they would protect the dealers, that the dealers would provide their own attorney in the event of an arrest, but that the Campbells would see to it that no one would testify against them as long as it was a state violation. It was further alleged that the Campbells were associated with a white fellow . . .

Pushback was to be expected—there was too much money at stake for the independents to give up Roxbury without a fight. One hot summer night, Johnny was drinking at Basin Street with Jimmy the Bear, who was out on a brief parole. Alvin Campbell and Deke Chandler came in and excitedly pulled Johnny aside. They were having some problems with the proprietor of a joint on Blue Hill Avenue—one Black Sam.

Alvin had spotted Black Sam holding court out in front of his unlicensed bar, surrounded by a crowd of hangers-on. It was a perfect opportunity to take him out, but it would be a difficult shot.

"How many cars you got?" Johnny asked.

Alvin Campbell would be acquitted of murdering three people—after Johnny Martorano killed the main witness against him.

"Two," said Alvin. Johnny nodded and told the Bear to go with Deke Chandler. They would be in the crash car, just in case. He and Alvin Campbell went out into the alley next to Basin Street, and Johnny grabbed a handful of dirt and rubbed it on his face to darken it. Then he tore apart a burlap bag and wrapped it around his head. He got into the backseat of Alvin Campbell's car and lay down. There was a loaded carbine on the floor.

A few minutes later, on Blue Hill Avenue, Alvin braked the car to a stop. Johnny popped up from the backseat, drew a bead on Black Sam, and fired. Black Sam fell to the sidewalk, wounded, shot in the shoulder. It would have to do—there were too many onlookers, and not enough time, to get out of the car and finish Black Sam off. This was his lucky night. The two Campbell cars then roared off north, toward downtown, toward white Boston. Black Sam's near-death experience never made the papers.

THERE WAS ANOTHER holdout named Nelson Padron. He was older, a cocaine dealer who owned a bar, lived in Sharon, drove a Mercedes convertible. The Campbells told him they were in charge now and it was time to negotiate new terms—in a public place, if Padron was concerned about his safety. They agreed on Slade's. A white fellow named Johnny Martorano came along, just in case there was a problem, which there was.

Padron had brought a gun to the sit-down—not a good way to win friends and influence people, as the McLaughlins had learned several years earlier at the Ebb Tide. Johnny pulled back Padron's coat, grabbed the revolver out of his belt, and began pistol-whipping him with it.

"We thought about killing him right there," Martorano said, "but there were too many witnesses."

Then Deke Chandler had an idea. While Johnny continued beating Padron, Deke ran outside, took out a switchblade, and slashed all four of Padron's tires. That way, when Padron tried to leave, the Campbells and Johnny could follow him in their car and eventually pull up alongside his Mercedes and shoot him—with no witnesses.

When Johnny finally tired of beating Padron and told him to screw, Padron bolted for his car. Nobody rushed after him, since Padron couldn't get far on four flats. As they leisurely walked back out onto Tremont Street, they saw Padron tearing off in his Mercedes, throwing off a shower of sparks as he rode the rims of the sports car. Everyone started laughing, and Nelson Padron lived . . . to get shot by Johnny another day.

JOHNNY MARTORANO WOULDN'T turn twenty-nine until December 1969, but already his life was changing. No nightclub lasts forever, and it was time to close Basin Street South. The city's new hot spot was the Sugar Shack.

One way or another, a lot of Johnny's old friends were gone. The Roxbury gang no longer existed. Wimpy Bennett and his brothers were dead, their killers, Frank Salemme and Stevie Flemmi, on the lam. Peter Poulos, the third guy who'd left town with them, had just been murdered by Stevie in the desert outside Las Vegas. Jimmy the Bear would soon be back in prison.

Joe Barboza was a free man, briefly, although he, too, would soon be back in stir, this time in California, for murdering an unemployed mechanic in a dispute over stolen securities. Most of Barboza's little crew had either been wiped out or absorbed by In Town.

Johnny found himself spending more and more time with the crew from Somerville. He'd never met Buddy McLean, but now he was hanging with his successor, Howie Winter. Like Buddy, Howie was an ex-marine born in 1929. Johnny had first met Howie in the mid-sixties at the various clubs in Boston, and the two men quickly discovered that they had a lot in common, including an avid interest in betting on pro sports, especially football games.

Howie Winter in custody in Boston, age 28, 1957.

Howie owned several parcels of land on Winter Hill, and George Kaufman had moved his operations to Howie's garage at the corner of Broadway and Marshall Street. Jimmy Martorano was out of prison, and he fit well with Howie, too. They liked talking about real estate. Both had the same idea about the South End of Boston—they thought it was going to come back. If they could just get into the right locations, Howie and Jimmy agreed, they could start making some real money.

JOHNNY MARTORANO HAD a date, with a nurse.

It was an old high-school classmate from Milton, the girl he'd once taken to Andy's cottage in Scituate in the winter, and whom he had tried to keep warm by taking an ax to his father's living-room set to provide some wood for the fireplace.

He'd run into her somewhere and had noticed she still wasn't wearing a ring, so he asked her out. The Sugar Shack seemed like a nice spot for a first date. They treated Johnny Martorano like royalty—there he truly was "Bwana Johnny," a nickname then used only by a few close friends, as a sort of inside joke until thirty years later, when the defense lawyers for crooked FBI agent Zip Connolly tried to resurrect the old moniker to destroy his credibility.

It was September 24, 1969. As usual at the Sugar Shack, Johnny didn't see a lot of white faces, but that was okay. But Johnny did notice one white guy, who was scowling at him. It was a slight, bearded thirty-four-year-old pimp from Philadelphia known as "Touch." His real name was Jack Banno, and, although Johnny Martorano didn't know it, Touch was on the run from the Campbells.

Early the previous Sunday morning, Deke Chandler was making what had become his usual rounds in Roxbury, looking for nonaffiliated drug dealers to muscle. Chandler spotted one of the guys on his target list, a black cocaine dealer named Rat, sitting in a car with Touch. Deke swaggered up to the passenger side of the dealer's car, and quickly got into a beef with the pusher, as Touch sat in the middle between them.

One of Touch's whores later told the police, "He didn't tell me all the words that were passed between the two of them but it had to do with cocaine, that is what Touch told me. It had to do with dope. There were threats . . . he couldn't come here with any kind of cocaine without the Campbell brothers' okay. . . . That is when Deke pulled out his pistol."

After that confrontation, Touch was terrified that the Campbells were going to kill him. He'd seen too much. He could put Deke, an ex-con, on Blue Hill Avenue with a .45. Or so he told his woman. Apparently, things had not been going well for Touch, as the police discovered after his murder. Touch had been banned from the Sugar Shack after running up a tab of $27.99 "without funds." He also owed the owner $135. He didn't have a car. He'd lost $3,200 in an after-hours card game. He was drunk or stoned most of the time.

But somehow, this night Touch was back inside the Sugar Shack, staring at Johnny Martorano and his nurse. Johnny wasn't exactly hiding—a BPD report the next day noted that "John Martorano was seen in the Sugar Shack early 10:30 or 11:00 P.M. with a female, on Wednesday."

JOHNNY AND HIS date were leaving around 11, through the back door, when suddenly, out in the alley, Touch jumped him, with a knife. He wasn't big enough to take on Johnny in any kind of physical confrontation, so he was probably high on something. They struggled, rolling around in the alley, until Johnny was finally able to get his own knife out and stab him. Johnny didn't have a gun with him that night—he was, after all, out on a date—but out of habit he was carrying a blade.

Soon Touch was falling down, trying to get up, keeling over again, bleeding, still swearing at Johnny. Johnny gave the keys to his car to the nurse and told her to bring it around. He got Touch into the backseat and was wondering what he was going to do with him now. He was bleeding, but the wounds didn't appear to be life-threatening.

Johnny started driving through the South End. He saw an alley behind the Diplomat Hotel on East Berkeley Street and figured this was as good a place as any to dump Touch. He pulled the car into the alley, opened the back door, and dragged him out of the car. The plan was to leave him there in the alley until somebody could find him and call an ambulance.

All of a sudden, though, Touch got one final burst of

strength—a second wind. He started yelling "Mother-fucker!" and lunged at Johnny. Johnny pulled out his knife again and stabbed him until Touch fell over. The last word Touch ever spoke was to Johnny Martorano.

"Motherfucker!"

TOUCH'S BODY WAS discovered around 3 A.M. The dead pimp's personal effects included $49 cash and a pawn ticket dated September 2 from Hudson Jewelers on Stuart Street for a $250 ring. According to the autopsy report, he weighed 145 pounds, and had been wearing an orange shirt with matching orange socks and a tan sports coat. His body was identified at the Southern Mortuary by "Candy, colored female," one of his two women.

Candy, who was twenty-three years old, turned over to police a letter she'd handwritten to Touch the night he died, complaining how badly he was treating her in his attempt to make more money. Touch was dead before she could deliver it to him.

"Dear Daddy," it began. "You made me your woman for three years so how can I cope with just being your whore? Do you remember when I first meet [sic] you? I thought here is a man, my man so how can I let him down? Touch when you come for me as my Man and Pimp I will be ready ready Ready. Love, Candy."

IN THEIR REPORT to the Boston police, the FBI noted that Martorano was likely involved in the slaying: "It is suspected that [REDACTED] either killed BANNO himself or took him to MARTORANO. MARTORANO was also the last person seen with Ronald HICKS, victim of a previous murder involving [REDACTED]."

MARTORANO NEVER WENT out on another date with the nurse. But he didn't worry that she would ever go to the police.

"She knew it was self-defense—she saw Touch come after me first. And I never heard from any cops about it, either. They don't question you if they're going to arrest you. And they didn't have any witnesses. The thing is, nobody missed Touch."

Except maybe Candy.

6

The Winter Hill Gang

LAWYER: Jimmy Sims, Howie Winter, Joseph Mc-
Donald, did any of those persons have a relationship to an entity known as "Winter Hill"?

MARTORANO: Yes.

LAWYER: And what was the relationship to Winter
Hill?

MARTORANO: There was a gang in Winter Hill and
that was the gang.

BILLY O'SULLIVAN WOULD be dead before he could
call in the marker Johnny Martorano owed him for
killing a guy in Billy O's after-hours joint. But one of
Billy O's underworld pals would parlay the unpaid debt
into the formation of a gang that would someday rival the
Mafia for power in Boston's underworld.

When Frankie Salemme and Stevie Flemmi went on the
lam in September 1969, in South Boston Donald Killeen
may have thought his troubles were behind him, but they
were only beginning. And it was homegrown trouble—
the Mullens, that loosely knit gang of younger criminals.

The more the Mullens saw of the Killeens, the less

impressed they were. Holed up in the Transit Café in the Lower End, appearing occasionally on West Broadway, bleary-eyed, their faces splotchy, beer bellies hanging over their belts, the Killeens just looked like another crew of toothless tigers, project rats taking bets on the dogs when they weren't sucking down dimeys and musties—half–Pickwick Ale, half Narragansett beer drafts. Donald Killeen didn't even live in Southie anymore. He'd moved out to the suburbs. He was pushing fifty. His two top guns were both over forty—Billy O and Whitey Bulger.

On the other side, the Mullens were led by Paulie McGonagle, who had a twin brother, as well as another brother on the fire department who was dating a blond dental hygienist named Catherine Greig. The gang also included an Irish-born ex-marine named Pat Nee, and Buddy

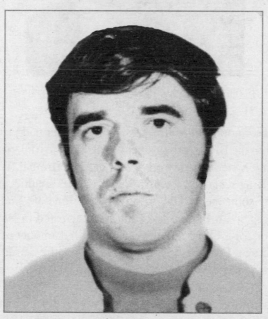

Pat Nee, Irish-born member of the Mullen gang in South Boston, a friend of Johnny's.

Tommy King, a Mullen, murdered by Johnny, 1975.

Roache, another hard drinker whose brother had just gotten onto the BPD. Perhaps the toughest of the Mullens was Tommy King, an ironworker and career criminal. Whenever King's name was mentioned in the Southie underworld, someone would bring up the time he and two younger South Boston kids had been arrested in Newton in 1960 for robbing a pharmacy of a large amount of cash and drugs. Even then, Southie was a good place to deal black-market prescription pharmaceuticals. A fourth guy in the crew—Paulie McGonagle—escaped.

One of the younger Southie guys who'd been arrested had a broken jaw. In those pre-Miranda, pre-ACLU days, the Newton cops took him into a back room at headquarters. They were working the kid over, trying to beat the name of the fourth guy out of him. He was screaming out in agony every time they smacked him in the jaw. In a nearby cell, King started yelling at the cops to send in their best guy, and they'd have at it, one-on-one.

Tommy King offered the cops a deal. If he prevailed, he said, the cops would lay off the kid. If the cop decked him, King would give up the name of the Southie guy who got away.

As another Southie mobster recalls the story:

So the captain figures he's got a guy who's never lost a fight, a sergeant. They send him into the cell with Tommy, but King takes him—can you imagine anything remotely like this happening today? Well, when it's over, the sergeant limps out of Tommy's cell, and now the captain is pissed, and he tells his guys to start really working over the kid with the broken jaw. But the sergeant intervenes and says to the captain, hey we had a deal with this guy, he won fair and square. So they lay off the kid, Paulie McGonagle gets clean away, and Tommy King does a couple of years. That was Tommy King. He was tough.

There were other Mullens, too, including one who would go on to be elected president of the Boston City Council. As they grew older, other Mullens would become ward bosses, or bus drivers, or barroom owners. In short, the Mullens were a true cross-section of South Boston, but in the early 1970s the only thing that mattered to Donald Killeen was that they were young and tough and that there were too many of them.

Killeen figured his best play was to eliminate the Mullens' leader—Paulie McGonagle. Whitey got the assignment. He knew the make, model, and license number of Paulie's car, a Volkswagen. On November 18, 1969, Whitey spotted the car and opened fire, killing the occupant as he pulled into a parking space outside the McGonagles' home on East Fourth Street. It was Paulie McGonagle's twin brother.

Next one of the Mullens, Mickey Dwyer, had a few drinks and went over to the Transit Café. Donald Killeen's brother, Kenny, soon stumbled out of the barroom, and Dwyer jumped him. In the ensuing struggle, Kenny Killeen bit off Dwyer's nose. The maimed Mullen ran off screaming toward the Broadway station as Killeen spat out his nose into the West Broadway gutter and then unsteadily made his way back into the Transit Café for a celebratory round.

The party was in full swing by the time Donald Killeen returned. After he was told what had happened, his first question was: What happened to the nose? When none of his crew seemed to know, he ordered them outside to find it, which they eventually did, covered with dirt and grime in the gutter.

They gingerly brought Dwyer's severed nose back inside, and Donald Killeen told his bartender to wash it off in the bar sink. Then Killeen filled a Styrofoam cooler with ice, wrapped the nose in a couple of cocktail napkins, and tossed it on top of the ice. Finally Donald Killeen called a cab and told him to take the cooler down to the emergency room at Boston City Hospital, hand it to somebody, and say that "Mickey's nose" was inside. They'll know what to do, Killeen assured the cabbie.

Donald Killeen went back inside the Transit and took a second gun out of the desk in his second-floor office. After this, he knew, there would be even more trouble.

THE FBI WAS aware of all of this. Flemmi was gone, on the lam, but Whitey Bulger had filled in FBI agent Dennis Condon. In January 1971, J. Edgar Hoover had personally sent a memo to the FBI office instructing his Boston office to develop Whitey as an informant.

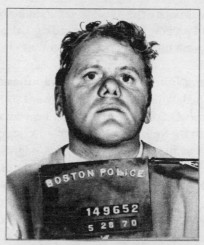

Mickey Dwyer, a Mullen whose nose was bitten off by
Kenny Killeen, and then reattached at Boston City Hospital.

At the time, Whitey was still legally residing with his
mother in the South Boston projects. In reality, he spent
most of his evenings with his girlfriend, Teresa Stanley,
who had four towheaded children by a Southie street
drunk. Like Billy O, Whitey had a no-show public job—he
was on the Suffolk County payroll as a courthouse custo-
dian for $76 a week. He was barely known outside the
South Boston underworld. Yet J. Edgar Hoover had taken
an unusual interest in Whitey. He always took personal
care of any requests from House Speaker John W. Mc-
Cormack, just as he had when Zip Connolly wanted to
join the FBI a few years earlier.

The Speaker was no stranger to the Boston underworld.
In the 1920s, as a state senator, he'd sued the Boston Police Department on behalf of his clients, the Gustin gang
of bootleggers. McCormack's brother Eddie, better known
as "Knocko," was a 300-pound bookie who owned a
block-long barroom in Andrew Square.

Facing an air force court-martial in 1952, Whitey had

so brazenly dropped the name of the then house majority leader McCormack to his commanding officer that the captain wrote it up in a report that went into Bulger's permanent military file. During his nine years in the custody of the Federal Bureau of Prisons, it was Speaker McCormack who had made sure that the wayward son of Southie never got too deeply into trouble as he was transferred from Lewisburg to Atlanta to Alcatraz to Leavenworth.

Throughout his forty-six years in Congress, Speaker McCormack had always been a friend of the Bureau, voting to extend its investigative and arrest powers across state lines, then later protecting its budget in good times and bad. As he retired in January 1971, McCormack only needed one or two more small favors from the director. One was to keep an eye on Whitey Bulger, his bank-robbing constituent. Whitey's younger brother Billy, after serving eight years as a state rep, had just been elected the new state senator from Southie—the position that had earlier been held both by the future Speaker McCormack and later by the brother of early Southie gangland boss Dan Carroll. The boyos were keeping the seat in the family.

AFTER THE NOSE-BITING incident at the Killeens' bar in February 1971, Buddy Roache of the Mullens arranged a sit-down at the Colonial Lounge on West Broadway with Billy O and Whitey. Whitey later told Dennis Condon how Buddy Roache had brusquely informed them that Donald Killeen was finished and that if they didn't switch sides, he and Billy O would be killed as well.

A violent argument ensued, ROACHE drew a weapon and was thereafter shot by O'SULLIVAN. ROACHE was seriously wounded and hospitalized. After this shooting, BULGER and O'SULLIVAN had expected retribution on the part of ROACHE's associates. BULGER had been extremely cautious but O'SULLIVAN underestimated the group.

In the aftermath of the Roache shooting, the Boston police got an early indication of just how much political protection Whitey already enjoyed. Detectives took the glasses that had been on Roache's table before the gunplay and dusted them for fingerprints. They found those of two ex-cons—Whitey and Billy O.

The detectives went to South Boston District Court, where Billy, by his own admission, already wielded considerable influence, to obtain arrest warrants. But the clerk-magistrate refused to issue them. The cops were amazed, and wrote up a report, much of it in capital letters, to indicate their dismay. It was sent directly to the police commissioner, who happened to be an ex–FBI agent himself.

Whitey was never charged in the Buddy Roache shooting. It was the beginning of a pattern.

A MONTH OR so later, on a Saturday night in March, Billy O had dinner at Jimmy's Harborside with his wife. Afterward, Billy O dropped her off in front of their house on Savin Hill Avenue in Dorchester and parked his car on the street. As he walked back toward his house, Billy O noticed a group of younger men walking rapidly toward him. They all had their hands in their pockets. Billy O knew what that meant—they were carrying.

Unarmed, Billy O turned and ran into the street. So did his pursuers. Billy O was heading for a vacant lot, and he almost made it. But he tripped on a manhole cover in the street and fell to the pavement. The Mullens caught up with him, pulled guns as he struggled to get up, and shot him four times in the head.

The next day Billy O's wife told reporters she had "no idea" who might have murdered her forty-three-year-old husband. Sure, she said, he enjoyed a wee small taste of the creature now and again, but never at home. And although Billy O sometimes muttered about these long-haired hippie types you saw on the Common nowadays, she told reporters that as far as she knew her late husband had "no enemies."

KENNY KILLEEN, DONALD'S brother, was known to the Mullens as "Balloonhead." But he was capable enough, and he didn't mind delegating authority. After Billy O's demise, Balloonhead decided to bring in more outside talent. This time he and his brother went to an old-time South Shore hood named Ben Tilley and hired him to make a bomb to plant under the hood of one of the Mullens' cars.

The Mullens got a tip and paid Tilley a visit at his house in Quincy. He was outnumbered and outgunned, so he immediately turned over the bomb to them and apologized.

"Nothing personal, guys," Tilley said. "It was just business."

They took the bomb, disabled it, and then left most of it, still looking quite ominous with all its dangling wires, on the porch of Kenny Killeen's bayfront home on Marine Road. However, he didn't seem to get the message, so the Mullens decided to take sterner measures.

On weekend mornings in the summer, Balloonhead would take the morning papers out onto his back porch and enjoy the fine weather while reading the papers and watching the boats. Soon the Mullens had their own boat in the harbor, monitoring the Killeen porch. The Mullen Navy had a walkie-talkie, which was used to communicate with the Mullen Army back on dry land. The Mullens had two cars parked on N Street, within shooting distance of Kenny's porch. One car was legit, and that was where the shooters sat, smoking cigarettes as they waited for Balloonhead to go outside onto his porch. The second car was stolen, wiped clean of prints, and parked directly in line to the porch. In the backseat of the second car was a rifle, a 30-ought-6, and a sandbag the sharpshooter could use to balance it on while drawing a bead on Killeen's head.

"We'd get the word from the boat that Balloonhead has come out onto his porch, and we'd run to the other car, wearing gloves," one Mullen said. "Twice we had him in our sights, but each time one of his kids came out. The third time, we had him cold. I fired, but the bullet hit the wrought-iron rail fence outside his house. He was hit by bullet fragments in the hand and somewhere else, but he was a marine, he knew what to do. He dropped and stayed down. But that was the end of him in the gang. He announced his retirement, instantly. He never left the house again for months. We stopped calling him 'Balloonhead.' Kenny's new nickname was 'Ben Bolt,' because he was bolted to his house."

FBI AGENT DENNIS Condon kept reaching out to Whitey Bulger, but the feds' courtship of him seemed to be going nowhere. In terms of inside information, he was no Stevie Flemmi. On July 7, 1971, Condon reported that Whitey "still has some inhibitions about furnishing information . . . if his productivity does not increase, consideration will be given to closing him out."

Whitey had more pressing matters on his mind than cultivating a relationship with the FBI. The Mullens were still hunting him and Donald Killeen, and Whitey told Condon he "was convinced if they did not make a move, they would be eliminated."

Whitey knew who he needed to see about making a move of his own, and it wasn't J. Edgar Hoover.

JOHNNY MARTORANO WAS now hanging out in a new joint. Basin Street was history. His new place was a small bar on Columbus Avenue in the South End, Duffy's Tavern. It was a temporary headquarters, because next door his brother Jimmy was constructing a new club with Howie Winter that they had named Chandler's. Buildings on Columbus Avenue cost next to nothing in 1972, because the South End was still mostly slums, its property values depressed by both the nearby public-housing projects and the rooming houses that attracted alcoholics slowly drinking their way to the bottom—the Pine Street Inn, the last resort of homeless winos in Boston.

Jimmy and Howie had been able to purchase a large building from the Boston Redevelopment Authority on the corner of Columbus and Dartmouth streets. In what would eventually become one of the city's more fashionable neighborhoods, they planned to open a club on the ground floor. On the four floors above their planned restaurant/lounge, they were putting in twenty-eight high-end apartments they planned to rent. When they bought the old building, one of the tenants was a barroom, and they quickly snapped up the liquor license.

As convicted felons, neither Jimmy nor Howie could own a liquor license, and even though Johnny could have held it in his name, that didn't seem wise, either. So the license for Duffy's Tavern, which would be transferred to Chandler's after the construction was complete, was held in the names of Jimmy's wife and Howie's daughter.

While the main part of the building was being renovated, the partners decided to keep the bar going. Duffy's Tavern was a small place, with maybe fifteen barstools and a handful of tables. One night in the spring of 1972, Johnny was sitting at one of the tables in Duffy's by himself, killing time, when he noticed someone walking across the room toward him.

The guy appeared to be in his early forties, with a very light complexion, blond hair, and blue eyes. He was dressed sharply, wearing a suit and tie, which pegged him as someone who was not from the South End. He stopped at Johnny's table, extended his hand, and smiled.

"You may not remember me, Johnny. I'm Jimmy Bulger. Billy O told me to come see you if I ever had a problem."

Johnny studied the man in front of him. He vaguely recalled maybe meeting him once before, one night at the Attic. But he said his name was Jimmy. Johnny seemed to remember that the guy in front of him had been introduced by another name—was it "Whitey"?

Johnny Martorano smiled at the guy with two names.

"Any friend of Billy's is a friend of mine," Johnny said and invited him to sit down and have a drink.

Whitey looked like a gangster-politician in that suit. He says he wants to meet with Howie Winter. He says, I have to get this thing in the Town resolved. That was what they all called Southie—"the Town." He showed respect. He knew how to ask for a favor. You knew he wasn't going to go see the Mafia because if Jerry Angiulo intervened he'd want to take over everything. I hadn't really been following what was going on over there in Southie, none of us had. But Whitey must have thought things weren't going well, or he wouldn't have reached out to me, to set up a meeting for him with Howie.

Whitey had figured out a way to end the war between the Killeens and the Mullens that didn't end with his own murder. The only way to accomplish that would be to dispose of his boss, Donald Killeen. Whitey naturally wouldn't even consider getting involved in such a plot unless he had a deal in place with the Mullens, who disliked him for a very good reason—he'd been trying to kill them, and vice versa.

Whitey needed someone to broker the deal for him, which was where Howie Winter came in. Howie knew the Mullens—Whitey had told Condon that much, months earlier—and they could be expected to go along with whatever Howie asked them to do. When they weren't stalking the Killeens, the Mullens were truck hijackers and tailgaters. They also burgled a lot of warehouses. They always needed a place to sell their truckloads of hot merchandise, and that was where Howie Winter came in. He was the Mullens' biggest fence, and once they got paid, the Mullens often stayed in Somerville to get drunk, recycling their profits back into various Winter Hill gin mills. It was a win-win, at least for Somerville.

Naturally Howie and the others in Somerville liked the Mullens a lot—they were earners. Whitey wanted Howie to guarantee that if he set up Donald Killeen, the Mullens wouldn't come looking for him next.

There was one other major sticking point. Once Donald Killeen was dead, Whitey wanted to merge the two crews, with himself as the boss. It was certainly an audacious suggestion, eliminating your own crew chief and then taking over the more powerful gang that had handled the murder on your behalf. But Whitey's pitch was that it would be in everyone's interest to halt the bloodshed. All the other gangs in Boston were consolidating—why shouldn't Southie's? As long as Southie was divided, it would be easy pickings for In Town. Stevie Flemmi and Frank Salemme might be gone, but sooner or later somebody else would move in to fill the vacuum. And ultimately, that couldn't be good news for Somerville, or for the remaining independents, like Johnny.

Howie agreed to arrange a sit-down for Whitey and the Mullens, but Whitey wasn't taking any chances. He didn't know many people from In Town, but one he had become friendly with was J. R. "Joe" Russo from East Boston.

Whitey asked Russo to check with Howie, just to make sure he wasn't walking into a trap. Russo made the call to Winter Hill and then reported back to Whitey that Howie had assured him everything was on the level. Less than a decade later, Whitey would be telling his FBI handlers how much he despised the Mafia, but in 1972 when his back was to the wall, he had no qualms about seeking their assistance—any port in a storm.

> The sit-down was at Chandler's, which we'd just opened. It was after hours, early one morning. For the Mullens, it was Pat Nee, Weasel Mantville, and Tommy King. I don't know where McGonagle was. Whitey was the only one on the other side. Howie was the mediator. He told them, he'd just been through one of these wars, and it made no sense. Everybody'd be better off if it got settled. At the end of the night I guess they had a deal.

Donald Killeen now lived in Framingham, and that was where they would get him. May 13 was a Saturday, and it was his son Greg's fourth birthday. His parents bought him a toy fire engine as his present. Shortly after 9 P.M., with the sun long down, Donald Killeen got a phone call. He told his wife he wanted to buy a newspaper, and went outside to his 1971 Chevrolet Nova.

"Several men charged the car," the *Globe* would later report, "rammed a submachine gun into the driver's side, and fired sixteen bullets."

Inside the house, Killeen's ten-year-old daughter heard the shots and thought they were fireworks. Killeen had seen the Mullens advancing on him, in a group, just the way they had with Billy O. Like Billy O, he'd been caught flat-footed. He died reaching into the glove compartment for the .38-caliber revolver police later found under his body.

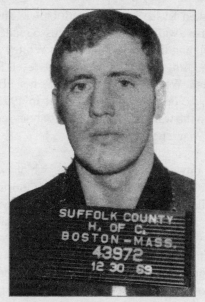

Weasel Mantville, a Mullen who died in the 1980s.

The next day, at the funeral home, a large bouquet arrived for Donald Killen from a Brookline florist, collect.

The card read, "Au Revoir."

JOHNNY MARTORANO WAS making ends meet, barely. Chandler's had just opened, and his name was on the payroll, if not the liquor license. But his women and his children were costing him a fortune every month. None of the mothers of his children worked. He was responsible for at least two rent payments, car payments, utility bills, wardrobes, and more. Everything that cost money, Johnny Martorano had two of.

He now had two daughters and two sons—his second son, Vincent, had been born in 1970. Johnny was now remarried, to Vincent's mother. They'd gotten hitched in New Hampshire.

Meanwhile, his first ex-wife, the former Nancy O'Neill, had remarried.

Her new husband was some guy from East Milton, he was a little older than me. I knew him. He'd been a friend of Wimpy Bennett's. I was visiting the girls one day, and I asked Jeannie how she was getting along with the new guy. Of course kids never really like their stepparents, I understand that. But she didn't care for him much at all, so I decided to have a private chat with him. I told this guy, if you ever lay a hand on either one of the girls, I'll shoot you in the head. Jeannie and Lisa didn't have any more complaints after that.

About the same time, Barbara got sick, and I asked Nancy to take in my son Johnny. He lived with his sisters maybe six months—they're still really close, after all these years. Barbara and Nancy always got along well, surprisingly I guess.

Everyone had to be supported. And there were other expenses as well—Johnny continued giving a couple of hundred a week to Stevie's common-law wife, Marion Hussey. That was what friends did for each other, when somebody had to go on the lam. And Stevie was, after all, Johnny's best friend

Johnny Martorano's life had become a country-music song—"Livin' here, lovin' there, lyin' in between." The new Mrs. Martorano was riding him hard all the time, inquiring in rather caustic terms where he was sleeping all those nights when he didn't come home.

"Life was a party, but you know, I couldn't have paid for everything with a 9-to-5 job, and I've never had one of those." So Johnny was hustling. He had some money out on the street, at a couple of points a week. The afternoons he'd spend at whatever track was open, along with most of his friends. Then he'd drive back to the South End, where he hung out nights. Duffy's Tavern was a dive—after last call, if nothing else was going on, Johnny would sometimes turn out the lights and sit by himself in the dark with a pellet gun, shooting the rats one by one as they slithered out of the walls.

Duffy's quickly became popular among the local boosters as a good place to unload their shoplifted merchandise. The way Johnny figured it, he was merely a pawnbroker without a license. He paid his thieves as much as they could have gotten at the pawnshops on Washington Street under the Orange Line. The only difference was that Johnny didn't have to let the cops periodically check out his shelves full of tagged swag.

Soon a continuous stream of junkies was showing up at Duffy's, lugging shopping bags full of obviously stolen merchandise. They boosted so much women's apparel Johnny finally got some clothing racks, which he used to set up his own version of Filene's Basement in the cellar. He paid the boosters between 10 and 15 percent of the price on the tags, then put the stolen clothes on sale for one-third of the label's list price, subject to haggling.

"That was enough of a markup so that I could make a profit and give a lot of stuff away," Martorano said. "It's an easy way to make friends. Somebody comes over, and you bring out a rack of fur coats and tell them, pick one or two out for yourself. It's something people remember. Gets 'em in good with their girlfriends, maybe even their wives."

Most of Martorano's boosters were black, but his best one was a white schoolteacher with a black boyfriend who Johnny knew from Roxbury. During the summer and school vacations she'd crisscross the country, hitting high-end department stores, stuffing the goods into cheap suitcases she'd send back to her boyfriend, who would call Johnny to come pick up the stuff.

Another regular booster at Duffy's was the head of an all-night cleaning crew in the downtown office buildings. He'd come in every few days with a couple of IBM Selectric typewriters, the best of that era, which usually retailed for about $300. The cleaning-crew boss wasn't greedy, he'd just steal one or two every week, from different buildings he cleaned. At $40 apiece, Johnny couldn't get his hands on enough Selectrics to keep the basement stocked. He also bought whatever stolen jewelry or gold he could pick up, and then moved it along for whatever markup he could get.

But no matter how fast Martorano made, or stole, money, he was falling further and further behind, even though Chandler's had become an immediate success as soon as it opened. Jimmy Martorano and Howie Winter had been right—there were enough affluent white people in the South End now to support a decent club.

Eventually they shut down Duffy's Tavern. Then they rented the old Duffy's space to Joe McDonald, one of Howie Winter's partners in Somerville. Joe Mac, as he was known, set up his son-in-law in a new liquor store. As

Joe McDonald, added to the FBI's Most Wanted List in 1976, at different points in his life.

for Chandler's itself, it quickly became the place where both Howie and Johnny conducted a lot of their business. For their Boston associates, it was a more convenient location than the garage on Winter Hill that served as Howie's hometown headquarters. And the ambience was a lot more upscale than it had ever been at Duffy's Tavern.

Howie and Johnny weren't formally hooked up yet, but it was moving in that direction.

WITH THE MURDER of Donald Killeen, Whitey Bulger was now on top of the rackets in South Boston. But that wasn't nearly enough for Whitey. Like Howie Winter and a host of other Boston gangsters, he was another one of those guys born in 1929—just a couple of years too young to have fought in World War II. The gangsters born in 1929 were forever trying to prove to the slightly older World War II vets in their neighborhoods that they were every bit as tough as they were, even if they hadn't gotten the chance to battle the Japs and the Nazis the way Jerry Angiulo and Louie Grieco had.

Whitey was a World War II buff, always reading military history books and later buying videotapes about the war. But his greater regret was that he had wasted so many of his prime robbing years in prison. Now he wanted to make up for lost time, and so he had another idea he wanted to bounce off Howie Winter and Johnny Martorano. He arranged to meet them at Chandler's to discuss a business proposition.

Whitey's pitch to Howie and Johnny was simple, and irresistible. He said the city was full of "independent" bookies, taking action but not paying anybody for what he called protection. In Town couldn't get all of them, so the time was ripe for another gang to move in and start grabbing the unaffiliated bookmakers.

Whitey had obviously worked out his spiel beforehand,

and he delivered it flawlessly. Like any good speaker, he began with a joke. His mother, he said, had actually come up with the proposal he was pitching them.

"My mother says to me, Jimmy, stick to gambling. If they pinch you, the most you can get is one, maybe two years. She says, don't rob no more banks, Jimmy. I can't handle another thirty-year sentence. I'm tired of visiting you in prison."

Howie and Johnny chuckled. It wasn't true, of course. It was Whitey's late father and younger brother Billy, the state rep and now state senator from Southie, who'd made the early trips. And later, as James Bulger Sr. aged and Billy had to assume the responsibilities of a father with a new baby every year, it was a sportswriter for the *Globe* named Will McDonough who would stop by Leaven worth whenever the Red Sox were playing the A's in Kansas City. Another Southie guy who had made several journeys to dreary Leavenworth was a homosexual bar owner from Southie, Hank Garrity. According to a 1973 FBI report, Garrity was one of the first tavern owners in Southie to start paying Whitey for "protection"—$500 a week. So Whitey's story about his mother's prison visits wasn't true. But the way he embellished this personal anecdote was almost . . . charming.

He then regaled his fellow gangsters with various prison stories—mostly about Alcatraz, the Rock—that in the coming years they would hear over and over and over again, at the garage on Marshall Street. Having softened them up, Whitey utilized another ancient rhetorical technique. He flattered his listeners.

Whitey said he envisioned this new gang of theirs as a group of "working partners." Everyone would be "capable." It wasn't going to be like In Town, with its hierarchical structure—Jerry Angiulo holding court at the Dog House or Café Pompeii, a guy who'd never even personally killed anybody, barking out orders to Larry Baione, who'd then dispatch his made men to tell the "associates" to do something. . . .

In this new gang that Whitey envisioned, everyone would have notches on their guns—real notches, not by proxy.

Whitey wasn't disrespecting In Town, he stressed, glancing at Johnny, the only one at the table with any Italian blood. But this mob would have none of the Mass-card-burning nonsense and all the rest of the mumbo-jumbo about "this thing of ours." There would be plenty of business opportunities for both In Town and this new crew, Whitey explained, and nobody would have to step on the other guys' toes.

LAWYER: Is there an area in Boston called Winter Hill?

MARTORANO: Yes, Winter Hill is a section of Somerville, Mass.

LAWYER: And where is Somerville again in relation to Boston?

MARTORANO: Just outside of Boston.

LAWYER: Winter Hill Gang, why did it get that name?

MARTORANO: A bunch of guys from Winter Hill.

LAWYER: Were there any particular requirements to be part of Winter Hill?

MARTORANO: No.

LAWYER: Did you have to be Italian. You are Italian, right?

MARTORANO: No.

LAWYER: Didn't have to be Italian. Did you have some Italians as part of Winter Hill?

MARTORANO: Correct.

LAWYER: Did you have some people who weren't Italian?

MARTORANO: Correct.

The way Whitey saw it, there were five guys who weren't with In Town who were especially capable, and who should be working together. Three of them are sitting here tonight, Whitey said. Howie, Johnny, and himself.

He proposed two other Somerville guys, who had long been hooked up with Howie in some of his rackets, mainly numbers. One was Joe McDonald, who had already been cut in on the Columbus Avenue project. Joe McDonald was a taciturn killer, solid as a rock. Born in 1917, Joe Mac was another one of those World War II guys. He'd been serving on the USS *Indianapolis* with his brother when it was torpedoed by a Japanese submarine in 1945. Bobbing with hundreds of other men in the oil-slick waters, he'd watched as sharks closed in on the helpless, floating sailors. Joe Mac's brother had been one of those devoured by the sharks, as Joe watched helplessly. After he was rescued and sent back to Pearl Harbor, Joe Mac had immediately volunteered to go back out on the next warship headed for Japan.

Joe McDonald was a man's man. I loved him. I liked to think of myself as being just like him. You know, since Joe died, I've tried to find out more about what he did in World War II. I've asked everybody who knew him, and all I can find out is that he just never talked about it to anybody. But boy, he was tough. And you could count on him—totally, absolutely. The only problem he had was alcohol. Most of the time he was fine, but he was a binge drinker. He lived on Marshall Street, too, just down from the garage. We called Joe's place the Fire House, because that's where we hung out when we were waiting to hit somebody. We'd have spotters out looking for the guy we wanted to hit, and when they'd see him, they'd use walkie-talkies to call us—give us the alarm.

Sometimes Joe wouldn't show up at the garage in

the morning, and you'd go down to see him at the Fire House, and his family would say, 'He's sick.' That meant he was on a bender.

Joe Mac made a lot of money, but when it came to spending it, he was like Wimpy. Ten bucks could dress Joe for years. One time, he was in the can, and his older brother Leo was out, and Leo sent him $50 for sneakers and to buy a few things at the commissary. Joe sent the money back to Leo. He said, "I don't need anything in here. They got everything in here for free."

In 1960, Joe and Leo McDonald robbed a dairy in Stoneham with a third man. The McDonalds were quickly arrested, but the third man got away. After their convictions, the judge called the McDonalds into the courtroom and demanded the name of the third man. Leo haughtily refused and got hit with another ten years. Then Joe was brought in and offered the same deal. He shook his head.

"I can't tell you, judge," he said. "The reason I can't tell you is because I wasn't there. You convicted the wrong man."

McDonald was shipped back to prison, with no additional time. He'd handled it perfectly.

About '63, Joe's doing time for the dairy robbery in one of those minimum-security-prison forest colonies, and he just took off. He wanted to help out Buddy in the gang war, and he was one of the Hill's top guns. I heard later, he's the one who took the acetylene torch to the balls of one of the McLaughlins. Another time, I heard he buried a hammer in a guy's skull. So he lasts on the street until 1966, but then he gets into a brawl in some barroom on Com Ave in Brighton, and the cops come, and he shoots it

out with them, and they don't take Joe Mac 'til he
runs out of bullets.

They ship him back to prison, and now he's got
this extra time on and after for the escape and the
shootout. But he goes to the prison law library every
day, does the research, and all by himself, pro se, no
lawyer, he gets the original conviction overturned.
Then, since he shouldn't have been in jail in the first
place, how can he have "escaped"? And you can't
charge him with shooting at the cops because they
were trying to get him for a crime he didn't commit.
So he walked. It was pretty amazing what he did.

The fifth partner in the gang would be Jimmy Sims, born
in 1935, the wheelman everyone wanted to work with on
a hit. He'd been the driver on the hits on both Hughes
brothers. He was a car-stealing whiz, the quickest thief in
Somerville, which was saying a lot. He could grab a Ford
in thirty seconds. Despite the age difference with Joe Mac,
they had been partners for years. He was a member of
Teamsters Local 25—all the Somerville guys were. They

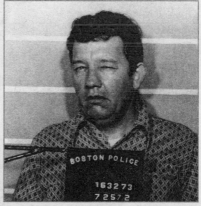

Jimmy Sims, a partner in the Winter Hill Gang, vanished in 1987.

owned Local 25 and its president, Billy McCarthy, who would one day become national president of the International Brotherhood.

Jimmy Sims was an Irish kid, an orphan, did time, reform school, Walpole, the usual. He was a very good thief. Besides being a Teamster, he had another trade—he was a steeple jack. He could go up a steeple and tear it down, one brick at a time. He was another guy that liked to drink—Howie always said he was worse than Joe when he got going, but I never saw it.

He used to hang around the Playboy Club, and Joe Namath's place downtown. He was tight with Jimmy Flynn, another Teamster from Winter Hill who later

Jimmy Flynn, a Winter Hill associate and later high-ranking official of Teamsters Local 25.

became the boss of the Local 25 movie crews. Flynn even wangled himself a bit part in *Good Will Hunting*. He was the judge, which was pretty funny, considering he'd been tried for the murder of Brian Halloran, which of course Whitey did. I can still remember both of 'em, Sims and Flynn, swaggering into the Playboy Club, dressed in full-length mink coats.

LAWYER: Other than thinking somebody is a good guy or somebody might be a good earner, were there any requirements to join the Winter Hill Gang?

MARTORANO: No, these were neighborhood guys, army, navy, marines, or just from the neighborhood. No membership or none of this.

LAWYER: You didn't have to take oaths or any of that?

MARTORANO: No oaths, no.

LAWYER: You didn't have to go through this rigamarole of the Mafia?

MARTORANO: No.

Whitey proposed that everyone keep their own separate rackets. Whitey would still have the bars in Southie. Sims and McDonald wouldn't have to cut anybody in on their truck hijackings, not to mention their increasingly brazen robberies of stamp and coin dealers. Howie and his Somerville crew could still control numbers and horse-racing bets in what *Look* magazine once described as the All-American City. Meanwhile, Johnny would retain his boosters and his bank scams and whatever else he was doing with the Campbell brothers in Roxbury.

Everybody would still have their "associates." The associates just wouldn't be cut in on the new sports gambling. That racket would be reserved for the partners. That was where the real money was going to be from now on, Whitey explained.

LAWYER: And you were also doing a shylocking business at the time, were you not?

MARTORANO: Minimal.

LAWYER: Goes hand in hand with gambling, doesn't it?

MARTORANO: Once you're in gambling, you end up in the shylocking business.

LAWYER: Weren't you a gambler yourself?

MARTORANO: I was a gambler. It's a different thing.

What this new gang first needed to do, Whitey continued, was find bookies to "protect." Then they could start moving the bookies they controlled away from numbers, and toward sports. Whitey reminded them that the state was starting its own lottery. For the time being, there would be only one drawing a week, on Saturday night, but the future seemed obvious. At some point the state would have the numbers racket wrapped up tight, under a different name of course.

The politicians would say that the money was going for "local aid" to the cities and towns. The take from the new numbers games would be "for the children." This new Massachusetts State Lottery would be controlled by the state treasurer, Bob Crane, a close political ally of Whitey's brother. Soon, at Billy Bulger's annual St. Patrick's Day roast in South Boston, Whitey's brother would be introducing Crane as "the biggest bookie in the state."

He wasn't kidding.

Once the state got into it, you could see numbers start to crumble. It was slow at first, because the state didn't pay off like nigger pool. When you won in the state lottery, you had taxes taken out of your money, there was no way around it. But even before the taxes it was less. When I was in numbers, I would use Doc Sagansky for the layoffs—all the big bookies did, Abie Sarkis, Bernie McGarry. Doc used to pay $800 for $1 on three numbers, $5,000 for four numbers. Before the state lottery, everybody always used the same number—that's how the *Record* could put it in the paper every night. It was based on the early races, that's why you couldn't play the number after 3 in the afternoon. If Suffolk was open, you used their numbers, if not, somewhere in New York. Aqueduct, maybe. By 4:30, 5, you had three of the four numbers, you could start sending out the runners.

Whitey explained to his future partners how dogs and horses were all right—Howie made a nice living controlling that action in all the bars in Somerville. And in Southie, Whitey himself handled dogs in the summer. It was one of the rackets he'd been involved in with Billy O. But all that was for old guys. The horses and dogs weren't on TV. The next big thing in gambling was going to be sports, specifically, the National Football League. The games were on TV every Sunday, and everybody watched them. Everybody wanted to bet on pro football, even squares. They all thought they were experts. They were ripe for the picking.

Outside of Nevada, the NFL didn't allow gambling on its games. So the mob wouldn't have to worry about this new state lottery commission eventually pushing them aside, the way it would be doing with the numbers.

So far Whitey had been the affable, self-effacing gladhander they'd come to know. But when he outlined how the proceeds would be cut up, it became clear that he wasn't planning on being the junior partner for long.

Of the five partners, four would each get one-sixth of the proceeds. The fifth partner was Whitey, and he would take a third. After all, he explained, he had more expenses. He still had all these younger guys, the Mullens, to take care of back in Southie. Even though they were no longer in open revolt, "the kids" remained restive. His third, after he got through cutting it up with the Mullens, would actually be more like 5 percent.

Whitey asked Howie and Johnny to consider how different his situation was from theirs. All his enemies were not only alive, they were still hanging out in the same neighborhood with him. Whitey hadn't won his gang war in the same way that the other partners had won theirs, by wiping out the opposition. That would come later—Whitey didn't come right out and say that, but that was the impression he left.

It was an easy sell. One-sixth of something was better than one-third of nothing. It didn't take them long to figure out how they would grab the bookies. They would send out their own guys, their "associates" as Whitey preferred to call them. Their associates would find bookies to bet with, and as long as they won, they'd collect and keep playing. Once they lost, they'd just tell the bookie, "Fuck you, I ain't paying."

If somebody from In Town showed up to collect, you'd know the guy was with the Angiulos. You'd pay what you owed, and cross that bookie off your list. If nobody came by to threaten you, then somebody—usually Johnny and Howie—would show up to tell the bookie about his new partners.

The bookie would now be splitting 50-50, but only on the profits, not the losses. Say a bookie lost $10,000 one week—the gang would not be on the hook for $5,000. If the bookie wanted to borrow the $10,000, the Hill would be there to loan it to him, at a point a week—$100. Then the next week the bookie makes, say, $30,000. He repays the Hill the $10,000 loan and is left with a profit of $20,000. He would then owe the gang half of his overall profit—$10,000.

Whitey's other idea was that they would offer to back bookies who wanted to get into betting on football. Long-term, that turned out to be the Hill's biggest mistake. In the numbers racket, everything was fairly predictable, especially if you could control the daily winner by manipulating the handle at the track—usually Suffolk Downs—that was used to establish the daily number. But Whitey and the others were novices at sports betting. They failed to take into account that if you hit a bad patch in sports gambling, even the bank—the gang—was going to be hemorrhaging such large amounts of cash that they, too, would have to go to bigger shylocks, and in Boston that meant Jerry Angiulo.

The way we considered it was, think about two people—one is a bookmaker you know and the other is a gambler you know. Guaranteed, the bookmaker is going to be living in a better house than the gambler. Because long-term the odds are on his side. As long as a bookmaker is patient and has enough money to ride out a bad stretch, in the end he wins. Bookmakers got no big edge in any one particular game. If you're a gambler, you can win anytime. You can hit a streak and keep winning for weeks. But in the end, greed takes over and you lose. It happens every time. What's the old saying? "All horseplayers die broke." It's so true, and it applies to sports bettors, too.

In the beginning, the Hill had visions of going around to their bookies every week—guys like Dick O'Brien on the South Shore, Tommy Ryan in Cambridge, and Charlie Raso on the near North Shore—and cutting up huge pots of cash, 10 grand here, 20 grand there. They'd be rolling in dough, and with any luck, they wouldn't have to risk shooting anybody.

Now they just had to close the deal with Jerry Angiulo. Meeting as usual at the Dog House on Prince Street,

Angiulo and the new gang leaders, Howie and Johnny, quickly hammered out an agreement. From now on, all bookmakers had to be connected with either In Town or the Hill. In other words, it was open season on independent bookmakers. Angiulo knew he couldn't control every bookie anyway, and this way, he was partnering up with a group that might otherwise cause him problems down the road. The likelihood of an eventual war would be greatly diminished if everybody was making money, working together, more or less.

But before they left, Angiulo gave his two new, younger partners some prescient advice: "If you get into betting on games, make sure you got a barrel of money, 'cause you're gonna need it."

> Jerry had it figured out a lot better than we did. He was financing bookies; all he cared about was one point a week on the money they owed him, the interest—the vig, as it's called. He would back a guy who backed sports. Guy loses his shirt and has to borrow a hundred grand from Jerry, it's a point a week—a grand a week, forever. Jerry wasn't into sports gambling, he was into shylocking.

Just as Howie and Johnny weren't paying close enough attention when Angiulo mentioned that barrel of money they'd be needing, they likewise ignored the other tip Angiulo offered them, about a guy he'd heard had been hanging out at Chandler's lately.

"Stay the fuck away from Tony Ciulla," the underboss of Boston said, not as a threat but as friendly advice, from one businessman to another. "He's no fuckin' good."

Later on, they couldn't say they hadn't been warned.

CHANDLER'S BECAME A hot spot, mentioned in the city's gossip columns. When the 1973 gangster movie

The Friends of Eddie Coyle was being filmed in Boston, actor Robert Mitchum hung out there nightly, along with his driver from Local 25, Fat Harry Johnson. As someone who'd done time himself almost thirty years earlier on a trumped-up marijuana charge in Hollywood, Mitchum fit in well with the Chandler's crew.

Also in the cast, both in the movie and at Chandler's, was Bobo Petricone, Buddy McLean's old pal who'd moved to Hollywood, changed his name to Alex Rocco, and become an actor. With his role in *The Godfather* behind him, Bobo was now back in his hometown, playing a bank-robbing gangster who bought guns from Mitchum's title character.

Mitchum was a John Wayne type, a two-fisted drinking cowboy. Howie and I are having dinner with him one night in Chandler's and some cops come in and serve both of us with subpoenas for the grand jury.

Fat Harry Johnson, Mitchum's driver
during the making of *Eddie Coyle*.

Howie is real embarrassed, and he apologizes to Mitchum, and Mitchum just laughs and says, "I'm just glad they didn't serve me."

Another guy from the movie who was in Chandler's all the time was Peter Yates, the director. You know that scene at the end of the movie when they take Mitchum to the Bruins game and get him drunk, and then Peter Boyle shoots him in the head from the backseat? Before they shot it, Yates asked Howie for his . . . insight, I guess you'd say. Scene turned out pretty well, don't you think? Very realistic.

In addition to the nightly socializing, a lot of business was conducted out of Chandler's. As Jerry Angiulo had heard, one guy who had started hanging around was a local swindler and degenerate gambler named Fat Tony Ciulla. A few years earlier, he'd tried to run a past-posting

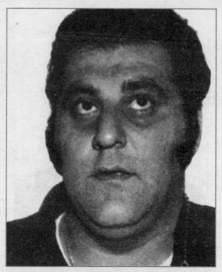

Fat Tony Ciulla, the race fixer who eventually went into the Witness Protection Program.

scam on a Mafia bookie—that was how Angiulo had gotten to know, and intensely dislike, Ciulla.

Fat Tony was always working on a new grift. One of his more successful flimflams involved a large diamond pinkie ring that he always carried with him in a velvet-lined box from the high-end jeweler Shreve Crump & Lowe. Whenever he found a suitable mark, Fat Tony would offer to sell him his prized possession. To show what a trusting soul he was, Fat Tony would hand the Shreve box to the mark and tell him, take it to a jeweler, get it appraised, and then bring it back to me.

The mark would quickly find out the stone was genuine, worth maybe $30,000. He'd bring the box back to Fat Tony, who'd quickly stick it back in his pocket. After much negotiation, they'd finally agree on a very reasonable price and then Fat Tony would give the mark back the ring—except, of course, it wasn't the same ring. It was in an identical box from the same store, and the stone was in the exact same gold-plated setting. But

Bobby Gallinaro, "Bobby G," a Somerville bookie and associate of Howie Winter.

instead of a diamond, the mark would have bought himself a zircon.

Whatever money Fat Tony could steal, he blew at the track. He had to place all his bets at the track, because bookies refused to take any action from him. Fat Tony was a pariah. On the first night that he had appeared in Chandler's in 1972, it was to settle a betting debt with one of Howie's top bookies in Somerville, Bobby Gallinaro. Fat Tony's brother-in-law, Eddie Ardolino, was a friend of Johnny's from the old days at Basin Street. So Martorano asked Ardolino to bring his wayward in-law around to Chandler's to settle up his debt to Bobby G.

As Howie and Johnny sat at a table, Eddie Ardolino appeared in the doorway of Chandler's. Behind him stood a hulking, unshaven, shabbily dressed man. He was six feet five inches and had to weigh at least 300 pounds. It was Fat Tony Ciulla. He was only twenty-eight years old, but he

Eddie Ardolino, Ciulla's brother-in-law, who warned Howie Winter against doing business with Fat Tony.

looked decades older. They walked over to the table and Fat Tony pressed a bulging letter-size envelope into Ardolino's hand. Ardolino then handed the envelope to Howie as Fat Tony bowed his head, to avoid making eye contact.

"There's $2,000 in there," Eddie Ardolino told Howie. "That's all he's got and he borrowed this from his mother." He shook his head. "I'm telling you, Howie, don't ever do nothing with this guy. He's a big piece of shit."

Within a couple of weeks, though, Howie was often huddling in a back booth with Fat Tony. Like Ciulla, Howie loved the horses, and both owned a few. Tony had been fixing races, or at least trying to, ever since he was a kid. He'd done time for race fixing in Rhode Island, and he'd also been arrested at least once at Suffolk Downs. But now he claimed to have worked out a system. Johnny was wary; he trusted the judgment of both Jerry Angiulo and Eddie Ardolino. But they all needed money.

JOHNNY MIGHT BE hanging out in a slightly more up-scale neighborhood now, but sometimes he had to deal with an issue from out of the past—like Nelson Padron, the Roxbury drug dealer he'd pistol-whipped at Slade's for the Campbells.

In February 1973, when Padron was about to go away on an income-tax-evasion rap, he got into his head that he was going to settle a few old scores before he left, starting with Johnny Martorano.

One Saturday night, a woman Martorano knew came running into Chandler's and told Johnny that Nelson was in Roxbury telling people he was going to get Martorano. It wasn't the first time Johnny had heard that Nelson was shooting his mouth off, so all night he kept a close eye on the traffic outside on Dartmouth Street. Finally, after midnight, he saw Padron's silver Mercedes convertible glide past Chandler's.

Johnny wordlessly nodded at Nicky Femia, one of

Barboza's old crew who happened to be drinking at Chandler's that evening. They hurriedly left the bar and got into Johnny's car, Femia at the wheel, Johnny in the back with a carbine.

When Nelson comes back around down Columbus and turns right onto Dartmouth Street, we pull up beside him and I let go with the carbine. The next day it was in the papers that the cops said they'd found six bullet holes in the car. But I know I only had time to shoot twice, before Nelson stopped the car. We had to keep driving.

Poor Nelson, he was hit pretty bad but somehow he managed to drive all the way to Mass. General, and then he crashed the Mercedes into an abutment. He was on the danger list for a while, and with all the bullet holes, the cops had probable cause to search his car. They found a bag of coke, an unregistered handgun, and $2,400 cash in the car. I still remember the headline in the *Herald*: "He's riddled by bullets, is arrested."

From then on, whenever I saw Nelson, he was on a cane.

In the daytime, the gang still congregated at Howie Winter's garage—Marshall Motors. Chandler's was a nicer place to hang, but it couldn't accommodate that many wiseguys. It would have been too obvious. So the garage in Somerville was the most logical place for the gang to have its headquarters, and its location soon gave the new mob its name—the Winter Hill Gang. The fact that Howie Winter was one of the bosses of the gang was nothing more than coincidence.

In the front of the building, there was an actual garage, run by Johnny's brother Jimmy and Johnny's old friend George Kaufman. Yet another hood born in 1929, the mild-mannered Kaufman first served as a liaison to the gang members in prison or on the lam, and later to the Jewish bookies from whom "the Hill" would extract tribute.

In the back of the building were the "offices" of Howie and Johnny. Nobody who owed money ever wanted to be taken back there. On the wall was a poster of two vultures perched on a dead tree in the middle of a desert, with one vulture saying to the other, PATIENCE, HELL, I WANT TO KILL SOMEBODY.

Next to his desk Howie had a trapdoor built into the floor, leading to the unfinished basement. What the trapdoor was used for was left to the imaginations of his visitors, most of whom owed the Hill money, and all of whom had heard chilling stories about the gang.

Farther down Marshall Street, Winter owned a house. He lived upstairs and for a nominal rent allowed the other gang members to use the ground floor as a more informal clubhouse than the garage—the Pad, they called it. Joe McDonald's Fire House was a few doors south.

With so many known hoodlums congregating in the area, even the Somerville police couldn't totally ignore the comings and goings. Occasionally they or the state police would raid the garage. So all the mob's hardware— guns, silencers, stolen cars, etc.—had to be stashed elsewhere. For that purpose, the gang rented a bank of garages a few hundred yards away, at the top of Winter Hill. The garages were particularly useful because the stolen cars—the ones that would be used on hits—could be brought into the garages through a back alley that was not visible from the street. The Hill called the stolen cars "boilers" because they were so hot.

The garages were also where shotguns could be sawed off, and bodies occasionally dismembered.

WHITEY BULGER WAS the only original partner who didn't have some ties to Somerville, but he, too, quickly

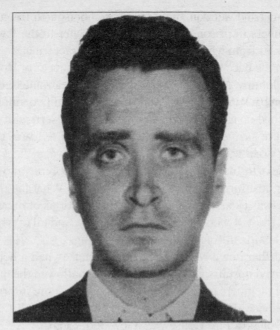

Jack Curran drove Whitey's car back to Southie
each day after Bulger arrived at the garage.

began spending at least a few hours at the garage every
weekday. From the start, though, he was a man apart.
Everyone else parked at the garage, but Whitey would always get out across Broadway from the garage in the supermarket parking lot. He always insisted on driving himself,
but he brought with him one of his older Southie guys, Jack
Curran, who would then drive Whitey's car back to Southie.

After getting out of his car, Whitey would pull down
his hat and wrap his coat collar up around his neck before
walking across the street, in case any cops who had the
place under surveillance hadn't figured out that he showed
up there every morning at the same time. He'd leave the
garage the same way around 3 P.M., crossing Broadway
and getting back into the driver's seat, while Curran slid
across the seat to the passenger's side.

As time went on, more and more hoods frequented the garage. As the old saying went, if you were indicted, you were invited. Now that the gang war against the McLaughlins was a fading memory, Charlestown guys started stopping by, as well as Teamsters from Local 25, and ocassionally Whitey Bulger's still-uneasy Mullen allies. Black guys from Roxbury occasionally came by to pay their respects to Johnny. The garage was also a good place to get their cars fixed. George Kaufman didn't ask any questions about bullet holes, or dark, sticky stains on the floorboards.

The Hill had long been home to many of Boston's more

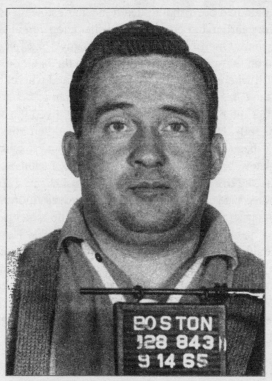

Tommy Ballou, a colorful Charlestown hoodlum murdered in 1970.

colorful gangsters. One of Howie's closest associates from Charlestown was a guy named Tommy Ballou. Ballou always carried two personal possessions: a $100 bill and a longshoreman's grappling hook.

If he ever got in a barroom brawl, Ballou would try to get face-to-face with the guy he was taking on. Before his foe could jump him, Ballou would pull out his C-note and throw it up in the air. Usually, the other brawler would be at least half drunk, and would pause just long enough to watch the bill float to the floor, then lean over to pick it up. Which was Tommy Ballou's cue to grab his grappling hook and sink it into the other guy's back, thereby ending the fight.

Ballou had been shot to death in Charlestown a couple of years earlier, but other colorful characters remained on the scene. One of the Local 25 wiseguys had once decided on the spur of the moment to rob the bank on Winter Hill where he had his own accounts, and where, much like the *Cheers* bar, everyone knew his name.

After the robbery, the hood quickly realized the extent of his folly. He drove straight to a drug-addled physician who'd been stripped of his license to practice, and who had lately been working under the table, including supplying the drugs that Fat Tony Ciulla sometimes used to fix horse races. The hood ordered the quack to break his leg, then set it, and forge a set of medical documents indicating that he'd been wearing the cast for weeks. That way he could "prove" he couldn't have robbed the bank, despite what all the eyewitnesses said. He beat the rap, although he would later be indicted in Local 25 shakedowns.

LAWYER: What was Mr. Bulger's role in the gang?
MARTORANO: Intimidating people, mostly.

Many of the hoods, even Mafia members, stayed around the garage to socialize while having their cars serviced by the garage crews who worked for Kaufman and Jimmy Martorano. Sometimes the other mobsters would wander back into the gang's offices, jangling their car keys. If they were too loud, Whitey would jump up and order them to stop shaking the keys. He couldn't take it, he said. It reminded him of the "screws" at Alcatraz.

Local women—some wannabe molls, others just salt-of-the-earth neighborhood types—would regularly stop by with home-cooked food for the boys. Whitey seethed whenever any female wandered into the garage. He talked even more about women than he did about Alcatraz, or about taking massive doses of LSD in CIA-sponsored experiments while he was in prison in Atlanta in the late 1950s.

"Women should be subservient," Whitey would say, over and over again. "He who controls the purse strings controls everything."

At which point, the Somerville guys would surreptitiously steal glances at one another, trying not to let Whitey see their smirks. This guy had obviously never met their broads. They figured he was just running around with project girls from Southie who didn't know any better. Like Teresa Stanley, his longtime girlfriend. When they were out for dinner, Whitey never allowed her to have more than two drinks, so the other guys in the gang would wait until Whitey went to the men's room, and then they'd let her gulp down a couple of quick ones. Once Teresa was half in the bag, she'd start mouthing off to Whitey, and that would really drive him over the edge.

When it came to women, Whitey tried to practice what he preached. One time, a couple of the Mullens were over at his apartment in Quincy. They were all sitting at the kitchen table when suddenly Whitey yelled at one of his girlfriends to bring him his slippers.

She obediently complied with his order, bringing him

the slippers and offering them to him as he sat at the table with his men. Whitey glared at her.

"I want you to put them on for me," he said, barely controlling his rage. The woman knew better than to talk back to him. She immediately dropped to her knees and crawled under the table. Then, after struggling to remove the tight-fitting boots he always wore outside, she gently placed the slippers on his feet.

Later on, I heard he told people he was afraid to have kids because of all the LSD he'd taken in those CIA prison experiments in Atlanta back in the 1950s. Remember all those scare stories they put out in the '60s about LSD causing chromosome damage?

But I can tell you he had at least one kid—a son. I never knew the girlfriend or the kid, because as far as I could tell he had nothing to do with them. But around 1973, one morning Whitey comes into the garage and says, My son died. It was a sudden thing, he says. The boy was about six at the time. He says I know you guys will probably want to do something, and I appreciate the thought but it's not necessary. That was it. He never missed a day for the funeral, or the wake, or anything. Never mentioned the kid again, either.

I read a story recently that described Whitey as a "doting dad." Maybe, but I never saw it.

Everyone at the garage noticed Whitey's boots early on. Whitey claimed he wore them so that he could conceal a blade, a big Bowie knife, in the boot. As a convicted felon, he couldn't get a permit to legally carry a gun. Everybody understood that. In fact, Whitey's knife was good for business, because sometimes Whitey would suddenly stride over to the garage wall, pull the knife out of his boot, and begin stabbing the concrete blocks. It made quite an impression on more than one reluctant deadbeat who'd been summoned to Marshall Street. But as time went on, they began to realize there was another reason Whitey preferred boots.

His boots all had built-in lifts—high heels. He was using them to add two or three inches to his height. Whitey wasn't as short as his politician brother Billy, whom a judge would someday dub "the corrupt midget." But in his stocking feet Whitey wasn't much over five feet seven—perhaps two or three inches taller than Billy.

Most of the hoods who hung around the garage shared the usual guys' locker-room banter. If they weren't discussing an upcoming score, they were talking about women, or sports, Whitey shunned such small talk. He preferred to discuss books—especially his reading list at Alcatraz. He liked to quote Machiavelli, and Sun Tzu's classic *The Art of War*. But perhaps the book he mentioned most often was *Mein Kampf* by Adolf Hitler.

I didn't even know what *Mein Kampf* was until years later. But every time I'd see him, with that blond hair and those blue eyes, I'd think how perfect he would have looked in an SS uniform in one of those World War II movies. He would have had to play a colonel, of course. He was already wearing the boots and he liked to click his heels, like Colonel Klink in *Hogan's Heroes*. The only difference was, Whitey was serious.

For a gangster, Whitey was a very strange guy.

In his infrequent lighter moods, Whitey would talk about his youth in South Boston, how he had tried to model himself on James Cagney, whose Warner Bros. gangster movies he would sit through all day, trying to pick up

Cagney's mannerisms. He wanted to be Rocky Sullivan in *Angels with Dirty Faces,* or later Cody Jarrett in *White Heat*—without suffering their ultimate celluloid fates, of course.

"I got my first gun when I was sixteen," Whitey used to tell them. "I went in to rob a liquor store and the guy behind the counter laughed at me, because I looked like I was about thirteen. He told me to get the fuck outta there, so I shot him in the leg before I ran out of the place."

We used to laugh when he mentioned he modeled himself on Cagney. Because the first gangster movie that came to our minds when we thought about Whitey sure wasn't *Public Enemy* or *The Roaring Twenties.* We thought Whitey was Richard Widmark in *Kiss of Death.* You know, Tommy Udo—he's giggling as he pushes the old lady's wheelchair down the stairs. That's the kind of gangster Whitey was, not that I was complaining. I'm not kidding when I say it was good for business, at least the business we were in, to have somebody as insane as Whitey around the garage. People were afraid of him. Nobody even wanted to be in the same car when he was driving, he was out of control behind the wheel. Poor Jack Curran—he always said he was scared stiff coming over from Southie, the way Whitey was cutting in and out of that bumper-to-bumper traffic on the old Central Artery. Jack would just be hanging on for dear life.

Another of Whitey's obsessions was his failed flight back in 1955–56, after his indictment for that multistate string of bank robberies. He would recall his aimless driving across the country while on the lam with a young girlfriend. She had quickly begun to nag him, demanding that he turn around and drive her back home to Dorchester.

After their return, it hadn't taken long for H. Paul Rico to make the pinch.

"Next time I have to go on the lam," he would say, "I'll be ready."

Indeed, as early as 1977, Whitey was already setting up fake identities for himself, taking the names of male infants who had died shortly after their births in 1929 and getting driver licenses in their names. As he said over and over again, he had no intention of ever going back to prison.

Despite his peccadilloes, the rest of the Hill quickly realized that Bulger was a capable guy with more than a few skills that would come in handy. Next to Jimmy Sims, he was the quickest car thief in the crew. He had impeccable police sources. Early on, he came up with a list of state police "undercover" license plates, which enabled the Hill to know if they were under more than the usual surveillance. He was a fearless driver, even if he did scare Jack Curran out of his wits.

More than anyone else at the garage, Whitey was into gadgetry. He loved going to the local cop shops and checking out the latest technological advances. He'd show up on Marshall Street with some new toy, like an infrared gun sight, or a tiny telescope that would fit into the palm of his hand, with which he claimed he could check out cops who might have the garage under surveillance. Whitey would demonstrate how the telescope worked by palming it while he raised his hand as if to scratch an eyebrow. He would then report on what was sticking out of a shopper's bag in the supermarket parking lot across Broadway. Nobody ever quite figured out what the telescope's real utility might be to the gang, but everyone agreed it was definitely impressive.

Whitey also mastered walkie-talkies and police radios. The Hill always tried to plan ahead, and one thing they knew they would need on any hit was a good crash car—somebody behind the boiler in which the shooters were riding. The crash car's job was to take out any pursuing police vehicles in an "accident," so that the killers could make good their escape.

With Whitey in the crash car monitoring the police bands, and able to radio ahead to the main boiler, the odds of a successful escape were a lot higher. In fact, they theorized, perhaps eventually they could switch to a system of two crash cars—one with Whitey listening in to the cop chatter, and then a regular crash car behind him. After all, even the local cops might get suspicious if a gangster in a car full of police radios suddenly got into a traffic accident with a police vehicle on its way to the scene of an organized-crime hit.

In 1972, these were mostly theoretical considerations. But they wouldn't be for long.

THE FALL OF 1972 was not an ideal time to begin a football-betting business. The Miami Dolphins were on their way to an undefeated season, and like most sports fans, bettors tend to be front-runners. They naturally go with the favorites—in 1972, Don Shula's Dolphins. Soon the Hill's bookies were awash in red ink.

The actual process of rounding up bookies had gone smoothly. After identifying a bookie as an "independent," Johnny and Howie would show up at his place of business, usually a barroom.

Martorano: "Do you know who we are?"

Bookie: "Yes, I've been expecting you."

Martorano: "We're your new partners."

Bookie: "Fine."

Martorano: "If anybody else tries to do this to you, let us know and we'll take care of it."

As their losses mounted, the Hill decided to change the line from 11-10 to 12-10. The way the line worked was, if you bet $100 on the Dolphins to win by three and they won by four, you got $100. If the Dolphins won by less than three, you lost, and you owed the bookie $110. Theoretically, if the bookmaker could fine-tune the spread, he would have enough bets—action—on both sides so that he finished in the black no matter who won the game.

But the only people losing in 1972 were the bookies who had to take the bets against the Dolphins. Finally, the Hill ordered its bookies to go with a 12-10 line. That might have worked if they'd controlled every bookie in the country, but of course they had no such monopoly. The bettors simply began switching to the remaining "independents," or for the cost of a long-distance phone call placed their wagers out of town. As bad as business had been before, now it was worse. Plus, Larry Baione, Jerry Angiulo's muscle on the street, was another fanatical bettor, who'd play with anyone and everyone he could. So the new line was costing Larry money, too. Everybody was pissed at the Hill.

The line was quickly shifted back, but not before the Hill decided to make an example of one of their bigger bookies, who had cut his line back to 11-10 before he got the okay. He was "fined" $100,000, which he didn't have. So he went to Jerry Angiulo to borrow the money.

By this time, the Hill had also turned to Angiulo to underwrite the losses he'd warned them to prepare for. So when the bookie reached out to Angiulo, Jerry called Howie and Johnny and asked them to come over to the Dog House. His proposal: he would "loan" the bookie the 100 large, only he would just keep the dough to reduce the Hill's debt, which was by now well over six figures.

Howie and Johnny didn't care much for that deal. They needed cash, too. They held out for half of the $100,000— 50 grand. Eventually Angiulo gave in, but he didn't like it.

"A guy comes to me for a hundred grand, out of which I then have to pay other guys who already owe me more than 100 large another $50,000 cash. How can it be that I get some money I'm owed paid back to me and I'm still out another 50 large? I think I'm getting fucked on this deal."

Which he was. In a few months, though, Jerry Angiulo would come up with a way for the Hill to make it up to him.

Indian War

LAWYER: You agreed to help Mr. Angiulo, isn't that right?

MARTORANO: Yes.

LAWYER: So you didn't hate the Mafia like you testified earlier, did you?

MARTORANO: I didn't say I hate the Mafia. I get along with them. I wouldn't be part of it.

LAWYER: Well, you got along with Mr. Angiulo well enough to agree to kill for him, didn't you?

MARTORANO: He convinced us it was a mutual problem, that that guy could hurt friends of ours also if he would hurt friends of his.

LAWYER: But it was primarily at Mr. Angiulo's request, isn't that right.

MARTORANO: He was indirectly asking for help. . . . There was a meeting and he was waiting for us to offer our help.

JERRY ANGIULO HAD a problem, and his name was Al Angeli. It was the winter of 1973, and the Mafia underboss of Boston invited his new associates, Howie

Winter and Johnny Martorano, to the Dog House. Angiulo got to the point very quickly. Al Angeli, or "Indian
Al," as he'd been known since his early days as a boxer,
was out of control.

Angeli, who had shortened his family surname from
"Notarangeli," was originally from Somerville. Most of
his business was now centered in the Medford-Malden
area. His arrest record dated back to 1952, when he was
fifteen, and over the years he'd been mixed up in the
usual assortment of rackets—arson, gaming, drugs. He'd
served time, but he'd also made a lot of money—at age
thirty-five, he owned pieces of at least three barrooms in
Boston and Cambridge. He was an earner, and appeared a
likely candidate for eventual induction into La Cosa Nostra. He personally knew a lot of people in In Town, including Angiulo, for whom he was a protégé of sorts, although
that was a word, like mentor, that the egomaniacal Angi-

Indian Al Angeli, murdered by Johnny in 1974.

ulo would never have used to describe his relationship to anyone, even his own sons.

But Indian Al couldn't wait his turn. He decided he could muscle in on the Mafia's bookmakers and get away with it.

Indian Al set up his own headquarters "in town" at the North Station, at a bar on Causeway Street called Mother's. It was right under the old elevated Green Line, less than a mile from 98 Prince Street, and fewer than two miles from Marshall Street. The location itself almost

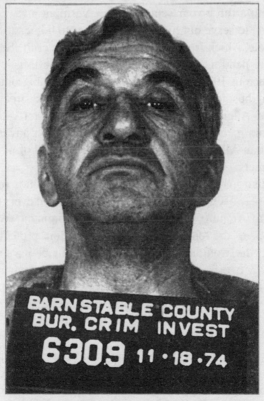

Jerry Angiulo, age 55, near the height of his power.

seemed like a provocation, a gauntlet thrown down to both big Boston mobs.

Angeli put together his own little crew, including his brother, Indian Joe, and various other wiseguys he'd done time with, another ex-boxer or two, assorted Mob wannabes and hangers-on and most significantly, at least two capable guys—killers. He was particularly close to his brother Joe—Al wore a large pinkie ring given to him by Joe, with a white gold setting and a large diamond in the center surrounded by smaller diamonds.

Indian Al was an experienced torch, although he botched a 1970 firebombing of a ski resort in Vermont and ended up with a three-year sentence. But Vermont allowed Indian Al to serve out his sentence closer to home, at MCI-Walpole, which is always a good place to recruit shooters for any pending gang war in Boston. As he finished his sentence in 1972, Indian Al was trying to hang onto his betting business until he could get back on the street. But one of Angiulo's bookies, Paulie Folino, a forty-seven-year-old gambler from Watertown, had taken advantage of Indian Al's incarceration to peel off several of his best customers.

Indian Al's crew started threatening Folino, telling him to lay off their customers. Folino reported everything back to Angiulo, along with editorial comment: Wasn't this one of the reasons he paid In Town for "protection," so that he wouldn't have to worry about being shaken down by two-bit wiseguys like Indian Al? And where the hell did a guy in prison get off, telling Paulie he couldn't take bets from people who were desperate for someone to cover their action—someone who would pay off if they won?

In the North End, Jerry fumed, but he wasn't prepared to go to war. He had a lot of headaches, starting with the fact that the first tell-all book about In Town was about to

Fat Vinnie Teresa wrote the first Boston mob
tell-all book in 1973, *My Life in the Mafia*.

come out—*My Life in the Mafia,* by the aptly named Fat
Vinnie Teresa, a rotund rat who wasn't really in the Mafia, not that that had stopped him from selling his story to
the highest bidder. More important, Larry Baione was
about to begin a short jail sentence of his own, and Joe
Russo, his other top gun, was already behind bars. But
Angiulo still wasn't that concerned. After all, how much
trouble could Indian Al really stir up while he was still in
the can?

Plenty, as it turned out. In August 1972, the state Department of Correction was just beginning an experimen-
tal new program—weekend furloughs for convicts. It was
one of those liberal reforms so popular at the time in
Massachusetts. It was supposed to reintegrate criminals
back into society, thereby reducing recidivism. Indian Al
got one of the first weekend furloughs and used it to hook
up with an ex-con, a guy from the old Wimpy Bennett–
Stevie Flemmi Roxbury crew. They grabbed Paulie Folino off the Indian Ridge Golf Course in Andover and

killed him. Folino may have been the first, but he was certainly not the last victim of Massachusetts's weekend furlough program.

A few days later, with Indian Al back in prison, Folino's brand-new white Cadillac El Dorado showed up at Logan Airport, but the body wasn't in the trunk. His corpse didn't turn up until October, in Boxford, about 150 yards off a main road. Indian Al hadn't even shown Paulie Folino the respect of properly burying him. Angeli had strangled Folino by wrapping a rope around his neck and then tying it to his hands and feet, which were pushed up underneath his body. For a while, Folino would have been able to keep his legs underneath, but slowly he would have tired. As he let go, the rope would tighten, slowly and painfully garroting him. It was an old-style hit. They had tortured Paulie Folino. As one state cop told reporters, "He died the hard way."

Indian Al was sending a message, and now it was Jerry Angiulo's turn to respond in kind. Indian Al was released from MCI-Walpole on the day after Christmas in 1972, and now he was moving around Boston again.

"He killed my guy," Angiulo explained to Howie and Johnny.

Jerry was looking for a sympathetic ear. He said Al would be gaining momentum now that he was out, and that if he'd come after him, he'd come after us, too. Mainly, Jerry was looking for us to do something for him without him having to ask directly. We told him we'd check around and get back to him. So we did. We talked to our guys, we asked Sal Sperlinga, who knew Indian Al, and Charlie Raso, who'd been doing some work for him. Charlie said he was staying out of whatever happened, but he confirmed that Angeli was out of his mind. It was insane what he did—if you whacked somebody who was with In

Sal Sperlinga, the Hill's connection to
Somerville City Hall, murdered in Magoun Square in 1979.

Town, you had to expect they're going to come after
you. And just killing Paulie scared Al's own bookies,
too, because they have to figure, the Indian is willing
to kill them too. None of it made any sense.

Howie and Johnny went back to the North End a couple
more times and finally agreed with Jerry that Indian Al
would have to go. The Mafia still wasn't their cup of tea,
but they figured Indian Al had it coming. He'd started it,
after all, by killing Paulie Folino. And now the Hill would
finish it, by doing a favor for their new partners.

Both the Hill and the Mafia would have crews out looking for him, but it was tacitly understood that the heavy
lifting would be done out of Somerville. In Town under
Angiulo had become a one-trick pony: if anyone crossed

them, they would demand that the guy come down to the North End, and then they would kill him. It had worked for decades, from the ambush of South Boston hoodlum Frankie Gustin in 1931 right up to the time when they murdered Joe Barboza's bail collectors in the Nite Lite in 1967. But Indian Al knew Jerry Angiulo too well to fall for that old trick.

He would stay out of the North End, and In Town wasn't much good beyond their own turf. As Frankie Salemme put it later, "They couldn't find their way off Hanover Street."

LAWYER: The Mafia was a much more powerful criminal group, if you will, than the Winter Group, right?

MARTORANO: Possibly.

LAWYER: They had more than five members, didn't they?

MARTORANO: Sure. Maybe more people. More money.

LAWYER: More guns?

MARTORANO: Maybe.

LAWYER: More shooters?

MARTORANO: Maybe.

Jerry Angiulo gave Howie and Johnny mug shots of Indian Al—he had a beard, and favored long leather coats and flashy jewelry, including both the pinkie ring from his brother and a gold chain with a small gold horn attached. In his packet of information, Angiulo included all of Indian Al's addresses, those of his associates and brother, and also the make and model of his car—a brown Mercedes.

The goal was to whack Indian Al before he knew they were after him, to catch him flat-footed.

The Hill set up a war room in Joe McDonald's Fire House. They put shifts of surveillance cars out on the street, all equipped with Whitey's new-model walkie-talkies, looking to spot Indian Al's Mercedes. Everyone had their own people out on the street, working shifts. Somerville, Southie, what was left of the old crews in Charlestown and Roxbury—the Hill really had become an amalgamated gang.

Next they would need guns, lots of guns. Before he went on the lam in 1969, Stevie Flemmi had stashed an arsenal in the basement of the Commercial Street restaurant owned by Bobby LaBella—Bobby the Greaser.

The Mafia was likewise looking to pick up a few machine guns. So Frankie Salemme's brother, Jackie, went down to Commercial Street. Jackie Salemme told Bobby the Greaser that Frankie was asking him to turn over Stevie's grease guns to In Town. Bobby the Greaser shook his head.

"Frankie didn't give me the guns, Stevie give me the guns."

Johnny made the next visit to Bobby LaBella's café.

"Sorry, Johnny," he said. "I gotta hear it from Stevie." So Stevie was called in Montreal, where he was still hiding out, working nights in the print shop of the *Montreal Gazette* under the alias of Robert Lombruno.

After Flemmi personally phoned the okay to Bobby the Greaser, Johnny returned to the basement and picked out a grease gun. It was a cheap but lethal World War II–era .45-caliber submachine that got its name from its resemblance to the standard garage mechanic's tool.

Everyone agreed that whenever they finally caught up with him, the hit on Indian Al would be handled by the Hill's "working partners"—Sims driving, Johnny and another guy from Somerville shooting. Whitey Bulger would follow in a crash car equipped with multiple police radios.

Then they set up their hit bags—bulky canvas mailbags with various weapons: pistols, carbines, sawed-off shotguns, even a couple of grenades, just in case something went wrong and they had to make a run for it. Johnny always took along a ski mask. Jimmy Sims preferred a plastic Halloween-type mask.

For what they had planned, the Hill laid in a new supply of "boilers." Mostly they were four-door Fords—they looked like police cars and their ignitions popped quicker than Chrysler or GM vehicles. They'd use a shimmy to unlock the front door, then stick a dent-puller into the ignition and pop it. After that, all you needed was a screwdriver to turn the engine over. It was a lot faster than hot-wiring a car.

With any luck, it would be over very quickly—a one-and-done. Once they hit Indian Al, the rest of his gang would probably fade.

LAWYER: You didn't know Mr. Notarangeli well enough to recognize him in person, is that right?

MARTORANO: I never met him.

LAWYER: So you agreed to kill a man you never met?

MARTORANO: Positively.

LAWYER: And you were going basically on the description of other people, isn't that right?

MARTORANO: Yup.

LAWYER: You weren't sure enough the first couple of times that you killed people who weren't Mr. Notarangeli, right?

MARTORANO: Well, he was driving his car, dressed in his coat, and had long hair like him and a long beard like him. Somebody said over the radio that that's him, so I took it to be him.

Just after midnight on a Thursday in March 1973, the walkie-talkie crackled at the Fire House. As usual, they had Indian Al's bar, Mother's, staked out. It had been a slow night, and one of the spotters had noticed what he presumed to be Indian Al's brown Mercedes out front of the bar on Causeway Street. Within minutes, a stolen Ford was heading down the McGrath/O'Brien Highway from Somerville toward the city. Sims was driving, with Johnny in the front seat and another guy from Somerville in the backseat. Johnny was cradling Flemmi's grease gun, and the guy from Somerville had an AR-15.

It was up to a Charlestown hood, John Hurley, to make sure that it was Indian Al getting into the Mercedes. The fingerman stood under the elevated Green Line and watched from the Causeway Street shadows as a guy in his early thirties with a beard and a long leather coat got into the driver's seat, followed by two other people. Hurley radioed to the hit Ford that he had positively ID'd Indian Al.

But it wasn't Angeli. Although Johnny and the others in the boiler didn't know it, the driver of the Mercedes was actually the head bartender at Mother's, a thirty-year-old guy named Michael Milano. His duties included opening and closing the bar, tallying the receipts for the evening. Milano had just bought a used dark red 1966 Mercedes, of which he was very proud. In the dark it looked like Indian Al's brown Mercedes.

Other than taking a few bets if no one else was around the bar, and moving small amounts of stolen merchandise, Milano wasn't in the rackets at all. He was a typical Boston bartender of the early '70s—a few days later, police searching his apartment in Brighton would find gambling slips, small amounts of cocaine and marijuana, and a handwritten note from somebody saying "Save an oz. for me."

Another fact that the Hill shooters were unaware of: sitting in the backseat was a thirty-four-year-old friend of Milano's whom he had just hired as a new bartender at Mother's. The new bartender's twenty-three-year-old

John Hurley of Charlestown served as the fingerman
on the (botched) Michael Milano and Indian Joe hits in 1973.

girlfriend was in the front seat beside Milano. Their plan
that morning was to return to Milano's apartment in Brighton for a game of chess. Leaving the bar, they took with
them three 12-ounce bottles of Schlitz beer.

LAWYER: And he had people in the car with him,
isn't that right?

MARTORANO: Yeah.

LAWYER: And you didn't care if you took out other
people at the same time you were taking out your
target, isn't that fair to say?

MARTORANO: Yeah, sure, we were concerned about
that.

LAWYER: Not concerned enough to stop you from
doing it, isn't that right?

MARTORANO: Not—we kept going, yeah.

LAWYER: And in fact one of the people in that car
was a woman, isn't that right?

MARTORANO: Turned out to be.

LAWYER: You didn't care, did you?

MARTORANO: Sure, I cared.

Milano's Mercedes left North Station, winding its way around to Storrow Drive, with the boiler remaining an inconspicuous distance behind. Milano got off by mistake at Kenmore Square, then headed down Brighton Avenue, around St. Elizabeth's Hospital, and onto Sparhawk Street. He was almost home to his apartment.

It was time for Sims to take the Mercedes, before it crossed Market Street and got too close to Brighton Center and a lot more witnesses. At the light, Sims pulled up alongside and Johnny and the guy from Somerville opened fire, Johnny spraying the front seat, the other guy the back. It was all over in a matter of seconds. Sims floored the boiler and headed back to the garage at the top of Winter Hill.

In the Mercedes, the new bartender slumped in the backseat, unconscious, critically wounded. In the front, the woman looked over at Michael Milano, slumped against the steering wheel. The woman later told police she'd thought some of the local punks were throwing rocks at the car, but then the car windows exploded, and she was hit in the shoulder.

"I ducked until the shots stopped and I was fine and I looked at Michael and said, 'Are you okay?' and he was just about breathing."

But not for long. Milano had four bullets in him, and less than three hours to live. He had $120 cash in his pocket when he died.

It wasn't until the next day that the Hill found out that they had shot up the wrong car. The Boston police quickly figured out what had happened—or at least why. The organized-crime squad informed homicide detectives that Indian Al "or his brother has been leaning on the local bookies to the extent that Angiulo has called him."

What the cops didn't know was that it wasn't In Town, but Winter Hill that had handled the hit. So it would go into the books as an unsolved Mafia murder, a case of mistaken identity.

At the garage on Marshall Street, everyone was philosophical. Shit happens.

JOHNNY FOUND OUT listening to the news on the radio. They said there'd been a shooting in Brighton, and a bartender had been killed. His first thought was, *There was another shooting last night?* Then he realized what had happened. The problem was, now Indian Al would know that someone was after him. They would never catch him off guard again. This was going to be a war.

Johnny blamed it all on Hurley. He wanted to kill him. But he knew the other guys would veto it. He'd been with them in the Charlestown war. But because Hurley blew that ID, five more people would end up dead, and even more wounded. None of it would have happened if they'd caught up with Indian Al first.

The other guy in Milano's car was paralyzed for life. We threw a fundraiser for him later at Chandler's, although of course we couldn't tell him why we felt so sorry for him and wanted to help out so bad. He's dead now, but when the feds were trying to settle all the cases I was involved in, they had to seek him out—he had moved to California. They told him who'd shot him, and his response was that he wasn't mad at anyone anymore. He'd gotten religion, I guess. I'm very appreciative of that.

The next day, Johnny and Howie returned to the Dog House. Angiulo had more names, addresses, photos, and license numbers for them. One guy Jerry wanted badly was Frank Capizzi, a loudmouthed thirty-eight-year-old North End native. He was now living in Winthrop, and he, too, had a Mercedes. Every morning he dropped his two young children off at Winthrop Elementary School. Whitey Bulger began looking for him.

One morning in early March, Capizzi had just dropped off his children at school and was heading into the city on Chelsea Street when Whitey pulled alongside and reached across the seat, came up with a revolver, and opened fire on Capizzi. He didn't hang around to finish the job, though, and Capizzi was able to turn off the main road and then abandon his blood-stained, bullet-riddled car a few blocks later. Blood oozing from his leg, Capizzi limped off to hail a taxi. A few minutes later, Mrs. Frank Capizzi reported the car stolen from in front of their home in Winthrop. The cops didn't buy it and arrested Capizzi after they found an unregistered handgun a witness had seen him toss across a fence near where he had left his Mercedes.

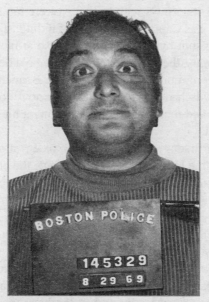

Frank Capizzi of the North End was shot by both Whitey and Johnny in 1973—and survived.

In a letter to a judge many years later, Capizzi recalled his children's reaction later that day when they saw the family car abandoned on a side street in East Boston.

"One of the most traumatic memories for my bright children was seeing the automobile they had been in ten minutes before full of bullet holes . . . [I was] frightened beyond words."

The only witness to the actual shooting provided nothing of use. The driver was hatless, he told police, and "was not a kid."

After the near-miss on Capizzi, the Angeli crew went to ground for a while. The Hill still had cars out, on the prowl, but it was days before they got another break. On the evening of March 18, everyone was hanging out in the Fire House playing cards when somebody spotted Indian Al on the waterfront. He was eating dinner at the Aquarium restaurant on Atlantic Avenue with three other guys. Two of the other guys with Indian Al were familiar to the Hill—one was Capizzi, finally out of hiding, still limping after being shot by Whitey Bulger. Also at the table was Sonny Shields, the Roxbury plug-ugly who'd been acquitted in 1969 of murdering the last of the Bennett brothers, Billy. Shields had gone mod, his hair now down to his shoulders, and that night he was sporting a hipster's long brown coat.

The fourth guy at the table was older, about fifty, a stranger to the Hill lookout who had made the others.

It was just about 7 P.M. when the four men left the Aquarium and climbed into a 1972 Buick sedan owned by a Chelsea garage. They didn't even notice the 1971 Ford trailing behind them, and behind the Ford, a crash car driven by Whitey Bulger.

In the Ford was the usual Winter Hill first team: Sims driving, Martorano next to him in the front cradling Stevie Flemmi's grease gun, and in the back the guy from Somerville with his AR-15. The Angeli car took off down

Commercial Street, obviously heading toward North Station, and Mother's, less than a mile away.

This would be a tougher hit than Milano. Commercial Street was narrower, it was earlier, and there was more traffic, which meant more potential witnesses. And they only had a couple of minutes. There were no long traffic lights, either; they would have to fire from a moving vehicle, at another one.

As they approached the coast guard station, Sims floored the stolen boiler and pulled out around, in order to get alongside the Angeli vehicle. The Hill guns were pointing out the windows, ready to fire. But just as Sims made his move, from Henchman Street another car suddenly turned left onto Commercial, pulling directly alongside the Angeli vehicle.

"Fuck," said Sims, but he had no choice. He swung into the opposite lane and cut in front of Indian Al's vehicle, forcing it to a stop. The Somerville guy's rifle was still pointed out the side window when Johnny swung his grease gun back inside and started firing through the back window of the stolen Ford. The Somerville guy dove for the backseat floor as Johnny continued shooting into the Angeli car. For the nighttime job, he was using tracer bullets, and behind the Buick in the crash car, Whitey Bulger swerved to keep his car out of the line of fire.

At the nearby coast guard base on Commercial Street, some on-duty guardsmen had just finished watching a rerun of *The Wild Wild West*. Suddenly outside they heard what sounded like a real-life shootout at the OK Corral.

By the time the coast guardsmen ran outside, the boiler was long gone, and so was the car that had cut in front of Sims. Angeli's bullet-riddled Buick was stopped on the street, its motor still running. Inside the car, they saw the driver slumped over. He was moaning and coughing up blood, with only a few minutes to live.

Once they were sure the shooting had stopped, Capizzi

and Shields scrambled to open the passenger-side doors. Almost comically, they bumped into each other as they tried to figure out which way to flee, before finally taking cover behind a parked moving truck. Then they decided to make a run for it, heading south back toward the Aquarium, stopping and turning around every few seconds to make sure no one with a gun was following them.

Then a fourth passenger opened the back driver's side door, jumped out, and took off running down the alley next to a restaurant named Giro's. That was Indian Al. He was wearing a brown scally cap.

The driver was Al "Bud" Plummer, of Andover, a forty-nine-year-old World War II veteran. He was dead on arrival at Massachusetts General Hospital. In the Andover town directory, Plummer listed himself as a "steamship clerk." He had no police record, but the cops noted that although he hadn't worked in two years, Plummer "lives in a high-priced area of the town and owns two expensive automobiles"—a Cadillac and a Thunderbird. He was also known to play golf with "well-known professional athletes" at the Indian Ridge Golf Course from which Paulie Folino had vanished eight months earlier.

He left behind a wife and two children. Police reported that Plummer had $451 cash in his pocket when he died.

LAWYER: Was it the right thing to do to kill Mr. Plummer?

MARTORANO: Well, at the time I thought so. He was part of the gang that we were having a problem with.

LAWYER: Well, what was it about him being part of the gang that gave you, allowed you, or caused you to believe it was the right thing to do, which was to kill Mr. Plummer?

MARTORANO: Well, the guy that we were looking for is in Plummer's car.

Sonny Shields and Frank Capizzi soon turned up at the emergency room at Boston City Hospital. Capizzi's lawyer also appeared. Shields, shot in the side, got himself patched up and then promptly vanished, not to be seen again for months. Capizzi was more seriously hit, in the back, but the next day he signed himself out of BCH and likewise fled.

Thirty years later, in a letter to a federal judge, Capizzi would describe how he and his family had spent the next few months of their lives.

"[We] drove crisscrossing the U.S. and Canada for over 20,000 miles. We were without a destination. Desi and Frank [his children] had the job of cleaning festering wounds and picking out bits of lead from my back as they surfaced."

The morning after Plummer's murder, outside his café on Commercial Street, Bobby the Greaser was sweeping up the broken glass from the previous night's shooting off the sidewalk. As he worked, he was muttering to himself about Johnny Martorano, loud enough for anyone within earshot to hear.

"Fuckin' Johnny," he was saying. "You give him a gun, and the next thing you know, he leaves you with a big fuckin' mess to clean up. Stevie's gonna hear about this, goddammit, whenever the fuck he gets back to town."

Two days later, the Chelsea Police Department got a report of an abandoned Ford behind the New Market Restaurant on Beechum Street. It didn't take long for the cops to figure out who had left it behind—its back windows were shot out. The owner reported that missing from the brown sedan were five quarts of J&B Scotch and three yellow hard hats. The Scotch was long gone, but the hard hats were stashed in the garage at the top of Winter Hill. The Hill never knew, those hats might come in handy someday.

•   •   •

LIKE SHIELDS AND Capizzi, Indian Al was now officially on the lam. He fled to Eugene, Oregon, with his family. He sent a letter to the public school his children had been attending in Winchester asking that their academic records be forwarded to Oregon.

But the rest of their little crew still didn't seem to have figured out just how overmatched they were. The next break for Winter Hill came from South Boston. Tommy King, one of the Mullens who had now thrown in with Whitey Bulger, got a call from a guy he knew from prison—Ralph DeMasi.

DeMasi was unaware that it was the Hill, not the Mafia, that was hunting down his friends, and he was equally oblivious to the fact that his old friend from South Boston was now an associate of the new consolidated gang. DeMasi still considered himself a friend of King. Now he wanted to know if King could get him some weapons, to use against In Town.

DEMASI ARRANGED TO meet King that Friday evening, March 23, at Linda Mae's, a popular restaurant on Morrissey Boulevard in Dorchester with a big parking lot. The Hill would be waiting; DeMasi was considered a capable individual and thus would have to be eliminated.

Driving DeMasi that evening was a thirty-two-year-old South Boston stevedore named William O'Brien. Like King, he had met DeMasi in prison, at MCI-Walpole. O'Brien had served several years for killing another man named O'Brien in a drunken brawl in a Southie tavern. O'Brien was on his way to his ex-wife's apartment in South Boston to pick up his ten-year-old daughter Marie for the weekend.

After the meeting at Linda Mae's, O'Brien and DeMasi went back out to their car. At Linda Mae's, O'Brien had bought a birthday cake for Marie, which he placed carefully in the backseat before he drove off. DeMasi was sitting beside him in the front seat. They were heading north toward Southie on Morrissey Boulevard when suddenly a Ford pulled alongside them. Again, it was the first team, the Hill's working partners—Sims was driving; Johnny and the guy from Somerville were shooting. Johnny's target was the driver; the Somerville guy would aim for DeMasi. They'd disposed of Stevie's grease gun, and Martorano was now firing a .30-caliber carbine with a 30-round banana clip. As usual, Whitey was behind them in the crash car.

"I thought someone was taking target practice on the road," DeMasi recalled in a letter he sent to a federal judge thirty years later. "It was my good friend John Martorano."

DeMasi was taking literary license. Martorano didn't know either DeMasi or O'Brien, whom he had killed instantly with his shot to the ex-con's head. O'Brien slumped forward on the steering wheel, dead, and the car came to a sudden stop. DeMasi was wounded in the chest, arm, and shoulder. As soon as the car stopped, DeMasi jumped out and flagged down a passerby who drove him to the emergency room at Boston City Hospital. He stayed just long enough to get himself patched up, but left before the cops could arrest him for a parole violation.

Meanwhile, at the East Fifth Street home of O'Brien's ex-wife, his ten-year-old daughter kept looking out the window, anxiously awaiting the arrival of her father. Finally, she heard the doorbell ring. Marie ran out to open the door, but instead of her father, she saw two stone-faced Boston police officers.

O'Brien also left behind a girlfriend who was nine months pregnant. She would soon give birth to a son who would never know his father.

THE NEXT AFTERNOON, a Saturday, Ted Harrington, the federal prosecutor who headed the Justice Department's organized-crime task force in Boston, called a press conference. For the benefit of the Sunday newspapers, Harrington denounced the wave of machine-gun violence sweeping the city.

"These men show an utter disdain for the lives of innocent people," the future federal judge said. "In all three of these incidents automatic weapons have been used and bystanders could have been hurt."

The next Wednesday, O'Brien was buried out of Gate of Heaven Church in South Boston. The Boston police organized-crime squad staked out the church, assuming that the fugitive DeMasi would make an appearance to pay his final respects to his deceased pal. The cops were right. DeMasi did show up, but he was still taking no chances, even in a house of God. He was carrying a loaded .38-caliber revolver when he was arrested and sent back to Walpole on a parole violation.

EX-BOXERS ALWAYS SEEMED to end up in the rackets in Boston. And they seemed to have a much higher mortality rate than hoodlums who hadn't made it to the Golden Gloves. John "Jake" Leary had never done much in the ring, but he'd grown up with the Notarangelis, so his next career move was obvious.

But when the bodies of his associates started piling up, he, too, fled Massachusetts. There was talk later that maybe Leary was looking to buy guns in Florida. But unlike Indian Al, Capizzi, and Shields, Leary let someone know where he was hiding out—in a beachfront apartment in Fort Lauderdale.

· Joe McDonald knew Leary, so he and Jimmy Sims immediately started driving south on I-95. Flying would have been quicker, but they couldn't carry firearms—let alone an entire Winter Hill "hit kit"—onto a commercial flight. On the evening of April 3, Leary was cooking dinner in his Broward County hideout when he heard a noise near the front door. He wasn't concerned; who could possibly know he was hiding out in South Florida?

Leary left the kitchen and walked into the living room, where he saw Joe McDonald, armed with a revolver, trying to sneak up on him. Jake Leary threw himself at McDonald and they went down in a heap, pummeling one another on the linoleum floor. But McDonald had the gun, and he quickly got off a shot. Wounded, the younger man rolled off him, and Joe jumped up and emptied his gun into Leary's face. The autopsy showed Leary was shot five times in the head. Fort Lauderdale police described it as a "gangland hit."

Back in Medford, Leary left a widow and three small children.

LAWYER: Can you pronounce Indian Joe's last name? I always had difficulty with it.
MARTORANO: Notarangeli. I'm not sure.
LAWYER: For now let's call him Indian Joe. Do you

Indian Joe Notarangeli, murdered by Johnny in 1973.

> believe you had a good reason for killing Indian Joe?
>
> MARTORANO: Yes.
>
> LAWYER: What reason did you believe was good enough to kill him?
>
> MARTORANO: Well, they had killed another guy before this. That's what the retaliation was for.

Al Angeli's brother, Indian Joe Notarangeli, had never shortened his surname. He was thirty-five, a year younger than Al, and he hadn't been seen at Mother's, or anywhere else, in weeks. But Indian Joe knew he couldn't hide out forever. Like everyone else in what was left of the gang, he believed In Town was hunting him. So he needed an intermediary, someone tight with the Mafia, but not of them. Someone of stature, someone from the old neighborhood— Somerville. It would have to be someone In Town respected. Indian Joe could think of only one such person who might be able to straighten out this thing for him and his brother.

Howie Winter.

Indian Joe reached out to his own Somerville guy, Charlie Raso, who'd been with the Angelis off and on in recent years, and Raso passed the message to Sal Sperlinga, who ran numbers in Somerville for the Hill. Indian Joe had left a number for Sal to call him back, at 3:45 the next afternoon. Sal showed the message to Johnny and smiled. Everything was falling into place.

"We call him," said Sal, "and then we kill him, and hopefully that ends it."

Johnny thought for a moment. He'd been thinking about trying something for a while now, and this seemed like the perfect opportunity. Johnny wanted to figure out where Indian Joe would be calling from, and then hit him right there, in the phone booth. It was an old underworld tradition, dating at least as far back as 1932. One of Dutch Schultz's torpedoes, the Irish-born Vincent "Mad Dog"

Coll, had gone crazy, and was kidnapping gangsters and shooting up Harlem. On the run, the twenty-three-year-old killer reached out to the biggest Irish gangster of the day, Owney Madden, and gave Owney a phone number where he could be reached at a certain time, after dark.

Owney used his phone-company sources to find out the location of the pay phone—a drugstore at Eighth Avenue and Twenty-third Street. Then he called Dutch Schultz. As Mad Dog harangued Owney Madden in the phone booth, a limousine pulled up and two well-dressed guys with Thompson submachines got out. One stood guard outside the drugstore, and the other gunman calmly walked inside and almost cut Mad Dog in two. The coroner dug fifteen slugs out of his body.

THE PROBLEM WITH Indian Joe was that the Hill only had a number, not the address where it was installed. But they assumed it was a pay phone. Back then, pay phones were everywhere, and most of them would accept incoming calls.

So Johnny called up New England Telephone and told a story he'd worked out in his mind before he called. It took a few minutes, but he finally got a supervisor on the line. Johnny told him that his kid had just called him. His car had broken down. Johnny told the supervisor that his son had given him the phone number of the pay phone he was calling from, but before the kid could tell him where he was, he got cut off. His three minutes must have been up. But he never called back, Johnny said. "You know these crazy kids today," Johnny explained with a sigh. So Johnny told the guy that it would really help him out if he could find out where the phone was, so that he could go pick up his son.

THE PAY PHONE was in Medford Square, at the Pewter Pot, a busy coffee shop in the heart of the square, on High

Street, which was a narrow two-way street, not much more than a lane really, with parking spaces on either side.

Medford Square was only about two miles from the garage, so a couple of guys were immediately dispatched to scout the location. The pay phone was just inside the front door, but that was the only good thing about the Pewter Pot.

Pulling this one off would make the Commercial Street hit seem easy. But it was too tempting, knowing exactly where Indian Joe was going to be, and at what time. Joe was very cautious. He hadn't been seen since the night the bartender was killed in Brighton. It might be months before the Hill got another opportunity like this.

They went up to the garage and picked out a green '71 Ford Galaxy sedan. It had been stolen in Framingham on March 25.

Johnny would of course handle the hit, but this time he wanted Joe McDonald behind the wheel. Sims was good, but for this one Martorano wanted an even cooler head. Some of the guys at the garage called McDonald "Yup," because that was how he answered every question. Can you take the guy yourself, Joe? Yup. Is the job doable? Yup. Can you unload the hot merchandise? Yup, yup, yup.

The next afternoon, April 19, Joe McDonald was behind the wheel of the boiler. Tommy King, the ex-Mullen, was driving the crash car. They had various other guys on the street, just in case. At least a few customers—potential witnesses—were always hanging out at the Pewter Pot. Johnny was wearing a disguise—one of the yellow construction worker's hard hats that they'd taken out of the Ford that was used in the Plummer hit.

To further confuse any witnesses, Martorano was wearing a white meat cutter's coat and a fake black beard.

The big problem was that narrow two-way street with parking on either side. If somebody double-parked in the wrong place, they might have to abandon the car and make a run for it. Then they noticed another problem. As McDonald pulled into a legal space on the street a couple of doors up from the Pewter Pot, he and Johnny saw a cop standing in a doorway across High Street. Johnny didn't like the layout. The vibes weren't right.

"How's it look, Joe?" he asked.

"Looks good," said McDonald, nodding. He picked up the walkie-talkie and inquired of the spotter as to whether "he" was where he should be. The answer was yes, but suddenly Johnny was antsy again. He recognized the spotter's voice—it was John Hurley, the same guy who'd mistaken the bartender Milano for Indian Al a month earlier.

"Are you positive?" Johnny asked Hurley via walkie-talkie.

"I'm positive," he said. "It's him."

JOHNNY THEN TOLD Hurley to come out to the car. He wanted to speak to him face-to-face. Hurley walked out to the boiler and leaned in and told Johnny again that it was Indian Joe. Johnny nodded silently. He couldn't afford any more mistakes, especially when he was walking into a place with witnesses, some of whom might be both with Indian Joe and armed. With both Johnny and Joe Mac watching him, Hurley assured them that this time he was sure he was right.

"You better be," Johnny told him.

JOHNNY LOOKED AT his watch. It was 3:45. Sal would be calling the pay phone right about now. Johnny still didn't know if Indian Joe had anybody with him. They'd killed some of the crew, and others had run off, but some things you could never be certain of until you walked in and started shooting.

Johnny turned to McDonald: "If you hear more than a couple of shots, come in after me."

"Yup," said Joe McDonald.

Johnny got out of the car, holding a .38-caliber snub nose revolver in his hand in the pocket of his butcher's coat.

He pushed open the coffee shop door and saw Indian Joe standing at the second pay phone on the wall, talking into the receiver, making his pitch for mercy. Johnny walked right up to him, raised his gun, and fired twice at Indian Joe's heart. The restaurant was crowded, and some of the other customers started screaming as Indian Joe, his eyes wide with shock, dropped the phone and crumpled to the floor. But Johnny Martorano didn't hear them.

All he was thinking was, *Get out, get out.* He turned around, then walked out the door slowly. He left the Pewter Pot as casually as he could, walked back to the Ford, and got back inside the front seat. McDonald, who would be described by witnesses as having "stubby fingers," had kept the motor running.

"Okay?" asked McDonald.

"Let's go," said Martorano.

"Yup," said McDonald.

About a mile outside Medford Square, on the way back to Somerville, Johnny spotted an unoccupied phone booth. He told McDonald to pull over, which meant the crash car and another one behind it also had to pull over. Martorano walked over to the phone booth, deposited a dime, and called a Somerville number. He wanted to check back in with the garage to make sure everything was okay—no large hits shaping up on the day's numbers.

As Martorano placed the call from the phone booth, Tommy King pulled up in the crash car alongside Johnny's boiler.

"Johnny," he yelled, "you know that the state police

will have their helicopter up in the air, don't you?" Its
landing pad in East Cambridge was at most three or four
miles from Medford Square. "Maybe we should get going."

Johnny hung up the phone. They got going.

NOW THERE WAS only one—Indian Al, the guy who
had started the whole war. No one had seen him in months.
He had obviously taken a powder. There was no pressing
need to look for him. The war was over, his bookies now
all belonged to Winter Hill—Jerry Angiulo couldn't very
well argue that point, not after all the carnage. And sooner
or later, Indian Al would have to come home.

And then they would kill him.

It was eight months before the call came from Indian
Al, in early 1974. It was almost a year since they'd killed
Michael Milano by mistake in Brighton. Angeli had re-
turned from Oregon just before Christmas, flying into
Logan Airport.

He met his mother in Cambridge, then drove with her
to Gloucester where they had lunch. He told her he'd
found Jesus, and that everything was straightened out, but
she was not convinced. Shortly thereafter, he moved into
the house owned by his late brother Joe's wife, until he
could find a place for his own family. He also visited Jake
Leary's widow, telling Jake's eleven-year old daughter
that he was "homesick" for Massachusetts.

Soon, Al Angeli decided he would reach out to the
Hill. He apparently didn't know who his brother had been
talking to on the phone when he was shot to death. Indian
Al still hadn't figured out that it was the Hill rather than
the Mafia that had wiped out his gang. When he finally
spoke to Howie, Indian Al told him he had money, and
that he wanted a sit-down with Angiulo, in a public place
naturally, with Howie vouching for his safety. Indian Al
wanted to straighten everything out, once and for all.

When Howie called In Town with the news, Angiulo was pleased. For the meet, he suggested his usual restaurant in the North End, Café Pompeii. Howie and Johnny picked Indian Al up at the Northgate Shopping Center in Revere. They'd never laid eyes on him before, but compared to his mug shots, he looked at least a decade older. He had a shopping bag with him, but mostly Indian Al wanted to talk about the Lord. He'd found Jesus. John 3:16. He was saved.

In the North End, they brought him inside the café, to Jerry's table, in the corner of the restaurant. No one was allowed to sit at the tables immediately around him. It was less about physical safety than about not wanting to be overheard—or bugged. Indian Al tried to give Jerry a hug, but Angiulo refused to rise from his seat. Howie and Johnny sat down at a nearby table, watching and listening in silence.

"Mr. Angiulo," Indian Al began, "I'm sorry. . . ."

Jerry Angiulo just sat there, scowling. He lived for moments like this. He'd never been a strong-arm, and now he lived in a seaside mansion in Nahant. But he still reveled in playing the tough guy, the Mafia don. His top guns, Baione and Russo, might be away, but he still had these other guys, from Somerville, his secret weapons sitting a couple of tables away. In Providence Raymond Patriarca might be "the Man," but on Hanover Street Gennaro Angiulo called the shots, and he never let anyone forget it.

Johnny and Howie listened as Angiulo berated Indian Al in unbelievably foul language, telling him how he now had to make sure Paulie Folino's family was taken care of. With a real hitman sitting two tables over, Angiulo shamelessly took credit for all the work of the Hill. It was at moments like this that Johnny realized that the Mafia was no place for anyone with a mind of his own. Who needed a "boss"?

Finally, Indian Al pushed the bag across the table to Jerry Angiulo.

"There's 50,000 there," he said, and Anigulo nodded. Jerry smiled weakly and told Indian Al that everything was okay now, and that he should stay in touch—but only with Howie. Don't call me again, Jerry ordered. Ever. You want to open a nightclub or any other fuckin' thing—I don't give a fuck what you want, after what you done to Paulie Folino, I don't need to ever be talking to a piece of shit like you. You wanna do anything from now on, you call Howie. You clear it with Howie. *Capisce?* Then he nodded at Howie and Johnny and they stood up. It was time for Indian Al to go. As Indian Al and Howie went on ahead, Johnny lingered behind at Jerry's table.

"I leaned in close to Jerry and told him, 'You deserve an Oscar for that performance.' What I was really saying to him was, maybe Indian Al believed that bullshit, but don't ever try anything like that on me, because I know better.

"In the car, Howie told Indian Al to stay in touch with Sal Sperlinga. He figured Sal knew Indian Al better than we did, so he'd be more comfortable with Sal."

HOWIE AND JOHNNY drove Indian Al to his sister-in-law's house and then returned to the Dog House. Angiulo was sitting at a table. He'd split the $50,000 into two equal piles. One he pushed across the table.

"Expenses," Angiulo explained.

That was the way they all preferred to look at it. It wasn't really murder-for-hire, this was just settling up . . . for out-of-pocket costs. Jerry just wanted to show his respect and appreciation for a job well done, and the Hill couldn't very well turn it down because that would be a slap in the face to Jerry Angiulo. Not to take the $25,000 would be showing disrespect to In Town.

LAWYER: You certainly didn't have $25,000 worth of expenses, did you?

MARTORANO: We just threw it in the pot. There was a lot of expenses, a lot of equipment, a lot of walkie-talkies. There was a lot of equipment.

LAWYER: But it had nothing to do with expenses. He just paid you to do it, isn't that right?

MARTORANO: Not at all.

LAWYER: After expenses, the rest was just the fee for killing him, right?

MARTORANO: It wasn't a fee for killing him, but we took the money.

LAWYER: And that was half of the money Mr. Angeli gave to Mr. Angiulo for not killing him, right?

MARTORANO: Right.

Back at 98 Prince Street, Howie Winter took the $25,000 and stuffed the wad of bills into his winter overcoat.

"Now you can kill him for killing Paulie," Angiulo said.

INDIAN AL STILL didn't get it. His sister-in-law had watched out the window as he was dropped off in front of her house by a dark car with two men inside—Howie and Johnny. Once Indian Al was back inside Joe's house, he went straight to the kitchen and started making phone calls.

"Everything is fine," he told someone. "I want that nightclub."

He was beaming as he hung up. He told his sister-in-law that everybody could come home now. Indian Al then called his wife in Oregon. He said he would be meeting someone for breakfast, but did not say who.

Despite his apparent relief, Indian Al decided to move out of the family house and into the Holiday Inn on the Lynn-Peabody Line. After he checked in there, his sister-in-law drove him to Cambridge, where he rented a small white car. But he didn't call the Hill.

After a while, Jerry started calling us every day, yelling, "Where the fuck is that no good motherfuckin' motherfucker? I want him dead! I want this over!" We told him, we aren't even sure where he is. We also told him, this ain't the kind of thing you can rush. You start trying to pressure a guy to set up a meet, he's going to figure out what's up.

Finally, on February 21, Indian Al reached out to Sal. He wanted another sit-down with Jerry.

Johnny went up to the garage at the top of Winter Hill to see what boilers were available. He settled on a Ford coupe.

On the last morning of his life, Indian Al met a guy who'd been holding onto some of his late brother Joe's effects. They drove to a warehouse in Woburn and Indian Al sadly went through a couple of his brother's steamer trunks. They drove back to Winchester and he ran into a cop he knew. He told the cop he had straightened everything out with Angiulo and that he'd soon be opening a "diner" in Magoun Square in Somerville—in the heart of Winter Hill territory.

Back at the Holiday Inn, Indian Al ate an early dinner of clam chowder and shish kabob, leaving a one-dollar tip. The total: $8.20. He went back to his room and at 5:21 P.M. made his final telephone call, to Jake Leary's widow. When cops later asked her where she'd been that evening, she told them she'd just started a new program at Diet Workshop.

A few minutes later, Indian Al was picked up again at the Northgate Shopping Center by Sal and Johnny. This time Indian Al wasn't carrying a bag, only a Bible. Johnny got out so that Al could sit in the front seat—the death seat. Johnny climbed into the backseat.

Johnny saw the Bible, and suddenly he remembered an old western starring the guy he'd been drinking with nights at Chandler's—Robert Mitchum. The movie was *Five Card Stud,* and Mitchum played a preacher with a hollowed-out Bible in which he carried a hidden gun. Just when the villain thinks he's got the drop on Rev. Mitchum, he opens the Bible and pulls out the gun and kills the bad guy. Johnny kept a close eye on Indian Al—and on his Bible.

Indian Al climbed in the front seat and didn't say much. He wasn't acting like Robert Mitchum. He seemed like a beaten man. Once they got onto an open stretch of road, Johnny took out his gun and shot Indian Al once behind the ear, and then he fired a second time into the base of the neck. Johnny was usually a one-bullet guy, but this was too important. This was the end of the war. Neither Johnny nor Sal said anything as they drove back to the garage at the top of Winter Hill.

As always, Whitey was in the crash car, with the scanners and a walkie-talkie. For this hit, Whitey was trailed by a second crash car, a boiler. They weren't taking any chances now at the end.

A bunch of guys were at the garage, waiting. They took the body out of the coupe, wrapped it in a heavy moving-company blanket, and put it into the trunk of a Ford sedan that had been stolen from a supermarket parking lot in Dorchester the previous day. Johnny told the guys to empty Al's wallet and to strip all the jewelry off his body. It was supposed to look like a robbery. Johnny grabbed the Bible himself and opened it, just to make sure. It wasn't hollowed out, of course. This wasn't the Wild West, it was Winter Hill. Johnny tossed the Bible to one of the other guys.

In the dark, the four-door with Indian Al's body in the trunk was driven to the Bunker Hill projects in Charlestown. Everyone knew it wouldn't take long for some project rats to steal it for a joyride. Two Townie kids, ages sixteen and fourteen, quickly noticed the popped ignition, but either failed to notice, or more likely didn't care, that the trunk lock had also been popped. They drove the stolen Ford into the North End and back before the cops spotted them and turned on the blue lights.

The joy-riding Townie kids hit two parked cars before they were pulled over. The cops had the car towed and eventually the popped trunk was noticed. Someone opened it and immediately saw Indian Al's body, wrapped in the moving-company blanket. At the Northern Mortuary, the coroner ruled that he'd been dead only a few hours.

That evening, when the Boston homicide detectives returned to headquarters on Berkeley Street from the Northern Mortuary, they found an FBI agent waiting for them—John Connolly, who'd recently been transferred back to his hometown after making a headline-grabbing arrest in New York. According to the police report, the cops "exchanged information" with Connolly.

A couple of days later, Indian Al's wife showed up at the Holiday Inn in Peabody with his three children, a daughter and two sons. After telling the clerk that her husband had had an accident, she paid his bill with a credit card. From his late brother Joe's home, she called the Boston Police Department.

"She was interested in her husband's property. Stated he wore a ring he had been given by his brother Joseph before Joe died. . . ."

The ring was gone, as was the gold chain with the small gold horn that she also inquired about. That was the last the cops heard from Mrs. Angeli.

For a few weeks, life returned to normal at the garage. Everybody relaxed and concentrated on their own rackets. But then suddenly they got the word from Montreal— Stevie Flemmi was coming home.

8

Glory Days

LAWYER: In or about May of 1974, did any other individual join the group, become another one of the principals in the Winter Hill Gang?

MARTORANO: Yes.

LAWYER: Who was that?

MARTORANO: Stevie Flemmi.

LAWYER: And Mr. Flemmi, how was it that he joined up and became one of the principals in Winter Hill in or about May of 1974?

MARTORANO: He was a fugitive for the four or five years before that. When he returned to Boston, he joined us right away.

LATER, IN COURT, under oath, Stevie Flemmi would say that he never wanted to come back to Boston, that he was happy living as a fugitive in Montreal. But he never could quite explain why he kept calling H. Paul Rico, using the alias Jack from Boston, leaving a number for Rico to call him back at in Canada.

After Salemme left the West Coast and returned to New York in late 1969, Stevie had traveled to Las Vegas with Poulos and a woman, all the while planning to murder Poulos at some point and bury him in the desert. Poulos had seen too much, knew too much, and he would fold under pressure—of that Stevie was certain. But before Stevie could eliminate him, he was almost arrested during a routine traffic stop by a Nevada state trooper.

"He had all kinds of material in the trunk," Salemme told the congressional investigators in 2003. "He said he had a shovel and a rope and all that shit in there. He had a gun under the seat."

The cops eventually let Flemmi and Poulos go, and soon after Flemmi shot him in the head, eliminating a possible witness to the murders of Wimpy and Walter Bennett. But there was a problem. When Stevie got the body into the Clark County desert, he realized it was not like the World War II movies he'd seen as a kid about the Desert Fox and El Alamein.

"He couldn't put him under," Salemme recalled. "He said, the desert's not soft. I said, what were you thinking, [that] it's the Sahara? I said this is Nevada, this isn't North Africa."

By early 1970, they were both living in Manhattan, in different hideouts. "I was living in an apartment," Salemme said, "and *The Man of La Mancha* was playing right across the street. That's the year it was."

Every week or so, the two fugitives would get together on a park bench in Central Park and exchange gossip from back home. They were waiting for something to break. Unbeknownst to them, so was a young FBI agent from Boston named John Connolly. He had worked his way back from San Francisco to New York, but he still wanted to return home. His father was sick. Connolly spoke to H. Paul Rico all the time, and after he retired in 1970, to Dennis Condon, who was now the "fugitive coordinator" in the Boston office. Connolly could no longer count on his political connections. Speaker McCormack had retired, and by 1972, J. Edgar Hoover would be dead. From now on, Connolly would have to advance on merit, or more likely, by figuring out a new way to put the fix in.

Fortunately, he had Rico and Condon pushing for him. Both of them wanted Connolly back in Boston. In their new post-FBI retirement careers, they would still need eyes and ears in the Boston office, a go-to guy who operated the way they did, who could be counted upon to look the other way . . . for a friend . . . if the price was right. Who better to fill such a role than young John Connolly?

Flemmi was also in contact with Rico, before and after his retirement from the Bureau. Stevie would call in as "Jack from Boston" and leave a message for Rico. If he wasn't in the office, Flemmi would leave a number and Rico would return the call . . . as "Jack from Boston." One nickname—it was a lot easier, only having to remember a single moniker.

Finally, in 1972, Rico figured out a way to get Connolly back to Boston. Connolly would collar Frank Salemme—after all, as a kid, Connolly had known the older Salemme at the L Street bathhouse in Southie. They were only five or six years apart in age. It wasn't beyond the realm of possibility that Connolly could pick him out of a crowd, even in Manhattan. The only problem was, no one wanted Flemmi caught with Salemme. Stevie was on the team. So Flemmi would have to leave New York before Zip could make his miraculous pinch.

Salemme later explained what happened next with Flemmi: "One day he shows up in Central Park and tells me he's leaving, he doesn't know where he's going but he's leaving. He might have even said, I might go to Montreal. But he said, I'm getting out of here, it's too hot down here."

Naturally Salemme wanted to know if something was up.

"We got in kind of an argument about it . . . how come

so sudden, what did you hear, did you hear anything? It was too spontaneous. It didn't make sense, that two or three days before, nothing, and this day, bing, he's going to leave."

Years later, when they were both jailed in the Plymouth House of Correction, as part of discovery, Salemme was given FBI documents detailing his movements in 1972. One report, filed by fugitive coordinator Condon, mentioned Flemmi and Salemme having an argument in New York.

"There's only one person it could be," Salemme said. "It's so singular."

Stevie left New York for Montreal. Meanwhile, fugitive coordinator Condon began sending Connolly one detailed report after another on where Salemme might be.

"It was shortly thereafter," Salemme said, "that I was bumped into by John Connolly on Eighty-third Street and Third Avenue."

Frank Salemme after his arrest in New York City in 1972.

Almost thirty years later, Dennis Condon would be on the witness stand in federal court in Boston. Frank Salemme's attorney would ask the now-retired fugitive co-ordinator if, after Salemme's capture, he had ever sent any FBI offices anywhere any reports about the possible whereabouts of Stevie Flemmi.

"No," Condon replied.

AS RICO HAD predicted, Bobby Daddieco was no Barboza. But he was enough to sink Salemme. Connolly got his transfer back to Boston, and in Superior Court, Cadillac Frank got thirty years for the Fitzgerald bombing. He ended up in Walpole with Jimmy Flemmi. Joe Barboza was in solitary, talking about recanting his testimony in the Deegan murder trial, and then later recanting his recantation.

Stevie, meanwhile, took trade-school courses in photoengraving—later, at the garage in Somerville, Flemmi told the others that he'd wanted to learn how to make counterfeit currency. He remained in contact with both the FBI and his friends in Somerville—Johnny Martorano and Howie Winter.

Brian Halloran, murdered by Whitey in 1982.

Everything was being taken care of back home for Stevie. But he had nobody to hang out with. However, Johnny and Howie had a connection to the Montreal underworld—a heavy boozer and drug user and all-around hard-luck hood named Brian Halloran. He was more a friend of Jimmy Martorano's, but he was also tight with some Irish gangsters from Montreal, among them the brother of Eddie Johnson, the goalie for the Boston Bruins. They'd robbed a bank in Somerville together. They'd all gotten arrested, but they were still tight.

So we all drove up to Montreal one night, me and Howie and Brian Halloran, to see Stevie. Must have been late '71 or '72. I remember I had a new Lincoln and that's the car we took. So we introduced him to the Johnson brothers. We only spent the one night there. I don't think Stevie ever did anything with the Johnsons, because, knowing him the way I do now, if the Johnsons had hooked up with him in anything, they would have ended up in prison, and they never did.

Back at the garage, Whitey, one-fifth of the partners, was getting one-third of the profits. The plan had been for him to cut it up six ways, with the Mullens, but somehow the money never quite trickled down the way it was supposed to. But whatever Whitey made, it wasn't enough. He was forty-three, the same age as Howie, and twelve years younger than Joe Mac, and he was still trying to make up for all that lost time in prison. By 1973, the Boston FBI reported that Whitey had been told by unnamed agents to back off his heavy-handed shakedowns in Southie, a warning that seemed to indicate that the Bureau still had hopes of recruiting him as an informant.

Whitey didn't like whacking up his proceeds with the Mullens. The first to go was Paulie McGonagle. Whitey talked Tommy King into helping him out on the hit. First Whitey went to a bank and got a number of new $20 bills. Then he and Tommy went to Paulie McGonagle and showed him the cash, telling him it was counterfeit and would he like to buy some.

Paulie, amazed at the quality of what he believed were the queer bills, immediately said he'd take as many as they could sell him. They made a date to meet early the next morning at the corner of O and Third streets. Whitey pulled up in his car, with Tommy King sitting beside him. Paulie McGonagle jumped in the backseat and King handed him back a briefcase. As Paulie opened it, King drew a gun and shot him in the head.

Now that he was dead, Whitey wanted to make Paulie "do the Houdini," as the Westies of New York's Hell's Kitchen used to say. As Whitey well knew, if the cops aren't 100 percent certain that there's been a murder, they seldom go all out. A missing person, at least if he's an adult and especially if he has a long criminal record, never receives quite as much attention as a dead body. And the cops wouldn't find McGonagle's body until 2000. He just . . . disappeared.

They buried him on Tenean Beach in Dorchester. Then Whitey dumped his car off a dock in Charlestown—a swerve to point the finger at Charlestown criminals. Finally he threw McGonagle's wallet into the water, making sure to immediately drop an anonymous dime to the police so that they could fish out the wallet before it sank to the bottom.

All in all, the McGonagle hit was a good piece of work. Whitey was already beginning to perfect some of the techniques that would serve him well in the years ahead— devious plotting, making the body disappear, planting evidence that pointed away from himself, and, in this case, laying the groundwork for a future hit. Throwing in with Whitey on the McGonagle hit, Tommy King had started down the path that would lead to his own murder. He had shown himself capable of shooting someone from his own crew, someone he knew well. Over the next few years, Whitey would often remind the others at the garage of Tommy's treachery, neglecting to mention who had actually concocted the plot to eliminate Paulie McGonagle.

ON THE OTHER hand, it was a lot of work, not to mention risk, for Whitey to kill somebody basically by himself. So for his next victim, Whitey decided to bring in his Somerville partners. Spike O'Toole was one of the last important McLaughlin Gang members still at large in Boston. He'd been arrested with Georgie McLaughlin back in 1965. He was the sole survivor of the McLaughlin hit squad that had wounded Jimmy Flemmi in Dorchester.

> Spike O'Toole was given a pass when he got out of prison. Somebody spoke up for him, probably Larry Baione, who'd done time with him. But then we start hearing from Eddie Connors, down at the Bulldog Tavern on Savin Hill Avenue. He's talking out of school, Spike is. I never liked him; he shot the Bear. Howie didn't like him 'cause he was with the other guys during the war. So Spike starts drinking, and when he drinks, he gets to talking about retaliating. He's gonna kill Howie. Whether he really means it, who knows, but we do know, he's in the Bulldog night after night. He's a dangerous kid, he shoulda got shot already, and this was an excuse to do it. I mean, we're not going to let him kill Howie. That's why Spike had to go. Why'd Connors tell us? He might figure he doesn't want any trouble with us. Suitcase Fidler was his partner.

Suitcase Fidler was an older Charlestown hood with a dodgy reputation in the underworld. During the gang

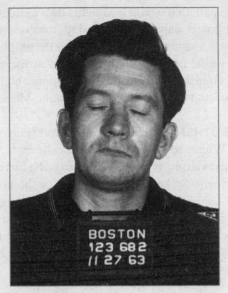

Spike O'Toole, murdered by Johnny in 1973.

war, he'd gone back and forth between Somerville and Charlestown, and had somehow managed to survive, if not thrive. One time he was in prison, and his family was broke. The Fidlers went to the veterans' agent of the city of Boston, a guy named Birmingham, and he filed a phony welfare application for the family. This was before 1968, in the days when each city or town, not the state, was responsible for all welfare payments in the municipality.

Somehow, it was discovered that Birmingham had falsified documents to get the Fidlers on general relief, as it was called. He was indicted and charged with welfare fraud. As his lawyer he hired a young state rep who pulled a few strings and got the charges dismissed. It was Billy Bulger, Whitey's younger brother.

Billy didn't make a lot of money off such cases, but he did make friends, for himself and for Whitey. In 1968, during the race riots following the assassination of

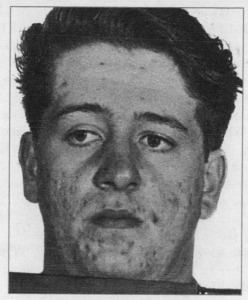

Kevin O'Neil, Whitey underling, acquitted on
murder charges in 1969.

Dr. Martin Luther King Jr., several Southie youths were
arrested for stabbing a black guy to death in front of his
girlfriend on D Street. Their first trial ended in a hung
jury, but then one of the Southie thugs, Kevin O'Neil,
hired Billy as his lawyer. The charges were dropped. Like
Birmingham, O'Neil owed the Bulgers.

IT WAS DECEMBER 1973. The decision had been made
to whack Spike O'Toole. Once more they set up shop in
Joe Mac's place, the Fire House, waiting for the call from
Eddie Connors. They were hanging around, playing cards,
with the boiler right outside Joe's house, ready to go. They
also had cars moving around Dorchester, looking for him.

Finally, the Hill sent somebody into the Bulldog and he
spotted Spike. They drove over immediately—for a hit so
close to Southie, Whitey Bulger insisted on driving.

They watched Spike unsteadily leave the Bulldog, and he reeled down to the corner to wait for the bus. He hadn't been out of prison that long and the fact that he didn't even have a car yet obviously meant that he was broke. But over the years, O'Toole had proved himself a capable guy and nobody felt like taking any chances. He was standing behind a mailbox at Savin Hill and Dot Avenue when Whitey pulled up in the boiler. Johnny let him have it with a grease gun—shot Spike right through the mailbox—and O'Toole fell to the ground, perforated. He'd been dead drunk; now Spike O'Toole was just dead. But Joe Mac jumped out of the car anyway, ran up to O'Toole, stood over his body, and lifted his ski mask. Assuming that Spike was still technically alive, Joe Mac wanted Spike to know that he had been killed by Winter Hill. After showing his face to Spike, Joe Mac pulled the mask back down and fired twice into Spike's head.

"I just wanted to make sure he was dead," he explained later.

Back in the car, Whitey had other concerns. A pedestrian had heard the shots, and foolishly had started crossing the street toward the boiler. In the dark, Whitey reached for a gun, then realized he didn't have one. He settled for pointing his index finger at the concerned citizen, enough of a warning to get the guy to keep moving, away from the car.

Later, back at the garage, Whitey told the others he'd learned a very important lesson.

"Never again do I go out on a hit without a gun," he said.

GEORGE KAUFMAN GOT a call one day in the garage from Bobby Daddieco's sister. She said her brother wanted to talk to him. George said sure, and soon Bobby was on the line. He was in the Midwest, in very loose federal custody, and he wanted everybody back in Boston to know that it was only Frankie Salemme he hated and wanted to get even with, not Stevie.

Kaufman realized what Daddieco was getting at, and told him it would be better if he spoke directly to Howie Winter.

Daddieco calls Howie and tells him, no way is he interested in testifying against Stevie, but he needs to get away from the feds, and he's got no money and no wheels, and he could sure use a truck. Howie says, I think that can be worked out; we'll get a truck for your sister, and she can get it to you. Howie tells him that if Stevie comes back, we'll pay you every week, through your sister, to stay away for six months, until we can get the charges dropped.

Up in Montreal, Stevie was ecstatic. The Hill bought the truck and came up with some cash for Daddieco's sister. Next they got a lawyer, Bob Dinsmore, who would

A smiling Stevie Flemmi returns to Boston in 1974.

represent Stevie when he returned to Boston to turn himself in. Johnny called a Statie he knew from Enrico's to handle Stevie's surrender; they didn't want any hero cops deciding to shoot it out with the dangerous fugitive. Then they arranged for a bail bondsman to handle Stevie's initial court appearance, when he would be charged with both the murder of Billy Bennett and the bombing of John Fitzgerald's car.

I mean, we didn't figure Stevie would even get bail. How could he, with those charges, and the fact that his partner's already been convicted of the bombing? Plus he's been on the lam all these years. But then he walks into the courthouse, a big smile on his face, with all the newspaper photographers taking pictures of him, and two hours later, he's out on bail. Now, of course, what we didn't know then was that all the time we thought we were the ones setting up the surrender, it was really the FBI that was doing the heavy lifting for Stevie. We took him back to the garage for a party, and nobody was suspicious. We all just said the same thing: "Damn, what a lucky bastard!"

Flemmi knew that there was one guy who might wonder a little more intently than the others about Stevie's sweetheart deal, especially since he had so much time to think about it, sitting in his cell down at MCI-Norfolk. Cadillac Frank Salemme was definitely the guy most likely to put the pieces together. After all, years earlier, down at the Office, the Man—Raymond L. S. Patriarca—had always warned Salemme to watch his back with Flemmi.

"He went to my house and saw my first wife when he got bailed," Salemme recalled, "and I'll never forget this, strictly the dog-and-pony show. He's my man, he's this and that, he broke down crying. And there I was saying, he'll do the right thing, L. S., and L. S. telling me Stevie's a phony. But he did go to the house and make the appearance, because he knew it would get back to me, and I'd take the attitude well, at least he's back, maybe he'll do something now, but nothing."

LIKE WHITEY BULGER, Stevie Flemmi was determined to make up for lost time. In Town made some overtures to him about joining the Mafia, but Stevie figured the opportunities were better in Somerville. And they were. Tony Ciulla had finally figured out how to fix horse races and not get caught.

At the beginning of his career, Fat Tony had drugged horses. Years later, in state prison, his partner Billy Barnoski wrote an essay about their early days fixing races at county fairs. He called his story "The Swinging Dick Derby." In it, Barnoski's first-person narrator recounts giving the favorite horse so many drugs that by the time the race went off, his penis is dragging on the track.

There's all kinds of ways to fix a race. You can past-post—bet after you know the winner. But with technology that got harder, plus you can get killed for that. On the dogs, they'd cut their nails, which slows 'em down. You can win a race by drugging a horse or two, but the problem is, they drug-test after the race, and then they throw out the results and usually somebody gets arrested. It's a lot better to control the jockeys—however you can. That's what Ciulla learned from experience. Drugs, bribes, hookers—Ciulla figured out which buttons to push with the jockeys.

How it worked was, Ciulla would get the racing forms ahead of time, and he'd determine which of his jockeys was in which race. If he had two or three jockeys in one race, the opportunity was there to

Billy Barnoski, Fat Tony Ciulla's partner.

make some money. If they were riding favorites, that was better, because you want to stop the favorites and then bet the long shots. Obviously, long shots are where you can make some real money.

If you've got the favorites stopped, then you bet all the combinations of the horses that have a shot—quinellas, trifectas, exactas. We'd tie up the betting windows for a half hour before post-time, betting every possible combo. They call it wheeling—you "wheel" the three or four combinations that have a chance. We could wipe out the pool for $2, and win 20 grand. The problem with wheeling was, it was labor-intensive. To make it work, you need a bunch of guys at the track, because bookies don't take that kind of action; it's too complicated. Bookies only take win-place-show. We had to have a lot of guys at the tracks.

Another thing you have to worry about: horse players can read the forms. They know how long a race should take, depending on the field. If you've got a bunch of horses that should be coming in at, say, 1:01 or 1:02, and then the winner comes in at 1:08 or 1:10, a lot of people are going to figure out that something is going on. Maybe even the steward. But hell, chances are the steward's betting too. They're like everybody else—they just want to know if the race is "live," and who they should bet on. "Live" is a track word. It means your horse has a good shot, in our case a real good shot.

The other problem was that after you win a string of races, the word goes out, "Don't take no more horses from that guy." The bookies shut you off, good-bye. Bookies know what's happening. The "live" horse becomes what they call an "order" horse. "Order" means watch out, something's going on.

The Hill needed bookies, to bet straight up on Ciulla's fixed races. Sometimes they used "beards"—guys who weren't connected, or at least weren't known to be with the Hill. Suddenly they would go on these incredible winning streaks, until the day came when the bookies refused to take any more action from them. Soon the Hill was inquiring of everyone they did business with, do you know any bookies we can bet with?

One of the guys they approached was Richie Castucci, the Revere hustler and owner of the Ebb Tide, Joe Barboza's old hangout on the beach. Now, in the swinging seventies, Castucci was running strip joints—the Surf and the Squire—moving a thousand cases of beer a week, pulling in above and beyond the cover charges and the hookers and the $15 "champagne cocktails." It was serious money and the Hill had a piece of it. They were also

Richie Castucci, Revere wiseguy,
murdered by Johnny Martorano in 1976

involved with Castucci in other scams, one of which involved bootlegged 8-track rock tapes.

Castucci was another degenerate gambler, who'd been
a high-roller in Las Vegas since the late 1950s. He was
such a regular that he attended Sammy Davis Jr.'s wedding to Swedish actress Mae Britt there in 1960. None of
Castucci's show-biz connections meant anything to Winter Hill. They only cared about finding more bookies.
Castucci told Johnny that he knew a guy in New York,
Jack Mace, who could handle all the action they wanted
to give him.

So we hit this guy Jack Mace three or four times, for
big money. Finally he calls me up. He says, look, if
you're going to do this to me, you gotta give me
some real action too. See, he was big enough that he

could lay off a lot of the "live" action we were giving him, but why should he do it if we're not giving him a chance to make some money, too? I understood. At least he wasn't cutting us off, period, which is what a lot of them had already done. Mace says, if you want to keep betting the horses with me, give me some sports action too. And that's when we started getting into the heavy stuff. We thought we were playing everybody for suckers, but what we didn't realize is that they were sucking us in, and in the end, we're the ones who got suckered.

But while it lasted, it would be boom times for the Hill. Their top bookmakers were bringing in big money. Sometimes during football season in the fall, the Hill would split up $75,000 in a good week, and that was just the partners' cut.

Soon everyone was driving a new car. They had jewelry, and so did their girlfriends and wives. Joe McDonald always had access to as much stolen jewelry as they wanted. Soon the partners were dipping into the till to buy one another jewelry or gold chains on their birthdays.

In December 1975, the other guys presented Johnny with a five-carat diamond pinkie ring. It was beautiful, but Johnny wanted an even more ostentatious setting. He took it down to the Jewelers' Building on Washington Street and had a guy he knew resct the diamond. From then on, Johnny never took the ring off his finger.

They kept expanding—after killing Indian Al, they inherited his territory in the Merrimack Valley. It wasn't long before the Lowell Police Department was noticing new people sitting down with the city's top bookmaker, Jackie McDermott, an affable ex-pressman for the *Lowell Sun*. After killing Indian Al, they had ordered McDermott to a meeting at the Holiday Inn on the Somerville-Charlestown Line—the same motel where Wimpy

Bennett and Stevie Flemmi had worked out a truce with Buddy McLean in early 1965 during the Irish Gang War.

McDermott was ushered in to see the new bosses. He only had one question: Why was Indian Joe hit in such a brazen way, in Medford Square?

"We wanted," said Whitey, "to show everyone how easy it was."

Now the Hill was moving around Lowell, setting things up. One of the new guys who called himself "Nick," the Lowell police reported, "is believed to be John V. Martorano."

The Lowell police knew of the reputation "Nick" had in Boston, and one night a plainclothesman approached McDermott and asked why he wasn't carrying a gun, now

Jackie McDermott, Lowell bookie,
murdered by Billy Barnoski in 1988.

that "Nick" was in town, putting things together for the Hill. Jackie McDermott waved off the cop.

"Guys like Nick," he said, "if they want to get you, they're gonna get you, whether you're carrying or not."

There were no problems in Lowell.

NEXT, EVERYONE AT the garage was buying houses. Stevie purchased one in Milton for Marion Hussey and her family, which now included three of his children, although Stevie insisted that on the birth certificates, she list her ex-husband rather than him as the father. He'd known guys like the late Spike O'Toole who'd been lugged into court for nonpayment of child support. Stevie didn't need any of that shit. After all, he was doing the right thing by his second family, moving them out of the city. None of them would have to worry about the Boston public schools anymore. Then he built a swimming pool in the backyard.

Finally, he bought the house next door for his parents and moved them out of Mattapan, which had "tipped" a few years earlier. Once his parents were settled in, Stevie called Frank the Trapper to install a large hidden compartment in the house where he could stash some more of his weapons.

Meanwhile, Whitey soon had a house on Silver Street in South Boston. Howie Winter got a house on Madison Street in Somerville.

Johnny bought two houses, one for his second wife and her son Vincent, the other for Barbara and Johnny Jr. Nancy might have gotten one, too, except that she was remarried. It wouldn't have looked right.

I couldn't put the houses in my own name. That would have been asking for trouble. So for my second wife I used Charlie Raso. It was on Main Street in Medford, a shack basically when I bought it. I think I paid 50 grand, put down 5 or 10 as a down payment, and Charlie took the mortgage, which I paid every month. Then I gutted the place, used subcontractors working under the table. That way you can launder cash and increase the value of the property and you don't leave a paper trail, which means the IRS can't come after you later. If they ask you, Why is the house so much more valuable now than it was when you bought it, you just say, It's the market. Everything's going up.

For Barbara and Johnny, I used George Kaufman as the straw, because I bought in Chestnut Hill, his general neighborhood. I think I paid 90 grand for that place—20 down and a $70,000 mortgage.

One day in 1974, Johnny and Stevie were driving around Brookline Village and Johnny decided to stop in at George Taylor's jewelry store to check out the inventory.

Inside, Johnny introduced Stevie to Taylor, and then Taylor brought over a new employee, a beautiful young blonde named Debbie Davis. Her father owned the service station across the street. After World War II he had brought back a German war bride, Olga. The Davises had a lot of kids and not much money. Before they left that day, Johnny noticed Stevie whispering something to the teenager, and that she was giggling back at him, like they were both in high school.

"So I'm the one introduced Debbie Davis to Stevie Flemmi. Not one of my better matchmaking efforts."

ANOTHER OF JOHNNY'S interventions on behalf of romance proved more successful, and long-lasting. One night one of the regulars at Chandler's, a successful businessman whom Johnny looked up to, walked in frowning, a dejected look on his face. Johnny invited him over to his table for a drink and asked him what the problem was.

He said he was just thinking about this girl who lived down the street, and how she was going out with another guy. And she had told him, if she wasn't tied up, she'd love to go out with him. I think she was afraid of this guy she had been dating. Now, this guy I'm sitting with is not just a customer of mine, he's my friend, you follow me? So I told him, maybe I can do something for you. Give me a day or two.

He left and I saw Alvin Campbell sitting at the bar. So I said to Alvin, do me a favor, go see this guy—the girl's boyfriend—and tell him to pack his bags and get outta town. I think the guy knew Alvin's reputation, which didn't hurt the situation. After Alvin had a chat with him, he ran away. I was surprised. I didn't think he'd leave, it was strictly a bluff on our part.

A couple of days later, my friend comes back into Chandler's, and now he's got a big smile on his face. He says he's got a date with this girl, now that the boyfriend is gone. As of 2010, they are still married.

Call me Cupid.

Tony Ciulla would follow the race circuit—living in hotels near wherever the meet was. A couple of times a week, he'd call Johnny from the hotels and give him the next batch of races that he'd fixed, and how they should bet them.

Eventually, Ciulla started buying thoroughbreds with Howie. This put him even deeper into the gang. Through straws, Ciulla eventually purchased a horse named Spread the Word.

It was a $30,000 horse that Fat Tony had somehow figured out how to run in $10,000 races. So we could win some really big money on Spread the Word. But we could only do it a few times before the tracks figured it out, so we had to make the races count. We had guys out everywhere when Spread the Word was running. This one guy, Jerry Matricia, he was from Boston but he'd moved to Vegas. We had him bet on Spread the Word—told him to just bet as much as he could, and then call us before the race, so we'd know how much we owed him if he lost. Spread the Word won, and so did Matricia—$90,000.

The problem was, before we could get somebody out to Vegas to collect, he went into the casinos, figuring he could use our money to win a few grand more for himself. You can imagine what happened next—he gets down 5 or 10 thousand, panics, tries to get it all back and loses everything, the whole 90 grand. Then he starts running, because he's afraid. That's the kind of problem you're going to get when you have as many guys handling cash as we did.

Another time Ciulla paid off a jockey to lose and he won. Double-crossed us. We lost a bundle. Joe Mac went crazy, he wanted to hit the guy and bury him in the back stretch at Suffolk, as a lesson to all the other jockeys. I think Ciulla even testified to that in court. But it ended up Howie and Barnoski went out and gave the guy a slap and told him, "If we ever pay you again to lose a race and it looks like you're gonna win it, then you just better make sure you don't, even if you have to jump off the fucking horse."

The Hill was making big money with Fat Tony, but Ciulla was addicted to gambling. It didn't matter how much he made fixing races, he was always in the hole, because he couldn't stop wagering. Winning just gave him more money to lose on the races and the games he couldn't fix. It was the thrill of the action that turned him on. Through the Hill, he could finally place bets on his fixed races, but he was still losing everything he made and more, betting on sports with Hill bookies like Bobby Gallinaro. So Ciulla went back to working his old scams, upgrading his old diamond-ring bait-and-switch. Now he was using bars of gold.

Fat Tony knew a guy named James Sousa, and Sousa knew a dentist who had a lot of cash he was looking to invest. Ciulla gave Sousa some gold samples to show the dentist. Just as in the diamond grift, the gold was of high quality, and the dentist went for it.

Sousa arranged to meet the dentist in the parking lot of what was by now the Star Market on Winter Hill, across Broadway from the garage. The dentist would bring cash, which Sousa would take in exchange for a crate full of what was supposed to be gold, but was in fact bricks. But that wouldn't be a problem, because after the transaction Barnoski was supposed to arrive, gun drawn. According to Ciulla's plan, Barnoski would rob the dentist and steal the crate of "gold," so that the dentist would never know he'd been scammed.

Ciulla's setting this up on his own and we know nothing about the details. The problem comes when he realizes he needs a second gun for the score, so Ciulla's running around Marshall Street looking for somebody, and he runs into Joe Mac. Joe says okay, he'll be the second gun. But when they get over to the parking lot, everything goes wrong. The dentist has his ten-year-old kid with him, and he brought a gun himself. When he sees Barnoski and Joe Mac with guns, he starts shooting. Doesn't hit anybody, but everybody's running for cover and screaming. Joe and Barnoski manage to escape, but Sousa gets arrested. Ciulla grabs the dentist's kid—to protect him, he says, that's his story later, and drives him around the block. But it's still kidnapping, and the dentist knows Sousa, who knows Joe was there. That's our problem. Now Joe is jammed up.

So Tony came into the garage with Barnoski, and by this point there's a John Doe warrant out for kidnapping the kid. Sousa's in a panic, he wants money for an attorney, he's afraid of jail, he knows Barnoski and Ciulla. I didn't think Ciulla would hold up.

Ciulla and Barnoski were told to leave and the partners convened a summit. Johnny immediately made a pitch for killing Ciulla, on the grounds that the whole crazy stunt was his idea, and because he was the one who snatched the kid. But he knew Howie would never sign off on hitting Ciulla. They owned horses together. So Sousa would have to go.

A few days later, Barnoski brought Sousa to the garage, and then left. Johnny and Stevie would handle this one. They told Sousa to go into the back office and wait for them. It was the middle of a weekday, since Sousa was supposed to pick up some money from them, during regular banking hours. Sousa wasn't worried. After all, there was a full crew of mechanics and body-shop guys working in the garage. To make sure nobody could hear the shots, Johnny had somebody start up the large motors in the repair bays. Then he sent the workers out for lunch early. Finally he put someone on the door to the office.

Johnny walked into the back office as Sousa watched him. Suddenly he drew a .38-caliber revolver from his coat pocket and shot Sousa in the head. Sousa slumped over in the chair, dead, and blood immediately started gushing from his head. Stevie rushed in and grabbed a paint bucket to catch the blood before it spilled onto the floor and made an even bigger mess. Johnny threw the gun down and changed into different clothes—the ones he'd been wearing when he shot Sousa were bloody, and there was gunpowder all over them.

Joe McDonald's brother Leo arrived with a sleeping bag to wrap Sousa's corpse in. Joe McDonald and Jimmy Sims came by and loaded the body into the back of a car, which they drove to Boxford. Sousa's body was never found, and probably never will be. The two guys who disposed of it, Joe Mac and Sims, are both long gone.

Sousa had a court date coming up pretty soon. Barnoski shows up, pretends to be surprised when Sousa is a no-show. He goes up to Sousa's wife and says, "Where is your husband? Everybody is looking for him." Then he gives her some cash and tells her, "If you get in touch with him, have him call me."

Since he had come back from Montreal, Stevie Flemmi seemed different. More serious. And preoccupied—sometimes he'd be sitting in a room with the others, and they'd eventually notice that he was just staring off into space, and hadn't said a word for a half hour. Yet he and Whitey somehow seemed to hit it off. They were the two Hill guys who were actually from Boston, the city itself. Stevie told the feds later that he first realized Whitey's potential one day when they were shaking down an independent Jewish bookie. Whitey grabbed an ax and so thoroughly frightened the bookie that he fainted.

But Whitey and Stevie had more in common than their propensity for sudden violence. Unlike everyone else in the gang, members and associates alike, they barely drank. They didn't smoke. Stevie was into what passed in the 1970s for health food. He enjoyed Japanese cuisine, but whenever he talked the other guys into joining him at a Japanese restaurant, he'd lecture them about the health hazards of sake. Some mornings he would bring a box of cornflakes to the garage. But he refused to drink milk, so he would take a bowl of cereal over to the sink and run tap water over it. Then he would eat it—with a fork.

Stevie had also become a bit of a hypochondriac. He was obsessed with "germs," constantly washing his hands. He hated shaking hands with anyone. Whitey was the same way. The younger guys in the gang quickly learned that if they didn't want Whitey and Stevie around, all they had to do was cough into their hands a few times. Whitey and Stevie would quickly excuse themselves for the rest of the day, or evening. Stevie didn't smoke marijuana anymore. He seemed to have nasal problems—he was always sniffing, so much so that even Whitey would grow exasperated with him.

Increasingly, Stevie seemed to care, as Salemme put it, "only about his money and his women, not necessarily in that order." He had set up Marion Hussey in the house in Milton, but he was also spending a lot of time with his new nineteen-year-old girlfriend, Debbie Davis. She had a sister named Michelle who had dark hair—"my Ava Gardner," Stevie would call her, as if she had any idea who Ava Gardner was. She was thirteen. Then there was Deborah Hussey, Marion's daughter. Stevie was her common-law stepfather. She was thirteen when Stevie started raping her.

There were other young girls, too, in South Boston, where Stevie seemed to spend more of his time than in Roxbury, now that his old neighborhood was overwhelmingly black. He still had a flag planted in Roxbury—the Marconi Club on Northampton Street, into which Johnny had also invested. But Flemmi spent less time there as the years went by. Increasingly Stevie and Whitey kept to themselves, which was just as well. From what they were starting to see and hear, the rest of the gang at the garage didn't really want to know what Stevie and Whitey were doing in their spare time.

IN 1975, WHITEY and Stevie reported a problem in Savin Hill, the Dorchester neighborhood between Whitey's Southie and Stevie's Roxbury. It seemed that Eddie Connors, the career criminal and proprietor of the Bulldog Tavern, had been bragging to the customers on the other side of his tap about how he'd set up Spike O'Toole for the Hill.

> The only guys we ever heard this from were Stevie and Whitey. Later on I learned that Eddie had been arrested on an armored-car job, but I don't know if they were somehow involved and wanted to shut him up. By then, Stevie and Whitey were like Ike and Mike. And they told us, this time they wanted to be the shooters. They wanted to kill Connors together. Maybe it was going to be their bond, or maybe they wanted to have something on each other. I'm not sure. All I know is, it was a Southie thing. They even wanted to use a Southie car instead of one of our boilers. It was a sedan, I remember that.

It was Howie's name that Eddie Connors kept dropping when he was telling his patrons about setting up Spike O'Toole—or so Stevie and Whitey said. So Howie called Connors at the Bulldog and said he had to discuss something important with him, on a safe phone, which in those days meant a pay phone.

Howie didn't let on what he wanted to talk about, just said it was imperative that they talk. Finally, Connors gave him a phone number Howie could call him at in a couple of nights. Johnny used the same song-and-dance he'd employed before the Indian Joe hit—calling the phone company and finally getting a supervisor. Once again, Johnny spun a tall tale about his son's car breaking down, and how the boy had run out of change before he could give him the address where he was stranded. The supervisor was only too happy to oblige.

This pay phone was at a gas station at the corner of

Morrissey Boulevard and Freeport Street, not far from the Bulldog. Johnny was driving the Southie car. There was a hill right behind the station—a good place for Johnny to park.

The next day they would read in the papers that several hundred yards down the boulevard, hundreds of cops had been attending a formal dinner at a local banquet hall. But they were off-duty, and loaded, and none of them heard a thing. But then Whitey noticed a Metropolitan District Commission (MDC) police speed trap on Morrissey

Eddie Connors, Dorchester bar owner,
was shot to death in a phone booth in 1975.

Boulevard, which could have conceivably presented a problem.

Whitey quickly spotted another phone booth and told Johnny to pull over. He called in a report of a bank burglary in progress down in Quincy. He knew that would get their attention. A couple of minutes later the MDC cops were heading south toward Quincy at about 90 miles an hour, blue lights flashing. Johnny started the boiler and they resumed their journey to the gas station.

JOHNNY PULLED THE Southie boiler over on Freeport Street and watched Whitey and Stevie scramble up the hill. Then he heard a volley of gunshots, after which they came running back down the hill. They jumped in the car and Whitey said, "He's gone." Johnny turned onto Morrissey Boulevard, heading back toward Southie. He wasn't in any hurry, considering that it was a stolen car and they still had the murder weapons with them. Suddenly, from the backseat, Whitey yelled, "Pull over."

"I want to drive," he told Johnny. "I know this area better than you do."

Johnny got out and climbed into the backseat.

IT WAS 1975, and Southie was in turmoil. Court-ordered school busing in Boston had begun a year earlier, and the epicenter of the city's white resentment was South Boston. Whitey's brother Billy, the state senator, sometimes showed up outside South Boston High School to lead the protests as the buses full of black students from Roxbury arrived in the morning. Stones were often hurled.

The situation on the streets in Southie quickly degenerated into total anarchy. The police grew so frustrated that one Saturday night off-duty members of the Tactical Patrol Force, which bore the brunt of the daily street battles, taped black duct tape over their badge numbers. Then they invaded the Rabbit Inn on Dorchester Street, where the rioters often congregated in the mornings after pelting the cops with stones. The first cop through the door slapped an unloaded throwdown on the bar—to provide some scrap of evidence that they had been threatened. Then the rest of the cops swarmed inside and beat the shit out of everyone inside the Rabbit Inn.

The most enthusiastic proponent of forced busing was the *Boston Globe,* then owned and operated by wealthy Ivy League–educated Yankees from the tonier suburbs—"social-planning liberal do-gooders," in the words of Johnny's former in-law, City Councilor Dapper O'Neil. The *Globe* daily lectured its blue-collar city readers on their duty to obey the busing decrees of the federal judge, who lived in Wellesley. The new Democrat governor, who lived in Brookline, a town that was almost totally surrounded by the city but with a school system that had not been ordered to integrate, agreed with the *Globe* and the judge that the lower-middle- and working-class white population of Boston must obey the law as laid down by their suburban betters.

Whitey Bulger was not a particularly political person. His only known instance of political activism came in 1970, when his brother was running for an open state senate seat after eight years in the House. Despite the fact that Billy's opponent barely represented a threat, Whitey told anyone who would listen that he was planning to kill the bum who had the temerity to run against Billy. Testifying before a congressional committee in 2003, Billy Bulger said that he had tracked Whitey down and told him to immediately desist in his "madness."

Five years later, apparently, no one was around to dissuade Whitey when he got the idea of shooting up the *Globe* presses. The broadsheet was published on Morrissey Boulevard, a few hundred yards from where Eddie Connors had been gunned down. The *Globe* in those days was immensely profitable, and powerful, and its presses, at street level behind plate-glass windows, were visible symbols of the *Globe*'s clout. The whole operation—the presses, the smug bow-tied editors and reporters, even the green delivery trucks—was a constant grating reminder of the suburban political establishment's domination of the poor whites of South Boston.

The *Globe* was so despised in Southie that on the night that the TPF wrecked the Rabbit Inn, the patrons who hadn't been taken by ambulance to the emergency room of Boston City Hospital would call only the *Herald American* to get their side of the story out. They didn't trust the trust-funded reporters of the *Globe* to tell the truth.

Finally, Whitey decided to strike a blow for the Town. One night in October 1975, he and some of his crew drove down Morrissey Boulevard to the *Globe*, where he opened fire with a high-powered rifle on the presses, shattering the plate-glass windows.

The next day, the editorial-page editor from Cambridge, the editor from Lincoln, the governor from Brookline, and the judge from Wellesley all once again denounced the outrageous lawlessness among the white Roman Catholic working classes of Boston.

DESPITE HIS BRIEF foray into civil disobedience, Whitey was still more interested in settling his own personal scores. Next he wanted to get rid of Tommy King, another of the old Mullen gang. Whitey had been bad-mouthing him for years at the garage, dropping hints about how Tommy had to go, but no one else cared. He'd been in on the Donald Killeen hit in 1972, then Paulie McGonagle's murder, and a couple of other murders since then. He had set up Ralph DeMasi perfectly and had driven a crash car on the Indian Joe hit. He could get the job done and he kept his mouth shut. In other words, he was capable.

Plus, Tommy fit better with the Somerville guys than Whitey did. He was an ironworker, and he'd done time in

Walpole with Jimmy Flemmi. He liked to drink. Tommy King didn't spend much time at the garage—he was a Southie guy through and through. He hung out more at Chandler's than he did at Marshall Motors. But the general consensus was that, although he might not be the sharpest knife in the drawer, Tommy King was Good People.

Later on, there were stories that he'd perhaps bested Whitey in a barroom brawl in Southie, but Whitey knew that as far as his Somerville partners were concerned, getting drunk and rowdy was hardly considered a capital offense. But in the fall of 1975, with South Boston and other city neighborhoods convulsed by rampaging mobs, Tommy King was beginning to unravel. He had taken to hanging out with his own crew of drug-ravaged ex-cons, Walpole warriors as everyone in the Hill still derisively called them. King himself was drifting into drugs—mostly speed, after marijuana the most popular drug in Southie in those precocaine days. He was living on black beauties and green hearts.

Whitey finally came up with the ostensible reason he needed to convince the rest of the Hill to join him in eliminating troublesome Tommy. A student of underworld history, Whitey decided to use the same story that got Dutch Schultz killed in Newark back in 1935—that he was planning to kill a crusading prosecutor named Tom Dewey. Forty years later, Whitey inserted a different cop's name— Eddie Walsh.

The Hill had the same reaction that "the Commission" in New York had in 1935. No way could they allow such an assassination to happen. It wouldn't just be bad for business, it would be fatal.

THERE WAS NO love lost between Johnny and Eddie Walsh, the first cop who ever arrested him, back in 1960. But with the daily street battles across much of the city, the cops were stressed to the breaking point. A gangland hit on a BPD deputy superintendent would be the final straw.

On the other hand, the Hill's other partners knew how much Whitey hated Tommy King, so they wanted to check out his story very carefully before they moved against one of their top hands. The problem was, Whitey was the only one of the partners from Southie, which had always been a world apart, even before busing tore the Town apart.

Johnny went to another one of the Hill associates from Southie and asked him what was going on. He confirmed that Tommy had been terrorizing Southie, and added that he was certainly capable of killing a cop. Other people said the same thing. Reluctantly, at the garage, a death sentence was handed down for Tommy.

IT WAS WHITEY'S plan. Eddie Connors's partner, Suitcase Fidler, was still out there. He, too, was capable—the

Alan "Suitcase" Fidler, Charlestown criminal,
Eddie Connors's partner.

Mafia had dispatched him to California in 1970 to hunt Joe Barboza. So the Hill told Tommy that they were going to have to take out Suitcase before he came looking for all of them. They said that, once again, the Bulldog would be staked out and that the next time Suitcase showed up, Tommy King would walk in and shoot him—just the way Dutch Schultz had gotten it, from a guy named Charlie the Bug, at the Palace Chophouse in October 1935, along with his guys named Abadaba and Lulu.

The other guys would be waiting in the car, just in case there was trouble.

LAWYER: Mr. King had participated in murders with you, had he not?

MARTORANO: And the day he got killed, he thought he was participating in another one. . . . Whitey had come to me many times and wanted to kill Tommy King, and I said no many times.

LAWYER: Mr. King was a friend of yours, was he not?

MARTORANO: I was friendly with him.

LAWYER: You considered him a friend, did you not?

MARTORANO: Not a big friend. I was friendly with him, yeah. You know, just not a close friend.

Tommy didn't like Whitey any more than Whitey liked him, and there was some concern that he wouldn't buy the Suitcase Fidler story, especially in his paranoid, drug-addled state of mind. Which may have been why Whitey insisted that Johnny come along—Tommy trusted Johnny. On the night of October 25, 1975, Johnny drove over to Carson Beach from the garage with another guy from Somerville. Whitey was already there, waiting in a stolen car. Johnny and the other guy from Somerville jumped into the backseat, which meant that Tommy would have to get into the front seat.

Tommy King arrived wearing a bulletproof vest. He was ready to walk into the Bulldog and shoot Suitcase. Then Stevie arrived with the guns. He handed one to each guy in the car, giving Tommy his last. Just in case, Tommy's revolver didn't have bullets, only blanks. Stevie walked away and Whitey backed the car out. He had barely turned south toward Savin Hill when Johnny leaned forward and shot Tommy in the head.

Driving back to Somerville, Johnny Martorano felt queasy. Whitey always knew the right buttons to push with Johnny, and this time the button was, we can't allow a cop to be killed.

But Johnny couldn't help thinking how Whitey first got Tommy King to kill Paulie McGonagle for him, and now he had gotten his partners to kill Tommy for him. In three years, Whitey had certainly come a long way from Duffy's Tavern. The question neither Johnny nor anyone else in the gang was quite ready to ask was, How much further was Whitey planning to go?

WHITEY'S EVENING WAS just beginning. He had the task of disposing of King's body. They had another stolen car ready, and they dumped King's body in the trunk and then drove to the beach at the Neponset River under the bridge to Quincy. They buried King's body there.

Then they took Tommy King's car and went looking for his best friend, Francis "Buddy" Leonard, another Mullen, a small-time hoodlum from Southie. A decade younger than Whitey, he'd grown up in the same public-housing project as the Bulgers. He was a friend of King's, and would try to find out what happened when Tommy turned up missing. But he never got the chance. Whitey and his crew grabbed Leonard as he left a barroom, drunk as usual. They got him into Tommy King's car, then shot him in the head. They abandoned King's car, with his friend's body in it, in the Boston Housing Authority project where Buddy Leonard and Whitey Bulger had grown up together.

The next day, King's wife reported him missing. His car soon turned up, with Leonard's body in it. The police were supposed to think that for some reason King and Leonard had had a falling-out, and that after shooting his pal, King had fled. The cops quickly got a tip that Whitey had actually killed him, in a dispute over a hijacked truck. On the police incident report, Leonard was described as a "tailgater" by trade. In other words, no

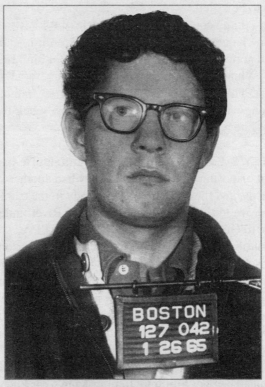

Francis "Buddy" Leonard, small-time Mullen gang member, murdered by Whitey the same night Tommy King was clipped in 1975.

great loss, whoever killed him. The cops had more pressing matters to deal with, namely the daily antibusing street
rumbles.

> From then on, whenever we'd drive across the bridge
> into Quincy, Whitey would say, "Tip your hat to
> Tommy." That's how I knew where he was buried.
> They finally dug him up in 2000, after I decided to
> help the government against Whitey and Stevie.

One day in the fall of 1975, Whitey called everyone to-
gether at the garage for a big announcement. FBI agent
John Connolly wanted to sit down with him. Whitey didn't
mention that he'd been talking, off and on, with FBI agent
Dennis Condon since 1971, or that he'd known H. Paul
Rico since the early 1950s.

As usual, the Boston FBI office had been playing fast
and loose with the rules. There was a new agent named
John Morris. When he was transferred to Boston, he
bought a house in the suburbs near Dennis Condon's home.
It wasn't long before they were riding into Boston together
every morning. Soon John Morris was coming up with
novel ways to develop informants.

Eddie Miani—better known as Eddie Miami—was a
small-time associate of Richie Castucci, the Revere hustler who had business with both the Hill and the Mafia.
Morris tried to recruit him as an informant, but Eddie
Miami wasn't interested. So Morris went to his house one
night and planted a "bomb" under his car, then called Miami to warn him that the FBI had been tipped that the Hill
was planning to blow him up. Miami didn't bite, but inside
the corrupt organization, Morris got points for trying.

Unlike Eddie Miami, Whitey was a natural as an FBI
informant. Zip, as Whitey would famously nickname John
Connolly, still owed Whitey Bulger's brother Billy. Six
years older than Connolly, Billy had provided one helping

hand after another to Zip throughout his life—first helping him get into Boston College, then securing Speaker Mc-Cormack's recommendation to J. Edgar Hoover that led to Connolly's appointment to the FBI.

> Whitey told us his brother Billy set it all up. Zip asked Billy how he could pay Billy back for all he'd done for him. And Billy said, "Keep my brother out of trouble." We said go ahead and meet him, and be a good listener. Whitey meets him at Wollaston Beach in Quincy. Whitey sneaks into Zip's car and they have a discussion and Connolly tells him they're just after In Town, not us. This is what Whitey tells us anyway.

Back in Somerville, everyone gave Whitey's new relationship with the feds a thumbs-up. After all, Johnny had Trooper Schneiderhan, although nowadays he always took Howie along with him for the meetings. Two-on-ones were always preferable in maintaining control of any situation, but with a cop there was another reason as well. As long as there was a witness, no one could ever accuse Johnny—or Howie—of ratting out the gang.

> Next Whitey comes back and says he wants to introduce Stevie to Connolly. I thought that was a good idea, to have two of us meeting with one of them, just like Howie and me with Schneiderhan. Obviously, none of us had any idea that Stevie had been a rat all those years. I don't even think Whitey knew, not at that point. See, when Stevie came back, in '74, and we were going to bring him in with us, Whitey asked me, "Was Stevie ever made?" I told him not as far as I knew. But the point is, if Whitey'd been in the loop with the FBI at that point, he would have known about Stevie. Later on, when we were in jail together, after he'd been disclosed as a rat, Stevie

always said he'd been blackmailed by the FBI—that
he didn't want to go back to work for them when he
came back, but they told him if he didn't they'd rat
him out to us. I never believed him, not that the FBI
was above that kind of thing.

In 1998, Flemmi testified that back in 1975 Whitey ap-
proached him and said that Connolly wanted to meet him.
The introduction would be handled by Dennis Condon.
They met in what Stevie described as an "obscure" coffee
shop in Newton. Flemmi asked about H. Paul Rico, and
Condon said he was fine. Connolly listened attentively.

"It was like a transition," Flemmi said.

At first, all the information seemed to be flowing in the
direction of the Hill. Zip would tell Whitey, don't do business with this guy, or don't say anything around that guy.
He was telling them, in so many words, who was an informant.

Soon, though, Zip inserted himself more directly in the
gang's affairs.

There was this company, Melotone, that had juke-
boxes and cigarette vending machines. Their warehouse was in Somerville. Howie had some machines
too, and he wanted to start a route, you know, like a
paperboy route. We went to this Melotone guy, Joe
Levine, and he misinterpreted it. We just wanted to
do business. We weren't looking for trouble. He went
to the FBI, and Zip got wind of it, and he went down
there to the warehouse and he told Levine, well, if
you wanna go through with this, you'll have to join
the Witness Protection Program, and we'll have to
relocate your family, and change their names. Levine
didn't want to do that, of course.

Whitey, meanwhile, comes to the garage and tells
us we gotta back off. Awhile later, Joe Levine comes

by the garage. We didn't know if the feds had wired
him or not, but just to be on the safe side we told him
we weren't interested in doing business with him
anymore, period. Afterward we talked it over and
we all agreed, this FBI thing is working out pretty
good for us. We could have walked into a trap there.

In court in 1998, Flemmi was asked what Connolly had
said to the owner of Melotone. "It was probably a threat. I
don't know. I wasn't there. All I know is what the results
were."

LAWYER: What is your recollection about any conversation that you had with either Bulger or Flemmi
about giving things to John Connolly?
MARTORANO: Any chance we got to give him something, give him something.
LAWYER: Did Mr. Bulger and/or Mr. Flemmi ever
say that they, in fact, were giving Mr. Connolly
things?
MARTORANO: At all times they said they took good
care of him.

Zip's next save came in Norfolk County, where Johnny's
classmate from St. Agatha's School, Bill Delahunt, had
just been elected district attorney. An ex-con named Francis Green owed $175,000 to a finance company with ties
to the Hill. Whitey, Stevie, and Johnny got the assignment, on spec. Whatever they could squeeze out of Green,
they'd get a cut of. They tracked Green down to the Back-
side restaurant in Dedham.

As soon as Johnny walked in, he noticed Delahunt
standing at the bar. He walked over and they exchanged
pleasantries, then harsher words. New on the job, an ex–
state rep from Quincy, Delahunt didn't need to be seen at
a popular restaurant chatting up one of Boston's more

notorious mobsters. Delahunt detested Whitey and Stevie, and the feeling was mutual. Later, Whitey would go
out of his way to make up damaging stories about Delahunt, which Zip dutifully included in his 209s.

"I didn't mean to embarrass Billy that night," says Martorano. "In retrospect, he was right about those guys, and I
was wrong. I just didn't know yet how bad they were."

Meanwhile, Whitey and Stevie had found a table, and
Green had joined them. As Johnny jawed with Delahunt,
Whitey was making Green the proverbial offer he couldn't
refuse.

"If I don't get my money, I will kill you. I will cut your
ears off. I will stuff them in your mouth, and then I will
gouge your eyes out."

The next day Green went to Delahunt, but given the
circumstances, the new district attorney handed the case
off to the FBI. And in what was becoming their standard
MO, the feds did nothing. Dennis Condon personally
handled the brush-off, describing Green in the first sentence of his report as "a convicted swindler," and adding
that Whitey was trying to collect for a woman, "a friend
of theirs." He did not mention the threats.

THE MAFIA HAD never stopped looking for Joe Barboza. Finally, they found an ex-con he'd served time with
who was now living in San Francisco. This was the opportunity In Town had been waiting for all these years. In
February 1976, as the Animal left his alleged friend's
apartment in San Francisco, a white van pulled up alongside him and the panel door opened. Whitey's old friend
J. R. Russo stepped up with a rifle and gunned him down.
A few years later, a drunk Larry Baione would be recorded
by the FBI describing Russo as a "genius with a fucking
carbine." Back in Boston, Barboza's last lawyer told reporters, "With all due respect to my client, society has not
suffered a great loss."

Two months earlier, the Animal's paperback autobiography had been published. In it, he described Johnny Martorano as a great friend, but misspelled his name as "Marterano."

For a few hours after the murder, until he turned up in Boston, Martorano had been suspected by some cops of having taken care of his former friend—another favor for In Town.

"I would have killed him if I'd known where he was," Martorano said. "He certainly fit the criteria."

PATSY FABIANO WAS always the weak link in Barboza's gang. A decade earlier, when Barboza was arrested

Patsy Fabiano, Barboza associate, murdered by the Mafia a few weeks after his old boss in 1976.

on the gun charges, he had tried to convince the cops to lock Patsy up, too, so that he wouldn't get shot.

Even after Barboza's murder, Fabiano remained in the Mafia's crosshairs. He'd backed up Barboza's testimony in the Deegan trial. He was trying to go straight, running a candle store, Wicks 'n' Sticks, in the Burlington Mall. He was more than $100,000 in debt when he got a call from the North End. The boys had a business proposition they'd like to run by him—and hey, no hard feelings about the Animal, right?

On March 30, six weeks after his former boss's murder, Patsy stopped by the garage to say hello. He said he had to pick up some linguine because he was having dinner that night with some of the guys from In Town. The next morning Fabiano's body was discovered in his new Buick in a parking lot in the North End. He was in the front seat, on the passenger's side—the death seat. He'd been shot four times in the head with a .32.

Patsy's wallet still contained a large amount of cash.

JIMMY MARTORANO WAS minding his own business. He was still running Chandler's, and he was also spending a lot of time down on the waterfront. He rented an apartment above the Rusty Scupper, a popular singles bar on Commercial Street, with a Yale-educated accountant named John Callahan. Callahan was a high-powered businessman by day. At night, though, he could usually be found either in some Irish bar or hanging out with the local element at places like the Playboy Club . . . or the Rusty Scupper. Brian Halloran, the hard-drinking Winter Hill associate, was another guy who ran with the Rusty Scupper crew.

Callahan had gone to work for World Jai Alai, a Boston company that ran frontons in Florida and Connecticut. When H. Paul Rico retired from the FBI in 1976, it was Callahan who got him hired as World Jai Alai's chief of security. After all, who better to keep the mob at bay than a crusading G-man?

Meanwhile, Dennis Condon was also about to retire, and would soon go to work in the administration of that new Democratic governor from the suburbs who supported busing so enthusiastically—Michael Dukakis.

Dukakis, a "card-carrying member of the ACLU," as he would later describe himself, wanted to make it even easier for state prison inmates to get weekend furloughs. More than a decade before Willie Horton derailed Dukakis's 1998 presidential campaign, his first administration was embroiled in one disastrous weekend furlough after another.

No matter how incorrigible, any prisoner was eligible, as Jimmy Flemmi discovered one Friday in 1976 when he was released from MCI-Norfolk for a weekend on the town. The Bear immediately took off for Boston, to settle some old scores, starting with his ex-wife.

Fortunately for Mrs. Flemmi, she wasn't in her Hyde Park home when the Bear arrived, so he settled for strangling her cat and tearing the place apart. Then he vanished, not to be seen again for three years. This time, Jimmy Martorano wouldn't get arrested for helping the fugitive Jimmy the Bear. Like everyone else, he now knew enough to steer clear of the Bear.

But even though Jimmy Martorano didn't know it yet, he had another problem. The FBI was lining him up. They'd done a lot for the Hill, and now it was time to claim a scalp.

My brother was doing a little shylocking, not much, but some. He knows this guy who loaned $2,000 to his own brother, who ran a bar in Revere. Now this guy figures out his brother will never pay him back, so he asks Jimmy if he can say he got the money

from Jimmy Martorano. That way maybe his deadbeat brother will get scared and pay it back.

In other words, it was a favor. Well, of course the
brother still doesn't pay it back, so the guy asks Jimmy
if he can send somebody over to the bar to scare his
brother. Jimmy didn't want to get involved—what
does he care about this one way or the other? But
Brian Halloran heard the story and he decided to go
up to Revere on his own. As usual, he's drunk, and
he pulls a gun on the bar owner and steals $445 out
of the register. The bar owner runs to the FBI, and
John Morris takes over the case and they arrest Halloran and my brother.

Still, Jimmy Martorano wasn't that worried. If he was
needed, his friend said he would be willing to testify he
hadn't borrowed any money from Jimmy. That way, Jimmy
and Brian Halloran might be facing state robbery or as-
sault charges, but not a serious federal rap like extortion.
In a Suffolk County courtroom, at worst they'd be looking at months, not years.

One morning, at the garage, Jimmy mentioned he was
going into the city to confer with his attorneys. Whitey
and Stevie asked if they could tag along and Jimmy said
sure. They overheard the entire discussion of Jimmy Martorano's defense—including the name of his surprise witness.

The next morning, agents Morris and Connolly barged
into the home of the guy who was to be Jimmy Martorano's defense witness. Panicking, he ad-libbed a different
story where the $2,000 had come from. He said he got it
from his wife. He mentioned nothing about asking for a
favor from Jimmy Martorano.

So Jimmy's witness was out. If he told his original
story under oath, Zip and Morris would be sworn as witnesses to impeach his credibility. A few months later, in

June 1976, Jimmy Martorano was convicted on the federal charges. Halloran inexplicably beat the rap, although by that time he was already in prison on weapons charges.

Nobody ever put two-and-two together until everybody was in jail together years later in the late '90s. As part of discovery, the feds gave everybody an FBI letter of commendation to Zip for getting one conviction of a so-called major Winter Hill figure in 1976. Well, there was only one conviction of anyone that year—my brother, Jimmy.

I was gone by then, but after they saw the document, somebody asked Stevie, why'd you rat out Jimmy Martorano over nothing, just to allow your pal Zip to win a few Brownie points with his bosses in Washington?

You know what Stevie said? He said, "Somebody had to go, and Jimmy did good time."

9

The Bubble Bursts

LAWYER: You weren't afraid to punch somebody, right?

MARTORANO: Not if it was called for.

EVERYTHING STARTED TO go wrong for the Winter Hill Gang in 1976. For three years or so, ever since Tony Ciulla had started fixing horse races, they'd been in an economic bubble—their assets rising wildly, out of all proportion to reality. They were making money here, there, and everywhere. The local cops were their friends, they had total protection in Somerville, they owned an FBI agent, they were getting along with the Mafia—what could possibly go wrong?

Like all bubbles, though, this one would end badly, in ways that no one in the gang could have ever imagined.

Johnny was in charge of keeping the sports gambling books. His partners didn't like bad news, especially during football season. With an open line of credit from Jack Mace, they bet heavily. Their long-distance phone bills were astronomical. They were always calling Vegas, looking for an edge. One of the race-fixing guys out there was an old Boston hand named Mel Goldenberg. He had a handicapper known as "White-Haired Jack from Pittsburgh." Another guy they used was Bob Martin. He was supposed to be bigger than Lefty Rosenthal, the Vegas gambler Robert DeNiro played in *Casino*.

Sometimes their guys in Vegas came up with good information, and the gang collected. Sometimes.

I'd go to the garage every Monday morning, and they'd all be staring at me as I walked in. They didn't want to know, did we win this weekend? They wanted to know, how much did we win this weekend? That's the way they thought. You gotta remember, we weren't six Einsteins, we were six shylocks, gamblers, bank robbers—you know what I mean. Regular guys.

One thing that was always strange to me was how little Whitey knew about sports. It's one thing not to care about watching the games on TV, which neither he nor Stevie did. But they didn't even know what a double play was in baseball. And Whitey had no understanding of odds. I could never figure out why he wanted to get into sports gambling in the first place when he didn't understand odds. Sometimes on Fridays, Whitey would ask me, who are we rooting for this weekend? And I'd say, the Patriots. And Monday morning I'd come into the garage and he'd say, all right, the Patriots won, I saw it in the paper. So we won, right? And I'd have to explain it to him, Well no, we didn't win, because the Patriots were six-point favorites, and they only won by three, so we lost. But he never got it, no matter how many times I explained it to him.

It was practically un-American how little he knew about sports. I even called him un-American to his face a couple of times. He just laughed.

Anyway, how the money worked was, if we took a big hit, we'd just borrow money from ourselves. I could always get cash from Joe McDonald—he handled the money for the "old" Winter Hill Gang, which was him, Howie, and Sims. At the end the new Hill owed the old Hill a half million. I borrowed 200 grand from myself, Whitey threw in 60, Stevie 20, and of course eventually we owed Jerry Angiulo $250,000. It didn't seem like such a big problem because when I lent the Hill 200 grand, I was paying myself a point a week vig—two grand. That's a lot better than you can get in a bank, right?

But the reality was, every week I had to come up with over ten grand just to pay the vig to everybody. Five grand to old Winter Hill, which I mainly gave to Howie Winter Jr., $2,500 to Jerry Angiulo, $2,000 to myself, $600 to Whitey, $200 to Stevie, and another grand or so to various other guys.

But remember, we didn't lose every week. A lot of weeks, we came out ahead—way ahead. So I'd come into the garage Monday and say, okay, we're up a hundred grand this weekend. Now, what do we want to do, do we pay down the balance on what we owe, or do we just whack up the 100 grand right now? You can guess what the vote was.

Then Tony Ciulla got arrested. The first one to go down was one of his jockeys, a guy in New Jersey. At Suffolk Downs, the jockeys might have stood up, especially the ones who'd been slapped around. But in New Jersey, names like Barnoski and McDonald didn't inspire quite the same respect as they did on their home turf.

The jockey gave up Ciulla, and he was arrested on a parole violation. Everyone knew it was only a question of when, not if, he'd flip. At the garage, Johnny didn't even have to state the obvious, that he had told them so—that they should have whacked Ciulla when they had the chance, not Sousa. Now there was going to be trouble. The only question was, how much.

JOE MCDONALD AND Jimmy Sims had more immediate concerns. Like all the other partners, they had always continued operating their own separate rackets, one of which was robbing coin and rare-stamp dealers. In 1974, police in California found a stamp dealer they'd held up who was willing to testify against them. Joe Mac and Sims took off for California, where Joe Mac once again barged into a home and gunned down the witness, whose name was Raymond Lundgren.

"Jimmy Sims told me about it later," Martorano recalled. "He said, that Joe is one crazy bastard the way he just keeps walking into somebody's house in a strange town with a gun in his hand."

The FBI was drawn into the robbery case because McDonald and Sims had moved the stolen stamps across state lines. On April 1, 1976, the FBI put Joe McDonald on the Ten Most Wanted List—for interstate transportation of stolen goods, but not murder. It didn't seem like such a big deal at first. Joe Mac went on the lam—to Chelsea.

One reason they weren't concerned was because they had grown to rely on their own personal FBI agent, John Connolly, as a literal Johnny on the spot. Whitey and Stevie were giving him information in return, but everybody assumed it was routine stuff. What they didn't know was that Whitey was handing the feds all kinds of dirt on every underworld figure in Southie who wasn't on the Bulger team. As one of the Hill's lawyers put it later, "With the Italians, Stevie was mainly providing gossip—so-and-so's going to a wedding, or somebody was opening a restaurant on Hanover Street. With the Irish from Southie, Whitey was giving Zip addresses, telephone numbers, license plate numbers. He was already letting the FBI do his dirty work for him, weeding out the competition."

All we knew was that Zip was taking care of us, in-directly, because of Whitey. We told Whitey, any-time you have the opportunity to do something for him, whatever it is—cash, airline tickets, anything—you tell us and we'll get it for him.

So Whitey comes to the garage one day and tells us, Zip wants to give his wife a ring. Now, I know Joe's got some stolen jewelry, so I went to see him in Chelsea and I picked out a nice diamond ring—two carats. I paid him two grand, out of the kitty, but the stone itself was probably worth 6 or 8 grand. The only problem was, it was in a man's setting, but Whitey took it to a jeweler and got it reset. Zip was pretty happy. I figured it was the least we could do. I mean, when Howie and I went to see Schnei-derhan, I always brought an envelope with at least $1,000 in it. I'd just leave it there for him, no name on the envelope or anything. I didn't want to embar-rass him.

Jimmy Martorano had always managed Chandler's, and after his conviction nobody else in the gang had any inter-est in actually running the place. It was too much like work. There was only one thing to do, the same thing they always did when they got tired of operating a business. They torched it.

The Boston police organized-crime unit and the fire department's arson squad quickly began investigations.

As usual, nothing came of the probes, and the Hill col-lected on the insurance. The money came in handy. Not only had they lost the income from Ciulla's race fixing, now they had to support Joe Mac and Jimmy Sims on the lam. And Zip Connolly notwithstanding, some of his fellow feds were actually looking for Joe and Jimmy. The Hill had to get them out of town, and they did, in the fall of 1976.

I went down to New York to see Jack Mace, Castucci's friend, the guy we were betting with. He had an apartment in the Village, Washington Square. I gave him $14,000 cash for a year's rent, including utilities, telephone, everything, so Joe and Jimmy didn't have to put their names on anything. I didn't tell him who I was putting in there, but I did tell him, don't tell anybody about this. Nobody.

But Jack Mace did. He told his associate in Boston, Richie Castucci, and Castucci put two-and-two together. Joe McDonald and Jimmy Sims had to be the guys in New York. And then Castucci told the FBI. He, too, was an informant. Castucci had been recruited back in 1969 at the Howard Johnson's in Revere, when Boston FBI agents told him that his wife had been involved in an affair with Mafia soldier Salvatore "Mike" Caruana, who would become a major drug trafficker before vanishing in the early 1980s.

In a later lawsuit against the U.S. government, Castucci's widow would deny the affair. But according to a 1970 FBI report, Castucci had thanked the G-men for telling him that Caruana "stole his wife. He stated that if he was a guy who carried a 'piece,' or was violent, he would kill Caruana for doing this."

Six years later, Castucci found himself in a precarious situation. He was with the Hill, he was with In Town, and he was with Mace, who was connected to the Gambino crime family in New York, although no one in Somerville knew that yet. Castucci had put Mace and the Hill together, and now the Winter Hill Gang was betting thousands of dollars a week with Mace. Sometimes Johnny would send down a doorman from the old Chandler's to settle up with Mace at LaGuardia Airport. Depending on the weekend's outcome, the doorman would either deliver or pick up a bag of cash. If the doorman wasn't around, sometimes Castucci would make the pickup or delivery at the garage.

The problem for Castucci was that his handlers in the Boston FBI office trusted Zip Connolly. Why shouldn't other agents know who their fellow feds were talking to? After all, if you couldn't trust a brother agent, who could you trust? And this wasn't exactly a shoplifter they were hunting—Joe McDonald was a Ten Most Wanted fugitive.

So the other agents in the office tell Connolly what Castucci came up with, and Connolly tells Whitey. Whitey comes to the garage and tells us that Castucci is a rat, and he's told the FBI where Joe Mac and Sims are. I think my first words when I heard it were, "That motherfucker!" I never liked the guy to begin with. He was a swindler, a past-poster, a card cheat, just no fucking good. But I didn't figure him for a rat.

Still, it's pretty easy to figure out what happened. Mace is just talking out of school—he's not a rat, not on this anyway, although we found out later, he was in fact an informant for the feds down in New York. So he mentions it to Castucci, not knowing the significance of what he's telling him, and Castucci, that motherfucker, he runs right to the feds with it.

There was only one way to settle up with Castucci now. Later, it was suggested that Castucci was killed because the Hill owed Mace $150,000, but just a few weeks earlier, Johnny had sent his guy down to LaGuardia with some money that the Hill owed him. Altogether, Mace had already collected $400,000 from Winter Hill.

Castucci rocketed to the top of the Hit Parade because he had ratted out Joe McDonald and Jimmy Sims. Still, at the garage, the thought did occur to everyone, why pay any more money to a guy who's about to get hit in the head? Being a rat cancels a debt—that was one of the Hill's rules to live by. And to die by.

THE FIRST THING Johnny did was call the apartment in the Village and tell Joe and Jimmy to clear out. He'd fill them in on the details later, but the most important thing was to get out of New York. And Johnny mentioned one other thing to them, that Whitey had insisted upon. Johnny told them to never, ever tell anyone that they got a heads-up to leave. If anyone asks, he said, just say you had a feeling. Zip was already starting to sweat this one. This tip was worth more than a diamond ring, a whole lot more.

IT WAS DECEMBER 30, 1976, cold and snowy in Somerville. Johnny called Castucci in Revere and told him he was a little short from the holidays but wanted to get Jack Mace at least $60,000. His guy wasn't around to make the flight to New York, Johnny said, so would Richie mind coming over to the garage to pick it up?

Johnny had the money in small bills, so Castucci would have to count it. He told Castucci that Whitey would take him down to the Pad—the gang's apartment—and that he could take as long as he wanted to count it.

Once inside the Pad, Whitey got Castucci seated just inside the front door at a round table, with his back to the door. Whitey was facing the door on the other side of the table, directly across from Castucci. Johnny waited a couple of minutes, until Castucci got settled in and started counting the bills. Then Martorano walked in with a gun,

Leo McDonald, Joe's older brother, a Hill associate.

the usual .38-caliber snub nose revolver, approaching Castucci from the side. Johnny put the gun right up to his forehead and pulled the trigger. Castucci never knew what hit him. There were no last words.

When Johnny fired, across the table Whitey flinched. Next Stevie arrived, and he and Whitey began the cleanup. Joe McDonald's brother, Leo McDonald, then showed up. Johnny told him to go down to K-Mart and buy a sleeping bag to wrap the body in—the same duty he'd had after the Sousa murder two years earlier. A half hour later Leo returned with a cheap Walt Disney sleeping bag covered with pictures of Snow White and the Seven Dwarfs. It cost maybe six dollars.

"You can pay me later," Leo told Johnny, and Johnny smiled and nodded. He'd just killed a guy for Joe Mac, and now he owed his brother Leo six bucks.

They waited until it got dark, which wasn't long on one

Richie Castucci's body in the trunk of his Cadillac
after his murder by Johnny in 1976.

of the shortest days of the year. Then they lugged Castucci's body out to his Cadillac and put it in the trunk. Wearing gloves, Johnny drove Castucci's car back to Revere, with Leo behind Johnny in his own car. Johnny dropped the Caddy off in some parking lot over by the water and then he and Leo drove back to the garage.

The cops found Castucci's body in the trunk a couple of hours later.

THERE WAS HELL to pay at the JFK Federal Office Building. The FBI couldn't allow its informants to get whacked. It was bad enough that Castucci had been outted, let alone killed. Even though it was a holiday week, an interagency meeting was immediately convened of all the various federal law-enforcement agencies—FBI, Justice Department, DEA, Customs, Secret Service. Zip Connolly was among the attendees.

One after another, everyone was asked: Who could have

done this? Where was the leak? Finally they got around to Zip Connolly. Zip spoke slowly, for emphasis. Already a lot of the other feds looked up to him, for his success in recruiting such high-level informants. Zip explained how he'd been working his sources. He said they'd told him that Castucci had owed the Mafia a lot of money, and In Town didn't like that he was planning to pay off his debts to the Hill first. Now he was dead and the Hill was out a lot of money. So obviously they had no reason to kill Castucci. Good old Zip, always taking care of "his Irish," as he called them, even while he was simultaneously trying to save his own hide as well.

"It was the Mafia," Zip explained. "Winter Hill doesn't kill like that."

Afterward, Zip frantically told Whitey again that he had to make sure that Joe McDonald didn't let slip what had happened. Whitey asked Johnny to get in touch with Joe. Whitey and Stevie wanted a sit-down with Joe Mac, to reinforce the message of how important it was to keep his mouth shut. But Joe Mac refused to meet with them. He'd always had less use for Whitey and Stevie than anyone else in the gang, but now he was being stubborn.

"I never found out what the problem was," Johnny said. "Maybe Joe had a premonition about them."

BUT IT WASN'T over yet. The Hill found out something it hadn't been aware of. Jack Mace was with the Gambino crime family. It was now a Mafia thing, in other words, and protocol had to be observed. New York called Jerry Angiulo and asked for permission to come into Boston to handle a piece of business—namely, collecting the $150,000 the Hill owed Jack Mace.

Jerry was bullshit, 'cause he didn't like New York guys coming into his town. But he had to play along, too. So he gives it the okay, and he sets up a date for

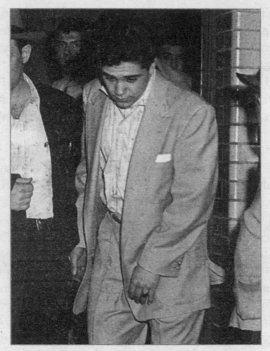

Angelo "Sonny" Mercurio, FBI informant
and the Mafia's liaison to Winter Hill.

us to meet them. At first I thought of telling them,
we gave Castucci the money before he got killed.
But why lie? So I decided to handle it another way. I
call every gangster I know and asked them to come
over to the garage at a certain time, before the New
York guys arrive, although I didn't put it that way.

Sonny Mercurio was the liaison between us and
In Town, so Jerry told Sonny that he had to bring the
New York people over. I told my people, when you
see these guys coming in with Sonny, I want you to
take a good look at 'em and try to remember if
you've ever seen them hanging around the garage or
anywhere else.

I rounded up everybody—the Campbells from Roxbury, Whitey's guys from Southie, the Charlestown longshoremen who'd been with the Hill in the war, and of course everybody from Somerville. It was a tough-looking bunch, sixty or eighty guys, and there weren't nearly enough chairs for so many of them, so they were just milling around. I thought a picture was worth a thousand words. A few theatrics could save a lot of trouble, maybe even lives.

Anyway, Sonny arrives with three guys, forty, fifty years old, dressed up. They're playing their roles— Mafia guys from New York—just like we're playing our parts. So we make them run the gauntlet, walk past our guys, who are all staring at the New York wiseguys. That got them a little spooked, even before Sonny brought them into the office. Howie's got the trapdoor next to his desk open—that sends a message, too, like we might throw their bodies down there if they get out of line, after we've shot them. It was mainly me and Whitey who did the talking.

The guy that was speaking for them was a member of the Colombo family.

He says, "We're here to collect the $150,000 you owe Jack Mace." He says, "Maybe you didn't know he was with us." And I says, "Maybe you didn't know that I rented a place from him in the Village for two of our guys who are on the lam," and he told Castucci, who went to the feds.

It doesn't matter how we found out, Johnny said, all that matters is that we did. We took care of Castucci, Johnny went on, and I don't know what you're planning to do about Mace, but I'll tell you right now, if we see him, we're going to whack him.

The Colombo soldier was an up-and-comer, and he was used to being treated with respect, especially by guys who weren't "made." But Johnny was addressing him brusquely, not at all deferentially. And as Johnny, and sometimes Whitey, spoke, they noticed how the soldier's eyes kept drifting over to that open trapdoor next to Howie's desk.

"As far as we're concerned," Johnny told him, "the debt's cancelled."

The Colombo soldier paused for a moment to consider how to extricate himself from this situation with his skin intact.

"Well, you know," he finally said, "we didn't know any of this." Now he was the one being deferential. "This kind of changes everything."

Then he stood up and nodded at Sonny Mercurio. The sit-down was over.

LAWYER: And the LCN representatives at this meeting agreed not to collect on the debt, isn't that right?

MARTORANO: They couldn't collect the debt so they agreed not to collect the debt.

LAWYER: Well, if the LCN wanted to collect a debt, even from you, they could do so, couldn't they?

MARTORANO: No, they couldn't. They didn't.

LAWYER: The Winter Hill organization couldn't afford a war with the LCN, isn't that right?

MARTORANO: We told them we're not paying. You want us to take care of Jack, we'll take care of Jack, because he's still a problem for us. They said never mind. You don't owe it no more.

Later on, Sonny Mercurio tells me that once they got outside and back in the car, the top guy from New York said he was just glad to get out of the garage alive, and boy, had they ever misread that situation. Jerry was happy, too. He didn't want New York thinking they could come up here and push anybody around. It would have been bad for business—his, ours, everybody's.

I think maybe that was the pinnacle of the Winter Hill Gang. One thing's for sure. Everything was downhill from there. Everything.

Melotone had been a near disaster, but Howie Winter wasn't giving up on vending machines. His next move was pinball. The machines were in some of the clubs in Somerville, but officially they'd been illegal in the city since 1954. Howie wanted them everywhere, and to do that, he needed to get them legalized.

That was a task for Sal Sperlinga, Indian Al's old friend, who ran the numbers in Somerville. He was a smoother guy, the good cop to Howie's bad cop. That was why Indian Al had reached out to him. He was glib, almost a politician. And he was close to the pols—it was Sperlinga who in August 1977 got the Board of Aldermen to legalize the machines. The vote was 9 to 2. Later the state police investigated allegations of $10,000 cash changing hands at City Hall, but no one was ever indicted.

Once pinball was legalized in the city, the Hill realized it had a new problem. At least nominally, Somerville was now wide-open. Clubs and bars could now contract with any vending-machine company, although of course Howie didn't see it that way. He figured that since he'd made the capital investment—"spent a bundle," as he told the owner of one rival company—then he alone should enjoy the fruits of the monopoly he had paid for.

"I'm giving you two days to get your machines out of the city," Howie was later quoted in court as telling the manager of one vending-machine company. "I own this city. You're all done. As far as Somerville goes, you're out of business. If you don't [quit], I can get rough and I can get plenty rough."

One of the club managers Howie tried to muscle was

seventy-five years old. He worked at the Disabled American Veterans Post in Ball Square. The Hill had gotten away with so much for so long that they never considered what might happen next. The people Howie was trying to muscle started marching down to East Cambridge, to the office of the Middlesex district attorney. They apparently didn't understand that it wasn't healthy to do that; unlike most of the people the Hill had been dealing with, they were legit. They were law-abiding citizens.

Howie Winter had picked an unfortunate time to tangle with civilians. The district attorney was sixty-seven years old and afflicted with a debilitating disease that had left him unable to speak. He had a primary coming up in 1978, and younger challengers were already lining up against him. He badly needed some scalps. He also had an ambitious young first assistant named John Forbes Kerry, who

Howie Winter under arrest in Somerville in 1977.

understood the publicity value of bagging a big-time gangster or two.

Howie Winter and Sal Sperlinga were arrested on October 20, 1977, and charged with extortion. Hours after the arrests—and a subsequent John Kerry press conference—the Somerville aldermen held a special meeting at City Hall and voted unanimously to halt the licensing of all pinball machines in the city.

I think Howie wasn't paying enough attention because he was more concerned about Ciulla. Fat Tony had sold the horses he owned with Howie, and then they'd let him out of prison. His brother-in-law, Eddie Ardolino, came by the garage to warn us not to talk to Tony, because the feds had wired him up. Plus Joe and Jimmy are still on the lam. So Zip tells Whitey who tells Howie the district attorney is coming after him, and that he had better go down to the DAV Post and get this straightened out, apologize or whatever. Same with the other places him and Sal tried to muscle. But I think what happened was, Howie was so preoccupied trying to keep everything else together that he just left it to Sal to patch everything up, and whatever Sal did wasn't sufficient.

The bottom line is, Howie and Sal end up getting indicted.

In November 1977, Johnny got more bad news. Deke Chandler was murdered outside his Roxbury home by a twenty-three-year-old Mattapan punk. Chandler, thirty-eight, was stabbed in the heart and shot repeatedly in the head. The slaying had nothing to do with organized crime; it was a dispute over Chandler's girlfriend.

In the newspaper accounts of his slaying, Chandler was described as a "lieutenant" in Boston underworld circles who had "strong affiliations with high-ranking organized-crime chieftains in Somerville and Boston."

JOHNNY WAS THE next one to get into trouble with the law. Dick O'Brien was a major bookmaker in Quincy, one of the Hill's top earners. The state police tapped the phones in one of his South Shore offices and soon had enough evidence to run in everyone in his organization on gaming charges. They even got Johnny, taking a call from one of O'Brien's underlings about a problem, and then answering, "I'll talk to you when I see you."

Dick O'Brien, South Shore bookie who later lived
near Johnny in Florida.

They were planning to play that tape in court. They said it proved I was one of the two bosses, with Dick O'Brien. They had me on tape, so it was hard to deny. I get ordered to go to state police headquarters at 1010 Com Ave and have a voice-print made, you know, to see if I'm the same guy as the one whose voice they got on the tape.

I call Schneiderhan and that's when I get lucky. He's still in the AG's office on Boylston Street, and he's going to be doing the voice-print. But he tells me he can't just fix the case, he's got to have the documentation that it's not me. So I asked him, "What do I do?" He tells me I have to go to my dentist and have a bridge made that I can stick in my mouth when he's giving me the test. The bridge changes the oscillation or something like that in your voice. So I wrote down what Schneiderhan told me, and then I go to my dentist and tell him what I want. He does it and then when he's finished he's washing his hands and he says, "I don't even want to know what you're going to do with that bridge but just let me know if it works."

It worked; my voice sounded totally different with the bridge, so now they have no evidence against me, and I'm the only one they really care about, not Dick O'Brien and his guys. Another problem, the Staties only had a warrant to record business on Dick's phones during bookie business hours, 12 to 2 and 6 to 8. But one of the cops, who got into worse trouble later, was taping everything. So their evidence was tainted. But after all this time, and effort, they still needed a scalp, so they offer me a deal—everyone gets four months, and I have to pay a $30,000 fine. So I took one for the team. With everything falling apart around me, I couldn't afford to be off the street for that long, but what else could I do?

Johnny Martorano ended up doing three months at the Plymouth House of Correction in 1978. When he got out, he found the underworld landscape shifting even more. Joe McDonald and Jimmy Sims were still fugitives, hiding out in Florida—Sims in the Keys, Joe Mac in Daytona Beach. Jimmy Martorano was in prison. Howie Winter and Sal Sperlinga were looking at serious time in the state pinball case.

Whitey Bulger and Stevie Flemmi were still free men.

ONE MORNING AT the garage, Johnny arrived to find a telephone message. Fat Tony was out on bail, and just as his brother-in-law had predicted, he was reaching out to Johnny, to get him on tape. Fat Tony wanted to call Johnny at Pal Joey's, around the corner on Broadway from Marshall Street. Johnny called his attorney, Marty Weinberg, and Weinberg said he wanted to be there when the call came in. Massachusetts was a "two-party" state—it was against the law to record a phone conversation without permission of both parties—but there was no reason Johnny couldn't tape his half of the conversation.

Tony calls me in the bar, and he keeps bringing up "the stuff we did." It was obvious he was trying to get me to admit that we'd fixed all those races. I wouldn't bite; I'd known for months not to talk to him about anything important. He just kept saying, "You remember what we did." I told him, "Tony, I have no idea what the fuck you are talking about. I thought you were calling because you had something that would help get my brother out of prison. I don't know about any of this other stuff you're talking about."

Finally Tony gave up.

They were all running around with much younger women now. At age forty-three, Stevie Flemmi had a veritable harem—in addition to the endless string of pickups and one-night stands, he had his common-law wife, Marion, and his now sixteen-year-old stepdaughter, Deb Hussey. He was also supporting Debbie Davis, age twenty-two.

Whitey Bulger had Teresa Stanley, in addition to whatever teenaged girls he could lure from Cardinal Cushing, an all-girls parochial high school on West Broadway. One of them was fifteen years old. Her name was Tammy. Whitey was also sleeping with a dental hygienist, Catherine Greig, who happened to be the ex-sister-in-law of two of his murder victims, Paulie McGonagle and his twin brother.

As for Howie and Johnny, they were involved in much more serious relationships with younger women. At the age of forty-eight, Howie now had a twenty-four-year-old girlfriend, Ellen Brogna, who was brought in before the pinball grand jury in East Cambridge. She took the Fifth Amendment. How could Howie not love a girl like that?

Johnny, now thirty-eight, had taken up with an eighteen-year-old girl named Patty. She was from Ball Square, the Somerville neighborhood where Johnny had spent the first eleven years of his life.

I think I met her when I was with Howie's son, Gary. Yeah, I was twenty years older than she was, but her parents always liked me. I went to see her mother, because she was the one who called the shots in that family. Her mother's name was Loretta. She was Sicilian. Patty's father was, I think, English. I told Loretta, Patty and I might be going on a vacation soon, six months tops. Patty had been running with a bad crowd, she'd dropped out of high school, so I told her mother, I think it'll be better if she gets out of

Somerville for a while. Her mother said, okay, as long as Patty's with you, I know she'll be safe.

We were together for the next twenty years. And we're still friends.

The pinball trial started in Cambridge in January 1978. Howie never had a chance. The seventy-five-year-old veterans' club manager testified that one of his employees told him, "Winter and Sperlinga said for him to get out of the business or they would break his legs and other things."

Faced with near-certain conviction, Howie decided to roll the dice and take the witness stand himself. It was a fiasco. On cross-examination, Winter said he was in the real-estate business, but was forced to admit that he had no office and had made only one sale in 1977, of a condominium in Medford, to someone whose name he couldn't seem to remember.

"I'd have to check with my lawyer," he said.

Then there was the question of all his various addresses. The prosecutor asked him about the Somerville address he'd given the state police when they arrested him. He said it was his daughter's house. Then he said he voted out of a second Somerville address, but actually lived in Medford and had a driver's license issued to his brother's home in Billerica. His wife, he said, lived in Lexington.

"Do you live in Somerville, Mr. Winter?" the prosecutor asked him.

"Sometimes," he replied.

"Did you live there last night?"

"No," said Howie, "I did not."

BOTH HOWIE AND Sal were convicted on all counts. The judge sentenced Howie to two nine-to-ten-year terms, to run consecutively. Sal got the same nine-to-ten-year sentences, but the judge stipulated that Sperlinga's terms would run concurrently because he was "only a follower."

Sal would be eligible for parole in three years, Howie in six.

The judge was apparently swayed by a handwritten note Howie had passed the judge before sentencing, asking for mercy for Sal: "I respectfully request that in considering sentence for Mr. Sperlinga, Your Honor keep in mind that he never had much to say and that he never raised his voice and also that he is the sole support of his eighty-two-year-old mother."

The judge told Howie, "I respect you, Mr. Winter, for the motion you filed."

THE RACE-FIXING TRIAL would be next. The feds had records of all the phone calls Ciulla had made from the hotels he'd stayed in at the tracks where he'd been fixing races. The phone records included dozens of calls to Johnny's various addresses. For witnesses, they would have Ciulla and jockeys who'd been threatened by various members of the gang. Everyone was going to be indicted, from Howie Winter to the transplanted Boston gamblers in Vegas who'd placed bets for them to the actual runners, guys like Sid Tildsley, the owner of El Sid's nightclub on Winter Hill.

Even Whitey Bulger and Stevie Flemmi were jammed up. They'd helped Johnny find bookies to take bets on the fixed races. But they had an out—the FBI. Zip was now on their payroll. John Morris was his supervisor, and he, too, would soon be on Whitey and Stevie's pad. Morris would later recall being introduced to both of Zip's prize informants at the same time—in itself a violation of FBI policy, which required that informants always be interviewed separately, so that they would not know who the other informants were, or what stories they were telling. There was one additional problem with Whitey and Stevie, Morris testified.

"I wasn't sure," he said, "if they knew they were informants."

Now Whitey and Stevie needed a favor—a big favor. And Zip came through. He and Morris went to the head of the organized-crime strike force, Jeremiah O'Sullivan, and told him that it was absolutely imperative for Bulger and Flemmi to remain free. The feds were planning an ambitious strike against In Town. They were going to wire Jerry Angiulo's headquarters, the Dog House, and they needed informants who could tell them how to get inside, and where to plant the bugs.

Of course Whitey had never once set foot inside 98 Prince Street, and he still owed a big favor to one of Angiulo's top enforcers, J. R. Russo. Stevie by his own admission had no use for Angiulo and his crew and avoided them whenever possible. But Zip made the pitch to O'Sullivan that only they could provide the inside information needed for the bugging to go forward. And he added that Whitey and Stevie hadn't really been involved in the race-fixing scheme. That was only the other guys, the Somerville crew. Zip had their word on that. Zip didn't mention Ciulla's testimony that they had shared in the profits. That would have been off-message.

O'Sullivan finally agreed to cut Whitey and Stevie out of the indictment. They would be listed, but only as "unindicted coconspirators." Zip hurried back to Southie with the good news. Then it was up to Whitey and Stevie to break the news to Johnny Martorano.

Remember, other than them, by then I'm the only Hill partner left in Boston. I wasn't suspicious at all when they told me Zip had kept them out of the indictment. I was happy for them, and I was happy for me. I needed somebody back here to keep an eye on things—and to keep the money coming to me. By then, I knew I would have to go on the lam. You get tried with a bunch of other guys, chances are everybody's going to get convicted. I figured, I'll go to Florida and hang out maybe six months, like I told Patty's mother, until the trial is over, and then I'll come back. If they're acquitted, which I doubt but you never know, I can probably get the charges dismissed. If everyone else is convicted, I'll plea bargain for less time. I wasn't thinking it was the end. You figure, if you're a gangster, sooner or later you go to jail. Everybody does.

Going on the lam was, and still is, standard operating procedure. The reason was succinctly summed up by Sonny Mercurio when he was called as a witness during the 1997–98 hearings before Judge Wolf. Sonny was asked why he always left town when he was about to be indicted.

"Power of the lam means you get a lesser sentence," he said. "I advocate everybody run away."

THERE WAS A lot to do to get ready to run away. First of all, Johnny needed new IDs. There was a guy who had a connection in the Framingham branch of the Registry of Motor Vehicles—Framingham John, they called him. On his new driver's license, Johnny became "Richard Aucoin."

Next he set up a couple of safe houses, where he could hide out if he ever had to come back to Boston. One was an apartment in Medford that belonged to an ex-cop. Then, from an old girlfriend, he rented a room in Winthrop. That would be his main safe house. He bought furniture and dropped off a full wardrobe. He gave Stevie Flemmi his Winthrop phone number, the number Stevie passed on to Zip, who put it in the FBI report that Johnny wouldn't read until 2009.

Then Johnny drove to Florida with Patty, who would be accompanying him when he finally began the six-month "vacation." They scouted out motels. Returning to Boston, Johnny introduced Stevie to Trooper Schneiderhan. That was what you did when you took it on the lam. When Stevie was a fugitive, he'd turned over his grease gun to Johnny, for use in the Indian war. Now Johnny was returning the favor, giving Stevie a Statie. Next Johnny worked out a system with Stevie so that he could stay in touch with everyone using pay phones.

We'd first set up a system of codes when Stevie was on the lam in Montreal. Here's how it worked. I would write down KING JM LEAR—ten letters, get it? Like there's ten numbers, including zero. So 1 is K, 2 is I, 3 is N, and so forth. If I want Stevie or anyone else to call me, I give 'em the number of a pay phone near wherever I'm staying, only with letters as the code for the phone number. All of South Florida back then was in the 305 area code. So I'd say, I'll be at N-R-J, and then give the rest of the number. Only instead of giving the phone number in ten digits, I use the letters that correspond to the numbers. Stevie was KING SF LEAR. It's the way I communicated with everybody—my parents, my kids, George Kaufman. As it turned out, I was the one calling out 99 percent of the time. I'd always have rolls of quarters in the car, so I could always make a call whenever I wanted.

Zip was still proving to be a valuable addition to the gang—or at least to Whitey and Stevie. In the summer of 1978, unknown gunmen invaded a Summer Street nightclub known as Blackfriars. In an after-hours drug-and-cash rip-off, they shot five men to death, including one of the owners and a former TV-news reporter. The shooters have never been positively identified.

Whitey read the stories in the papers and got an idea

how he could make a score off the five murders. He called Zip and asked him if he could get the Boston Police Department to turn over to the FBI copies of their photos of the crime scene. Whitey was particularly interested in obtaining a few pictures of the murdered co-owner of Blackfriars.

Zip had the photos to Whitey within hours, and Whitey and Stevie quickly paid a visit to another local businessman, who they knew had owed $60,000 to the dead owner of Blackfriars. Whitey was his usual brusque self, informing the guy that he now owed Whitey sixty grand. Whitey, whose reputation by now preceded him, left the impression that he had murdered the five men, and didn't mind adding a sixth victim. "And if you think this is just a shake-down," Whitey added with a sneer, "here are some pictures we took of the guy after we killed him, before we left."

Props—sometimes Bulger used an ax, or a knife. Other times, some grisly black-and-white police photos would suffice. Whitey left with $60,000 in cash.

TONY CIULLA FIRST had to stand trial in New Jersey. He negotiated a deal with prosecutors, and part of the plea was that he could sell his story to the highest bidder, which turned out to be *Sports Illustrated*. The race-fixing scandal was *SI*'s cover story in the November 6, 1978, edition. Since they hadn't been indicted yet, the magazine didn't print the names of the Winter Hill Gang, but in open court in New Jersey a state judge ordered Fat Tony to reveal the names of his partners in Boston.

"Fellows that were partners of mine," Ciulla said. "One's name is Howie Winter. One name is John Martorano. M-A-R-T-O-R-A-N-O. Whitey Bulger. Stephen Flemmi."

AS 1978 ENDED, Johnny's flight plans were almost finished. He made sure all of his children had a good Christmas, because he knew he wouldn't be seeing them again for a while. He still had the six-month figure in his head, but he couldn't be sure how long it would take to get everything straightened out.

After all, Howie Winter had hoped to get out quickly, too. His lawyers had asked a new judge for clemency, presenting a petition signed by 4,000 residents of Somerville. Yet Howie was still languishing in state prison. And on February 9, 1979, he and Johnny Martorano and everyone else in the gang except Whitey and Stevie would be indicted.

I knew money wouldn't be a problem. I'd scouted out the Western Union offices down in Florida, plus there were always guys coming down from Boston. And I had my brother's friend, John Callahan. I'd gotten pretty friendly with him—I liked him. He struck me as a CIA-type guy, almost like a double agent, in the daytime a polished businessman in the boardrooms, at night wearing a leather jacket in the barrooms. I knew he had a condo in Florida, Plantation, and he said I'll do anything I can to help out.

I left before the indictment. At some point Whitey and Stevie told me the date the indictments were coming down, and I knew, the sooner I got out the better. See, if you get arrested, you have to jump bail and you lose that money, but more importantly, jumping bail adds an extra five years on your sentence. That's why everyone screws before they're indicted.

I hit the road right after Christmas 1978. Patty was with me. I had a brand-new Cadillac. Later on, I cut back to a Chevy-looking car, to be less conspicuous. I think I had maybe $10,000 cash, not that much but I could always get more. Whatever money you have on you when you're arrested, it's forfeited. So when you're a fugitive it's really not smart to carry a huge amount of cash. I'd get down to $2,000, then I'd start looking for another 10. But I didn't plan on being gone that long.

Besides, I had Stevie and Whitey looking out for me.

The Fugitive

MARTORANO: I went on the lam.

JUDGE: You did what?

MARTORANO: I became a fugitive.

PROSECUTOR: Went on the lam, I believe he said, Your Honor.

JUDGE: I think that is what he said. I want to make sure we all understand. Go ahead.

PROSECUTOR: You became a fugitive.

MARTORANO: Yeah.

JOHNNY MARTORANO AND Patty had a couple of suitcases with them when they hit I-95 in early 1979, heading toward the Sunshine State, that sunny place for shady people, as Graham Greene would say.

For the first few months they just drifted, a pair of tourists, stopping at different motels and hotels, crisscrossing the southern third of the state, from Fort Lauderdale to the Keys and across Alligator Alley to Naples and Fort Myers.

I would talk to George [Kaufman]. He stayed on top of my families. Initially I was getting money from Stevie and Whitey. Off and on, I was into sports betting, with Tommy Ryan, and Nicky Montaldo and Nicky Rais from Somerville. I always had 200, 300 thousand with George, and each week I'd add to it. Every so often Stevie would give George, say, $15,000. I never asked what it was for, I was just happy to have it. You know, on the lam, everything is different. All cash, you can't leave a trail, you can't work, or at least you can't work at a job that doesn't pay you cash. You need that cash coming in. I'm sure it's different now, since 9/11 you need identification for everything, you can't move around with no IDs anymore. After a few months, I switched my Richard Aucoin driver's license to Florida, and then I did get a credit card—I mean "Richard Aucoin" got a credit card. In those days, in Florida, you could walk into Sun Bank and put down say a thousand bucks cash. They'd give you a MasterCard and you had a credit limit of $500—half the cash you'd put down. Give 'em five grand, and your limit was $2,500. Even then you needed a credit card to rent a car. So if I had to rent a car, I'd just give 'em my credit card, so they'd have a number to put down, and then I'd pay cash.

I was doing okay. I was just waiting for the horse trial, I wanted to see how it went.

Not very well. They went into court in the summer of 1979. Howie Winter was the marquee defendant, with Jimmy Martorano, still serving out the federal extortion sentence, as the unlikely second banana. Fat Tony Ciulla spent seventeen days on the witness stand, detailing his banning from most of the racetracks along the East Coast, and how he had managed the career of that now infamous thoroughbred Spread the Word.

A jockey from Florida recalled being "smacked in the face" by Winter, and threatened with being "put in the trunk of a car." The prosecutor estimated that Howie Winter's "ring" had been grossing $40 million a year.

On July 11, 1979, Howie, Jimmy, and all of their code-fendants except one jockey were convicted. Howie was found guilty on forty counts, including racketeering, bribery, and violating the federal Travel Act, which prohibits making out-of-state phone calls in the commission of a crime. As evidence, the Justice Department cited Ciulla's damning phone records, including dozens of calls to Johnny Martorano.

At sentencing, Howie told the judge he'd rejected two overtures by the feds to become a witness. He said he refused to "make up lies like Ciulla did."

"I've had enough justice," Howie told the court. "What I would like is a little mercy."

The judge sentenced him to seven-to-ten years, on top of the eighteen-to-twenty-year state sentence he was already serving.

After the trial, I had to reevaluate my situation. Stevie and Whitey said wait awhile longer. Now I knew the worst I would get was 7-to-10, because that was what Howie got. In '81 or '82, my lawyer, Richie Egbert, said he could get this settled for not much time at all. But it seemed like something was always coming up, like a murder.

LAWYER: How long did you expect to be out and about?

MARTORANO: Six, seven months.

LAWYER: And it turned into?

MARTORANO: Seventeen years.

LAWYER: Did you ever have any discussion with Mr. Bulger and Mr. Flemmi about doing anything to take care of your situation?

MARTORANO: As far as looking for Ciulla?

LAWYER: Yes.

MARTORANO: I would have liked to have found Ciulla.

LAWYER: And if you had found Mr. Ciulla?

MARTORANO: I would have shot him.

Johnny and Patty were staying in Fort Lauderdale. But Johnny started spending a lot of time in the bars along the beach, and soon Patty was on him about his new female friends. Johnny wasn't married, but he might as well have been. He and Patty were living together—in one house. It was a lot different than dating. As a fugitive, he could no longer afford the multiple residences he'd maintained around Boston. Finally, he decided to quit the "sun-fun capital" of Broward County. He and Patty moved north and inland, to Orlando. They took out a twelve-month lease on a house and Patty started a one-year cosmetology course.

A few times, Johnny drove north to meet Stevie face-to-face in New York City. They always rendezvoused at the same place—the Marriott at LaGuardia Airport. But mostly Johnny stayed put in Florida.

With time on his hands, he took up motorcycles, Harleys of course. First it was a low rider, then a wide glide. He started making runs down to Daytona Beach, where he basked in the redneck ambience. He bought a twenty-two-foot boat, with a cabin and a single engine. The boat gave him somewhere to hang out on the weekends when Patty wasn't in school. During the week, Johnny would walk Daytona Beach, sometimes barefoot, back and forth for miles, people-watching, pondering his next move.

Must been late '80, early '81. I'm just walking, like I always did, and then, up ahead, coming in the other direction, I see Joe McDonald. I don't know which of us saw the other one first, but we hugged each other, and we went out for lunch and caught up on everything.

He had plenty of dough, he had his shy business back in Boston, and he had money in a no-tell motel in Chelsea. He was living in a furnished apartment, like a Guest Suites, nothing fancy, because he didn't need anything. I'd go see him, and one time I had to come down from Orlando to babysit him when he went on a bender. Back in Boston, he'd had his brother Leo. Leo would watch out for Joe when he'd go on a bat. But now Leo wasn't there, so I had to do it. I'd try to talk to him, but when he got to really drinking, it was like talking to the wall. Once he got on the hard stuff he was gone 'til it played itself out.

Later on, I'm in Plymouth, reading the 209s Zip filed, and there's Whitey, reporting back to the FBI that Joe's on a bender in Florida, and Johnny's watching out for him.

Jimmy the Bear Flemmi died of a drug overdose at MCI-Norfolk on October 16, 1979. The Bear was forty-seven years old. After his escape during a weekend furlough in 1976, he had remained free until earlier in 1979, when police arrested him while he was beating yet another woman in Baltimore. He was returned to prison in Massachusetts, where he soon died of an overdose of heroin. Stevie always claimed In Town gave his brother a hot shot to get rid of him.

Meanwhile, Stevie again moved his parents. The problem with Milton was that his mother had to drive down Blue Hill Avenue to get home from her job at Boston City Hospital. Earlier in 1979, at a stoplight, his parents had been jumped by a gang of blacks and severely beaten. A photograph of Mary Flemmi, propped up against her car, had run on the Associated Press regional wire, without references to her two gangster sons. There were reports that Stevie later bragged about having killed several of his parents' attackers, but he denied the stories. At least one of Mrs. Flemmi's muggers was later shot to death by a Boston policeman, and another died in a drive-by shooting.

Whitey told Stevie about a place for sale in what he described as a "safer" neighborhood—Southie. The address was 832 East Third Street, next door to Whitey's brother Billy, the president of the Massachusetts State Senate, at 828 East Third. It was a small house, but 832 East Third had a "sunporch," good for stashing machine guns and silencers, and for strangling young women.

SAL SPERLINGA HAD not been indicted in the federal race-fixing case. By late 1979, he was out on work release. He got a work-release "job" working for a Somerville alderman, whose brother was a state rep. The alderman had a print shop in Magoun Square, where he printed the Hill's weekly football cards—"to be used for entertainment purposes only," as they always said.

One day, down in Union Square, Sal had spotted an ex-con, a half-assed wiseguy named Dan Moran. He was the son of another ex-Somerville alderman. Sal told Moran to get out and stay out. Moran bided his time a few days, found out where Sal was hanging, and one Friday afternoon slipped into the alderman's print shop. In the back room, Sal was playing cards with the boys. Dan Moran shot him dead.

As of 2010, Moran was still serving a life sentence at Souza Baranowski Correctional Center in Shirley, Massachusetts.

BACK IN BOSTON, Zip Connolly continued to watch over Whitey. After Johnny's flight, the Winter Hill Gang was basically down to the two guys who weren't from Somerville. They decided to move their headquarters into Boston. George Kaufman had a new garage, in the West End, on Lancaster Street near North Station.

The animosities from the Irish Gang War lingered, and Georgie McLaughlin, another beneficiary of those Dukakis weekend prison furloughs, was moving around Charlestown, talking to the younger hoods, among them the son of the late Steve Hughes, murdered in 1966 by Stevie Flemmi and Frankie Salemme.

In early 1980, Whitey and Stevie decided on a housekeeping hit. Steve Hughes Jr., a paroled bank robber, had just pulled his car into a Charlestown public-housing project with his girlfriend and their child when he was shot and killed with a high-powered rifle—Stevie's trademark—from the roof of a nearby building.

An FBI informant reported the next day that young Hughes's killers were Whitey and Stevie, and that they had driven to Charlestown in a boiler they'd taken from George Kaufman's new garage on Lancaster Street in the West End. The FBI did nothing with the information, even though the garage was within five minutes' walking distance of their offices in the JFK building in Government Center.

Months later, two undercover state police were driving through the West End when they spotted a couple of organized-crime types lurking outside the garage. Intrigued, they staked out the garage and soon noticed a steady stream of underworld figures—both Mafia- and Hill-affiliated—paying their respects to Whitey and Stevie and their newest muscle, Nicky Femia, Joe Barboza's old driver and sidekick. One regular visitor from In Town was Phil Waggenheim, a veteran hitman.

The Staties got a warrant and put a bug in the garage. Across Lancaster Street, above a gay bar—the Boston Rifleman, an ironic name given Stevie's nickname—they set up surveillance. They were soon picking up conversations among the remaining Hill hoods. Unlike his bosses, Femia enjoyed junk food (as well as cocaine), and one day the bugs captured Whitey screaming at him when he returned to the garage from the nearby McDonald's on

Phil Waggenheim, shown here in a 1960 photo, was one of
Jerry Angiulo's highest-ranking non-Italian associates.

Causeway Street. Whitey even pelted Femia with french
fries as he warned Femia never to bring such "shit" into
the garage again.

Femia had been a suspect in the unsolved slaying of
five people at the Blackfriars nightclub on Summer Street
during the cocaine and cash rip-off in the summer of
1978 that Whitey had parlayed into a profitable score of
his own. When Femia went onto Whitey's payroll, Connolly filed several 209s absolving him of the Blackfriars
murders. Later, after Whitey fired Femia, Connolly filed

a new report, naming Femia as a prime suspect in the Blackfriars massacre.

The Staties were optimistic about their garage bug. It appeared they were on the verge of taking out what remained of the Winter Hill Gang. But in the summer of 1980, they noticed a sudden change in Whitey's demeanor at the garage. He began congratulating the state police on the efficiency of their speed traps on the Mass Pike. Whenever any gangster or drug dealer of any consequence showed up, they would leave the anteroom the Staties had bugged and go outside, onto the sidewalk. Finally Whitey stopped coming to the garage altogether. He began using the phones at the HoJo's on the Southeast Expressway in Dorchester. Whitey would show up, with Nicky Femia standing beside him, a small handgun tucked into his belt.

The Staties got a warrant to bug the HoJo's phones. Whitey suddenly stopped using them.

THE KILLINGS CONTINUED in South Boston. Louis Litif was an "independent," a bookie, a hustler. He was

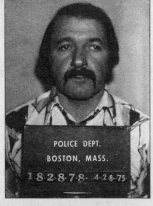

South Boston drug dealer Louis Litif got heavily into the disco scene before Whitey murdered him in 1980.

also one of Zip Connolly's handball partners at the Boston Athletic Club, and Litif realized early that drugs, not bookmaking, were the future of organized crime. He dressed flamboyantly, spending thousands of dollars on then-fashionable leisure suits, including, it was rumored, color-coordinated underwear. He began moving cocaine, starting small but quickly graduating to larger and larger amounts. He wasn't fucking around, either. At his barroom, he met a recalcitrant drug dealer and took him downstairs. As the dealer followed Litif into the basement, he yelled back at the bartender, "If I'm not back in fifteen minutes, come looking for me, 'cause I'm probably dead."

He was. Soon thereafter, the bartender, too, disappeared. His daughter went to the FBI, looking for answers. Zip Connolly was quite blunt.

"Honey, your father's dead. But don't worry. They got him drunk first."

The problem was, the bartender's family was destitute, and they couldn't collect on his life insurance policy without a death certificate, which they couldn't get without a body. Connolly told her that going to the Boston police might jeopardize some very important informants of his. He offered to handle the insurance company, which he did, with a single letter. Before his trial twenty years later on racketeering charges, Zip would deny ever writing such a letter, until the bartender's family produced a letter from the insurance company crediting "agent Connolly" with resolving the case.

> I sometimes wonder what my body count would have been if I'd stayed in Boston all those years. I can tell you, I wouldn't have minded killing Litif. I never had any use for that guy—he was just a jerk who wore a lot of gold. But some of the others that they killed. . . . I'd like to think that I could have stopped some of the later murders, especially of the women.

Whitey didn't need Johnny to handle Litif. This one was personal. Whitey was the boss of Southie, and Litif hadn't been authorized to kill anybody, let alone two people. Zip had been able to handle the bartender's daughter, but then Litif was arrested for the Matera murder. After making bail, the frightened Litif sought out a high-ranking Boston cop and offered to testify against Whitey and Stevie in return for leniency. Unfortunately for Litif, according to what Flemmi later told police, a second cop was present to hear the conversation—Litif's FBI handler, Zip Connolly. Louie Litif rocketed to the top of the Hit Parade.

Brian Halloran was out of prison, hanging around, snorting coke, drinking too much. On April 12, 1980, Whitey put him to work. Louie Litif asked his wife if he could borrow her car—"he said he had a bad stomach and wanted to get some Maalox tablets," was how Anna Litif explained it to a judge in 2009. He told her nothing about being summoned to South Boston, or that he was told to pick up Brian Halloran on the way to the Lower End. Their destination was Triple O's, which was the new name of what had been the Killeens' old Transit Café. Whitey had taken it over through a straw, Kevin O'Neil, the tubby, acne-scarred plug-ugly who had beaten a murder rap in 1969 after hiring Billy Bulger as his attorney.

Once they got to Triple O's, Halloran took Litif upstairs, to Whitey's "office." Whitey shot Litif in the head. Then he and Halloran wrapped a blanket around his body, brought Mrs. Litif's car around back, and put the corpse in the trunk. Halloran drove the car over to the South End and left it in front of Larry Baione's Laundromat on Shawmut Avenue. It was either a message, or a coincidence.

As for Halloran, he walked back to Triple O's and had a double. He owed it to himself.

•   •   •

THE STATIES WERE irate that their bugs kept getting blown. It has never been officially determined who tipped Whitey to the Lancaster Street surveillance, but the state police pointed the finger at the FBI. Lieutenant Colonel Jack O'Donovan, who had personally arrested Jimmy the Bear three times, was adamant in his demands for a meeting with the FBI brass. The feds were chagrined, probably because they realized that O'Donovan was correct. The state police were insisting that the FBI sever ties with the two mobsters who were now so palpably pulling the feds' strings. The FBI brass in Boston appeared on the verge of terminating Whitey and Stevie as informants.

So in late 1980, Zip Connolly and his ostensible boss, John Morris, swung into action. They wrote memo after memo to their superiors, lionizing Whitey. For Zip, it was already a matter of dollars and cents. Connolly had quickly grown accustomed to the cash payoffs he took from Whitey—in 2003, a secretary at the Boston FBI office would testify that in the late '70s, long before the advent of direct deposit, she once opened one of the lower drawers in Zip's desk and found "ten to twelve" uncashed FBI paychecks.

After discarding his first wife, Zip bought a condo in Southie from a convicted Bulger-affiliated arsonist known as Frankie Flame. To help defray costs, Zip took in a roommate—a DEA agent who worked with his brother. Zip furnished his new pad with stolen appliances from a store Whitey controlled, and even the deliveries were made by gangsters. He bought a boat. Later, he would purchase a second home on the Cape. Finally, Whitey had to warn him to stop spreading around so much cash in such a flashy manner.

Increasingly dependent on Whitey for both his professional and financial well-being, by late 1980 Zip was using his 209s to defend Whitey in ever more histrionic tones. In one, he dusted off an urban myth about Whitey doing a favor for a white Quincy cop, rescuing his wayward daughter from the clutches of an evil black pimp. Sometimes, he told the truth: he pointed out that Whitey had ratted out one of Johnny's old friends, Jimmy Kearns, when he was on the lam in Las Vegas after taking a contract from an El Paso cocaine dealer to shoot an assistant U.S. attorney.

On October 15, 1980, Zip and John Morris actually met with their gangland boss and then wrote a memo quoting Whitey as saying he was less concerned about being revealed as an informant than he was with the Mafia possibly killing him to take over his rackets. A business hit, in other words. Nothing personal. Besides, Whitey added, no one would ever believe he was a rat. Certainly John Martorano never did.

> The FBI always knew where I was, all those years. I didn't know it then, but I know it now. Whitey and Stevie told them. They kept tabs on me for the FBI. But they needed me to be free, so they could drop my name with Jerry. The Mafia understood what I was capable of, so whenever Jerry Angiulo tried to get Whitey and Stevie to agree to anything, they'd always say, we'll have to get back to you on that. We have to check in with Johnny first. They never told me what was going on. But they loved to drop my name.

LAWYER: You were a ruthless guy, weren't you, Mr. Martorano?

MARTORANO: I don't know.

LAWYER: You don't know?

MARTORANO: You don't act like I am.

LAWYER: Let's go back to reality here, Mr. Martorano. Your reputation for ruthlessness was well-deserved, was it not?

MARTORANO: Probably.

LAWYER: And when you say "probably," are you
being modest.

MARTORANO: I'm not the person—it has to be the
other person to decide that, not me.

Zip was desperate to protect his source—his source of
income. Next he wrote a memo saying that there was
speculation that he himself had tipped Billy Bulger to the
Lancaster Street garage bug, and that Billy had informed
Whitey. That was an indication of the seriousness of the
threat to terminate them, that Zip would reveal the name
of his real mentor, the senate president. But he had to move
quickly. The FBI was about to install bugs at the Dog
House, and the names of Stevie and Whitey would surely be
mentioned.

The only way to protect them from indictment would be
if they were listed as informants on the federal wiretapping
warrant. So in December 1980 both Whitey and Stevie
paid an unscheduled visit to the Dog House, so that they
could be listed as informants on the warrant, even though
in fact the most significant information was provided by a
Chelsea bookmaker who in return for his services would
later be pardoned by President Ronald Reagan.

After their visit to Prince Street, Zip wrote up a report,
summarizing the mundane information about In Town
that Stevie and Whitey had provided—"revenue was
down," an unsurprising development, considering the re-
cession that was gripping the nation. It just wasn't enough.
The FBI brass was ready to cut Whitey and Stevie loose,
so on November 25, 1980, Zip took his final shot. He
brought Whitey to a hotel room at Logan Airport, where
he met for four hours with the new head of the Boston
FBI office, Lawrence Sarhatt. Without ever mentioning
his days as a gay hustler in Bay Village, Whitey went on
at length about his deep respect for H. Paul Rico.

"SA RICO," Sarhatt wrote, "was such a gentleman and

was so helpful that he, Informant, changed his mind about his hate for all law enforcement. Additionally, he has a close feeling toward SA JOHN CONNOLLY because they both grew up in the same neighborhood in Boston and had the mutual childhood problems, as well as his deep hatred for La Cosa Nostra."

Whitey denied that anyone in the Bureau had tipped him to the Lancaster Street bug, saying the leak came from the state police, although he refused to name the trooper "because this source is not doing it for monetary benefit but as a favor to him."

Just for good measure, Whitey "also related that he is not in the drug business and personally hates anyone who does [sell drugs]. Therefore, he and any of his associates do not deal in drugs."

Sarhatt was new to Boston, but he instinctively under-stood that he was a fed being fed a line. In his report, he noted that he was "not certain" if Whitey was "telling the full story of his involvement."

As usual, Whitey was keenly aware of the bureaucratic turf wars among various law-enforcement agencies. So he took the opportunity to unload on Massachusetts State Police Lieutenant Colonel O'Donovan. Whitey said he'd met several times with O'D, as he was known, and that O'D had repeatedly expressed his disdain for the G-men for whom Whitey claimed to have such respect.

"He [O'Donovan] made very disparaging and deroga-tory statements about the professionalism of FBI per-sonnel. [Whitey] took great umbrage inasmuch as his association with the FBI has been nothing but the most professional in every respect."

Ultimately, Sarhatt recommended terminating Whitey and Stevie. But the final decision was up to Jeremiah O'Sullivan, the head of the Organized Crime Strike Force, who two years earlier had cut them out of the race-fixing indictment. Once again, at Zip Connolly's behest, O'Sullivan saved Whitey and Stevie.

Johnny was still on the lam in Florida, talking to John Callahan.

CALLAHAN HAD BEEN the president of World Jai Alai until 1977, when he was observed by Connecticut State Police at the Playboy Club in Park Square in the company of "known gangsters," one of whom was Johnny Martorano. Callahan had long since contracted what a cop would later tell the *Miami Herald* was "a bad case of gangsteritis," but now it would come back to bite him. The state of Connecticut quickly stripped Callahan of his license to operate a pari-mutuel —a betting pool—without which he couldn't run a fronton.

Callahan was out, and soon afterward World Jai Alai's longtime owners from Boston sold out to Roger Wheeler, a fifty-five-year-old native Bostonian who had made a fortune in high tech. Wheeler, who now lived in Tulsa, Oklahoma, paid $50 million, a reasonable price for a company that spun off $6 million clear each year. Wheeler got a loan from the First National Bank of Boston, where Callahan had once worked and was still well-regarded. As part of the deal, Wheeler had to bring in one of Callahan's associates to run the company. Suddenly, Callahan was dreaming of a triumphant return to World Jai Alai.

Given the nature of the business—gambling and cash—Wheeler wanted the best possible security. That was where H. Paul Rico came in. After his retirement from the FBI in 1976, Callahan had hired him as vice president of security as a favor to Rico's gangland associates. Rico quickly brought in more retired G-men, and after the ownership change, he hit it off with his new boss Wheeler. Rico was old-school FBI, and he knew how to act the part, just like Efrem Zimbalist Jr., Jimmy Stewart, and James Cagney before him.

Despite his security team's impeccable FBI credentials, Wheeler soon realized that his frontons were being skimmed. They weren't churning out nearly the $6 million annual profits that he'd been expecting, and needed, to pay off the note to the First. Wheeler started an audit, but before he could get far, a female World Jai Alai employee in Florida was brutally murdered in her apartment, along with her boyfriend. The boyfriend was killed first, hit over the head and then hanged from a shower curtain while unconscious. Then the cashier was dragged into the kitchen, to the sink. The killers looped the sash from her bathrobe around her neck and then fed it into the garbage disposal. She died of a broken neck. At the time, in December 1980, the double homicide was written off as another Miami drug deal gone bad. It remains unsolved; Miami-Dade's cold-case squad reopened the case in 2007 but got nowhere.

Meanwhile, John Callahan was hanging out at his condo in Plantation, and he decided to bounce an idea off Johnny Martorano.

I'd be out drinking with him whenever he flew down—he was one of the guys bringing down the money to me. George Kaufman managed my own money for me—I gave him 10 percent of whatever he handled, whether from the sports betting or anything Stevie and Whitey cut me in on, which was usually the deals I found out about. They'd give George my cut to get to me. Usually George would then give it to Callahan, and I'd get it the next time he flew down. Off-season, he let me stay at his condo in Plantation, and I could use his car. He didn't need them if he wasn't down there. So I was hanging with him, and he was always talking about his jai alai problems. I guess it was late '80, early '81, when he came up with a new idea.

He wanted to buy World Jai Alai, with Rico and his friend who the bank had put in as his partners. Once the deal went through, Callahan was going to cut the Hill in, for $10,000 a week, to provide protection against any of the New York families muscling in on the fronton in Hartford. They were particularly concerned about that one, because it was so close to New York. There was so much cash coming in, from the betting and parking lots, they could have skimmed it easy. The plan was to offer Wheeler good money—at least $60 million, probably more. Then they would sell off a couple of the smaller frontons and pay down the debt to a manageable level. So he asked us—meaning me, Whitey, and Stevie—if we'd be interested in handling the "protection." Naturally they loved the idea—$10,000 a week, steady.

Subsequently, the offer was made to Wheeler, but he wasn't interested. And from then on, Wheeler seemed more interested in getting the people who were stealing from him arrested. Callahan kept saying, he's trying to get us indicted.

In early 1981, the FBI finally installed the bugs, at both the Dog House and Larry Baione's "clubhouse" on North Margin Street. Within days, the feds knew they had more than enough to put Jerry Angiulo behind bars for the rest of his life.

In addition to the incriminating tapes, the underboss turned out to be a font of unintentional humor, profanely spouting off on everything from the untimely passing of a loanshark victim ("He can't be dead—he owes me

$13,000!") to the low IQs of the next generation of hood-lums ("I don't need tough guys, I need intelligent tough guys").

He fulminated against his own "college boy" son: "That's a fuckin' order 'cause you're a fuckin' idiot."

Just as Zip had expected, the Hill was talked about continually. But by using Whitey and Stevie as sources for the warrant, Zip had saved his friends once more. Angiulo bragged that Whitey, among others, was one of his hitmen, which of course he was, or had been, during the Indian War. But Zip quickly inserted a report into Whitey's file, flatly stating that "source [Whitey] is not a 'hit man' for Jerry Angiulo as has been contended."

One night, Larry Baione listened as Jerry Angiulo discussed the breakup of the Winter Hill Gang into territories.

"Whitey's got the whole of Southie. Stevie is got the whole of the South End. Johnny's got niggers. . . . Howie knows this."

In the long run, the bugged conversation most damaging to the Hill didn't even involve Angiulo. It took place at Baione's club on North Margin Street. One of his soldiers, John Cincotti, had been working with a relative of his, Jerry Matricia. It was the same Matricia who a few years earlier had disappeared from Nevada after losing $90,000 he had won for the Hill in Las Vegas betting on one of the fixed races in which Tony Ciulla had run Spread the Word.

Now Matricia had returned to Boston, and Larry and his fellow made man Ralphie Chong were concerned that if Whitey or Stevie saw Matricia, "they're going to hit him," as Baione put it.

Late one night, Matricia was brought to North Margin Street to speak with Larry, who had been drinking heavily, as he did most evenings. Baione began with a brief history lesson for Matricia.

"If you fuck someone that's friendly with us—just so

you understand me, do you know that the Hill is us? Maybe you didn't know that, did you?"

"No," said Matricia, "I didn't."

"Did you know Howie and Stevie, they're us? We're the fuckin' Hill with Howie. . . . You know that they're with us. You didn't know that?"

Matricia said he didn't know that. So Baione told him that from now on, whatever money he made with Cincotti would go directly to pay off his debt to the Hill.

"You understand?" Baione asked Matricia. "After all, you fucked them. These are nice people. These are the kind of fuckin' people that straighten a thing out. They're with us. We're together. And we cannot tolerate them getting fucked."

ALL THE BOSTON agents took part in the bugging operations, sitting in the cramped surveillance vans for hours on end in the dead of winter, monitoring the conversations as they were recorded. For such tedious, uncomfortable duty, most of the agents dressed casually, in sweatsuits and sneakers. But not Zip. At his retirement dinner at Joe Tecce's in 1990, another agent described Zip's daily arrival at the van, decked out in "tan slacks, Gucci loafers, velour shirt open to the chest with enough gold showing to be the envy of most members of the Gambino crime family."

Soon Zip Connolly had a new nickname, at least among the younger, straighter agents. They called him "Cannoli."

WHITEY AND STEVIE were kept apprised of the tapes' content—information they did not share with their "partner" down in Florida. One night, agent John Morris called Whitey and said he had a tape he wanted Whitey and Stevie to hear. The two gangsters rented a room at the Colonnade on Huntington Avenue and laid in a few bottles of wine for the heavy-drinking Morris. Morris arrived after business hours and played the tape for them—it was Larry Baione drunkenly threatening to kill Whitey and Stevie. Then Morris himself got drunk, so drunk that from then on Whitey and Stevie called him "Vino." Whitey ended up driving the crapulous G-man back to Lexington, with Stevie following behind. They kept the FBI tape he'd left behind. It would come in handy, if Vino ever got out of line, not that that was likely to happen, as alcoholic and as crooked as he had become.

Angiulo wouldn't know for months that he was fin-

Zip Connolly, left, arrests Jerry Angiulo's brother,
Frankie "the Cat," in 1983.

ished. It was tedious work, transcribing all those tapes. Angiulo would remain free until September 1983. So he went about his usual business, and one of his tasks was getting the Hill to start paying back the $250,000 they still owed him. He'd frozen the vig, and in return, Whitey and Stevie had promised to start paying down the principal at the rate of $5,000 a week.

They made one payment, then stopped again.

"Jesus Christ all fuckin' mighty," Jerry complained to one of his brothers, "why haven't these guys been in touch with me? I don't understand it. Fuck me maybe, they don't like me. They got a right not to like me. It's not a problem . . . but they been jerkin' me around."

And for a very good reason. Jerry Angiulo wasn't going to be on the street much longer.

JOHN CALLAHAN DECIDED he couldn't take any more chances. Roger Wheeler had to go. After the murder of his Florida cashier, Wheeler had decided to sell the fronton in Connecticut. It was just too close to New York, and he was sick of mobsters. He stepped up the audit. Callahan flew to Florida.

I think Callahan and I were having dinner at Yesterday's. It was a fancy French restaurant on Oakland Park Boulevard in Fort Lauderdale. We were up in this private dining area. The Plum Room, they called it.

He says to me, this guy won't take our money. We still have to stop him. We need to get rid of him. Can you help us?

I said no. On something like this, I'd have to check with my partners, Whitey and Stevie, but I didn't think they'd be interested because Wheeler was a legitimate guy. Killing somebody like that would bring down a whole lot of heat. Callahan says, tell them the deal, the $10,000 a week, it isn't dead. Rico says he'll propose the same deal to Wheeler's widow once he's dead. Then he starts telling me, you know this guy Wheeler cheats at golf. He knows I can't stand cheaters, that's why I never liked Castucci. So he's trying to push my buttons, only he doesn't do it nearly as effectively as Whitey and Stevie do. What do I care, some guy in Oklahoma cheats at golf?

It took a while for everything to fall into place. Despite Johnny's misgivings, Whitey and Stevie were immediately on board—in those precocaine days, $10,000 a week was awfully tempting. But there was more to whacking Wheeler than money, Johnny realized later. If the skimming investigation went forward, Rico was likely in jeopardy. And Rico was part of the original crew—the one Johnny would later come to consider the greatest criminal enterprise of all in Boston, the one that also included Whitey, Stevie, and Zip.

Once they were in, Whitey and Stevie inexplicably allowed Callahan to talk them into a terrible decision—offering the murder contract on Wheeler to Brian Halloran.

In January 1981, Callahan invited Halloran up to his apartment above the Rusty Scupper. Whitey was there, even though he didn't like Halloran, never had. He was a boozer, a cokehead. His brother was a state cop; Halloran was a complete fuck-up. And most important, he could put the finger on Whitey for the Litif hit. Whitey had taken to calling him "Balloonhead"—recycling the Mullens' old nickname for Kenny Killeen.

Despite all that, Whitey signed off on Callahan's decision to offer the contract on Wheeler to Balloonhead. After hearing the offer, Halloran immediately asked if there wasn't some other alternative. That was not the right answer. Whitey stood up and told Halloran they'd get back to him later. A couple of weeks after that, Callahan told

him to come back up to the apartment. There he handed
Halloran two hundred $100 bills—$20,000 in cash.

"We shouldn't have involved you to begin with," Callahan said. Halloran then went out and bought himself a
new car, parked it at Logan Airport, and flew off to Fort
Lauderdale for a two-week bender.

Callahan was also headed for Fort Lauderdale.

He tells me he's been talking to Whitey and Stevie,
that they're in, and they want me to handle it out in
Oklahoma. Nobody tells me nothing about Halloran
being offered the contract. Callahan says he's also
been talking to Rico, and Rico wants me to ask Joe
McDonald to help out. That surprised me, but I called
Joe, and he says, "Yeah, I do owe Rico a favor." That's
when he tells me how Rico set up Ronnie Dermody
for Buddy McLean back in '64. So here's Rico calling
in the marker almost twenty years later, and the guy
who's paying off, Joe Mac, isn't even the guy who
ran up the original tab, he's just doing it for his
friend who's been dead fifteen years now. But that's
how it worked back then, just like Whitey called in
the favor I owed Billy O.

So I got back to Stevie, and told him Joe's in.
Then I told him what equipment we'd need for the hit.
They sent it all down on the bus. Next thing Callahan
gives me a piece of paper from Rico. He's written
down all of Wheeler's addresses, where he parks his
car, everything. At the bottom there was a description of what Wheeler looks like—Rico said he had a
"ruddy complexion." A ruddy complexion—when I
read that I knew a cop had written it, an FBI guy.
John Callahan or anybody else would have said, "a
red face." "Ruddy complexion" is how an FBI guy
talks when he's trying to impress somebody, even
another cop.

So now we have to fly out there, to Oklahoma. I tell Patty, Why don't you go back to Boston to see Loretta? I told her, I'm meeting one of my kids at Disney World. She doesn't believe me, but what can I do, tell her I'm going out to Oklahoma to kill some guy? She'd go, "Yeah sure." It got so that I'd tell her a lie and she'd believe it. You tell her the truth, she says you're lying. I'm telling you, guys know exactly what I'm talking about.

Richard Aucoin and John Kelly—Joe Mac's alias—flew out to Oklahoma City on the same flight, sitting far apart. They rented a car, then drove to Tulsa, about an hour away. They changed motels every couple of days. All of Rico's information was solid, but they had to wait for the package to arrive at the bus station—handguns, a car-

The body of Roger Wheeler in his car in Tulsa in 1981. Crouching, wearing suspenders, is Tulsa police detective Mike Huff, who 22 years later would arrest H. Paul Rico in Miami for Wheeler's murder.

bine, a grease gun, silencers, bulletproof vests, ski masks, a shimmy, and a dent puller for stealing cars. It was the standard Winter Hill hit kit, minus grenades. In a bit of underworld humor, the package was addressed to "Joe Russo"—the Boston Mafia's top hitman.

Joe stole the boiler, popped the ignition, and we stashed it near the country club in a big apartment complex. Joe was sixty-five, but you'd think he was twenty-five. He was a ball of fire. One of his kids had gotten hurt real bad in an accident, so he wasn't even thinking about drinking.

Then I get an update from Callahan. Rico gave him a tee time for Wheeler at his country club, two o'clock Saturday. We drive out to the golf course, Southern Hills Country Club. We spot his Caddy, but remember, I've still never seen this guy. So we park a few rows closer to the club. I'm in full disguise—we'd picked up that stuff at a theatrical store in Tulsa. Full beard, sunglasses, a baseball cap.

Finally I see a guy coming down the hill from the club to the parking lot, might be Wheeler. I let him walk past our car, then I fall in behind him. If he gets in the Caddy, I clip him. If he goes to another car, I just keep walking. But it's him, he's getting in the car. He doesn't hear me, he's about to close the door but I grab it to keep it open. He jumps back in the seat, startled, and I let him have it, one shot, between the eyes, .38 snub nose. But when I fired, the gun exploded. The chamber flew open, the bullets fell out—I'd wiped them down as I was loading the gun, so there were no prints. I just left the bullets there on the pavement. I closed the door to Wheeler's car; I walked back to our car, got in, and Joe drove off.

LAWYER: Did he say anything when he got shot?

MARTORANO: Not that I heard.

LAWYER: Did he seem surprised he was going to die?

MARTORANO: I think it was too fast.

LAWYER: Let me ask you something, when you had the gun that close to his face, did you look at his eyes?

MARTORANO: No.

LAWYER: Did he look at you?

MARTORANO: I wasn't thinking about that, no.

LAWYER: What were you thinking about?

MARTORANO: Getting away with this.

They drove directly back to the apartment complex, dropped off the boiler, and got back into the rental car. Then they returned to their hotel, where Joe chopped up the .38 with a special saw that had been sent down from Boston. Johnny meanwhile was cutting up the false beard with some scissors, then flushing the pieces down the toilet. They'd driven by a marsh one day, and now they returned, Joe driving, Johnny throwing the pieces of the gun into the water.

Then they drove back to Oklahoma City, where they stopped at the bus station to check the hit kit. It would be shipped back to Fort Lauderdale, where Joe would store it, just in case. You never knew. Then Johnny flew back to Orlando, and Joe caught the next plane back to Fort Lauderdale.

I get home, I call Patty in Somerville, I tell her to come back home. A couple of days later, she's back and she's stewing, I can tell. Finally she says to me, I don't believe you went to Disney World to see your kid. I got no way of checking up on you, she says. She figured I was with another broad. It was a question of trust, and there was none. But like I said, under the circumstances, what was I supposed to tell her?

Callahan was pleased. He'd been afraid he was going to be indicted, but now he didn't have to worry. His next trip to Florida, he sat down with Johnny and told him he wanted to express his gratitude.

He said he wanted to help out on the expenses, and how did $50,000 sound? I told him it sounded good. It was like a bonus, a gesture of appreciation, like Jerry Angiulo with Indian Al. Both cases it was found money. I never discussed payment for killing with either Angiulo or Callahan. It was a favor. I mean, I took it, sure, but a hit like that—if you were doing it for money, it would have to be worth a million. I did it because Callahan was a friend. So I figured, Joe's gotta get half of it, because he's my partner on the deal. That leaves me $25,000, but Whitey and Stevie are my partners too, so each of them gets a third, the same as me. So I arranged for Callahan to get the money to the various parties. I think Leo McDonald got 25 grand for Joe, and then George Kaufman got the $25,000 and split it three ways. I ended up with, like, eight grand.

After that, every once in a while I'd ask Callahan, what's the update? Rico had said, once Wheeler's gone, we can try to buy the place from the widow. Callahan tells me he'd made another offer, but it was turned down again. I don't even know how hard they were trying, because once Wheeler was gone, Rico somehow won his son over, so he was back in tight with the owners.

Back in Tulsa, the investigation into Wheeler's murder went nowhere. The trails quickly led back to Boston and

Zip Connolly told Whitey and Stevie to dress up in suits and ties
before the FBI took their mug shots in 1981
to send to the Tulsa police.

Miami, but the FBI offices in both cities were less than
helpful to the Oklahoma cops. The Boston office finally
agreed to send down mug shots of Whitey and Stevie—
but when the photos arrived, the Tulsa police were amazed
that the two gangsters were wearing suits and ties, as if
the feds were trying to make them look as little like
Wheeler's killer as possible.

The FBI report on Wheeler's murder painted a remarkably unsympathetic portrait of Wheeler. The feds more or
less described him as an unscrupulous, tax-evading son-
ofabitch, a variation on Callahan's theme with Johnny
that he "cheated" at golf.

Tulsa police detective Mike Huff flew to Miami to interview H. Paul Rico in his well-appointed chambers at
the World Jai Alai fronton. Rico was obdurate, refusing
to answer even the simplest questions. He didn't even
bother to hide his contempt for the Oklahoma lawman.

"I walked out of Rico's office in a state of disbelief,"
Huff said in 2010. "I'd been expecting to talk to another
cop, and instead I ran into the Godfather."

•   •   •

AS MUCH AS the Boston FBI had done for Whitey, it had done at least as much for his younger brother, Sen. Billy Bulger. In the mid-seventies, Billy was stuck in the number-three position in the leadership of the state senate, with no place to go. Then, the senate president suddenly resigned in a scandal over an old $1,000 check. Even more fortuitously for Billy, the majority leader, a younger man, also from Suffolk County, was suddenly ensnared in a bribery case involving state building contracts. His name was Joe DiCarlo.

DiCarlo had a lot of clout, and was assured by the then U.S. House Speaker Tip O'Neill of Cambridge that he would not be indicted. But then the FBI abruptly reopened the investigation, flying Boston agents to Texas to interview new witnesses. DiCarlo was indicted and convicted, along with a Republican senator who served as his bagman.

Suddenly, in 1978, Billy Bulger was the president of the state senate.

Quickly, Billy began settling scores with his own enemies—and Whitey's. Whitey had been fired years earlier from his no-show janitor's job at the Suffolk County courthouse—his old boss and his top staff had their pay frozen in the state budget for five years. Jack O'Donovan, the lieutenant colonel in the state police who had complained to the FBI about Whitey's insidious influence on their agents, was targeted in an anonymous rider to the 1981 state budget that would have forced him and three other senior MSP brass to retire. The governor vetoed the provision, and Billy Bulger said he had no idea who had inserted the outside rider designed to end O'Donovan's career.

A Boston judge who refused to hire another crony of Bulger's had his staff slashed and "is now holding court in a Winnebago," as one of Billy's senate stooges joked, openly, at Billy's televised St. Patrick's Day breakfast.

The politically connected audience cracked up.

Jackie Bulger was the youngest Bulger brother. He'd graduated from high school and gone to work at a fish market in Roslindale. Eventually Billy got him a job at the courthouse, but the clerk's job Jackie wanted was occupied. No problem—the clerk was appointed to a judgeship, and Jackie became the clerk of the Boston Juvenile Court.

Jackie's ex-wife, too, got a job in the courts. His daughter went to work for her uncle Billy at the State House. Both Jackie's son and son-in-law got jobs with the Massachusetts Bay Transportation Authority. It was the same for everyone in the Bulger family. They all had state jobs—everyone except Whitey.

Soon Whitey, too, was feeling his oats. After the murder of Louie Litif, a reporter for the *Herald American* named Paul Corsetti began poking around, looking for a story. Whitey called the reporter anonymously, leading him on with tidbits of information. He offered Corsetti the whole story of Litif's slaying if he would meet him in a bar at Quincy Market. Whitey was waiting when Corsetti arrived. He introduced himself by saying, "I'm Jimmy Bulger, motherfucker." Then Whitey read the reporter a list of addresses where he lived and worked and where his young daughter attended day care. Finally he told the reporter the makes, models, and license plates of the cars he and his wife drove. Then Whitey abruptly got off his barstool and walked out without a word.

The next day Corsetti arrived in the city room wearing a holster on his hip, with a .38. Word traveled fast. Suddenly there was a lot less coverage of organized crime—in the *Globe* as well as the *Herald American*.

Billy demanded one of the state's coveted three-digit license plates. The Registry of Motor Vehicles gave him one, then when a relative of the original holder demanded its return, Billy was given an even lower three-digit plate— "to ease the pain," the Registry admitted.

Zip Connolly would now take new agents in the office to the State House to meet the man he described, accurately, as "the most powerful man in Massachusetts politics." The message was clear: when you retire, you'll have a job waiting for you—if you play ball with the Bulgers, both of them.

On his retirement from the FBI, Condon was hired by Governor Mike Dukakis, who more and more did whatever Billy Bulger told him to do. Also hired by the state was an ex-agent named Bob Sheehan, who once offered a gangster in his custody a machine gun and the keys to the Dog House, so that he could wipe out the Angiulos. Obviously, Sheehan was Good People. He transferred to a new agency, the Massachusetts Convention Center Authority (MCCA), which Bulger had set up to rebuild the Hynes Convention Center on Boylston Street.

To run the new MCCA, Billy engineered the hiring of the tin-whistle player in his Irish band, a former postman. It was a "nationwide search," explained the MCCA chairman, Billy's close friend, state treasurer Bob Crane. Next Whitey's stepdaughter got a job at the MCCA. At the garage run by the MCCA, one of Stevie Flemmi's old gangland associates from Roxbury was kept on, along with his brother, both of whom would soon be arrested for stealing cash. The suspicions of even Billy Bulger's tin-whistle player were aroused when the brothers both bought new Cadillacs on their $12-an-hour salaries.

Billy Bulger controlled the MCCA—whenever treasurer Crane had to do something for him, he would roll his eyes upward, toward the fourth floor of the State House, where the senate met, and Bulger had his offices.

"This is for the little man upstairs," Crane would say.

My daughter Lisa needed a job. We knew they were hiring. So an approach was made to the Bulgers to see if they could put her on the MCCA payroll like they'd done for everybody else. But they refused. Somebody, I don't remember who, told us it would look really bad if Johnny Martorano's daughter got hired by Whitey Bulger's brother.

But Billy wasn't the only pol at the State House. The House Speaker was Tommy McGee, from Lynn. He controlled one of the seats on the board—his appointee was Nick Rizzo, a big fundraiser for Paul Tsongas. Later on Rizzo went to prison for embezzling money from Tsongas's campaign when he ran for president against Clinton in '92.

So it was McGee and his guy Rizzo who got Lisa the job with the MCCA. Contrary to what you hear, the Bulgers had nothing to do with it.

Life went on in Florida. Johnny was driving a conversion van—customized inside, with more space in the back for hanging out in style than for hauling equipment. One day the van was stolen. It was finally recovered down in Miami, and "Richard Aucoin" had to go down to the police lot to retrieve it. He walked past one surveillance camera after another, rode down an elevator with several uniformed sergeants, and then had to have his photo taken by yet another camera before he could reclaim possession of his van. No one realized the resemblance between Richard Aucoin and the guy on the wanted poster, John Vincent Martorano.

Another time, on an interstate in a different southern state, Johnny Martorano was headed down an incline when he saw a massive roadblock at the bottom of the hill. He had no choice but to keep driving toward it. When he reached the roadblock, he casually rolled down the window and the cop leaned in.

"What's happening, officer?" Johnny asked.

"We're looking for a fugitive," the cop said, explaining that they were searching for escapees from a nearby prison.

"Well," Johnny said, "if you want to have a look, go right ahead."

Joe Mac, meanwhile, was hanging out in Fort Lauderdale with another Boston-area fugitive who was still involved in various small-time criminal activities in South Florida.

I never trusted this guy Joe was hanging with, he was from Peabody. I kept telling Joe, stay the fuck away from him, and whatever you do, please don't ever mention my name to him. I don't know why, I just thought he was trouble. Anyway, at one point, I don't hear from Joe for a while, and then suddenly he turns back up. He tells me, you'll never believe what happened to me.

He says this friend of his from Peabody got in some beef with some hoods up in Atlanta, and he needed some backup, and can Joe help him out? Of course Joe says sure, but something happened— these Georgia guys got the drop on them, and they locked them up in a closet for a few days. Had them both tied up, I don't know what for. Joe thought for sure he was dead, but somehow he got loose. I told Joe, What did I tell you? That guy is no fuckin' good.

Johnny and Patty were settling into a routine. They met some people from Montreal, and began visiting them occasionally. It was no problem getting back and forth across the Canadian border. Another family tradition became their annual trip to Hawaii, in February, right around the time of the Pro Bowl.

When I was in jail in Plymouth in 1978, I was playing softball and I met a guy. I'll call him Joe. He said as soon as he got out he was moving to Hawaii. His wife and kids were already out there. He said, if you're ever out there, give me a call, my number's in the book. So I kept in touch with him, and we started going out there every winter. His son was a good football player—played in the NFL for a while. He's moved back out there to the islands and is coaching now.

Anyway, "Joe" would make reservations for me every winter on Waikiki Beach. I used to stay at the Ilikai Hotel, and every morning, I'd go for a walk, just like I did in Florida. One day I'm walking along a big boat dock near the hotel, and I see that they're filming *Magnum P.I.* You remember that TV show, with Tom Selleck?

So they were between scenes, and I'm walking by, slowly, taking it all in, and all of a sudden, Tom Selleck yells over at me, "Hey you, you wanna be a walk-on?" It was just a casual, spur of the moment thing. I smiled and said, "No thanks, Tom," and I kept on walking. And he's just standing there for a few seconds, until he finally he yells at me again, and he runs up to me and gives me this look. And Tom Selleck says, "You know, you're the first guy who ever said no thanks, who didn't want to be on the show." I smiled and said, "Is that right?" and I kept walking.

Things had never been quite the same for Johnny's father, Andy, after Luigi's was padlocked in the wake of Margie Sylvester's murder there in 1964. Always self-employed, Andy ended up working as a restaurant-equipment salesman.

In 1980, Johnny got the word that his father was at the South Shore Hospital, and that he was dying. He couldn't go home to say good-bye, but Johnny did call him a few days before he died.

He told me he loved me—he'd never said that to me before. It meant so much to me to hear him say that. Then I remembered what Billy Vaughn said to me once. You remember Vaughn, he owned that real dive, McCarthy & Vaughn, on Dover Street. I was talking to Billy once, and he told me, Do you know how proud your dad is of you, Johnny? He told Billy, "Johnny is a man. He will help you or he will hurt you." Being a man, that was the only thing that mattered to Andy.

After Andy died, I got a call from Whitey. He said he wanted to express his condolences, but the real reason he called was to tell me that from now on, I should do all my communicating with Stevie. He said talking to Stevie was like talking to him. He said: Don't take it personally, I just don't like telephones. I'd already figured that out.

It wasn't the best time of Johnny Martorano's life. He'd have preferred to be back in Boston. But overall things could have been worse. There were no really pressing life-and-death issues he had to deal with down in South Florida.

But then Brian Halloran shot a guy in the head in Chinatown.

11

The Last Hit

BRIAN HALLORAN KNEW he was in trouble one morning in September 1981 when he walked out of his apartment in Quincy and someone took a shot at him. He knew too much, and he knew he knew too much. About Louie Litif, about Roger Wheeler—about everything. So Halloran did what he always did, whatever his mood. He drank, and he drank some more, and then he snorted cocaine. This time, he didn't sober up.

A few weeks later, in the midst of his latest bender, "Balloonhead" found himself sitting in a restaurant in Chinatown after last call, with Frank Salemme's younger brother Jackie and a drug dealer named George Pappas. When Pappas got up from the booth to make a phone call, Halloran suddenly stood up himself. He pulled out a gun and shot Pappas in the head, killing him instantly. Salemme immediately dove under the table, and as the other customers scrambled for cover, Halloran calmly stood up and walked out of the restaurant, leaving behind his car keys and his trademark scally cap.

Now Halloran really would have to go. Somehow he made bail, and as soon as Brian Halloran hit the street, he started playing let's make a deal. Whitey knew he had to get to him before he started dropping names. There was no alternative. But at least Halloran had done Whitey a favor, by committing the murder in front of Salemme. Jackie Salemme was with In Town, and now he was going to be a witness for the prosecution. Jerry Angiulo, still on the street as the FBI transcribed the Dog House wiretaps, didn't need Jackie cross-examined in open court.

The Mafia's need to eliminate Halloran wasn't nearly as pressing as Whitey's, but now, with the help of his G-man amanuensis, Zip Connolly, Bulger could lay the groundwork for what he had to do. On October 2, 1981, Zip filed the first of his many reports about the impending death of Brian Halloran: "Source advised that the Mafia want Brian Halloran 'hit in the head' to shut him up as a potential witness."

Halloran, meanwhile, had started talking to the FBI.

STEVIE FLEMMI WAS having girlfriend problems. Things just weren't working out with Debbie Davis, the beautiful blonde Johnny Martorano had introduced him to after his return from Montreal in 1974.

Debbie took up with a Mexican, or at least that was Stevie's story later. If she did, she should have known better, because one young man she'd flirted with a few years earlier had ended up shot in the head, his body dumped in the Blue Hills.

One night Stevie took Debbie out to the Bay Tower Room, at the top of 60 State Street near Quincy Market. They were bickering, and when the maitre d' came over to whisper in Stevie's ear that Mr. Flemmi had a call, Debbie sneered and then asked him who he had to talk to. Stevie was so angry that he told her—it was Zip Connolly, he said, an FBI agent he and Jimmy Bulger did business with.

Debbie soon began telling people about Zip. When word reached Whitey, he was beyond angry. It got worse. On St.

Patrick's Day in 1981, Debbie Davis's jailbird brother Ronnie was stabbed to death at MCI-Walpole. When Stevie showed up at the Davis home, Debbie began screaming at him, in front of at least one of her siblings: "Use your FBI friends and find out who killed my brother!"

Debbie Davis didn't have long to live.

On September 17, 1981, Stevie made sure his parents were out of the new house he'd bought for them in Southie, next to Billy Bulger's. Then on some pretext, Stevie drove Debbie Davis to Southie, and got her onto the sunporch where he and Whitey now stored the gang's arsenal. According to Flemmi's later story to prosecutors, Whitey was waiting with a rope, and he jumped on top of Debbie Davis, strangling her as Stevie watched. Then they stripped off her clothes and cut off her fingertips to prevent identification. Stevie used a pair of pliers to pull out her teeth, to prevent any identification based on dental records. Finally, they wrapped her body in a large sheet of plastic.

Even after she was buried, toothless, Whitey was obsessed with Debbie Davis's teeth. He ordered Stevie to get her dental records, and Stevie assigned the task to George Kaufman, who lived in Brookline near her dentist. Somehow Kaufman got them and gave them to Stevie, who then burned the records—with Whitey watching.

As the years have gone by, the stories about the circumstances of Debbie Davis's death at the age of twenty-six have grown ever more lurid. In a wrongful-death trial against the U.S. government in 2009, a lawyer for the Davis family quoted from a deposition given by Stevie Flemmi. Flemmi testified that before he and Whitey strangled her, they had tied her to a chair with duct tape, and that as Whitey waited behind her with a rope, Stevie "pulled her back, gave her a kiss, and told her she was going to a better place."

Actually, she was going down to the Neponset River marshes. They buried her next to where they had dumped

Tommy King's body back in 1975. Stevie told her mother Olga that she had run off to Houston under an assumed name. Then he started crying, and Olga ended up consoling him.

I hear from George Kaufman, Debbie Davis is missing. So the next time I was talking to Stevie on the phone, I asked him where she was, if he knew what had happened to her. He says, she's gone, she won't be coming back. He said they'd had an argument,

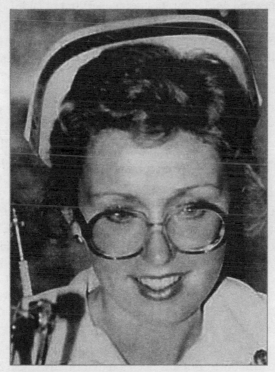

Catherine Greig, Whitey's dental-hygienist girlfriend,
who could have obtained a professional dental
tooth-extraction kit for Stevie to use
in later murders instead of pliers.

and he started strangling her, and it was an accident. I said, "How can an accident like that happen?" What a shame. What really happened I don't know, but later on he comes up with this other story for the cops about how Whitey was the one who strangled her. Who's going to contradict him? Debbie's not around anymore, and neither is Whitey.

What I do know is that Stevie had a tough time pulling her teeth with the pliers. So Whitey bought him a set of surgical dental tooth removers—probably had Catherine Greig get them, through the dental office she worked at. I guess it was kind of an inside joke between Whitey and Stevie, but from then on they did use the dental tools whenever they had to kill somebody and wanted the bodies to disappear. Stevie told me about it later.

BRIAN HALLORAN HAD sense enough not to go anywhere near the feds' organized-crime unit. He knew what Zip Connolly and John Morris were. Instead, he reached out to a couple of agents he knew from the labor-racketeering unit. He told them who had murdered Louie Litif—he was an eyewitness to that one.

Then there was Roger Wheeler. Callahan had told him about the Wheeler hit one night when they were out drinking at one of those Irish pubs in Quincy Market where they both spent so much time getting wasted. Halloran mentioned his earlier meeting with John Callahan and Whitey Bulger in the apartment above the Rusty Scupper. The agents from the labor-racketeering unit were impressed by the detail and consistency in Halloran's stories, and they started moving him from one safe house to another. But any decision to formally shield him, in the Witness Protection Program, was a decision that would have to be made by Jeremiah O'Sullivan, the head of the Justice Department's organized-crime task force.

He'd cut Whitey and Stevie out of the race-fixing indictment, and he'd kept them on as informants to protect them during the Dog House bugging. Now O'Sullivan did them yet another huge favor—he vetoed Halloran's entrance into the Witness Protection Program.

Of course, O'Sullivan could rationalize his decision. He was preoccupied with the pending Angiulo indictments. Halloran was a junkie charged with first-degree murder, who could provide only uncorroborated testimony. Still, everyone in the Boston FBI office knew exactly what cutting Halloran loose would mean.

Whitey dictated another report to Zip on April 23, 1982, saying, "The 'outfit' continues to be interested in having Halloran killed. Source advised that the 'outfit' consider Halloran to be a weak person and are concerned that he may make a deal with the DA's office to give up Salemme."

Among the honest FBI agents, there was shock over what was tantamount to a death sentence for Halloran. The U.S. attorney was William Weld, a future governor of Massachusetts. In federal court in 1997, Weld recalled what he was casually told by the number-two agent in the Boston office, Robert Fitzpatrick.

"You know, people always say there's a danger for this snitch or that snitch," Fitzpatrick had told Weld of Halloran's predicament. "I'm telling you, this guy—I would not want to be standing next to this guy."

THE GUY WHO was unfortunate enough to be standing next to Brian Halloran was named Michael Donahue. On the afternoon of May 11, 1982, Donahue was drinking with Halloran at the Pier, a barroom on Northern Avenue on the South Boston waterfront. Blocks away, Whitey was hanging out at the gang's new appliance store at F Street and West Broadway. It was simpler, moving hijacked appliances directly without having to worry about any fences, plus without a middleman the markup was higher.

There were never any complaints from the customers, several of whom were FBI agents, including Zip Connolly.

John Hurley, the Charlestown hood who'd fingered Indian Joe—and earlier the unlucky bartender Milano—dropped into the appliance store and mentioned casually that he'd just seen Brian Halloran drinking at the Pier. Hurley apparently had no idea what he was setting in motion, but Whitey immediately snapped to attention. Within an hour, he had Kevin Weeks stationed outside Jimmy's Harborside, across Northern Avenue from the Pier. Whitey arrived a few minutes later in a souped up blue Chevy that they called "the tow truck."

Among other things, the "tow truck" was outfitted with a specially built oil tank in the trunk. With the flick of a button under the steering wheel, Whitey could release enough oil from the tank onto the street to put any pursuing vehicle into a spin. Another button would release clouds of blue exhaust. The license plates were of course stolen. The hit car was usually stashed in a hidden garage in the Lower End, to be taken out only for tasks like this one.

By the time he was in the hit car, Whitey was wearing a brown Afro wig. In it, he looked a lot like Jimmy Flynn, another Winter Hill associate who was widely known to be feuding with Halloran.

In the backseat of the hit car was a second shooter Whitey had rounded up in Southie. Weeks later testified that the second man was wearing a ski mask, which no other witness ever mentioned, and which would have drawn attention on a sunny weekday afternoon in May. But by putting a ski mask on the second shooter, Weeks was relieved of the necessity of having to identify Whitey's backup. Later that would make it easier for him to return to South Boston after he served his brief prison sentence.

Whitey had given Weeks a walkie-talkie, and told him

that when Balloonhead left the bar, he should radio simply that "the balloon is in the air."

Halloran was getting a ride from his friend Donahue, a father of three sons. They both stumbled out of the bar, and Donahue walked across the street to retrieve his blue compact car. Weeks gave the signal as Donahue stopped in front of the bar to pick up Halloran. Just as Balloonhead got into the car, Whitey pulled up alongside Donahue's car.

"Brian," he yelled, and then he aimed his automatic carbine out the front window and began shooting at point-blank range. Mortally wounded, Donahue floored the car, and it lurched across the street, finally coming to a stop when it hit a building. Whitey pulled around and emptied the carbine into the car as Weeks sped off.

By the time the police arrived, Donahue was dead, and Halloran was going fast. The cops asked him who had shot him.

"Jimmy Flynn," he said, and then died.

THAT NIGHT, ZIP Connolly and John "Vino" Morris stopped by Whitey's condo to question him. Their question for him was, Do you have any beer? Whitey did, and plenty of it, good imported lager—Beck's. Weeks had already sawed up the gun and dumped the pieces off the Fore River bridge into Quincy Bay. The hit car was back in its garage. Vino mentioned that someone had gotten the number of the license plate. Whitey nodded and opened two more beers. Now he knew he'd have to get rid of the plates, and sooner rather than later.

After a while the two crooked FBI agents staggered out of the house.

"Thank God for Beck's beer," Whitey would say later. "Thank God for Beck's."

ONCE THE IMMEDIATE heat died down, Whitey decided to point some more fingers in the wrong direction.

First he and Zip made up a story that Charlestown wise-guys had heard that Halloran and his brother the state trooper "had met with Colonel O'Donovan"—another foe.

The next day Whitey floated a different trial balloon—maybe it was Jimmy Flynn and one of the Mullens who'd killed Donald Killeen, Weasel Mantville. Later Whitey named more Charlestown hoods, and invented a "backup van" with three more guys inside whom he didn't like. By July 7, it was all the fault of the state police because they "let the cat out of the bag."

ABOUT A MONTH after Halloran's murder, John Morris flew off to an FBI drug-training seminar in Glynco, Georgia. The married agent had a girlfriend in the office, Debbie Noseworthy, and he told her how much he wanted her to fly down—they could stay in his motel room, make it their own little love nest. The only problem was, he couldn't swing the airfare; his wife would be sure to notice an expenditure of that size.

One morning shortly after Morris left for the conference, Zip walked up to Debbie's desk in the FBI office and handed her an envelope he said came from her boyfriend. She opened it and saw ten $100 bills.

"Where did John get this?" she asked. He was always complaining about being broke.

"He's been saving it," Zip told her. "It was in his desk and he wanted me to give it to you to go down to visit him in Glynco."

John Morris was now officially on the payroll.

MEANWHILE, STEVIE CALLED Johnny Martorano in Florida and said he and Whitey needed to meet him in New York, face-to-face, at the usual place—the Marriott at LaGuardia. Richard Aucoin got there first, rented a room, and soon Whitey and Stevie arrived. It was a strictly business meeting. No refreshments were served. There was only one item on the agenda: John Callahan.

Whitey did all the talking. He was in his politician mode, making the case, point by point. He said, we killed Halloran for you; he was telling the FBI that you killed Wheeler. Zip told us. What Whitey didn't say was that Halloran had also named him and Stevie as being in on it. He also didn't tell me that they were the ones who approached Halloran first, to kill Wheeler, not me. They didn't tell me that Whitey was in the room when Callahan made the pitch to Halloran to kill Wheeler. Whitey also didn't tell me that Halloran was a witness to his murder of Louie Litif, which I had nothing to do with. Whitey was very selective with the facts, you might say, but what did I know? I'm on the lam. You're at a disadvantage in so many ways when you're a fugitive.

So Whitey goes on: the reason Halloran knew about how you killed Wheeler is because Callahan told him. Callahan! Your friend. Here's a guy you killed somebody for in Oklahoma, we all helped out. All he had to do was keep his mouth shut and we wouldn't be here today and Halloran and that other guy with him wouldn't be dead.

Whitey says, we told him—hell, Johnny, you told him, too—we told Callahan to stay away from that drunk asshole Halloran and keep out of those Irish pubs. Whitey was right about that, we did all warn Callahan to watch his step. Whitey was good at that kind of thing, mixing in facts with the lies. He was very effective.

Then he tells me, Zip says the feds want to talk to Callahan, so I'm asking you, Johnny, can you guarantee he'll stand up? I says, I don't think he'll talk, but I can't guarantee anything. Whitey says, well, if he does crack, Zip says we're all going to jail for the rest of our lives. At that point, I was convinced. It was clear Callahan had been talking, whether it was just to Halloran or to the FBI, I wasn't sure, but he had been talking about things he had no business talking about.

Whitey always knew what buttons to push with me, and this time he was pushing the rat button.

Finally, he asks me if I agree with them that Callahan has to go. What can I say? Callahan's my friend, but these guys are my partners. They're clever, they've proven they know how to handle the FBI, they're my lifeline with cash—one of my lifelines anyway. And they've already killed two guys to protect me, or so I think. I'm sick over the thought of my friend being killed, but I finally said okay. In for a penny, in for a pound.

So now Whitey says we need you to handle it, Johnny, down in Florida. There's too much heat on us right now back home. They'd already had to go in for mug shots that the FBI had sent down to Oklahoma—that was another one of those facts Whitey threw out there, which made the lies and evasions and half truths he was feeding me somewhat more believable.

Whitey's making the pitch, trying to close the deal, saying the cops in Boston are all over them, so it needs to be done somewhere else. Whitey tells me he's already been feeding stuff to Zip, trying to set it up so that when he gets hit, somebody else'll get the blame, Cubans, drug dealers. Again, he was telling the truth about that. I got a look at the reports later. But by now I am really distraught, that I actually have to kill this guy, my friend, who's been helping me out ever since I went on the lam. I mean, I reluctantly agreed to the hit, and I very reluctantly agreed to do it myself. Once I agreed, the meeting was over. No small talk. They left and I just sat there by myself, thinking. I always liked to take in a couple of shows when I was in the city, but not that day. I was sick at heart. I checked out immediately and caught the next plane back to Florida.

Johnny called Joe McDonald and they began planning. They'd take Callahan the next time he flew to Florida. By now there was a routine to Callahan's visits. Johnny was living in Fort Lauderdale at the time, so he would always pick Callahan up at the airport in Fort Lauderdale and then drive him to his condo in Plantation. They were planning to leave Callahan's body in the trunk of his own car, a Cadillac. But even though Callahan had given Johnny keys to both the car and the condo, Johnny couldn't pick him up in the Caddy, because Callahan might realize something was wrong. Johnny always met him in his own Dodge Ram conversion van.

So the hit would have to be done in the van. First Johnny and Joe laid down plastic rubber runners on the floor of the van. Johnny put beach towels on the captain's chairs, to soak up the blood. Rubber would have been less messy, but it would have been too obvious a tip-off. Then Johnny put more towels on the two back captain's chairs, and underneath the towel on the backseat on the passenger's side he placed a loaded .22, one of the guns left over from the Wheeler hit.

Then Johnny went to one of those downtown rent-a-stall garages in downtown Fort Lauderdale. He leased a double stall, with room for two cars. Then he drove to Callahan's condo in Plantation, picked up the Cadillac, and backed it into the garage.

On the day Callahan was to arrive, Johnny met Joe Mac at the garage and then they drove to the airport in separate vehicles, parking in the short-term garage. Joe Mac was watching the van while Johnny went inside the Delta terminal to meet Callahan. He'd caught the last flight of the evening out of Boston. It was about eleven o'clock on July 24, 1982.

He came off the plane and I picked up his suitcase and carried it back to the car. He got in the passenger side—it's my car, so I'm driving. I opened the back door to put his suitcase in, and that was when I picked up the .22 from under the blanket, reached around and shot him once, twice at the most, in the head. He slumped over, and I pushed him off the chair and onto the floor, where the rubber mat could catch any blood without it leaving a stain.

LAWYER: You didn't look into his eyes when you shot him in the head, did you?
MARTORANO: No.
LAWYER: Now sir, you just shot your friend in the head after a half-hour meeting with Mr. Bulger, who convinced you to kill your friend. How did you feel when you shot him in the head?
MARTORANO: I felt lousy.
LAWYER: You felt bad?
MARTORANO: I didn't want to kill a guy that I cared enough about to kill somebody for a year before.

Now we have to move the body into his own car, but the problem is, the garage is closed until 7 A.M., so Joe and I have to sit on my van all night. There's an all-night Albertson's supermarket right near the garage, so we drop the van in the parking lot there. But we have to keep an eye on it because if it gets stolen, I'm in big trouble. See, it's registered in my name— Richard Aucoin's name. It's not like the Indian Al hit, where we dumped the body in a boiler. That time it was a break for us that the car got stolen off the street. It confused everything for a while, which is usually what you want. But this time if they find the body in that car it can be traced right back to me. So Joe and I watched it all night from his car. I think we only left once, to get some coffee.

Next morning at seven, as soon as the garage opens, we're there. We leave Joe's car outside the garage, and back my van into the bay and close the garage doors and lock them. And that's when Joe thinks he hears something from Callahan, a moan or something. It was probably just some of those noises that bodies make sometimes after they're dead, but Joe didn't want to take any chances. He says, give me your gun, and he shoots Callahan a couple of more times, just to make sure he's dead.

Then we put his body in the trunk of the Cadillac. Joe took his watch and later on his way home he drove into Little Havana and stopped in a Cuban bar and left the watch in the men's room. We were hoping it would be found by a Cuban and then end up in a pawn shop on Eighth Street there. The cops are always checking the pawn shops, and if it ends up there, it backs up Whitey's story about Cubans. Joe also took his credit cards, and some papers from his suitcase and left everything in the bar there too, to make it look like a robbery.

Finally, we wiped the Caddy down, getting rid of any fingerprints. After it was clean I put on flesh-colored gloves to drive it down to the airport in Miami. I drove with the gloves on, except when I went through the tolls. The toll taker might not have noticed, but you can't take any chances. Joe followed me in his own car.

It was Whitey's idea for the body to be found. I

Johnny in his boat off Fort Lauderdale.

wanted to make him disappear. By then I had a twenty-eight-foot boat. I was living on the Intercoastal in Fort Lauderdale, at a place called The Pilot. I had my boat out back. All I would have had to do was take a nice day trip and get out far enough to dump him in the ocean. The sharks would have taken care of everything.

At Miami International Airport a couple of days later, the smell from the Cadillac became overpowering. Underneath the back of the car cops noticed a puddle from a gooey substance that was dripping out of the trunk.

Another gangland hit in the Sunshine State.

It made the papers, both in South Florida and in Boston. Patty read the stories. All Johnny told her was that perhaps it was time to hit the road again.

Back in Boston, Whitey and Stevie moved quickly.

Callahan had been involved in a number of business deals, and they went to as many of his partners as they could find. Callahan's business associates all got variations on the same theme: Callahan had died owing Whitey and Stevie money. In some cases, the partners turned over the keys to safe-deposit boxes. Whitey and Stevie even tried to shake down Callahan's widow, after expressing their condolences about John's unfortunate passing at the hands of those bloodthirsty Cubans.

> They grabbed a lot of dough. I think they may have even sent me a little, if I had any idea who they were shaking down. But if I didn't know about it, they didn't cut me in, and being right there in Boston, they had the ability to find out a lot more than I did.
> Later on, after I got back to Boston, I ran into one of Callahan's business partners who I'd known casually before I left. He told me Whitey and Stevie stole a half million off him. He said he'd always regretted not standing up to them, not throwing Whitey out of his office when Whitey came looking for dough. He said he could tell Whitey was lying, that Callahan didn't owe Whitey and Stevie a dime. I told the guy, you absolutely did the right thing, giving up the money, not going to the cops. He would have just gotten himself killed, trying to stand up to those guys. They had all the juice back then.

A few months later, Joe Mac called Johnny. He had one question: Was the jai-alai deal dead? He wanted Johnny to put the question directly to H. Paul Rico. Johnny had never met Rico, so he got Stevie to arrange a meeting. A few days later, Stevie flew down to Miami with one of his off-and-on girlfriends, an Italian woman named Janey. She'd been out of the picture during Stevie's Debbie

Davis period, but now she was back in the mix. Stevie left
Janey at the hotel and he and Johnny drove to the fronton
in Miami.

> Now, I'm not too crazy about going in there, you fol-
> low me? I mean, I know Joe isn't sending me into a
> trap, but Rico's FBI, or was, and he's hired all these
> other agents to work the fronton, to keep guys like me
> out, supposedly. But I gotta find out from the horse's
> mouth; I promised Joe. So we walk in there, me and
> Stevie, and we take the elevator up to this private
> dining room area. It's for high rollers; they got the
> betting windows right there. Stevie introduces me to
> Rico, we shake hands, sit down, and I say, "Joe
> wanted to ask you, is anything happening on the
> deal?" And he says, "Nothing's doing yet." And I
> said, "That's all I needed to know." I stood up and
> said to Stevie, "I'll be waiting for you outside. Take
> as long as you want." And then I said, "Nice meeting
> you, Mr. Rico."
>
> About five minutes later, Stevie comes out and we
> leave, walking very casually. I know he's got all
> these FBI agents there, but no one's making a move
> to collar me. And then I knew, I mean I really under-
> stood for the first time, that all the rumors about
> Rico were true.

In Boston, Whitey and Stevie kept busy. A bold group of
thieves, including several corrupt police officers, had broken in the Depositors Trust Bank in Medford on Memorial
Day weekend 1980, cleaning out hundreds of safe-deposit
boxes, including some that belonged to organized-crime
figures, including one of the Angiulo brothers.

Whitey and Stevie began an investigation of their own,
by kidnapping a guy out of a Charlestown bar whom they
suspected of being involved. He quickly gave up the name

of the architect of the multimillion-dollar burglary—a criminal jack-of-all-trades named Bucky Barrett. But the Depositors Trust crew also had clout—Bucky was tight with Frankie Salemme, who was still in state prison for the Fitzgerald bombing. When Salemme told him that he'd ripped off some guys from In Town, Bucky did the right thing and returned their loot. Cadillac Frank told Barrett not to worry about Whitey and Stevie.

"Jackals," he said, when Barrett visited him at MCI-Norfolk. "That's all those two are—jackals."

Whitey and Stevie had to lay off for a while, but they had long memories. In 1983, they had one of their minions dangle the lure of cheap, stolen diamonds in front of Bucky, and he walked into a trap in Southie. Soon Whitey and Stevie had him tied to a chair in the kitchen of a house belonging to a relative of one of the gang members.

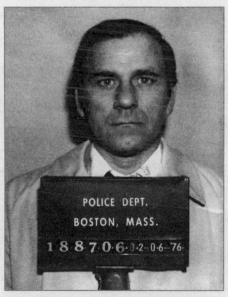

Bucky Barrett, murdered by Whitey in 1983.

They wanted all of the Depositors Trust loot, but Bucky told them a lot of it had been returned to the Angiulos. He offered them $60,000 that he had hidden under the refrigerator in his home. They gave him a phone and he told his wife to turn off the burglar alarm and to then leave the house. Whitey then sent a guy to Bucky's house to get the cash. Meanwhile, Barrett called a bar in Quincy Market and told somebody that he was sending a guy down in a cab to pick up $10,000 cash. Then he phoned a couple of other Charlestown hoodlums and asked them if they could help him out. They turned him down flat. Finally, Whitey told Bucky Barrett it was time to go into the basement.

He walked slowly down the stairs, Whitey following him, holding in his hand a Mac10 machine gun equipped with a silencer. Whitey put it to Bucky's head and pulled the trigger. Stevie then used his new dental kit to pull most of Bucky's teeth.

Some of the gang members dug a grave in the basement, and then Stevie's man, Phil Costa, arrived with quicklime, to make the body decompose faster. They spread a layer at

Phil Costa, the Flemmi associate who provided quicklime to hasten the decomposition of Barrett's body.

the bottom of the grave, threw the body in, and then poured what was left of the quicklime on top of the body.

The Barrett family never recovered from Bucky's disappearance. Over the next decade, two of his sons would commit suicide in the exact same way—by hurling themselves in front of Red Line trains.

STEVIE WAS HAVING more girlfriend problems, this time with Marion Hussey's daughter, Deborah, with whom Stevie had been having sex since she was thirteen. As she grew older, Deb Hussey had become a drug addict.

Marion Hussey, Stevie's common-law wife,
leaving court in 2009.

Stevie got her a job as a bar waitress in a rough organized-crime hangout on Geneva Avenue in Dorchester, and soon she was turning tricks.

In yet another wrongful-death lawsuit against the federal government in 2009, Marion Hussey testified how one day in 1982, she returned home from her job at a bank to find Stevie beating up Deborah. As Flemmi put it in a 2005 deposition, "She was doing a lot of things I didn't approve of." Marion Hussey described what happened next.

"I said to him, 'You've got to get her out of here.' That's when she said something about blowing him. She said, 'I've been doing it for years.'"

Marion Hussey threw Stevie out of the house he had bought for her. Stevie was irate, and there was a new number one with a bullet on the Hit Parade. She was twenty-four years old—the same age as Deb Davis when she was garroted.

Offering to buy her a new coat, Stevie lured Deb to the same house in Southie where they had killed Bucky Barrett. Whitey jumped her with a rope, breaking five of her ribs as he strangled her. This time Stevie helped out, grabbing one end of the rope as Whitey pulled the other end. After his stepdaughter was dead, Stevie again put his new dental kit to good use. Then they had one of their younger gang members, Kevin Weeks, dig another hole in the basement.

When Marion Hussey began asking questions about what had happened to her daughter, Stevie shrugged. He said he had no idea, but that he'd ask around.

A COUPLE OF years later, one of Marion's sons by Stevie was hospitalized after a bad head-on car accident. Stevie, who had never reconciled with Marion, showed up at the hospital. In court Marion Hussey described what happened next.

"We were arguing, because that's what we did," she

said. "I went outside to have a cigarette and he came after me. I said to him, 'You killed my daughter.' He was taken aback. He was in shock. He grabbed a pole, knees bent. He said, 'How could you?' "

In his 2005 deposition, Stevie admitted that he had had Deb Hussey murdered. But, he insisted, there were "extenuating circumstances." He did not elaborate.

Marion was awarded $300,000 from the U.S. government for the murder of her daughter by the FBI's two Top Echelon informants in Boston.

WHITEY AND STEVIE were shaking down drug dealers now, too. Stevie testified later that he and Whitey once got $5 million for "protecting" a single load. "Protection" mostly meant not tipping off their favorite cops.

Joe Murray was a career Charlestown criminal who

Kevin Weeks dug graves for Whitey's victims.

had gotten into large-scale marijuana smuggling. Bucky Barrett had been in his crew. Murray was storing tons of weed in a warehouse in the Lower End, and that was where he got a call from Whitey one day. Whitey told him he'd just gotten a tip that the cops were on their way to Murray's warehouse with a search warrant and that he'd better clear out pronto.

Whitey's tip, of course, turned out to be right on the money. A few days later, Bulger reached out to Joe Murray, telling him he wished he'd known that so much pot was being stored in the Town, because he might have been able to prevent the police raid altogether. Joe Murray took the hint; he had a new partner. The police raids ceased immediately.

Meanwhile, though, Whitey continued to feed Zip Connolly information about his new associate. He mentioned Joe Murray's barroom in Sullivan Square, the Celtic Tavern—"a sort of clubhouse for organized crime," as Whitey described it. In other words, it was a lot like Triple O's in South Boston. Whitey said Murray was "one of the best-kept secrets in organized crime." He could have said the same about himself, given the blackout the papers had given him since his threats against the reporter from the *Herald American*.

WHITEY DECIDED HE wanted to help the Irish Republican Army. After all, they generated a lot of cash from their sympathizers in the United States. All the gin mills in Southie and Charlestown and Brighton had clear jars on their bars next to the Slim Jims and the hard-boiled eggs, into which their patrons could drop their change for the cause of Irish freedom, or something. Whitey smelled a score, and put together seven tons of ordnance, as well as some bulletproof vests from the Boston Police Department, one of which was donated by Stevie's younger brother Michael, a Boston cop who worked as a crime-scene photographer. Joe Murray was in charge of shipping the arsenal across the Atlantic.

In Gloucester, the weapons were loaded onto a seventy-seven-foot fishing vessel, the *Valhalla*. Off the coast of Ireland, they were offloaded onto a smaller fishing boat, the *Marita Ann*. Pat Nee, who unlike the others really did care about his native Eire, was there to watch out for the gang's interests, along with a couple of lesser Southie thugs.

But the garda got a tip, and the Irish Navy stopped the ship. When the *Valhalla* returned to port, it, too, was seized. Whitey was livid; he suspected somebody had ratted him out. Eventually, his suspicions settled on one of Joe Murray's gang, a crewman from Quincy named John McIntyre.

After being arrested on a minor domestic charge, McIntyre began opening up to the Quincy police, and then to the DEA. He told them of his disdain for Whitey and the Southie gangsters who'd been on the *Valhalla*—"they got the Adidas jump suits, and they ain't got a speck of dirt on them. Every day they take two, three showers."

Still, he refused to mention Whitey and Stevie by name. Instead he referred to them only as "the two guys who ride around together."

Next, McIntyre told them about a drug ship, the *Ramsland*, that was headed to Boston carrying thirty-six tons of marijuana. Stevie testified later that he and Whitey's projected cut from their "protection" of *Ramsland* was to have been "about a million."

The *Ramsland* bust was handled by the DEA, and as a departmental courtesy, the DEA revealed the identity of the informant to the FBI. That was all Whitey needed to know. On November 30, 1984, another of the *Valhalla* crew members, a Southie guy, invited McIntyre to a party at the same house where Bucky Barrett and Deb Hussey had recently been murdered and interred.

The Southie guy dropped McIntyre off at the house,

and he walked in carrying a case of cold beer, expecting a good time. Instead, he found Whitey Bulger waiting for him. They took him down to the basement and tied him to a chair. Whitey tried to throttle him with a rope, but it was too thick and he couldn't finish the job. He then picked up a revolver and asked McIntyre if he wanted to be shot in the head.

"Yes, please," said McIntyre.

Sixteen months later, Joe Murray and Pat Nee were indicted for gunrunning. So was the late John McIntyre.

THE EXTORTIONS CONTINUED. A local contractor got into a beef over a fence with Kevin Weeks. Whitey Bulger summoned him to Southie and shook him down for $200,000. A real-estate agent was brought to Triple O's and ordered to come up with $50,000. He went to the FBI, and Whitey sent word to him to forget about it.

There was another Southie guy Whitey heard about who'd moved to New York and made a fortune in penny-stock boiler-room operations. That sounded shady enough for Whitey to decide that it was time to pull another Bucky Barrett the next time this guy came back to Boston for a visit. He had to have a lot of cash, right?

Another gang member called up the boiler-room guy in New York and asked him if he'd like to have dinner with the gangster who was becoming a legend in his own time—and mind. The penny-stock hustler was looking forward to the get-together until he got a frantic call from a different gang member he was acquainted with. The second gangster warned him that if he hooked up with Whitey, it might be his last supper. The boiler-room guy never set foot in the city again until 1995, when Whitey was safely gone.

An enterprising young Southie businessman named Stippo Rakes started up a new liquor store with ample parking on Old Colony Avenue, in between two large housing projects. Just as the store opened in December 1983, Whitey and Stevie paid a visit to his apartment. Stevie put a revolver on his kitchen table and picked up Stippo's two-year-old daughter and told him, "It'd be a shame if she had to grow up without a father."

Stippo sold them the liquor store for $60,000, then fled to Disney World with his family for a long vacation. When rumors began circulating that Whitey had killed Stippo, Bulger ordered him to return to Boston. He and Whitey spent hours standing at major intersections in Southie, waving to passing motorists, to prove that unlike so many others who had crossed Whitey, Stippo was still alive.

Two months later, Stippo's wife mentioned to her uncle, a Boston cop, what had happened. Within hours, Whitey was back in Rakes's apartment, accusing him of going to the cops.

"Bad fuckin' move," Whitey told him. Eventually, Stippo was able to convince Whitey he would never, ever think of going to any cops, especially his wife's uncle, who a few years later would be sentenced in federal court to six months for aiding two illegal gambling businesses.

Soon, business was booming at Whitey's liquor store. A large green shamrock was painted onto the front outside wall of the store. During election season, candidates jockeyed to get their signs prominently displayed in the South Boston Liquor Mart's front window. Having one that was visible from the traffic rotary represented an unspoken endorsement from the Bulgers. Every Christmas, agents from the Boston FBI office would stop by the Liquor Mart to pick up the booze for the office holiday party. Whitey made sure the G-men got the "professional discount."

As for Stippo, his career as a businessman was over. He took $3,000 of Whitey's money that was left and obtained a job for himself at the MBTA, the Massachusetts

South Boston Liquor Mart in the late 1980s.

Bay Transportation Authority, or, as the politicians at Billy Bulger's St. Patrick's Day roast always called it, "Mr. Bulger's Transportation Authority." Years later, when Stippo was called before a federal grand jury to testify about what Whitey and Stevie had done to him, he denied everything. He was indicted for perjury.

> The real criminal enterprise here was these four guys—Whitey, Stevie, Zip, and Rico. If you crossed them you got robbed, or whacked, or put in a hole or sent to jail so somebody could get a feather in their cap.
> Just to name a few examples, they robbed Stippo, they put my brother and Pat Nee in jail, the two Debbies ended up in a hole, and poor Bucky—he got robbed, killed, and put in a hole. Bucky hit for all three—he was a quinella.

Johnny's old gang was being thinned out, one way or another. Joe McDonald's Florida friend was arrested on drug charges in 1983, and Joe decided to return to Boston. He took the train north, with three Uzis in his luggage. When the train got to Penn Station, the FBI was waiting for him.

> I don't know who tipped them. Maybe Whitey, but I'm more inclined to believe it was the guy in Florida. He was in a jam, and remember, Joe was still on the FBI Ten Most Wanted List. That's a good catch. As for the guns, some people say he was planning to get 'em to the IRA. Hey, if it makes Joe look good, that's the story I'll go with, too. I have no idea.

Jimmy Sims was the next to be picked up. The feds caught up with him in Key West, where he'd been hiding out for years. He had family down there, and had been working as a commercial fisherman. He was brought back to Boston with all the charges against him consolidated.

One day in January 1983, he pleaded guilty in federal court to the race-fixing counts. The next morning, he was in Suffolk Superior Court to take the fall on various gambling and gun charges and even a few minor traffic violations, including running a red light on Columbus Avenue in the South End. He got four years total, to be served in state prison.

As Sims was taken from the courtroom in handcuffs, he asked the guards, "Do they have televisions in Walpole?"

JERRY ANGIULO WAS having dinner at Francesco's on North Washington Street on September 19, 1983, when FBI agents arrived to arrest him. As he was led away in handcuffs, he shouted back at the other patrons, "I'll be back before my pork chops get cold."

He wouldn't see the street again until 2007. In Town was on its way out. As for "the Man," Raymond L. S. Patriarca, he died of a heart attack in 1983 at age seventy-five while getting a blow job, at least according to underworld lore.

•   •   •

H. PAUL RICO was staying busy. Alcee Hastings was the first black federal judge in Florida, appointed by President Jimmy Carter. It quickly became apparent that he was utterly corrupt, and soon the FBI realized they had a perfect opportunity to take him down.

Santo Trafficante, the Mafia boss of Tampa, was coming up for sentencing in front of Hastings. What if the FBI could get an undercover agent masquerading as a mobster close enough to Hastings, or his bagman, to obtain enough evidence to indict him?

The only question was, did the FBI have an agent who could pass himself off as a top-level gangster? It didn't take long for the feds to come up with a perfect match— retired agent H. Paul Rico. Rico "pretended" to be a gangster, an emissary from Trafficante, and soon had more than enough evidence to end Hastings's squalid career on the bench.

Hastings was indicted, but a predominantly black jury in Miami refused to convict. However, he was then impeached in the U.S. House and convicted in a Senate trial. Hastings was removed from the federal bench, but in 1992 was elected to the U.S. House of Representatives from a majority-black district in South Florida. According to his Congressional website, Hastings is still known to many as 'Judge.'"

Special Agent Rico, meanwhile, was flown to Washington to testify before a Senate committee, which presented him with a commendation for his years of selfless service to the people of the United States of America.

COCAINE WAS EXTRACTING a fearful toll on Johnny's old friends back in Boston. Nicky Femia had been in the old Barboza crew. After the breakup of the old Winter Hill Gang, Whitey had brought him aboard as hired muscle. But Whitey couldn't abide his drug use, and later fired him.

By October 1983, Femia had graduated to heroin, and he tried to hold up an auto-body shop, of all things, in East Boston. Holding a gun on the owner, he was staring off into the distance, yelling at someone who wasn't there. That gave the shop owner long enough to grab his own gun and kill Nicky Femia.

Sid Tildsley was a Somerville associate of the old gang. He ran the Broadway barroom around the corner from the Marshall Street garage, known over the years by various names, among them the Peppermint Lounge, Pal Jocy's, and finally El Sid's. Tildsley was a runner for the gang during the race-fixing days, as was another Somerville guy named Bobby Duda. Both of them pleaded guilty and did short bits.

After Duda was released from prison, he got heavily into cocaine. One night he and Tildsley were drinking in a bar in Union Square when suddenly Duda pulled out a gun and shot Tildsley between the eyes. A few days later, Duda's body was found in a cheap motel room outside New York City. He had hanged himself.

Weasel Mantville, the old Mullen gang member whom Whitey had tried to blame for the Halloran hit, followed Femia's footsteps in graduating from cocaine to heroin. Soon he, too, was dead. Now Whitey could blame Weasel for anything.

The Campbell brothers also went down in 1983, on various gun and drug charges. Inside Alvin Campbell's suburban Boston home, cops found a veritable library of books and videotapes about organized crime. They also discovered clips about one murder in particular—that of Roger Wheeler in Tulsa, Oklahoma, in 1981. If the cops were still baffled by the slaying, Alvin Campbell certainly wasn't.

JOHNNY HEARD ABOUT all of this secondhand, sometimes from Stevie, but more often from George Kaufman.

Johnny had his own headaches, trying to support his various families. As the (absentee) father of the brides, he picked up the tabs for the weddings of Jeannie and Lisa. His son Vincent was attending a private high school in Beverly. Over four years, the tuition cost Johnny $100,000. He also had the monthly payments on the two mortgages on the houses in Medford and Chestnut Hill.

> I was in and out of the sports gambling business all those years. Basically I was bankrolling different guys. George handled most of it for me. He lived on Kent Street off Beacon in Brookline. I would call him at home and tell him to "meet" me in five minutes. That meant he would go to the phone booth by the 1200, and I'd call him there.
>
> I'd lend guys money, too. When Jimmy Sims got out of prison around '87, he wanted to get back into the sports gambling business. I got him $15,000. Then he disappeared. To this day nobody knows what happened to him. That's one murder nobody has ever confessed to.

After the Callahan hit, Johnny and Patty had gone on the road for about six months before settling down again in Pompano Beach in 1983. Johnny had met a car dealer named Jeff Jenkins, who quickly became one of his best friends.

But Johnny and Patty weren't settled in their new digs in Pompano Beach long before Stevie called with an urgent message from Whitey. Johnny had been spotted in a bar, and the report had gotten back to the FBI office in Boston. Zip just wanted to make sure that Johnny knew he had to hit the road again, and that he would be needing new IDs.

> That's one of the counts the feds got Zip on in the Boston trial, tipping me to the sighting. After that

Richard Aucoin was no more. I became "Vincent Rancourt." It was a name from a Canadian driver's license. I think I found it on Hillsborough Beach one day, in a wallet somebody lost. There were always a lot of Canadians on that beach. The good thing about the license was, there was no photo on it, so I could switch it down to Florida no problem.

In 1983, a city councilor from South Boston named Ray Flynn was elected mayor of Boston. Billy Bulger had briefly considered running himself, but even in the city he was distinctly unpopular, at least outside of Southie.

After Flynn's election, he was approached by Senate President Bulger. A former state legislator himself, Flynn knew how much he needed a powerful ally at the State House, to assure a steady stream of local aid to city coffers, and to make sure that any legislation City Hall needed would not be bottled up in committee or killed.

Billy sat down with Flynn, whom he had never much liked, considering him a publicity hound. But Billy said he was willing to let bygones be bygones, if only for the sake of the city. All he had was one small favor to ask of the new mayor.

Would the new mayor appoint Zip Connolly police commissioner?

Flynn recoiled. He was, after all, from Southie. He knew who Zip was, and what he was. He turned Bulger down flat, and instead gave the coveted job to another Southie native, a guy named Mickey Roache, whose brother Whitey and Billy O'Sullivan had shot and paralyzed in the Colonial Lounge on West Broadway back in 1971.

Billy Bulger never forgave Ray Flynn. His legislation was always hamstrung at the State House, and he became a butt of endless jokes every year at the St. Patrick's Day breakfast.

•   •   •

LEAVING POMPANO BEACH, Johnny and Patty hit the road in one of Johnny's mobile homes. In 1985 they settled down again at tennis great Rod Laver's development in Delray Beach. Then Patty got pregnant, and Johnny figured it would be better if she went home to Somerville and stuck close to Loretta until the baby was born.

Jimmy was born at St. Elizabeth's in Brighton. I called Stevie and told him to ask Whitey if he'd mind being Jimmy's godfather. Whitey said sure. Stevie and Whitey both went to the christening; it was at St. Anne's in Somerville. They sat in the back, didn't say anything. From then on, every Christmas Whitey would send Jimmy a $20 gold coin. He never saw Jimmy, but Whitey always sent him that gold coin every year.

After Jimmy was born, Johnny drove his mobile home north to New Jersey. There was a trailer park on the Jersey side of the Lincoln Tunnel where he always stayed when he came to the city. He told Patty to fly down to New York with the baby. He'd pick her up, and then they'd drive back to Florida together.

But when I picked them up and drove back to Jersey, Jimmy was just crying and crying and crying. He wouldn't stop. It got so bad we figured something had to be wrong. We finally took him to a hospital in Jersey City. They knew right away—they did a spinal tap. It was spinal meningitis. But they didn't have a trauma unit, so they wanted to send him to a bigger hospital, Bergen something-or-other.

Thank God I had a lot of cash with me, because of course I didn't have any health insurance. I had to pay cash for the ambulance, and then when we get to the hospital, we realize it's in a tough, tough neigh-

borhood. The hospital staff told us, don't wear any
gold in here or somebody might stick you up in the
stairwells. That was a problem because you had to
use the stairs. The elevators weren't going all the way
up, and they had Jimmy on the eleventh floor. The
security was so bad I was concerned Jimmy might
get snatched.

I talked to this Indian doctor who ran the unit,
and I convinced him to combine two single rooms,
so Patty and I could stay with Jimmy, on shifts, just
to make sure nothing happened to him. Plus I was
paying nurses cash—$100 per shift.

It was tough, watching a little baby that sick. And
I was concerned about Patty, too. She was frantic. I
was afraid she'd climb up on the roof and just jump
off.

We were there in that hospital for a couple of
weeks, and I'm telling you, the whole experience
made me realize what I'd missed with my other kids.
That's when I turned into "Mr. Mom." When I was
sentenced, that's what some of my neighbors in Boca
called me in their letters to the judge. Mr. Mom. After
Jimmy almost died, I wanted to spend as much time
with the kids as possible.

Back in Florida, Johnny and Patty decided to settle down
as best they could, considering their circumstances.
Johnny asked Jeff Jenkins if he knew of any houses for
sale. Jenkins told him that one of his neighbors in Boca
Raton had a brand-new house that he was looking to
unload.

But of course there was that old problem—I couldn't
own anything in my own name. I'd always told Jenkins I was a gambler. That's what I always told people I met in Florida if they asked me. Later on, I

Johnny with his son Jimmy at Disney World, late 1980s.

started saying that I was "retired." Hey, it was true in both cases, wasn't it? I also said I had ex-wives coming after me, looking to put attachments on anything I owned. So I asked Jenkins if he would mind holding the title to the house in his name. We were "partners."

In Boston, Whitey was becoming a legend. Gullible columnists for the *Globe* chronicled his supposed selfless exploits, giving money to priests, reducing street crime, and, most important, "keeping the drugs out of Southie," a phrase that was repeated over and over again. At the *Globe,* it became practically verboten to say anything negative about the gangster with the alleged heart of gold.

Always tight with a buck—Frankie Salemme referred to him as a "squirrel"—suddenly Whitey was flush with his new drug money. Whitey began smuggling cash out of the country. One time, he was stopped at the security gate at Logan Airport's international terminal as he tried to slip $100,000 cash through security onto a Montreal flight.

Whitey grabbed the satchel, took off running, and threw it to a guy he called "Kevin"—probably Kevin Weeks—who escaped. Whitey then found himself in a loud confrontation with a state trooper named Billy Johnson, a Vietnam vet. Johnson wrote up a report and forgot about it until the next day, when the executive director of the airport, a Dukakis appointee named Dave Davis, showed up at F Troop barracks and demanded that Johnson hand over any and all copies of the embarrassing report about the senate president's brother.

Johnson refused, and within days was stripped of his coveted Logan airport assignment. He would later commit suicide.

WHITEY'S LIQUOR STORE, the South Boston Liquor Mart, wasn't far from the *Globe* building on Morrissey Boulevard with the plate-glass windows that Whitey had once shot out during busing.

One morning a *Globe* photographer was driving north toward downtown when he noticed a city work crew outside Whitey's liquor store. They were installing parking curbs. Amazed, the photographer doubled back around, parked his car on a side street, and then shot a series of damning photographs showing city workers on city time doing a job for . . . Whitey Bulger.

Excited, the photographer returned to the *Globe,* quickly developed the shots, and turned the prints in to the photo desk. He expected them to run in the next day's paper—probably on the front page. But nothing happened. The blue-bloods at the *Globe* had their own code of omerta when it came to Whitey. The days went by and the photos never appeared.

A few weeks later, the photographer bumped into an honest FBI agent he knew. He gave him an extra set of the South Boston Liquor Mart photos that he had in his car, and the agent, as excited as the photographer had been, quickly returned to the FBI offices and showed off the photos . . . to John Morris. Morris quickly summoned Zip Connolly for a crisis meeting.

The next morning, the *Globe* photographer was again driving by the South Boston Liquor Mart when he noticed a new work crew in the parking lot. It was from a private company, and it was removing the curbs that the city crew had installed a few weeks earlier.

During one of the later trials, Kevin Weeks was asked how it was possible that for twenty years someone like Whitey Bulger could get away with committing so many crimes, up to and including murder? How, the prosecutor inquired, could such a scandal ever occur in America?

"We weren't in America," Weeks replied. "We were in Boston."

THERE WAS JUST too much money in drugs, especially cocaine, to settle for a mere "protection" racket. Soon Whitey and Stevie were setting up their own networks of dealers. Eventually there would be four "rings" in Southie, all controlled by Whitey, at arm's length of course. If he wouldn't talk to Johnny Martorano, he certainly wasn't going to issue orders directly to some junkie out of the projects.

Almost all of Whitey's dealers ended up on some public payroll or another. Some had two public-sector jobs, one on the day shift, where they were never seen except on pay day, and another on the overnight shift, which they would sleep through. Jobs on the MBTA were particularly prized—and costly to obtain. Not only did a T job mean you had a reason to be in various stations, where dealing drugs was easy, but the perks of a T job also included retirement on a full pension with full health benefits after only twenty-three years. Or you could just buy a job and immediately "take a fall" and go out on full disability. That only provided 72 percent of an employee's final salary, but it was tax free.

Soon, on federal wiretaps, agents would hear Whitey's cocaine dealers calmly discussing which option was preferable, the immediate phony disability pension at 72 percent, or a twenty-three-year no-show job with 80 percent at the end. The feds soon noticed the astonishing numbers of able-bodied younger and middle-aged men loitering on Castle Island in Southie during the warm-weather months. Why weren't they working? the agents would ask one another, until they realized most of them were "retired" from hack public-sector jobs.

Shocked by the sudden rise in cocaine use in Southie, in 1987 the DEA made a run at Whitey. They put a bug into the driver's-side door of his new Chevrolet Caprice. The quality of the audio wasn't great, but they did pick up snippets of him dismissing his old mob—"there is no Winter Hill Gang," he said.

It was the same thing Whitey was telling Zip. Howie Winter had just been paroled, and Whitey dismissed his old partner as "strictly a leftfielder" who expected to be paid for "protection" he couldn't deliver—a complaint many of Whitey's drug dealers would later make about their boss, not too loudly of course. On the DEA tapes, Whitey also complained about having to continue to send money south to Johnny Martorano.

LAWYER: Do you remember about how much money it was that you would receive every month?

MARTORANO: It was always different. Whatever I needed.

LAWYER: Was it like $500 a month or $700 a month?

MARTORANO: Probably ten thousand a month.

LAWYER: And did it remain a constant amount or
   did it fluctuate?
MARTORANO: It kept going down.

I had no control over anything. It was tough still being on the lam. The other guys had done their time
and were out. Even Joe Mac didn't get a long sentence. See, my theory was proven correct—if you
stay out for a while, they'll always cut you a deal for
less time. But for me, something was always coming
up; I was still out there. I always said, I did sixteen
years, one year at a time. I couldn't afford to go to
prison, even for a couple of years, because I had all
my families to support. Sometimes I'd want to turn
myself in, and Whitey and Stevie would say, oh no,
it's a bad time. Bad time for them, they meant—they
needed me out there, to keep the Mafia at bay. Then
they'd say, maybe you can come in—that's when
they were tired of sending me money. But I'd have
all these bills to keep paying, so I just stayed out.
They were getting rich, and I was getting poor.
   I never really understood how much money they
were making in drugs until one time Stevie was
down in Florida on vacation. We went to the Boca
Mall, and we were in this specialty shop where they
had these ceramic bulls by the Mexican artist Sergio
Bustamante. It was the kind of thing Stevie liked,
and it was his birthday or something, so I pointed at
one of the smaller Bustamante bulls, it was worth
about a grand or $1,500. I was thinking of getting it
for him, so I asked him if he liked it. He said yeah,
it's okay, but there's a much bigger one, which goes
for about 10 grand. He said Whitey had given that
big one to him—the one that went for 10 grand. At
first I was kind of embarrassed, that I'd been thinking of getting him the smaller one. But then I

started thinking—10 grand? For a ceramic bull? For a guy?

LAWYER: Later you learned that their business kept growing and growing, isn't that right? You learned they cheated you, in effect, right?

MARTORANO: Sure, but that's not my reason for being here because I could care less. I was happy with whatever I was getting.

LAWYER: Whatever you got, you still were upset with Mr. Flemmi for getting you less than you thought you should get, right?

MARTORANO: I was a fugitive. Whatever I got I was thankful for.

LAWYER: Well, didn't you have an agreement with Mr. Flemmi that he would share a certain amount of profits, correct?

MARTORANO: Yeah, but those agreements don't usually last after you're a fugitive.

LAWYER: You were never told by Mr. Flemmi that the Winter Hill Group was collecting money from extortions, isn't that right?

MARTORANO: He told me that they were ripping off drug dealers, not setting them up.

In Boston, the DEA was still trying to figure out how to improve the reception on their $50,000 state-of-the-art bug in Whitey's car when they suddenly heard him and some of the others trying to rip it out of the car. The agents quickly rushed down to the South Boston Liquor Mart to retrieve it.

Whitey and Stevie were very gracious to the cops. Stevie suggested if they needed information from anyone, just let them know "and we can wrap a rope around their necks." He didn't mention their expertise in wrapping ropes around people's necks, especially girlfriends.

"We're all good guys here," Whitey amiably explained to the DEA agents. "You're the good good guys and we're the good bad guys."

Every Christmas, the payoffs to the local constabulary escalated. Looking the other way for Whitey and Stevie was turning into a cottage industry for bent cops in Boston. One Christmas Eve, Whitey was sitting at a table in the back of the South Boston Liquor Mart, counting out cash from a huge wad and placing the large bills into envelopes that would be going out that evening.

He looked up at one of his gunsels and smiled.

"Christmas is for cops and kids."

GEORGE KAUFMAN TOLD Johnny about a younger guy, a kid from "the Lake" in Newton named Joe Yerardi— Joey Y, they called him. A tough kid, George said, good with his hands. He was doing some collection work for Chico Krantz, one of the Jewish bookies who paid "protection" to Whitey and Stevie. George was the liaison to the Jewish crowd, which was how he met Joey Y. Joey Y had another link to Johnny—he was working with the ex–Medford cop that Johnny had rented an apartment from when he first went on the lam.

> George said to me that if I had 50 grand I could spare that Joey could use it. He'd been borrowing money from Stevie, and from George, so they just took my 50, settled up with him, and from then on Joey Y was my guy. I just kept giving him more and more—he could always keep up the vig, a point a week. At the end he owed me $365,000—that's almost $4,000 a week in interest he was paying me. Of course by then he couldn't pay. He wasn't a bad guy, just a lousy businessman. If you're gonna be a shylock, you have to have an instinct about who you can lend money to, and who to stay away from. It's not

Joey Yerardi, Newton hoodlum,
borrowed $365,000 from Johnny.

that much different than a bank, except the interest rates are higher.

At one point, I spoke to Stevie, and I told him, I didn't mean to steal your guy. If you ever want any of this action, just let me know. But he wasn't interested. I wonder now if he knew even then that the feds were keeping an eye on Joey Y.

Anyway, I did get to know Joey Y fairly well as time went by, and I invited him and his family down to Orlando to meet me and Patty and Jimmy at Disney World. We used to stay at the Contemporary. And I meet his wife, this Iranian woman who acts like she's a princess, and I immediately notice she's wearing a seven-carat diamond ring. And then he starts telling me how he's living at the Four Seasons. And I said to him, "Joe, she's got a seven-carat diamond ring, you live at the Four Seasons, and you owe me 300 grand. There is no way this is going to end well."

By 1988, the two Bulger brothers were on top of their respective games. With Governor Mike Dukakis running for president, Senate President Bulger had become the de facto governor of Massachusetts. In 1988, four presidential candidates, of both parties, attended his St. Patrick's Day breakfast in South Boston.

During the presidential campaign, Billy Bulger's imperious control of state government began to be noticed. A reporter interviewed the judge whose court was gutted after he refused to hire one of Billy's cronies. Asked what kind of president he thought Dukakis might be, the judge replied, "How can he stand up to the Russians if he can't stand up to a corrupt midget?"

He was referring to Billy Bulger. Unlike Whitey, Billy did not use lifts in his shoes. He was five feet, five inches tall.

Joe Murray, the Charlestown drug dealer, was now in federal prison in Connecticut, convicted of gunrunning in the *Valhalla* case. In early 1988, he began calling Bill Weld, the former U.S. attorney who would be elected governor as a Republican in 1990. Weld was working in Washington as an assistant attorney general when Murray began calling him. Murray would leave him cryptic messages, always accurate, about who was doing what to whom in the Boston underworld. One day he named Brian Halloran's killers. He even mentioned a witness to the Halloran murder "who sits in a bar all day drinking and talking about it." Weld would pass the information along to the FBI, and back in Boston there would be no follow-up.

Finally, though, the Boston FBI office felt compelled to interview Murray. He was brought to Boston from Danbury for a debriefing. But at the direction of Connolly and

Morris, the agents dismissed Murray's information as "unsubstantial and unspecific allegations." They did, however, put into the record Murray's description of the situation in Boston:

> MURRAY said that WHITEY BULGER and STE-
> VIE FLEMMI have a machine and the Boston Police
> and the FBI have a machine and he cannot survive
> against these machines.

The Mafia was still reeling. The Angiulos and Larry Baione were gone, sentenced to long prison terms. Now In Town's mantle of leadership, such as it was, had fallen to a younger generation. They set up shop in a bakery in the Prudential Center called Vanessa's and Stevie Flemmi telephoned Zip Connolly. It had gotten almost too easy. Joe Russo was one of the wiseguys who used the bakery as a base of operations, but his old friend Whitey didn't think of giving him a heads-up. Business, after all, was business.

The feds bugged the back room of Vanessa's and soon

Ancient Boston gambling czar Doc Sagansky (left) paid
the Mafia $250,000 for the release of his diminutive associative,
Moe Weinstein.

they overheard the arrival of Doc Sagansky, the ancient bookie, and his seventy-five-year-old bodyguard of sorts, Moe Weinstein. The younger Mafia guys, with names like Vinny the Animal and Champagne Dennis, told Doc the days of paying a token $1,500 a month to Jerry Angiulo were over. So Doc Sagansky patiently tried to explain to them how the state lottery had destroyed the old numbers racket.

"Kid, I'm eighty-nine years old," he told the Animal. "Listen, take the business, will you please, and forget about everything."

The Mafia insisted Doc come up with some cash, and that until he did, they'd be keeping Moe Weinstein as a hostage. Then they left the two old men alone in the back room, with the FBI bug still recording everything.

"Moe," said Doc, "what am I gonna do now?"

"I guess you're gonna have to pay, Doc."

And the next day he did—$250,000 cash in the lobby of the Parker House. It would now be only a matter of time before the Mafia's next generation would join their elders in the custody of the Federal Bureau of Prisons. Doc Sagansky was called to testify before the grand jury, but he refused to talk. The habits of a lifetime eventually bought him six months in prison at the age of ninety-two. He did it, as they say, standing on his head, and finally died a free man, at the age of 101.

MEANWHILE, DOWN IN Florida, Johnny Martorano was having his own problems with the Mafia.

At the time, I'm in a sports-betting business with Bobby G. in Somerville and Richie Shea down on the South Shore. And we're getting a lot of help out in Vegas from this guy Joe Schneider—we called him Joe Schnitz. He was handling the "service" for us—he'd get us the lines before they came out in the papers, and make sure there were no surprises in the handicapping. He was valuable.

So these wiseguys out in Vegas threatened him and his family, said if he doesn't come up with 300 grand they're going to kill his family. It's two hoods from Vegas and this guy from Providence, the Saint they call him. Anthony St. Laurent, another rat for the FBI as we later find out. Anyway, Richie Shea calls me up and tells me Joe Schnitz is being shaken down, and can we do anything? I asked Richie, is he with us? And Richie says, yeah, so I told him I'll handle this. I called up Stevie and said, talk to Sonny Mercurio—he was our liaison to the Mafia. I told Stevie, you tell Sonny to tell the Saint to leave Joe

Anthony "the Saint" St. Laurent, Rhode Island Mafia member derided as "Public Enema Number One."

Schnitz alone, he's with me. Tell the Saint if anything happens to Joe Schnitz or his family, the same
thing'll happen to him or whoever did it.

Stevie for some reason puts it out to Sonny that I'm
on my way to Providence to kill the Saint. I never said
anything of the sort. But that's how it came out in all
those FBI reports I read ten years later. Nothing happened to Joe Schnitz, of course. I guess I was still the
Mafia's "boogey-man," as Stevie put it.

Finally, the *Globe* had to do something. It had become an
embarrassment, this continuous gushing about the Bulger
brothers, especially Whitey. A team of reporters was assigned the task of compiling a no-holds-barred biography
of the brothers, including Whitey's remarkable ability to
avoid indictment while almost every other major figure in
the Boston underworld was going down.

The *Globe* reporters sat down with John Morris, who
had long since been completely compromised. Whitey
and Stevie had paid him at least $8,000 in cash bribes. As
if that wasn't enough to hold over his head, they also still
had the old tape from the Dog House that he'd drunkenly
left behind in the room at the Colonnade Hotel. They
knew where he lived; one night they even had dinner with
Dennis Condon at Morris's house in Lexington. At the
end of the evening they'd given Morris $5,000 cash. In
short, they owned John Morris, and he didn't much like
his life anymore.

The *Globe* reporters bought Morris lunch and started
asking questions about Whitey. Morris quickly blurted
out: "You have no idea how dangerous he is."

Not for attribution, Morris gave them the whole story—
with his own sorry role in it naturally downplayed. Meanwhile, the rest of the Boston FBI office went into the usual
lockdown mode it assumed whenever Whitey was threat-

ened. Another *Globe* reporter, who lived in South Boston, was approached by an FBI agent who said he was delivering a message from Fat Tony Ciulla. The message: Be very careful what you write about Whitey, because he knows where you live and may very well decide to kill you.

It was a chilling message, but also somewhat suspect, because Fat Tony had long since vanished into the Witness Protection Program. There was no way of tracking him down to ask him if he'd ever said such a thing, and years later, when he did finally turn up, Fat Tony adamantly denied ever passing on such a warning.

The reporter and his family were temporarily relocated, and the *Globe* pressed ahead with the story. Billy Bulger reluctantly agreed to an interview, in which he said of his murderous, cocaine-dealing brother, "There is much to admire."

But the *Globe* was most interested in pursuing Whitey's connections to the FBI. When the story finally appeared in the fall of 1988, the *Globe* hadn't quite managed to nail down the official nature of the alliance, at least on the record. But the newspaper felt sure enough of its sources, namely Morris, to describe Whitey's ties to the FBI as a "special relationship."

It was a well-turned phrase. Special relationship. Everyone got it.

I heard about the *Globe* series, I think George or one of the bookmakers told me about it, that they were accusing Whitey of being a rat. I said no fucking way. But I called Stevie anyway and asked him what it was all about. He told me, Billy's up for reelection this year, and they're looking to smear him by smearing Whitey. Guilt by association. It was another button they were pushing that they knew would work with me—the smear button.

The DEA had never bought into Whitey's line that he was one of the good bad guys. So in 1989 they began another investigation, and this time they made sure that Zip Connolly's brother and Zip's old roommate, both of whom worked for the DEA, were kept far out of the loop. Instead, the DEA would work with the district attorney of Suffolk County, Newman Flanagan, and his crew of state police investigators. At the 1989 St. Patrick's Day breakfast, Billy made several disparaging remarks about Flanagan, in addition to the usual respectful recognition of Zip Connolly and a few stale jokes about Somerville— "Why don't they just build a wall around the place and give everybody inside three to five?"

The DEA began tapping dealers' phones in Southie, and soon had overwhelming evidence of a massive drug cartel in the Town, although they couldn't yet directly tie Whitey and Stevie to the rings. Still, the taps were full of references to "the white man," no-show state jobs, and the politicians who were selling them.

The DEA quickly figured out that all but one of the rings were run by old-style Southie strong-arms who more closely resembled traditional gangsters than they did modern cocaine dealers. They theorized that these ringleaders reported directly, if not to Whitey himself, then to someone close to him. The feds got a court order to tap Whitey's new cell phone, but almost as soon as the warrant was issued, Whitey stopped using his new toy for everything except the most cryptic messages. Like every other attempt to bring Whitey down, that cell-phone tap was somehow "compromised," as a federal prosecutor delicately put it later.

JOHNNY HAD BY now become a fixture in his neighborhood in Boca Raton. He still had a driver's license in the name of Vincent Rancourt, but everyone knew him as

Johnny and his mother Bess in Boca Raton, early 1990s.

"John." He used Patty's last name. He was just another middle-class family guy, very accommodating to everyone, always ready to drive the kids, his own and everyone else's, anywhere they needed to go. His widowed mother Bess came for visits, and Patty would take Kodachromes of Johnny and Bess in the driveway under a palm tree. Every month he gave Jeff Jenkins cash to make the payment on the mortgage. Jenkins and Johnny liked to hang out together, with their wives. Jenkins took things as they came and he didn't ask a lot of questions—until he had no choice.

One of the mechanics who worked for Jenkins came up to him one day at the dealership and said to him, You know that guy who's always hanging around here, I just saw him on *Unsolved Mysteries*. They described me as a "person of interest." Jenkins finally asked me who I really was, and I told him the truth—that I was wanted for racketeering and race fixing. Period. He said okay. Nothing changed.

Whitey was wheeling and dealing like always. Pat Nee had done a four-year bit in the *Valhalla* gunrunning case. When he got out of prison he was looking for new opportunities, so in 1990 Whitey set him up with a tough armored-car robbing crew out of the Lower End. They'd had a good run—until Nee threw in with them. On their final job, in Abington, the FBI was waiting for them. What made it even worse was that Whitey had given Nee a machine gun that he had used in the commission of a felony. Under the new federal sentencing guidelines, that meant another thirty years, on and after.

Pat Nee was going away for a very long time.

Billy Barnoski, Fat Tony Ciulla's muscle, had turned himself in in 1983, after four years on the lam. He was released from prison in 1987, and went to Triple O's, looking for work. Whitey took one look at his wild eyes, remembered his fuck-ups in the race-fixing days, and told him he would now be partners with Jackie McDermott, the Lowell bookie whom Johnny had brought into the fold after the Indian War.

Barnoski got deeply into cocaine, and early one morning in May 1988, he showed up at Jackie McDermott's house in Lowell and allegedly shot both McDermott and his son in the head. Jackie died, but the son survived to testify. Barnoski hired Johnny's lawyer, Richie Egbert, but a Lowell jury convicted him and he was sentenced to life in prison.

• • •

THE MAFIA IN Boston was trying yet again to regroup. After serving seventeen years in state prison, Cadillac Frank Salemme had been released. He began moving around again, meeting with various organized-crime figures including Johnny's younger brother, Jimmy. Salemme also sat down with his old partner, Stevie Flemmi.

Whitey was not happy about Salemme's overtures to Stevie. Whitey trusted Stevie as much as he trusted anyone except his brother Billy. But just in case, he soon decided that he needed a second stash of guns besides the arsenal on the Flemmis' sunporch across the courtyard from his brother.

After all these years, down in Providence the Office finally decided to grant the half-Irish Salemme his fondest wish—he would be officially inducted into the Mafia. But like Whitey, much of what remained of Angiulo's organization didn't think much of Salemme, never had, going all the way back to his Roxbury days with Wimpy Bennett.

As usual, it fell to Zip to stir things up, to keep the Italians at each other's throats. On June 19, 1989, he planted a front-page story in the *Herald* about how Cadillac Frank was preparing to crack down on dissident crews in the Boston Mafia.

Three days later, Salemme arrived—in a Mercedes, not a Cadillac—at the International House of Pancakes in Saugus. He had a meeting scheduled with some of his East Boston rivals. As he walked unarmed across the IHOP parking lot, a rental car roared toward him.

"Hey, Frankie!" someone yelled out the window, and then opened fire with a machine gun. Clutching his stomach, blood oozing from between his fingers, Salemme staggered into the IHOP and fell into a booth. Diners began screaming and running. A waitress warily approached Salemme as he grimaced in pain. She asked him if she could do anything for him.

"Yeah," he said, looking down at the blood on his hands and pants. "You could bring me some more napkins."

SALEMME RECOVERED, BUT not before several more bodies turned up. Eventually, what remained of the Office—namely, the Man's son, Junior Patriarca—decided that the only way to stop the fighting would be to hold a formal induction ceremony, bringing the various factions together in a traditional ceremony of Mafia mumbo-jumbo with a few burning Mass cards thrown in for good measure.

Even by latter-day Mafia standards, Junior was not an impressive godfather. Known variously as Abe (as in Lincoln, the suburban town in which he lived) and Rubber Lips (after the most prominent feature on his face), young Patriarca spent his days listening to Rhode Island radio talk shows, which he often called under assumed names that fooled nobody.

Given the events of the past decade, his organization was obviously riddled with informants. Yet Rubber Lips somehow convinced himself that news of this formal LCN induction ceremony—the first in New England in years—would remain secret. Sonny Mercurio got the first word to the FBI, but Zip made sure that credit went to Stevie and Whitey, which was okay by Sonny, as he testified later. Some things you don't want to be taking a bow for, Sonny told the judge, and this here was one of them.

The ceremony was scheduled for a Sunday in October 1989, on Guild Street in Medford. The owners of the house were away for the weekend. The FBI arrived first, on Friday night, and quickly wired the entire house. On Sunday morning, Joe Russo and Vinnie "the Animal" Ferrara arrived with platters of food—mainly meats and pastries—from the North End.

Vinnie Federico, a North Ender serving time at MCI-Shirley for killing a black man in a dispute over a parking

Raymond "Rubber Lips" Patriarca under arrest after
the taped Mafia initiation in 1989.

space, got yet another one of Governor Mike Dukakis's
weekend furloughs. On his furlough application, next to
"reason," Federico wrote, "family business."

Federico even brought a date, a twenty-nine-year-old
North End woman who worked for Mayor Flynn at City
Hall. She was sent downstairs to the basement to watch

TV. When the guys from Rhode Island arrived, a couple of them expressed concerns that they seemed to have been followed by an airplane. They had been. A leg breaker from Brockton thought he had spotted a cop in a phone booth. He had.

The FBI was everywhere. They got video and photographs of everything walking in, all of which would run in the Boston newspapers in less than two weeks. Eavesdropping in a nearby unmarked van, Zip was in his glory

Joe Russo under arrest in 1989.

as the ceremony began, with Junior Patriarca dusting off the clichés from a hundred Mafia movies about how "youse come in alive and youse go out dead."

Recording this induction ceremony would put Zip in a class all by himself. No one had ever done this—a crusading, courageous cop singlehandedly bringing down the Mafia in his hometown. At least that was how Zip was planning to pitch it. This had Hollywood blockbuster written all over it. Zip had remarried the previous year, and now his younger second wife, a former FBI secretary, was pregnant with their first child. He had his twenty years in for the federal pension and now Billy Bulger would get him a big job working for some state-regulated utility. And after this Mafia induction, he would be the most famous G-man in America.

When the ceremony was finished, Vinnie Federico yelled downstairs to his girlfriend that it was time to eat. As for Vinnie himself, he just picked at his food. He was heading back to MCI-Shirley, he explained, and they were planning their usual big Sunday-night feed. Vinnie went on, explaining that one of the Greek inmates at Shirley was a great cook. This weekend, Vinnie said, the Greek's menu included lobster, shrimp, and, for dessert, pineapple upside-down cake. The old-time goombahs from Revere, who'd done time in the hellhole that was the old Charlestown prison, couldn't believe what Federico was telling them about incarceration in the Dukakis era.

"You call dat doin' time?" one of the Revere guys said.

After everyone went home, or back to prison, Vinnie Ferrara was in a great mood as he cleaned up the house, telling one of his men what a beautiful fucking thing it had all been. The FBI bugs were still recording.

"Only the ghost knows what happened here today, by God," said the Animal.

Only the Ghost Knows—Zip had the title for his screenplay!

• • •

ZIP'S EUPHORIA DIDN'T last long. In August 1990, a combination of various law-enforcement agencies—pointedly excluding the FBI—began rolling up Whitey's drug rings in Southie. The arrests began before dawn on a Friday morning, when they picked up one mid-level dealer sleeping at his job at the city DPW yard. In the morning, he had been planning to punch in at his second job, at a state agency where hiring was controlled by the wife of one of Billy Bulger's loyal state senators.

In the morning, Zip was frantically working the phones to make sure Whitey hadn't been indicted. Why, didn't these people read the *Globe*? Didn't they understand, Whitey kept the drugs out of Southie.

That afternoon, the DEA held a press conference.

"For years the Bulger organization has told people there are no drugs in Southie," said the DEA agent in charge. "These arrests show that that's not true. These arrests show the people have been had by James Whitey Bulger."

Some of the arrested dealers were shipped down to the federal penitentiary in Danbury, where Rubber Lips Patriarca had been incarcerated since his arrest after the Guild Street induction ceremony. Rubber Lips knew who was being brought in, and when he saw one of the Southie guys, the Mafia boss of New England called him over. Without even introducing himself, Rubber Lips shook his head and began talking:

"You do know why you're here, don't you?" he asked the Southie cocaine dealer. "You got ratted out by your boy Whitey. He's been snitching for years."

DOWN IN FLORIDA, Johnny wasn't worried about the drug dealers. He knew nothing about any of that. But he was concerned about another problem, this one in Chelsea. A number of the Jewish bookies who had been paying "rent" to Whitey and Stevie for years were starting to feel the heat from a probe begun by the U.S. attorney's office in Boston, with subsequent help from the state police (but not, of course, the FBI).

The bookies had been laundering cash out of Heller's Café, under the Mystic Tobin Bridge in Chelsea. The feds started by targeting the barroom owner, a guy named Michael London. Once they had London's books, they knew exactly who they could take down for money laundering and income-tax evasion. It was now just a question of figuring out which bookies to flip first.

It was a guy named Chico Krantz who started the stampede. He used to drive a delivery truck for the *Herald*. Now I begin to get worried a little bit. He was one of the guys Joey Y was collecting for. What I'm worried about is RICO—the Racketeer-Influenced Corrupt Organizations Act. That's what they got Jerry Angiulo on. They hook you on a couple of recent crimes— predicate acts, they call them. After they've established them then they can drag in anything else, even if the statute of limitations has expired on the earlier crimes.

I remember when I first went on the lam, Whitey and Stevie told me they were getting out of the bookmaking business, that all they were gonna do now was "protection." I said to them, I don't get it. Bookmaking is a state offense, a year tops, in the House of Correction, which means three months, like I did in Plymouth in '78. "Protection" is extortion. That's a federal rap, ten years, and nowadays you gotta do 85 percent of a federal sentence. It didn't make sense to me, Whitey and Stevie exposing themselves like that, but then, I didn't know they had complete protection. Their problems with "protection" only started when their own protection began to break down.

In the fall of 1990, Zip Connolly suddenly decided to retire from the FBI. Times were changing rapidly—the Re-
publicans had swept the statewide elections in a landslide.
The cocaine busts, the dealers' state jobs, and Whitey's
increasing notoriety were among the many issues that had
infuriated the electorate. Nine of Billy Bulger's rubber-
stamp Democratic senators were ousted from office, and
the GOP came within perhaps 20,000 votes of taking
over the entire state senate for the first time since 1958.

Billy Bulger's clout was definitely diminished, at least
temporarily, and it was time for Zip to cash out while he
still could. Although both would later deny it, at the time
Zip told his friends that Billy had arranged a job for him,
as chief of security at Boston Edison. He succeeded another former FBI agent, and would in turn eventually be
succeeded by another G-man pal of Whitey's.

That agent, Nick Gianturco, was the host of Zip's farewell dinner at Joe Tecce's in the North End in December
1990. A camera recorded the event, and a copy of that
videotape was later found in Whitey's personal effects
when he became a fugitive four years later.

Among those in attendance at Zip's farewell dinner
were a number of high-ranking Boston cops, including a
future police commissioner and Eddie Walsh, that dear
friend of Zip's who made the first pinch on Johnny. Also
in attendance was a gangster named Arthur Gianelli—
Zip's brother-in-law, an underworld associate of Joey Yerardi's. Zip's second wife was also there, visibly pregnant
for the second time in three years. She would soon give
birth to twin boys.

Everyone lauded Zip's career as a lawman and gang-
buster. The number-two agent in the Boston office read
the letter that the then U.S. House Speaker John McCormack had written to J. Edgar Hoover on Zip's behalf back
in 1968.

The head of the Organized Crime Strike Force, a future

superior court judge named Diane Kottmyer, presented Zip with a bottle of wine and said, "John, they wanted me to say that that bottle came courtesy of South Boston Liquors, but I won't say that."

She didn't quite get the name right—it was the South Boston Liquor Mart—but Zip was ready with a quip of his own.

"No finer liquor store in the Commonwealth," he said, to gales of laughter and applause.

Finally, it was Billy Bulger's turn to laud his pal.

"Who's the personification of friendship in our community other than John Connolly? He's a splendid human being. He's a good pal. . . . John Connolly is the personification of loyalty, not only to his old friends and not only to the job that he holds but also to the highest principles. He's never forgotten them."

WHEN THEY BROUGHT Chico Krantz into court to plead guilty, he had more protection than any Boston mob witness since Joe Barboza. Uniformed marshals patrolled the halls outside the courtroom with M-16s. Once Chico was in the Witness Protection Program, the feds began raiding the other bookies' bank safe-deposit boxes. Eight of the Heller's Café bookmakers were indicted on money-laundering charges. A few of them flipped immediately and went into the Witness Protection Program. They testified that they had been paying "the Hill"— Whitey and Stevie—up to $3,000 a month in "rent."

Others, though, hung tough. Sooner or later, they figured, the laws' attention would wane, as it always had in the past, and then they could get back to business as usual. But this time it was different. At the urging of the feds, judges began denying the bookies bail, on the grounds that they were in danger, which they probably were.

Before their arrests, whenever he spoke to them, Stevie Flemmi would mention the words "Barney Bloom"—a bookie who'd been murdered in the 1970s, not by Stevie or the Hill, but by In Town. But it made Stevie's point, or so he assumed.

The bookies were not young men—most were in their sixties. It was tough on them, being shipped off to Allenwood for a few months and then brought back to Boston and given a second chance to testify. If they refused again, they'd be threatened with eighteen months for contempt of court—before their money-laundering trials even began.

"The government is turning everyone into rats," one bookie groused to his attorney in open court. "It'll become Russia."

A few weeks later, he flipped. Emboldened by what they were now reading in the papers, some of Whitey's extortion victims began coming forward. One guy was a Southie bar owner who had worked in a bank. Whitey had brought him to their convenience store, Rotary Variety, and demanded a "loan." Whitey had pulled a knife out of his boot and began stabbing empty cardboard boxes and calling this latest victim a "fuckster" over and over. In the end, the man paid Whitey $35,000, but then screwed up his courage and went to the FBI. He was fitted for a wire, but then the old pattern reasserted itself. Whitey refused to meet with or even speak to the guy. As usual, Whitey had gottèn a tip from one of the crooked G-men on his payroll.

But this time, what was even more significant was what didn't happen. The banker who had gone to the cops wasn't robbed or whacked or put in a hole or thrown in jail as a feather in somebody's cap. Whitey's grip on Southie was starting to slip.

I began to hear the word "amalgam." At first I didn't even know what it meant. But then I found out, and I became even more concerned. They were going to use some of those tapes from 1981, when Larry

Baione was saying, "We're the Hill and the Hill is us." It all went back to 1972, when the Winter Hill Gang was formed, and Howie and I sat down with Jerry and decided there weren't going to be any more independent bookies, that they have to go with either us or In Town.

So they got those tapes, from '81, and now we find out, they've also been bugging Heller's Café, and they have these wiseguys from In Town saying to the bookies, you either gotta go with Whitey and Stevie, or Vinnie the Animal. They got one Mafia guy on tape saying, Stevie can't carry Vinnie's jockstrap.

Once we know the questions they're asking in the grand jury, it's pretty obvious where the feds are going with their theory. They're going to say that the Hill and the Mafia are "amalgamated," that since '72 it's really just one gang. That means this time everybody's getting indicted, not just the Mafia, or us guys from Somerville. Looks like Whitey and Stevie could finally have a problem.

But still, I'm laying back. I mean, at that point all they got on me is the race fixing.

Whitey had always understood the necessity of staying out of the limelight. After threatening *Herald* reporter Paul Corsetti in 1981, he'd been pretty much left alone by the media until the *Globe* series in 1988. He and Stevie often did business standing on the sidewalk at the traffic rotary outside the South Boston Liquor Mart, but no media ever took their pictures. The cops knew what he looked like, as did a few reporters, but to the general public beyond the Broadway Bridge, Whitey was a wraith, a phantom, a legend.

No pictures, no story, or at least not nearly as much of a story—Whitey had long benefited from that journalistic fact of life. But his instincts finally failed him. In the summer of 1991, with so many of his bookies and drug dealers looking at serious prison time, Whitey should have been somewhere far, far from Southie.

But then one of his old associates won $14.3 million in the state lottery's Mass Millions drawing. It has never been clear exactly how Whitey engineered it, but he ended up with a one-sixth cut of the winning ticket, good for $120,000 a year before taxes. Every year for the next twenty years, Whitey would get a check from the state on July 1 for just over $89,000.

Not a bad "kiss in the mail," as the boyos on Castle Island would say. It wasn't a phony disability pension—white man's welfare, as such pensions were called in Boston's blue-collar neighborhoods. But the annual lottery payout would serve as the white man's welfare. Whitey's syco-phants at the *Globe,* sullen and silent since the cocaine busts eleven months earlier, sprang deliriously back into action. One even recounted the fable about how Whitey

Surveillance photo of Whitey at the lottery headquarters in Braintree, claiming his Mass Millions winnings in 1991.

"has delivered . . . beatings to people accused of dealing drugs in South Boston."

The downside to this latest score was that Whitey had to go to lottery headquarters in Braintree and present himself as a winner. The lottery had surveillance cameras in the lobby, and suddenly, thanks to the new Republican state treasurer, every TV network in the country had video of Whitey. His picture—in sunglasses and a white Red Sox hat—appeared on the front page of *USA Today*.

Now everyone in the country would know what Whitey Bulger looked like.

BILLY BULGER BEGAN a public-relations campaign to rehabilitate his image. No longer the all-powerful de facto governor, he now had to deal with someone in the Corner Office at the State House who was not a rubber stamp. Bill Weld, the former U.S. attorney, had been elected governor after spending hundreds of thousands of dollars of his private fortune on TV ads that morphed his Democratic opponent into Billy Bulger (and, by implication, Whitey).

Billy could no longer rely on the Boston press to restore the luster to his tarnished reputation. Outside the *Globe,* many in the local media were now too wary of either Bulger brother to cozy up to them. As for those who had spent decades cheerleading for them, their credibility was shot. So Billy had to seek out the national press. His first score came in the October 28, 1991, issue of *The New Yorker* magazine. The trials of Whitey's cocaine dealers were going on as the story was written, but no mention was made of the wiretapped complaints by drug dealers about the poor quality of the "snow" that someone named "Whitey" was peddling.

The *New Yorker* piece was picked up by *60 Minutes,* and in March 1992, CBS cameras recorded Billy's St. Patrick's Day breakfast, complete with the senate president joking about his brother's lottery win the previous summer. On September 17, 1992, almost 20 million Americans watched *60 Minutes*'s puff piece on Billy Bulger, complete with a fleeting reference to Whitey, so that Billy could say: "He's my brother. I care about him. I encourage him to come by all the time."

DICK O'BRIEN, THE South Shore bookie who had done three months with Johnny back in 1978, had by now also moved down to Boca Raton. He and Johnny saw a lot of each other socially. Soon the feds were looking for him, too, as part of their expanding bookie investigation. Stevie called Johnny and told him he needed to talk to O'Brien. They all agreed to meet at the Cracker Barrel in Okeechobee.

> I heard people say later maybe Stevie wanted to make a move on Dick, or me, or both of us, but I never thought so. He just wanted to get an idea what Dick was going to do when he got called to testify before the grand jury. Dick told him he'd go to jail, and I told Stevie, you can count on Dick. And they could—he ended up in Plymouth with the rest of us later, for contempt of court for refusing to testify. Obviously, though, Stevie had to be getting very concerned, to come to Florida to sit down with the both of us.

Later on, there was speculation that as the noose tightened around them, Whitey and Stevie had been on the verge of hatching another scheme, one that would have eliminated almost everyone who could testify against them in all of the murders that were still officially listed as "unsolved."

According to this version, widely circulated in the underworld, Whitey and Stevie first planned to take out Howie Winter. Since his release from prison on the race-fixing charges, Howie hadn't had much luck, getting involved in one ill-fated criminal venture after another. The fact that he would never rat on any of his codefendants did a lot toward solidifying his gangland stature as a stand-up guy, but it didn't help his prospects for shorter time whenever he came up for sentencing.

By 1994, Howie was broke and way behind in his taxes on the long-shuttered old garage in Somerville. He was living in Millbury. Meanwhile, Frankie Salemme was still moving around the city, hustling, trying to make up for his seventeen lost prison years. According to the supposed plan, Whitey and Stevie would first kill Howie, then call Johnny in Florida and tell him that Frankie had done it. They could always concoct believable stories as to why someone had to go.

Then Johnny would rush up from Florida, pick up some guns in Southie, and quickly eliminate Frankie—with the help of Whitey and Stevie, of course. Then, as soon as Frankie was dead, and a hole was dug for the body, Whitey and Stevie would shoot Johnny, too, and dump him in the hole on top of Cadillac Frank's body. That was another thing Whitey and Stevie had gotten quite good at over the years—burying multiple bodies in one location.

In one weekend, they could have eliminated the witnesses to all but a couple of their murders. Then they could have gone into court and pleaded guilty to racketeering, done three years, and ridden off into the sunset with their saddlebags stuffed full of all their millions in ill-gotten gains.

I don't know for sure if they ever planned anything like that, but it's certainly a plausible theory. They'd kill anybody to protect themselves, they'd long since proven that. And it would have tied up the loose ends, once and for all. But even if they had wanted to kill us all, by then events were moving too fast for them.

By 1994, it was clear that the feds were about to make their move. Whitey spent much of the year shuttling back and forth to Europe, stashing cash across the continent in various safe-deposit banks. One of his final public appearances came on election day 1994. Billy was being challenged for the senate presidency by a younger Democrat, Senator Bill Keating of Sharon, an old acquaintance of Eddie Connors of all people. Whitey held a sign on election day in Norton, down on the Rhode Island border, for Keating's Republican opponent. Whitey's candidate lost.

AT NIGHTS NOW, in his apartment in Quincy, with the bulletproof steel plate on what had originally been a sliding plate-glass door to his back patio, Whitey would sit at his kitchen table. In his neat Palmer-style longhand, he would write in his journals about the LSD experiments he had taken part in as a federal prisoner in Atlanta. He had written to Emory University in Georgia seeking copies of the medical records. It was clear that if he was arrested, this was going to be one of his defenses—that the feds had made him what he was today, with all their drugs.

"We were recruited by deception," Whitey wrote. "We were encouraged to volunteer to be human guinea pigs in a noble humanitarian cause—searching for a cure for schizophrenia . . . I was a believer in the government to the degree they would never take advantage of us. . . ."

The poor, innocent Whitey. He thought everything was on the level, or so he would have everyone believe now.

"It's 3 A.M. and years later, I'm still effected [*sic*] by L-S-D in that I fear sleep—the horrible nightmares that I fight to escape by waking, the taste of adrenaline, gasping for breath. Often I'm woken [*sic*] by a scream and find it's me screaming."

DESPITE THE OMINOUS turns the investigation was taking, Stevie seemed strangely unconcerned. He stashed some money offshore in the Grand Caymans, but he basically stuck to his usual routine, taking his annual summer trip to Montreal, knocking up a teenager, and helping one of his sons by Marion Hussey open a bar downtown.

IN THE FALL of 1994, Whitey showed up unannounced in Pompano Beach. Whatever the reason for his trip, it wasn't a social call. Johnny only found out about his visit when the father of a woman he knew bumped into Whitey on a staircase at a beachfront motel. He introduced himself as "Whitey from Boston." Johnny was perplexed that his partner hadn't called ahead to say he was coming down. So he phoned Stevie in Boston and asked him why his old pal was giving him the swerve.

> Stevie said, "Whitey doesn't want to bring any heat down on you." What heat? I said he's never seen his godson, this might be a good time. But Whitey wasn't interested. I wondered later if he was afraid I might try to kill him. Not then I wouldn't have, I didn't really know anything at that point.
>
> Now would be a different story. Wouldn't matter what the weapon was. I'd use anything that was in front of me, and if there wasn't anything, I'd strangle him with my bare hands.

Zip was earning a six-figure salary as a vice president of Boston Edison. His only headache was that his secretary didn't seem to like typing up the revisions he was constantly making to his screenplay. He and his growing family lived in a new mansion on a cul-de-sac in Lynnfield that he shared with his gangster brother-in-law. Summer weekends Zip spent at his second home on the Cape.

One day he ran into Frank Salemme on the street, again, and invited him up to his office in the Prudential Center. Sitting across a desk from the gangster he'd arrested on the east side of Manhattan back in 1972, Zip promised to warn Salemme as soon as the indictments came down, just as H. Paul Rico had done a quarter century earlier, so that Cadillac Frank could flee once more.

Among the first charged was Joey Yerardi. It wasn't part of the larger indictment; he'd just been named by some of the Jewish bookies as their collector. Before the cops could arrest him on extortion charges, Yerardi called Johnny in Florida and told him he was flying down.

By now, Joey Y owes me $365,000. He was panicking; he'd been calling people who owed him money from ten years earlier, that's how desperate he was. He'd told me he might be going on the lam, and sure enough, he does, and of course he comes to me for help. What can I do? I feel sorry for him. He told me he was broke, and at that time I was a little short myself. So I just took off my diamond pinkie ring and gave it to him. He didn't know anybody down there, so he had to take it to a jeweler and he got ripped off. I think he told me the guy gave him 10 grand for it. But what are you gonna do?

When you're on the lam, you always need an ace in the hole. And that's what that ring was for me all those years. That's what diamonds are for. You can always get cash for them when you're in a jam. So what the hell, the ring served its purpose.

Next I take Joey Y to Jeff Jenkins, and we get him a car, and then I set him up in a place in Hillsborough Beach, about ten miles away from my place in Boca. And then I make my big mistake—we go to this cell-phone guy I know and I buy Joey Y a cell phone. He's only supposed to use it to call me. So I'm filling out the paperwork, and I ask him, whose name do you want it in? He gives me one of his aliases.

That night, I start thinking to myself, am I out of

my mind, giving this fucking guy a cell phone, what
the hell was I thinking? Next day I took it back from
him, but I've already paid for it, got a year's contract
or something. So I decide, it'll be my second phone,
I'll just use it to call Patty at the house.

Zip Connolly got the word on December 23, 1994, that
the indictments were coming down after New Year's.
Whitey fled immediately, with Teresa Stanley. They spent
New Year's Eve in New Orleans, where Whitey registered
under his own name. Kevin Weeks tipped off Stevie, who
drove down to Randolph to tell Salemme. Cadillac Frank
immediately screwed to West Palm Beach.

Stevie, meanwhile, remained in Boston, moving around
the city openly. By January 5, 1995, Whitey was beginning
to wonder if maybe Zip had jumped the gun. What he
didn't know was that the feds had already arrested Jimmy
Martorano and Bobby DeLuca, a Rhode Island mobster
who, like Jimmy, had been spending too much time with
Salemme. Whitey was driving back to Boston from New
York when he heard a bulletin on the all-news radio station in Boston. Stevie Flemmi had just been arrested in
Quincy Market. Whitey immediately called Kevin Weeks
on a cell phone.

"I'm turning around," he said.

I got my own bad news— Joey Y has been picked up
in Boca. Now I'm in a real jam. I call up Dick O'Brien
and say, "I'm coming by to pick you up, you gotta
help me clear out Joey Y's house before the cops get
there." So we rush over and we're running through the
house, grabbing his records, betting slips, everything.
Actually, though, I'm more concerned about his car.
If the cops get the car, they'll trace it back to Jenkins,
and I'm done for.

So we get the car and drive away, and I think to

myself, maybe I got lucky again. But I forgot one thing: the cell phone. When the cops arrest Joey, they start running checks on anything in his name, or his aliases. And of course I'd used one of his aliases when I bought him the phone. So the cops get the call records on the phone I bought him, and all the calls are going to my house.

The cops told me later, when they went out to my house, the first thing that caught their attention was the fact that I was driving a car with dealer plates. Then they noticed that it was backed into the driveway. For easy getaway, in other words. Then they see me come out of the house, and one of 'em says to the other one, "Is that who I think it is?"

LAWYER: Fair to say that you weren't expecting that arrest, correct?

MARTORANO: I was expecting it for a long time, but it just happened at that time.

It was January 10, 1995, five days after the arrests in Boston. Patty had an evening class at the local community college. So her devoted "husband" decided after dinner to take young Jimmy and one of his neighborhood playmates down to the local Morrison's Cafeteria for some pie. John parked the van and stepped out with the two kids when he suddenly heard a voice behind him. It was Steve Johnson, he found out later, then a sergeant, now a lieutenant in the Massachusetts State Police.

"John?" said Sergeant Johnson.

"Johnny Martorano?" said another cop.

"I think you've got the wrong man," Johnny Martorano said.

"Really?" Johnson, backed by uniformed Boca Raton police, began advancing on him. "Let's check your arms, John."

They grabbed his arms and rolled up his sleeves and saw the tattoos he'd gotten all those years ago in Scollay Square. On his right forearm was a blue jay, and underneath it, the word NANCY. On his left forearm, a cross and underneath it the initials IHS—*In hoc signo.*

In hoc signo they had Johnny Martorano cold.

"Looks like you, John," one of them said. "You're under arrest."

They take me down to the stationhouse with the kids, and I've got my one call. Patty's in occupational-therapy class, so I call the mother of the other kid, Gail Silverman is her name. She comes in the station, shocked. I'm in handcuffs. I say to her, "I'm sorry about this Gail." Then I lean forward and whisper in her ear, "Tell Patty there's 40,000 cash under the floorboards in the bedroom."

12

"You Can't Rat on a Rat"

LAWYER: So you don't consider yourself a rat?

MARTORANO: Nope.

LAWYER: What is your definition of "rat"? Maybe you can tell the—

MARTORANO: Well, I am here to try to stop the people I perceived as rats from testifying against other friends of mine, including myself and my brother.

LAWYER: Okay, but the question is, What is your understanding of what a rat is, what you claim not to be?

MARTORANO: A rat is somebody that tells on somebody on things that they shouldn't tell on. . . . I know you can't rat on a rat.

LAWYER: When you say Mr. Bulger and Mr. Flemmi are rats, what do you believe they did to make them rats?

MARTORANO: They turned a lot of people in. . . . They were informants, period. They were Top Echelon informants and they had a number, just like a cop has a number on his badge.

LAWYER: You were offended by that, weren't you?
MARTORANO: A lot of things about them, yes.

AT THE BEGINNING of this final chapter, Johnny Martorano wanted to explain, in his own words, how he reached the decisions he had to make for himself and others during his years in prison.

"You Can't Rat on a Rat"—that's the title of this chapter, because that's what my twelve years in prison were all about, grappling with the question of how to stop these four rats—Whitey, Stevie, Zip, and Paul Rico. But at the same time I was determined to remain true to my own personal code, which tells me that an honorable man never informs on another man. I finally came to the conclusion that I had to speak up, and that by doing so, I wasn't violating the precepts that I have always lived my life by, because you can't rat on a rat.

To me, these people—Whitey, Stevie, Zip, and Paul Rico—they were the bottom of the barrel. You can be a gangster, or you can be a cop, but you can't be both.

My father used to say, a liar is worse than a thief. A thief just wants your possessions, which you can always replace. But a liar is trying to hurt you, personally, deliberately. To me an informant is the same as a liar—they just tell shit out of school, whispering behind your back. Sometimes what they say may be true, but if they got nothing new that day to pass on, a rat will just make it up. Believe me, when I was in jail, reading the old 209s that Whitey dictated to Zip, I saw that over and over again. A lot of the so-called incidents in those files about me and the other guys never happened. And it wasn't just gangsters that Whitey and Stevie lied about—they lied about honest cops, who by the way they hated more than gangsters, or anyone else. They lied about politicians, lawyers, businessmen—everybody who crossed them.

I always felt an informant should be stopped at any opportunity. As an honest man, it's your duty, your obligation, to stop them.

My whole life, I never ratted on anybody. That's what I mean when I keep saying that you can't rat on a rat. I said that under oath in Miami, at Zip's murder trial. I wasn't "ratting" on anybody, I was trying to stop these four rats from hurting anybody else—me, my family, my friends, anybody. And you know what? Since I started helping the government, none of these guys have hurt anybody else, have they?

I'm sure some people will say, Johnny's just trying to rationalize what he did, testifying for the government. I'm no angel, most people consider me a bad guy. I understand that. But with me, everything is up front. What you see is what you get. I'm not pretending to be anything I'm not. It's my belief that good men can do bad things. Take that as you will.

Whatever else I've done in my life, I think I played a pivotal role in ending this terrible evil in Boston, this rat partnership between my two ex-friends and those corrupt FBI agents.

People who don't like me will say, Johnny claims he's a stand-up guy, but he worked for the government. My answer to that is, this was a war. You know the old saying, "The enemy of my enemy is my friend." In this case, I had the same goals as the honest cops, the guys in the state police and the DEA and the Justice Department. We were all trying to weed out this cancer that was infecting the whole system.

Look, there are bad apples in any group. Who rooted out the bad priests in the Archdiocese of Boston? A lot of it was done by the good priests, who were appalled by what the bad priests were doing to those kids.

I feel like I was rooting out the worst apples. Again, I'm not trying to whitewash what I did. I'm coming clean here, just like I did in court. I regret an awful lot of what I did, but remember, a lot of the guys I killed were rats. A lot of the guys I killed had killed a lot of other guys, and probably would have gone on killing if I hadn't killed them first.

You may not believe this, but I'm a religious person. I've confessed my sins, and I believe I've been forgiven, by God if not by everybody else.

That's all I wanted to say.

IN JANUARY 1995, Johnny Martorano was moved to a new home—the Palm Beach County jail. By prison standards, it wasn't bad. He made his first court appearance in front of U.S. District Court Judge Maryanne Trump Barry, Donald Trump's sister. Among those in the courtroom was an FBI agent from Boston named Buckley, who had been Zip Connolly's last partner before Zip retired in 1990.

Buckley comes up to me and says, you were indicted in 1979. I said, "I don't know anything about that." He shows me the indictment and says, "There's your name, and your brother's name, and Howie Winter's name, and you're telling me you didn't know you were indicted?"

Donald Trump's sister asks me the same question, and I say, "Your Honor, I'm really not sure you have the right person here." She says, Okay, why don't you go back to your cell for two weeks and think it over?

In two weeks, I came back in and I told her, "Your Honor, I've checked the indictment, and it's me. I didn't know it was me they were looking for." I had to hold out for those two weeks, in order to avoid any new charges against myself and anyone who'd helped me—aiding and abetting a fugitive, that kind of thing. I had to at least try to act surprised. That way, I could back up my story, that I never told Patty anything except that I couldn't have any contact with anyone in Boston because I had all these marital problems, which of course I did have.

Next stop was the Miami/Dade jail, which wasn't nearly as posh as the Palm Beach lockup. Then he boarded the federal airbus—*ConAir* as they called it in the Nicolas Cage movie—for the flight back to Boston. Federal prisoners were housed at the Plymouth House of Correction—a new jail built since Johnny's three-month stay at the old one in 1978. He was still chained to his seat as the plane landed in Boston, when suddenly he heard someone yelling, "Johnny! Johnny Martorano!" He looked up and saw Pat Nee, shackled, shuffling through the airbus.

Nee had just gotten a break. A judge had thrown out the additional thirty-year on-and-after sentence he'd been facing for using a machine gun in the botched armored-car robbery in Abington. The gun had been given to Nee by Whitey, and subsequent testing had proved that the firing pin had been removed before Nee and his codefendants had taken possession of it. Nee's argument, which the judge had bought, was that if the gun couldn't fire, it wasn't really a machine gun.

Nee had slowly come around to the conclusion that it probably wasn't an innocent mishap that the gun was missing its firing pin. What if Whitey had wanted to make sure that the gang wouldn't be able to use it to es-

cape? After all, mere possession of it should have ensured
a virtual life sentence for his old rival Nee, in addition to
the other Southie wiseguys in the gang, none of whom
were shrinking violets themselves.

Now, Nee was being returned to prison to finish out his
much-reduced sentence, just as Johnny was arriving back
in Boston to stand trial. As Pat made his way down the
ConAir aisle, he yelled back at Johnny Martorano.

"I left you all my toiletries. You can have my sneakers,
too."

He wasn't kidding. I inherited Pat's sneakers. A good
pair of sneakers is a big deal at Plymouth—you
couldn't buy 'em at the commissary, only junk food.

I get down there, and the first person I see is my
brother, and my heart sank. I told him, this is the one
thing I always wanted to avoid—both of us in jail
together. That's why I'd kept him out of the sports-
gambling business, so he could stay clean. I told him
back then, in '72, I don't need you in a boiler beside
me, I need you right here, at Chandler's. Somebody
has to be here to take care of our families in case
something happens to me.

Then I meet Robert DeLuca, from Rhode Island,
Mafia, who was also in the indictment. There were a
lot of Charlestown guys in for various things. And
then I saw Stevie. At that point, he's still my friend
and my partner. I was in a separate case, I was facing none of the counts the other guys were indicted
for, illegal extension of credit, all that stuff. They
hadn't added me to the larger indictment. Only thing
they had on me was the horse case.

After turning around and driving back to New York the
night Stevie Flemmi was arrested, Whitey Bulger hit the

road with Teresa Stanley. They drove aimlessly around the country for a couple of weeks before Whitey called Kevin Weeks and told him to bring Catherine Greig to a Chinese restaurant in Weymouth. He was switching molls. Not only was Catherine twenty years younger, she had no kids or grandchildren, no one to miss, nothing to get homesick about. Catherine's closest relative was her twin sister, with whom she left her two black poodles, Nikki and Gigi. Whitey had made it clear to Catherine that the dogs were not included in his invitation.

At the Chinese restaurant, Whitey coolly said goodbye to Teresa and told her he'd call her. She never heard from him again. From a pay phone, she called her son-in-law, Chris Nilan, a former NHL hockey player. It was Nilan who Whitey had been on his way to visit in Montreal in 1988, when he had his run-in with Trooper Johnson over the bag full of cash at Logan Airport.

When Nilan arrived at the Chinese restaurant, he didn't recognize his mother-in-law. On Whitey's orders, she had dyed her hair white.

IN LATE JANUARY 1995, Whitey arranged to call his brother Billy at the home of one of Billy's favorite State House employees, a senate court officer—a uniformed door-opener—who was one of the few men in the building actually shorter than Billy himself.

Even though he was an attorney—an officer of the court—the senate president never reported that he had received a phone call from his brother, a federal fugitive. In 2001, Billy Bulger was called before a federal grand jury to answer questions about the call. Specifically, he was asked if he told Whitey he should surrender.

"I doubt it because I don't think it would be in his best interest to do so."

Did he ever consider turning his fugitive brother in?

"I don't feel an obligation to help everyone catch him."

Two years later, Billy was again questioned about the call, this time in a public forum, on live television, by members of a congressional committee. Once again, Billy Bulger was less than forthcoming about his conversation with Whitey.

"The tone of it was something like this," Billy said. "He told me, uh, don't believe everything that's being said about me. It's not true."

Not a single body of any of his victims had yet been disinterred, and yet Whitey was already pleading not guilty.

"I think he was trying to give me some comfort on that level and he—I don't know." Billy paused. "I think he asked me to tell everybody he was okay and, uh, then I told him, well, we care very much for you and um, we're very hopeful. I think I said I hoped this will have a happy ending. At the time there was no talk of the more terrible crimes."

AS THE MONTHS went by, more and more of Johnny Martorano's old associates arrived in Plymouth. Cancer-stricken George Kaufman had been indicted with the others, but he was allowed to remain free to die at home. After his death Kevin Weeks and another Southie guy went to his home to remove yet another stash of weapons Stevie had stored in George's attic. Weeks missed one automatic rifle, which came as quite a shock to the new owner of Kaufman's house when he stumbled upon it a few months later.

Frankie Salemme was arrested in West Palm in August 1995. Dick O'Brien was likewise brought north and thrown into Cellblock H after he refused to testify before the grand jury. Another of the Winter Hill bookies, Charlie Raso, soon joined them. Rubber Lips ended up in a different wing, along with Sonny Mercurio, who had gone on the lam after the Vanessa's bakery bugging but had since been arrested and returned to Massachusetts.

There was only one guy who wasn't there—Whitey Bulger.

I don't think I ever asked Stevie—where's Whitey? At that point, I just hoped he never got caught. I certainly had nothing derogatory to say about him, and neither did anyone else. At least not on our cellblock.

Richie Egbert was Johnny's original attorney on the race-fixing case. But as an old friend of Johnny's, Marty Weinberg quickly offered his services. And he came up with a plan. He told Johnny, just sit tight for a few months, and then we make our move. In August 1995, after seven months in confinement, Weinberg filed a motion for dismissal of the race-fixing charges, claiming that Martorano had been denied his right to a speedy trial.

An afternoon hearing was scheduled in front of U.S. District Court Judge Reginald Lindsay. To the prosecutors, Lindsay made clear his displeasure that the Justice Department had not officially charged Martorano.

It was about 3:50. The judge told the prosecutors, If you can't come up with an indictment by four o'clock, or an arrest warrant to hold him, he's outta here. He's pointing at me as he says this. A couple of the Justice Department guys rush out of the courtroom and the other prosecutors are just sitting there, along with me and Marty and the judge and his clerk and a couple of marshals. Tick-tick-tick. Nobody says anything. We're staring at the clock and then glancing at each other, me and Marty.

Finally it's four o'clock. The judge points his finger at me and says, "It's time. I'm leaving, and you're outta here." Marty and I bolted for the door. We didn't even wait for the elevator; we ran down eleven flights of stairs, down the courthouse steps, and out onto Devonshire Street. I had no money, so Marty throws me a hundred-dollar bill and tells me to call him at nine that night. Then we split up and head off as fast as we can go in opposite directions. Back upstairs, in the courtroom, the prosecutors are back with the warrant to hold me, but it's too late.

I'm walking fast, but then I realize, I have no idea where I am. I haven't set foot in Boston for sixteen years. I'm lost. I jumped in a cab and said, "Take me to Somerville."

He went straight to Patty's mother's house, on Morrison Avenue. He still had a few grand stashed there, which he picked up. Then he called his daughter Lisa, and she drove in from Quincy and picked him up. Then they headed down to the Cape where they enjoyed a leisurely dinner. Around nine, Johnny called his lawyer.

I told him, this is great being out. But Marty said, "I hate to burst your bubble, but we gave our word you'd be back at the courthouse at nine tomorrow morning if they came up with a new arrest warrant." Which they had. I asked Marty, how about if I just go to Florida for the weekend and come back Monday? He says, "If you're not back in the morning, Johnny, they say they're going to start knocking down the doors of all your families." So I went back, and then they put out a superseding indictment— there were a few of those over the years—and they added Joey Y to it. By then, George Kaufman had died, so basically they just put my name in the indictment wherever George's had appeared, because most of the time, whatever calls he was making to Joey Y he was making for me.

So I'm back in Plymouth and Stevie says, "What are you, crazy? Why'd you come back?" I said, "I didn't want to leave you here alone with all these guys." I figured the charges were still basically gambling and racketeering shit, nothing about murder. But it was time for me to make a deal with Marty to defend me on the new charges they'd tacked on. I needed money. Weinberg got me a severance from the others, which is the best thing to have, and everybody was putting in pretrial motions. I was going to sit with the rest of them in the hearings, so they didn't have to go through everything twice.

We all get visitors, and you can mill around and talk to the people visiting the other guys. Stevie had told me he and Whitey had set up this thing they called the "X" fund, which they use for miscellaneous expenses, buying guns, bribing cops, things like that. Now Whitey's gone and Stevie's in jail, so this kid Kevin Weeks, who hasn't been indicted yet, has control of the X fund. They got maybe a hundred grand in it. Stevie's seeing Weeks all the time, giving him instructions as best he can. So one day Stevie is talking to Weeks, and I yell over to Weeks, "Tell the other guy"—meaning Whitey—"I could use a little help."

Stevie nods, and so Weeks delivers 10 grand to Phil Costa, Stevie's guy, and Phil gets it to Loretta in Somerville, who sends it to Patty. I still needed 50 grand for Marty, but I knew somebody who'd help me out. You remember that guy I told you about from Chandler's—I sent Alvin Campbell down to threaten the boyfriend of the woman he ended up marrying. He was like a big brother to me. Well, I called that guy, he was and still is a good friend of mine. I told him I needed $50,000. He came through, no questions asked.

Whitey and Catherine were touring the country in Whitey's new Mercury Marquis, for which he had paid $13,000 on Long Island. Twice in 1995, cops pulled him over and ran his plates—once in Long Beach, Mississippi, and another time outside a Veterans Administration hospital in Wyoming. Both times the plates came back registered to "Thomas Baxter," who had no outstanding warrants. Whitey never even got a ticket.

Finally the couple settled in the bayou country of Louisiana—Grand Isle. They rented a duplex on the beach called It's Our Dream. They befriended a struggling Cajun family, buying them new kitchen appliances with cash—$100 bills. "Tom" carried the bills in a pouch, along with a pearl-handled knife.

Some nights "Tom and Helen" would drive forty miles to the Walmart superstore in Galliano. It was open all night, and during his stay in Louisiana Whitey used the pay phone outside to call at least five of his fellow former Alcatraz inmates—usually ex–bank robbers like himself. He would ask them for assistance in getting new IDs. It was surprising that "Thomas Baxter" had lasted as long as it had.

Whitey was restless. He'd been expecting that somehow, everything would get worked out, the way it always had in the past. But Zip had retired, and his brother's political career was drawing to a close. Billy was angling for the presidency of the University of Massachusetts as his golden parachute.

Billy parlayed his *60 Minutes* puff piece into a modest book contract, and now his memoir was about to come out. The book's title was *While the Music Lasts*. In it Billy defended his older brother against all allegations, saying that the evidence against Whitey was "purchased." James, as he called Whitey, "abhorred addictive drugs. . . . I *know* some of the allegations and much of the innuendo to be absolutely false. Other matters," Billy conceded, "I cannot be sure about, one way or the other."

In his memoir, Billy also discussed, at some length, Southie's hatred of informers. That was why Billy occasionally handed out a faux prize at his St. Patrick's Day breakfast, to someone who had crossed him, or Southie, which Billy had come to consider synonymous with himself. He called it the Gypo Nolan Award, named after the title character in the Liam O'Flaherty novel that John Ford made into the Academy Award–winning 1935 movie, *The Informer.*

In the book, Billy mentioned "informers" on page 4, "snitching" on page 11, and "spies" on page 171, but never in the context of his brother James.

IN LATE 1995, Whitey's frustration over the stalemate in which he found himself finally got the better of him. He knew that John Morris had been promoted, and that he was now the director of training for new agents at the FBI academy in Quantico, Virginia.

One afternoon he placed a call to Morris, and got through after identifying himself as "Mr. White." Morris immediately began taking notes, to be used in preparing a 302 incident report, perhaps because he suspected Whitey was taping the conversation. Whitey demanded that Morris use his "Machiavellian mind," as Whitey put it, to get a retraction from the *Globe* for its 1988 series, which he now believed was the beginning of the end of the Bulger hegemony in Boston.

Whitey also mentioned "ruining him and his family," as Morris later recalled under oath. Finally, Whitey hung up and phoned Kevin Weeks to brag about his call to Morris.

That evening, Morris's wife came to pick him up. He asked her if she remembered the $1,000 in cash that John Connolly had handed her back in 1981, when she was a secretary at the Boston FBI office. She'd used the money to fly down to Georgia and shack up with him at the FBI training session in Glynco, even though he was married to another woman? Did she remember that money? Morris asked her. Of course she remembered.

"It came from Bulger and Flemmi," he confessed. Once he got home, Special Agent Morris keeled over with a massive heart attack. Ten weeks later, on December 31, 1995, Morris retired from the FBI.

IN EARLY 1996, Governor Bill Weld's appointed board chose Billy Bulger as the president of the University of Massachusetts—another "nationwide search," as the State House joke went. That opened up the Southie state senate seat for the first time since 1970, when Whitey had openly threatened to kill Billy's underdog opponent.

Billy had already handpicked his successor as senate president. It would be Tom Birmingham of Chelsea. He'd only been in the legislature for three terms, but his pedigree was impeccable. His namesake uncle was a small-town Charlestown hoodlum who'd been shot to death in a rooming house in 1969. His father was the former veterans' agent for the City of Boston who'd been indicted for obtaining welfare payments for the family of Suitcase Fidler, the gangster/partner of the late Eddie Connors. The charges had been dismissed after the elder Birmingham had hired as his attorney one William M. Bulger, Esq.

With Birmingham as president of the senate, Billy now wanted his son, Billy Bulger Jr., to replace him in the state senate. And then perhaps in six or eight years, Billy Junior could follow in his father's footsteps to the presidency of the senate, or even better, someday succeed his father's pal, Joe Moakley, in John W. McCormack's old seat in the U.S. House of Representatives.

But there was a roadblock—the state rep from Southie, a former ironworker named Steve Lynch. Lynch boldly jumped into the special election to fill Billy's senate seat. Still, the Bulgers seemed to have everything going for them: at his final St. Patrick's Day breakfast as senate president in 1996, Billy insisted that everyone, including U.S. Senator John Kerry, wear a green Billy Bulger Jr. campaign button. Billy Senior worked the Red Line stations at rush hour with his son, an undistinguished attorney and even more lackluster candidate.

It was the first time since 1964 that Whitey hadn't been moving around Southie on election day. When the votes were counted, Lynch had crushed Billy Junior by a two-to-one margin. Billy Bulger Sr. couldn't even carry his own home precinct for his son. It was the end of the Bulgers in Massachusetts politics. None of them would ever run for public office again.

OF ALL THE organized-crime types in Plymouth, Stevie Flemmi was the only one who had never done any time, not even a few months in the House of Correction. And at the age of sixty, he was not doing "good time."

Stevie kept waiting for someone—anyone—to ride to his rescue. But nothing ever happened. He began covering his bed with pictures of the saints. Soon he took up with a burglar who was a Jehovah's Witness. For hours Stevie would lie on his back in the cell, softly moaning as the Jehovah's Witness massaged his feet. When he wasn't attending religious services of the Jehovah's Witnesses, he would spin out endless tales to his codefendants, often about Whitey and the FBI.

He told them Whitey's stories about LSD experiments in Atlanta were "bullshit," and that it was H. Paul Rico who'd made sure Whitey got time off for good behavior. He claimed the FBI had its own hit squad. He mentioned how Whitey always carried tiny tape recorders that he used to record all of his conversations with the FBI. Stevie talked about the Sunday-afternoon dinners at his mother's house, a few feet from the sunporch where the gang's machine guns were stashed, and where Debbie Davis was murdered. Stevie told them how any number of FBI agents, not just Morris and Connolly, had stopped by to dine with him and Whitey, and how Billy Bulger had joined them "plenty of times," a claim Billy would later unconvincingly deny.

The more Stevie talked, the more the other guys wondered. But at first, they couldn't even articulate what they were starting to suspect. Or maybe they just didn't want to.

WHITEY HAD BEEN gone from Boston for over a year. His Louisiana home, Grand Isle, was too deserted in the winter for Whitey's liking, so he and "Helen" went back on the road, only to return in May 1996. He again rented a house near his Cajun friends. Whitey continued paying his rent with $100 bills, and he still passed on his monthly copy of *Soldier of Fortune* magazine to his friends. But there had been a change in his favorite Cajun family since he left. Their father-in-law was living with them now, and he and "Thomas Baxter" didn't get along.

The father-in-law was appalled that Tom would brag in front of Helen that "I have control of my women." The two men also squabbled over the value of work, with the father-in-law bragging that he'd worked every day of his life since he turned fifteen.

"I never had to work," Whitey retorted. "I had people working for me."

IN 1996, THE FBI finally got around to interviewing Teresa Stanley and she gave up Whitey's alias. Kevin Weeks found out and got word to Whitey that he needed new IDs. In July 1996, Whitey and Catherine left Grand Isle and drove north, finally ditching the Mercury in Yonkers, New York. The feds soon had it staked out, but

Whitey never returned. When it was impounded, the feds discovered that Whitey had put 65,000 miles on it in the eighteen months he drove it.

By then, Whitey was holed up in Chicago, where one of his fellow former Alcatraz inmates was working for a mobbed-up local union. Whitey needed new IDs, and first Weeks posed Whitey's youngest brother, the court clerk Jackie, for the photos. But they weren't close enough, so Weeks flew out to Chicago to get new pictures of Whitey. Later Weeks shook a state police tail and got the new IDs to Whitey in Chicago.

Whitey and Catherine flew to New York, and then caught a plane to Europe. Neither has been seen in the United States since 1996.

THE JUDGE WHO'D drawn the racketeering case was Mark Wolf, and every time he had all the defendants in court together, he would ask the prosecutors if there were any "surprises" they were holding back. It was almost as if he were trying to drop a hint, and finally someone on the defense team picked up on it.

Before being appointed to the bench by Ronald Reagan, Wolf had been the first assistant U.S. attorney in Boston under Bill Weld. In other words, he'd been around in the office when the Dog House bugs were installed, and for at least a few of the occasions when Jeremiah O'Sullivan had gone out of his way to protect Whitey and Stevie.

Maybe Wolf knew something that he couldn't come right out and say. So finally, in early 1997, Frankie Salemme's lawyer filed a motion listing a number of names, asking the government to acknowledge whether any of them had been used as informants. The most important name on the list was Whitey Bulger. How could the government allow one of its own informants—one of its own employees—to take part in crimes with impunity, while arresting others who were involved in the same conspiracies? It was one of the lawyers who first mentioned the Fourteenth Amendment, but pretty soon everyone in Cellblock H couldn't stop talking about the Constitution's equal-protection clause.

At this point, Judge Wolf called everyone back into his courtroom and asked whether they were asking if just the names on their list were informants, or if they would prefer to have the names of all the informants the FBI had used in building its case? Now he was dropping an even broader hint.

The defendants immediately asked for all the names.

It was right about this time that the feds offered us a blanket deal. It could be they knew what was going to come out, or maybe they just figured it would be easier this way, for everybody. The way one of these deals works is, everybody in the indictment has to agree to plead guilty. The guys at the top end of the indictment, who are looking at the longest sentences, get a few years cut off. And the guys at the bottom get some time added on. But at least it's done, and you can get down to just doing your time and getting it over with.

So we all sat down, among ourselves, and everybody agreed to the blanket deal. Everybody except Stevie. He was adamant. He said, "I'm not going to prison." I said to him, "Where exactly do you think you are now, Stevie?" But I guess he knew he couldn't go into the federal system, because of all the people he'd be running into that he'd ratted out over the years.

So in the end there was no deal. It looked like we were going to trial.

As part of discovery, the FBI was already providing some ancient 209s and 302s to the defendants. With little else to do in Cellblock H, Johnny Martorano and Frankie Salemme in particular pored over the old documents. After all, they had both lived through the events described.

> Frankie noticed one particular 209 from 1967. Rico had written it. It contained a lot of "information of a singular nature," which was what the FBI always stamped on the bottom of the reports back in those days. They'd redacted the informant's name— blacked it out—but Frankie could put it together, because he was there back when it happened. So he says to Stevie, "You're the only one who could have known this, and that's your name that's blacked out up top as the informant." And Stevie goes, no no no, that ain't my name, that's Wimpy's. You know Wimpy was a rat, Frankie, that's why we killed him. And Frankie gives him this look and he says, Stevie, look at the date on this 209. It's April 1967. We killed Wimpy in January. Stevie just kinda hung his head.

Johnny Martorano's mother Bess was going downhill fast. One day in early 1997, he and his brother Jimmy were shackled together and driven to a nursing home in Quincy. She had Parkinson's disease and Alzheimer's. She looked at Johnny and smiled and said, "You're still the quiet one."

Two weeks later she was dead. Johnny asked to be allowed to attend her funeral, but was told that prisoners only got to see their dying parents once—either before or after they passed on. He hadn't known he had a choice.

Joe McDonald was the next to go. He died a free man, in his own bed, in Somerville, at age eighty. When he was released from prison, he'd tried to find out what happened to his partner, Jimmy Sims, who had vanished in 1987.

Joe Mac never did solve that final mystery, nor has anyone else. Jimmy Kearns, ratted out by Whitey Bulger when he was a fugitive in Las Vegas in 1979, died in federal prison.

The old In Town crew was dying off as well. Larry Baione passed away at age seventy-five from an intestinal disorder in 1996 at the federal prison hospital in Springfield, Missouri. Two years later, at the same hospital, Joe Russo died of throat cancer at the age of sixty-seven.

Johnny, meanwhile, sent a message to Patty in Florida, asking her to come up to Plymouth some visiting day soon, because he had something to tell her, and he wanted to say it to her in person, face-to-face.

I told her, you've been a great girl all these years, but it looks like I'm gonna be here for a while. You gotta get on with your life. She started dating a guy, married him, a good guy, he took wonderful care of her and Jimmy. She still lives in Florida, never left. It was tough, I loved her. I still do.

Patty still comes up to Boston every summer to visit her family. After I got out of prison, that summer she and her husband and Jimmy were staying at the Long Wharf Marriott. I asked Jimmy, "Can you bring your stepfather down to the lobby tomorrow, because I want to meet him."

See, when he started dating Patty, I don't think he knew about my . . . reputation. So it meant a lot to me for him to understand that I'm not Jack the Ripper. We met and shook hands and I thanked him for taking such good care of both Jimmy and Patty. Jimmy was really happy.

One day in 1997, they all filed back into Judge Wolf's courtroom for another day of hearings. The defendants—Johnny and Jimmy Martorano, Stevie Flemmi, Frankie

Salemme, and Robert DeLuca—all sat together in the jury box.

This day, Wolf announced he would like to see Flemmi and his lawyer, Kenny Fishman, alone in his chambers. In private, the judge told Stevie that the next day he was going to release his name—as well as those of Whitey and Sonny Mercurio—as informants. Wolf told him that this would be his final opportunity to work something out with the government, that is, to agree to testify.

That night, everyone climbed wearily onto the bus back to Plymouth—everybody except Stevie. They all thought he was gone for good. But after dinner, Flemmi bounded back into Cellblock H and announced that he needed to get everyone together because he had an announcement to make. They filed into a small room next to the visitors' area.

"I was an informant for over thirty years," Stevie said. "And so was Whitey. Wolf's going to tell you that in court tomorrow. But I wanted you to hear it from me first, because it's not what you think it is. Me and Whitey gave them shit and got back gold in return."

I was crushed. I mean, I loved that guy. Now I wanted to kill him and at the same time I was heartbroken. I know "mixed emotions" is a cliché but that's what I felt. Stevie said he gave them "shit"? We had the diagrams he gave the FBI of the Dog House so they'd know where to place the bugs. That wasn't shit. Neither was setting up Barboza to perjure himself about innocent guys—the ones who hadn't died in prison were still in the can at that point, thirty years later. It wasn't shit to get himself and Whitey cut out of the race-fixing indictment when all the rest of us went down.

Yeah, he and Whitey gave 'em shit all right—and I was the shit. Me and my brother and Howie and all the rest. And these two guys were the godfathers of my sons!

Stevie just kept trying to talk his way out of it. He'd come up with one lie after another. He started saying, well, I never hurt nobody but the Italians. I said, what about them fifty drug dealers in Southie? Remember, we were getting more 209s every day, I still haven't seen all of them, but these two guys were ratting out everybody, and not just gangsters either. And if Whitey didn't have anything on you, he'd just make something up, something bad, like he saw you snorting coke. And Zip would write it all down.

Stevie was dancing, but it just wouldn't fly no more, not after we started getting the 209s. He hurt everybody. At one point Stevie was complaining, he was supposed to get paid for all these reports, but Rico was stealing the money. And then a few minutes later he's saying he's not a rat. Him and Whitey, they were men without a country now. Billy Bulger's probably the only friend Stevie's got left.

It was killing me, thinking about what they'd done. Then on top of everything else, I started feeling guilty. This was all my fault. It was me who brought them both into the gang. Whitey came to me; I'm the one who introduced him to Howie. If I don't help him out 'cause I owed Billy O a favor, maybe the Mullens would have killed him and none of this happens. And then Stevie—sure, Howie helped him come back from Montreal, too, but I was the one who was pushing Howie to do it, whispering in his ear every day. If I'm not so hot to get Stevie back, the FBI wouldn't have been able to make it look like they had nothing to do with it. They're the ones who really brought him back, and that would have been obvious if Howie and I hadn't been hiring lawyers and bail bondsmen and arranging which cops he'd surrender to. I provided the cover for the FBI to bring him back to destroy us. It's all my fault, that's what I was thinking.

I says, well, fuck it, this is just too embarrassing. I don't want people to think I'm involved in this. I'm in tears. I loved this guy at one point but fuck it, I'll just kill him.

LAWYER: So it was at that point that you realized that Mr. Flemmi, Mr. Bulger were pretty much handing you up?

MARTORANO: They were handing everybody up.

LAWYER: Including you, right?

MARTORANO: Including me . . . I knew they were informants. That was enough.

LAWYER: And you knew these informants had been around you for twenty-five years of your life while you were committing murders, right?

MARTORANO: Right. . . . Now I know they could possibly implicate me, my brother, all my friends. That's why I came forward, not to save myself, because I took 10 extra years, but I tried to save a pack of people.

LAWYER: You did it for your friends?

MARTORANO: I did a lot for them, yeah.

LAWYER: So you did the right thing?

MARTORANO: I still believe I did. I mean, I didn't think anybody else got hurt by Flemmi or Bulger after the fact.

On May 22, 1997, after more than a decade of denials, the FBI officially admitted that Whitey Bulger had been an informant. Judge Wolf had already granted the defendants' motion for open pretrial hearings. In outing Whitey

as a rat, the government cited "unique and rare circumstances."

The hearings began with a parade of FBI agents, including Zip Connolly. But he took the Fifth Amendment,
refusing to testify. Outside the courtroom, he denounced
the rumors now swirling around him, issuing almost
daily denials of the stories that were appearing in both
Boston newspapers. He knew nothing about the FBI office buying all the booze for its Christmas parties at the
South Boston Liquor Mart. When it was reported in the
Herald that he had accepted free stoves and refrigerators
from Whitey's appliance store at F and West Broadway,
Zip denounced the front-page story as "an abject lie."

After the FBI agents came the gangsters. Anthony St.
Laurent, the Saint, who had had the run-in with Johnny
over his attempted shakedown of Joe Schnitz, complained
to the judge that he was in ill health and had to take "40,
50 enemas a day."

Suddenly the Saint had a new nickname: "Public Enema Number One."

The Saint was asked directly if he was an FBI informant.

"I take the Fifth," he replied.

It all made good copy in the newspapers, but it was clear
that all this was just a warm-up for the main attraction—
Stevie Flemmi. If, that is, he lived long enough to get to the
witness stand.

I think I could have killed him and gotten away with
it. I planned it out for a while. Even if they got me for
it, so what? I'm facing one murder charge instead of
twenty. Plus, if I don't kill him, for the rest of my
life—my life in prison—people who Stevie put in
jail will be asking me, "Why didn't you stop him
when you had the chance?" It was like with the

Campbell brothers. If I don't do something, other people are going to get fucked.

My plan was simple. I was three doors down from him. The doors are locked at 9 P.M., and at 6 A.M. they press a master button, and all the cells are unlocked. There were cameras everywhere, but that time of day, before dawn, it was real dark, too dark for the camera to catch anything but a shadow. What I would do is, I would go into his cell and either strangle or stab him, then pull the blanket over his head, and close the cell door behind me, locking it. Then I'd go down to the mess hall and get in line.

See, Plymouth was a boring place. They didn't have jobs there. They might find his body right afterward, but chances are they don't discover he's dead for twelve hours—until the first lockdown of the night, at 6:30. We talked about it, and one of the other guys offered to help me out if I needed any assistance.

But ultimately, I decided not to do it. Lotta people get stabbed in jail, you know, so they've gotten pretty good at saving guys who've been shanked. And they can bring back people you think you've strangled. If I'd had a gun I could have made sure, but that wasn't an option. It was too dangerous, if I tried to kill him and he survived. Then he's out the door for sure, and we're all done for.

It was a difficult situation for us to be in. Stevie's real scared by this point. We tell him, you're not our friend no more, but you're in this case with us, and maybe we can still win it. We showed him the decisions from the Scarpa case in New York, the Colombo crime family—it was the same deal, an FBI informant in the conspiracy. Did we have a good chance of succeeding? No. It was a long shot, and we know he's a rat, but we can't treat him like one, number one because he might get us out, and number two, because he might turn on us.

Remember, he's got other problems in jail besides being a rat. There's also a lot of guys from Southie locked up in Plymouth, and they know what Stevie and Whitey were doing with those young girls all those years. They hated the guy. We hated him too, wanted to kill him as much as the guys from Southie did, maybe more, but on the other hand we had to protect him, for our own case.

This is a guy who I know now has been ratting on me since I was twenty-four years old, and now I'm fifty-six, and I'm concerned that he's going to get me and everyone else I know one last time. It's not beyond the realm of possibility that if he starts talking about all the murders, he could walk out of Plymouth, no murder raps, no forfeitures, no nothing. And what if they bring Whitey back to corroborate his testimony against the rest of us? Stevie and Whitey could end getting away with everything, with all their money, living somewhere warm, and we're locked up forever.

Johnny had a childhood friend from Milton who was in the Secret Service. He asked him to come in for a visit—as an attorney, so that Johnny could invoke the attorney-client privilege if something went wrong. Johnny wanted his old friend's opinion of the cops' organized-crime strike force. Could he trust Dan Doherty, the DEA agent? And how about the state police—Tom Foley, Dan Duffy, and Steve Johnson? Obviously, going to the FBI was out of the question. The Secret Service agent vouched for the strike force. They're stand-up guys, he told Johnny. That was good enough for Martorano.

Next he needed a lawyer. Dick O'Brien was using Frank DiMento, who'd been around forever. He went back at least as far as Buddy McLean, and he'd even represented Whitey Bulger a time or two.

Johnny knew and respected DiMento, and of course O'Brien was a good friend, so nobody thought anything of it when Johnny started hanging around the visiting room talking to DiMento, even if Dick O'Brien wasn't around. Finally Johnny told Frank to call the strike force.

> I knew Frank was friendly with Fred Wyshak, the prosecutor who was handling the case. Frank vouched for Wyshak's integrity. Frank spoke to Wyshak and then got a message back to me at the jail from Wyshak: "Tell Johnny if he helps us I'll do anything I can for him."
> Frank told me, "If Fred says it, he means it." He was right. Wyshak was telling the truth.

Johnny couldn't say anything to anybody. But he'd gotten to like Robert "Bobby" DeLuca, the Mafia soldier from Rhode Island. Never having done anything with Flemmi, DeLuca had never been betrayed by him. So he became an intermediary, a go-between of sorts, between Stevie and the Boston guys he'd fucked.

It wasn't an easy assignment for DeLuca, having to commiserate daily with Stevie Flemmi. DeLuca detested him as much as everybody else. But for months DeLuca kept Stevie talking, fantasizing about winning the case and getting out. It was enough to keep Stevie from flipping. Under adverse conditions, DeLuca performed a real service for his fellow wiseguys. So one morning Johnny stopped by Robert's cell to give him a heads-up.

"Robert," he said. "I am going out that door before Stevie does. I am going to destroy him before he destroys us."

They called me in for a phony hearing or something like that, and that was it, I was gone from Plymouth. The state police had a little two-man jail set up at the academy in New Braintree. That's where they put me. They made a back room and I'd talk to them there every day—Doherty, and from the state police Tom Foley, Dan Duffy, and Steve Johnson. Some days Fred Wyshak and Brian Kelly from the U.S. attorney's office.

Frank DiMento was involved in everything, either in person or on the phone. He protected my position, totally. I never considered lawyers as having balls, but I ended up with two guys who did—Frank Di-Mento and Marty Weinberg.

So I'm in there talking to the strike force every day. I tell them what happened; I give them everything except the names. This is a proffer—if we can't reach an agreement, they can't use any of what I've told them against me. They made it clear from the beginning, you have to tell us everything, if you lie you get thrown out, sent back to prison, and prose-cuted for perjury, the way Frankie Salemme did later on. Plus they can then use the evidence in the confessions of murder against me.

From day one, I told them I would testify against Stevie and Whitey. I also told 'em, those are the only two I'll testify against. Because they're the rats.

Foley would say to me, at trial you would have to tell the truth, who was with you on all the hits. I said okay, but other than Whitey and Stevie all the names in these murders stay blank until the day I make the agreement, and the agreement has to be that I don't have to testify against anybody but those two. The only way I'm naming any of my friends is if I have a deal, in writing, that I don't have to testify against them, ever. And I told them, if you don't like my terms, then just send me back, because I'm almost done anyway.

Meanwhile, Judge Wolf's hearings are going on without me. Marty Weinberg is still there every day for me, because I don't know if I'm going to make a deal or not. Finally the feds got tired of haggling with me, so they sent me back, but not to Plymouth. I got shipped out to Otisville, a federal prison in New York, and they threw me in the hole.

In "the hole," Johnny Martorano only got out of his cell twice a week, for showers. It was solitary confinement. There was a hole in the cell door, and twice a week, on Wednesdays and Saturdays, he would stick his hands through the hole. The guards would then handcuff him, open the cell door, and take him down to the shower room.

Once he was inside, the guards would lock the shower-room door, and Johnny would stick his hands back through the hole in that door, and the handcuffs would be unlocked and removed. He would shower, after which he would stick his hands through the shower door and be handcuffed for the trip back to his cell.

I was in a good position, if you can ever call being in the hole a good position. They needed me to solve all these murders. They wanted to make a deal with me, but there was all kinds of pressure. The FBI was knuckling the U.S. attorney, they wanted to make the deal with Stevie, and then probably Whitey would have come back to corroborate everything.

But by then they were just too dirty for anybody to deal with, except maybe the FBI. The strike force finally went to Janet Reno—she was the attorney general then—and what they decided in Washington was, offer him twelve to fifteen years. Remember I'm still only looking at four-to-five, and by now I've been in almost four. They never thought I'd agree to it.

But I surprised them by accepting the deal. Because that's the only way I could stop Whitey and Stevie from going on ratting people out, myself included, but also everybody else I knew. In a lot of these murders, there weren't a lot of witnesses, so it's either gonna be Stevie or me who makes the deal. And if it's not me, and he ends up testifying against me and all my friends, what do I say to my brother? Or Howie? Or Pat? Or even Frankie?

They told me, well, you're gonna have to agree to also testify against any "corrupt officials." Meaning cops. I said I got no problem with going up against Connolly and Rico, but I would prefer not to go against Schneiderhan. He never hurt me. And I never did testify against him. They got him, but not through me.

But they knew how bad it would look, if I admitted to twenty murders, and I only had to testify against four people. So they came up with a specific target list. I had nothing to do with drawing up that list. It was a bunch of Whitey's guys from Southie that I would have to testify against. Sure, I said. I loved that list, because I'd never known any of those guys, let alone committed any crimes with them. So I was glad to say I'd tell the government the truth about anything I did with them, which was nothing.

The real list to me was still the same guys— Whitey, Stevie, and Zip, and, before he died, Rico. At Zip's trial in Miami, they tried to make a big thing out of all these guys that I didn't know.

LAWYER: The people that you agreed to testify against included George Hogan, correct?

MARTORANO: Never met him.

LAWYER: Patrick Linskey?

MARTORANO: Never met him.

LAWYER: John Curran?

MARTORANO: I knew him because he drove Whitey Bulger around. That's all I knew.

LAWYER: Why did you agree to testify against somebody you didn't know?

MARTORANO: That's the best way to agree.

LAWYER: You put one over on the government?

MARTORANO: No, they wrote the list. I didn't write the list. That was the South Boston crew in the '80s and '70s. I don't know nothing about them. I was gone.

LAWYER: So you did put one over?

MARTORANO: I didn't put one over. My lawyers made a good deal.

Johnny signed the agreement and was shipped off to Texas, to a special federal penitentiary with a wing called "the Valachi suite." Johnny hated the name, because he didn't consider his decision at all similar to the one made by Joe Valachi, the first Mafia soldier to turn rat, and testify before Congress. Back in the early '60s, Valachi had been trying to save his own skin, period, and had informed on everyone he ever knew.

It was going to take the feds awhile to put the whole package of plea agreements together. They had to get prosecutors in three states to sign off on the unsolved murders, many of them high-profile. In Massachusetts, they had to deal with elected prosecutors in two different counties, one a Republican, the other a Democrat.

In the meantime, Martorano's debriefings continued.

He was questioned by cops from three states, in addition to the various feds. He told them how Joe Barboza had confessed to him that he was planning to frame the four innocent men who would be convicted of the 1965 murder of Teddy Deegan. One of them, Joe the Horse Salvati, had been freed pending a new trial, but he hadn't yet been cleared.

Wyshak wrote a memo to John Durham, the new special prosecutor who had been appointed to investigate FBI corruption in Boston. Using Johnny's testimony, Durham asked a judge to release all the FBI files on the Deegan case. The smoking gun turned up quickly—a memo from H. Paul Rico to J. Edgar Hoover on the day after the Deegan murder, correctly naming the real killers.

The two surviving innocent men—Joe the Horse and Peter Limone—were finally exonerated, after thirty years in prison.

Down in Texas, the strike force would give Johnny names dating all the way back to the '60s. The feds wanted to know who was with which gang—In Town, the Hill, Roxbury, etc. If they'd been murdered, they would ask Martorano if he knew who had done it, and why.

MARTORANO: They pulled a list out of eighty people that I knew, and there was only five left by the time they showed me the list. Everybody else had been killed. And I was one of the few that survived, so we started going through that list to see how many people I knew anything about, what the situation was.

LAWYER: And this is a list that the government is interested in, if you can give any information on their deaths, right?

MARTORANO: Do you know this person or that person, whose side they were on. Most of the

people were dead, just to show you the context,
there was a lot of people that got killed them days.

It took over a year, there was so much stuff to settle.
Different counties, different states, and nobody ever
wants to make a deal with the hitman. Like I always
said in court, I had good lawyers.

When word got out about Johnny's deal, Zip Connolly
was frantic. Stevie Flemmi was about to take the stand,
and Zip began conferring on an almost daily basis with
Stevie's attorney, Kenny Fishman. Zip understood that he
was in serious jeopardy because of what Johnny Martorano
knew. Now it wasn't just his FBI pension or his Boston
Edison job at stake. He suddenly realized that he could end
up in prison. So Zip didn't need Stevie digging him an even
deeper hole with his testimony. It was important, for instance, that Stevie dummy up about how Zip had tipped
them to their impending indictments four years earlier.

When Zip was down on the Cape at his summer home
in Dennis, he'd never call Fishman from his house. He'd
drive around the corner to a pay phone to call. But then
he'd charge the call to his Edison credit card, establishing
the very paper trail he was trying to avoid.

Next, one of the longtime Bulger sycophants at the
Globe decided to make a run at Martorano's credibility.
Mike Barnicle, who referred to Whitey as "Jimmy" as
though they were close friends, wrote a piece in which he
quoted Eddie Walsh, one of Connolly's closest friends, as
saying that Martorano used blacks in Roxbury for "target
practice."

This accusation was so over-the-top that the U.S. attorney later denounced the statement as "made up" and
"fantasy." It turned out to be Barnicle's last regular col-
umn in the *Globe*. His career at the *Globe* came to an end
soon after when he was forced to resign in disgrace over

earlier transgressions and suggestions of plagiarism and outright fabrication.

AS THE MONTHS dragged on with no sightings of him in the United States, people who had known Whitey began coming forward, anonymously at first, then more openly as they realized that he wasn't coming back. And stories began to leak out—that Whitey was gay, or at least bisexual. By the time his mug shot was featured on *America's Most Wanted* for the twelfth or fifteenth time, it was practically gospel.

The strike force released a photo it had found in Whitey's personal effects. It was taken in the late 1980s, in Provincetown, where Whitey spent a lot of time, some-

Whitey in Provincetown in the late 1980s
during his Village People phase.

times with a woman, other times by himself, or with Zip. In the photo, Whitey was wearing a cowboy hat, and was bare-chested except for a leather vest. In his hands he cradled a long-barrelled rifle. Zip apparently understood how it would look to his superiors, his alleged he-man hoodlum supersource hanging out in the gay mecca of P-town. In one 209 report, absolving Whitey of any possible connection to a gangland hit, Zip mentioned that at the time of the murder, Whitey had been in Provincetown—"with a woman," Zip hastily added.

More stories came out. Gays began to remember how he used to hang around Jacques in Bay Village, the oldest transvestite bar in the city. An old tale that no one had ever dared recount when Whitey was around began to spread through the underworld. According to the story, shortly after he got out of prison in 1965, Whitey had started hanging out with Hank Garrity, the gay owner of the Pen Tavern who used to visit him at Leavenworth.

In those days in Southie, there was a dinner club called Blinstrub's. Occasionally Blinstrub's would book a fading show-biz act into the main room, and one weekend in 1965, the main attraction was Sal Mineo, who would later be murdered by a gay hustler in Hollywood. Between shows, the talent hung out upstairs. According to Southie legend, one night during Mineo's stand at Blinstrub's, someone had stumbled into the upstairs green room without knocking and had seen Whitey and Hank Garrity double-teaming the fading teen heartthrob.

Then everyone recalled Whitey's old Native American friend from Alcatraz, Clarence Carnes, the Choctaw Kid. When the Kid died penniless in prison in Missouri in the 1980s, Whitey paid to have his body exhumed from a pauper's grave at the prison. Whitey then had the Kid's body brought back to the Cookson Hills of Oklahoma for a proper Indian burial, which Whitey paid for and attended, also bailing the Kid's nephew out of jail as a sort of bonus goodwill gesture. The Choctaw Kid had died of AIDS.

Then there was Catherine Greig's younger brother. In the 1980s, David Greig sometimes accompanied Whitey around the Town. Hooked on Percosets, he would often nod off. But Whitey, who knew nothing about drugs except how much money they could generate, was clueless as to Greig's problems. He told his younger associates, "I think David has a vitamin deficiency." Whitey wanted to bring the kid into the gang, a sort of Kevin Weeks for Kevin Weeks. For once, everybody rose up in unison and told Whitey he was out of his mind. A short time later, David would be found shot in the head on Cape Cod in what was eventually ruled a suicide.

With Whitey gone, the rumors took on a life of their own. Even the cops started spreading them. The police in Tulsa, where Roger Wheeler had been murdered in 1981, finally put out a wanted poster in 2002.

"Subject said to have extreme bad breath," the Tulsa police warned. "Subject is traveling with female companion but may be found in homosexual communities/resorts or nudist facilities."

Look, I know what my brother and Pat Nee and a lot of other guys say about Whitey now. It's not a big deal to me now one way or the other, but you guys never did like Whitey, he did shit to you, and you have no way of knowing whether these stories are true or not, because everybody except Whitey is dead now.

All I can tell you is, I've heard the same stories, but in all those years I never saw it. He was weird, but not in that way. You think he would have been my partner if I'd thought he was gay? You think I would have shot people with him? Like Seinfeld says, not that there's anything wrong with that, but. . . .

Flemmi finally took the stand in August 1998. Jimmy Martorano had wisely pleaded guilty earlier, so the only other two defendants left in the courtroom were Frankie Salemme and Robert DeLuca.

By then, prosecutor Fred Wyshak had copious notes of Johnny's debriefings, and he started going down the list of murders Stevie and Johnny, among others, had committed together. Wyshak would inquire of Flemmi, Did you murder Eddie Connors? James Sousa? Richie Castucci?

Flemmi would look over at Fishman, who would hold out his right hand, all five digits pointing outward. Five as in Fifth Amendment.

"Assert the Fifth on that," Flemmi would reply to Wyshak.

Through Fishman, Zip was trying to protect not only himself, but also his hero Billy Bulger. Morris had testified weeks earlier that he had seen Billy at one of those Sunday-afternoon crime confabs at the Flemmis' house. Stevie brought up Morris's testimony himself, without any questions from either side, in order to deny that it ever happened.

"Just wanted to clarify that," he said.

When asked how he had learned of his pending indictment, he lied again. He didn't mention Kevin Weeks passing on the tip from Zip. Instead, he said Whitey had called him at his mother's house. No, he didn't know where Whitey was calling from. It hadn't occurred to him to ask.

In the jury box, Salemme fumed. Stevie was lying—obviously lying—to protect Zip Connolly and Billy Bulger. At the next break, back in the courthouse holding pen, Salemme grabbed the smaller Flemmi by the throat and began throttling him, screaming: "You piece of shit! You fucked me all my life and now you're screwing everyone around you! Fucking scum!"

The marshals had to pull Salemme off Flemmi in order to prevent yet another murder.

• • •

WYSHAK ASKED FLEMMI about how he must have realized at some point that Whitey Bulger wasn't going to ride to the rescue.

"I can't say that," Flemmi replied.

"You can't say that?" Wyshak said. "Well, he hasn't rescued you so far, has he?"

"He must be working on it."

Stevie Flemmi's mother died in 1999, leaving the home on East Third Street vacant. Two of Stevie's illegitimate sons by Marion Hussey got into the gang's "clubhouse" and found a hidden cache of $500,000 in cash. They blew through it in six months of nonstop partying, one of them would later testify.

The feds started tightening the screws on the families. Michael Flemmi, Stevie's cop brother, was convicted of obstructing justice on the testimony of his nephew, one of the Hussey boys, who, after learning that his father had murdered his half sister, decided to change his last name to St. Croix. Whitey's youngest brother, Jackie Bulger, was convicted of perjury after lying to a grand jury about visiting his brother's safe-deposit box in Clearwater, Florida. Catherine Greig's twin sister was also convicted of perjury and sentenced to six months' house arrest, after which she put down Catherine's two French poodles, Nikki and Gigi.

Down in Plymouth, in memory of the dogs, Robert DeLuca wrote a poem, "Who's Minding the Puppies?"

LAWYER: You were aware that both Florida and Oklahoma were death penalty states, were you not?

MARTORANO: I'm not sure if I was aware, but I am now.

LAWYER: Is it your testimony that you weren't aware at the time that you entered into this plea agreement?

MARTORANO: When I shot those people, I wasn't
aware. It didn't matter.

In September 1999, Johnny Martorano pleaded guilty to
ten murders in three different states. After the guilty plea
in Oklahoma in the murder of Roger Wheeler, Tulsa police detective Mike Huff flew to Boston to reinterview
Zip Connolly. He was ushered into Zip's office by the
taciturn secretary who spent much of her time typing and
retyping his still-unsold screenplay about the Mafia induction on Guild Street—*Only the Ghost Knows*.

"What do you know about Bulger and Flemmi?" Huff
asked Zip, who ignored the question and changed the subject.

"Did you know that HBO is going to make a movie
about me?"

Now it was Huff's turn to ignore Zip. "I know they set
it up," he said, "but nobody here will help me."

"Do you understand what I did?" Zip continued, talking as much to himself as Huff. "I took down LCN. I took
down twenty-eight guys, man. I'm proud of what I did.
You guys, you just don't know what it's like. That's why I
have to write the screenplay myself. I'm the only one who
can do it."

JOHN DURHAM, THE special federal prosecutor appointed to investigate FBI corruption in Boston, was closing in on Zip. Durham and his squad of out-of-town
FBI agents worked out of Worcester, rather than Boston,
to avoid even the appearance of association—and
impropriety—with the Boston office. Durham obtained a
warrant to search Zip Connolly's office in the Prudential
Center, where his agents seized the hard drive from his
computer. On it they found drafts of an anonymous letter
that Zip had written to Judge Wolf three years earlier,
questioning the credibility of several honest Boston police

officers who were potential witnesses against both Zip and his gangland bosses. Zip had printed his scurrilous screed on BPD stationery, to make it look like an inside job from police headquarters.

In Zip's office, Durham's FBI agents found reams of blank stationery from both the BPD and the *Globe,* which Zip also apparently used when sending out his anonymous hit pieces. Then the feds located several witnesses who were willing to testify that Zip had shown them early drafts of the anti-BPD letter he'd sent to Judge Wolf.

Now the feds had Zip cold on at least one obstruction

Zip Connolly, charged with murder,
at a court hearing in Miami.

of justice count. He was going to prison, even if he didn't realize it quite yet. At this point, it was just a question of gathering up even more evidence, and witnesses to testify against Zip. Johnny Martorano and John Morris, among many others, were already in the fold, and the next to join them would be Mafia boss Frankie Salemme.

Salemme pleaded guilty in 1999 to the racketeering charges against him. Now he could testify how Zip told him he, too, would be tipped off, and how the actual message was delivered by Stevie Flemmi at Salemme's home in Sharon. His wife had been there at the time—another potential witness.

As the original defendants were being packed off to prison, new ones were entering the federal pipeline. On November 17, 1999, Kevin Weeks and Whitey's money launderer Kevin O'Neil were both arrested and shipped off to a different federal holding pen, in Central Falls, Rhode Island. The newspapers immediately began speculating which Kevin would flip first. It was Kevin Weeks, after less than a month behind bars. Overnight his nickname in Southie went from Kevin Squeaks to Two Weeks, which was about how long he stood up. Now there was one more witness against Zip.

On December 12, 1999, Zip Connolly was finally arrested on racketeering and obstruction of justice charges. A few weeks later, at Weeks's direction, the state police began digging up the first of Whitey's death pits, at Florian Hall, where they found the bodies of Deb Hussey, Bucky Barrett, and the *Valhalla* crewman John McIntyre. Weeks had re-interred them there after the East Third Street house in which they were originally buried was sold in the Southie real estate boom to some rich squares from out of state.

IN THE FALL of 2000, Billy Bulger was still hanging on as president of the University of Massachusetts. And he

devised what he thought was a perfect way to shore up his increasingly shaky position. He would bring the first presidential debate of the 2000 campaign to his school. He was tight with both the Bush family and Senator Ted Kennedy, so Kennedy asked Vice President Al Gore to do a favor for him by agreeing to debate his GOP opponent at the UMass-Boston campus on Columbia Point. It was quite a feather in Billy Bulger's cap, lining up that first debate.

But Johnny Martorano had a surprise in store for Billy. He'd remembered something else during his debriefings.

They were always asking me different questions, to get me to recall things I'd forgotten. And one day it suddenly occurred to me, whenever we drove over the bridge from Quincy into Dorchester, Whitey would say, "Tip your hat to Tommy." Because that's where they'd buried him, under the bridge, on the banks of the Neponset River. Public land, like all the other places Whitey and Stevie buried bodies.

It was the same place they'd buried Deb Davis. So they started digging with backhoes, on the day of the presidential debate at UMass. I heard they had to pull all the curtains because you could see the backhoes out the windows in the hall where the debate was taking place. Billy is the first guy on TV as the debate begins. Millions of people are watching on TV. It's his big moment, and a couple of hundred yards down the beach, the cops are digging up more bodies of people his brother murdered.

LAWYER: Did you know the location because you actually put the bodies there?

MARTORANO: No.

LAWYER: Did you know that because someone told you?

MARTORANO: Yes.

LAWYER: Who told you?
MARTORANO: Whitey Bulger.

After all of his guilty pleas, and his testimony before the grand jury in Boston, Johnny spent most of the next six years in a federal penitentiary in North Florida. He did, however, have a date in a federal courtroom in South Boston on Northern Avenue, the same street where Whitey Bulger had gunned down Brian Halloran and Michael Donahue twenty years earlier.

Zip's federal racketeering trial was front-page news in Boston. He was still conducting himself like a "hero cop." His brother, the now-retired DEA agent, met him at the front door of the courthouse every morning and acted as his security, keeping the scruffy reporters and camera crews at bay. Zip originally retained a high-profile Boston defense attorney, who had successfully defended several corrupt politicians, including Billy Bulger.

As the evidence mounted against Zip, Billy Bulger's old lawyer suddenly bowed out of the case and was replaced by one of his junior partners.

When the trial began, Zip asked to be allowed to sit not at the defense table with his lawyers, but in the first row of the gallery, with his wife, as if he were a spectator at his own trial rather than the defendant. That was unusual enough, but on the first day of the trial, he walked into the courthouse with his three young sons, the oldest of whom was now thirteen.

Special prosecutor Durham built his case methodically. He played an FBI training video in which Zip had starred during his heyday as a gangbusting G-man. In it, Zip had lectured the new agents, "Never try to outgangster a gangster," advice he himself had obviously never heeded.

One of the first witnesses was Zip's ex-wife—spousal immunity doesn't apply after a divorce. She told of receiv-

ing the diamond ring Johnny Martorano had given to Whitey. John Morris testified under a grant of immunity. So did his ex-girlfriend and now wife, about how Zip had given her cash from Whitey and Stevie for her airline ticket to the Georgia love nest. They produced Zip's phone records, showing his calls to Stevie's lawyer, Kenny Fishman.

Johnny Martorano was flown north from Florida in a Learjet. But the strike force was nervous.

They started asking me, am I sure I told them about all the murders? Of course I'm sure—I had immunity, as long as I told the truth. If I lied about anything, I blow up the deal. Why would I lie? So they tell me, Zip's lawyer is making noises that I supposedly killed some girlfriend of Billy Kearns, a Roxbury guy, after I raped her. It's just more bullshit from Flemmi, and Zip believed it. You look at those 209s, and Zip believed everything they told him. All he knew was what Whitey told him, and he couldn't even keep that straight. He was always mixing up names and titles. Skinny Kazonis was "Slim" Kazonis. He never could remember the names of any politicians in Somerville. And now he's mixed up again, on this murder, or maybe Stevie Flemmi is feeding it to him, and he figures it's the only way he's got to dust me up. But I'm ready for it.

LAWYER: Is it your testimony that you don't kill women?
MARTORANO: Positively not.
LAWYER: But sometimes you have to, right?
MARTORANO: I never run across that situation.
LAWYER: How about Kathleen Murphy? Do you recall her?
MARTORANO: Don't know her.

Zip's lawyer then tried to spin a story about Martorano picking up Kathleen Murphy and taking her somewhere and raping her, before taking her home.

> LAWYER: Is it also possible that when she got out of the car, she said she was going to tell her uncle about what you had forced her to do?
>
> MARTORANO: Nope.
>
> LAWYER: Are you testifying that you did not kill this woman?
>
> MARTORANO: I don't even know the name . . . I would remember killing her.
>
> LAWYER: Even if it were in the '60s?
>
> MARTORANO: Even if it were in the '30s.
>
> LAWYER: Because you keep track of all your victims, is that right?
>
> MARTORANO: A single girl and killed her alone for a bad reason, I would remember.
>
> LAWYER: But you wouldn't want to admit it, would you?
>
> MARTORANO: I would admit it or lose my life if I don't.

The jury convicted Connolly on most of the counts; he was sentenced to ten years in federal prison. Johnny was flown back to prison in Florida.

Now time was running out for Billy Bulger. He had stacked the UMass board with his friends and cronies, and hired many of their relatives, or given lucrative contracts to their spouses. His annual pay was up to $359,000 a year.

As long as he controlled the governor—or at least had a good relationship with him or her—he could survive. But the acting governor, Jane Swift, a bumbling former Republican state senator, was forced out of the 2002 Re-

publican primary by Mitt Romney, a GOP golden boy and venture capitalist who had just guided the Winter Olympics in Salt Lake City out of near-bankruptcy.

Romney won in November over another female former state senator, a Democrat. Bulger sought a meeting with the governor-elect; perhaps he could charm Romney, the way he had the last three Republican governors. But Mitt's new aides, State House veterans, nixed any sit-down. This was one governor Billy Bulger wouldn't own, and he knew it. In the waning days of her administration, the lame-duck Swift decided to appoint Kenny Fishman, Stevie's lawyer, to the superior court bench. Then she picked the brother of Billy Bulger's top aide at UMass for a district-court judgeship on Nantucket. It looked like a going-out-of-business sale.

By December 2002, Billy was on the ropes. The House Committee on Government Reform and Oversight was investigating FBI corruption in Boston. The surviving victims of Joe Barboza's perjury had finally been freed from prison after wrongfully serving more than thirty years. Like Billy Bulger a decade earlier, they had been featured on *60 Minutes*. Now they were suing the federal government for over $100 million, and with their elderly wives, they had made quite an impression before the congressional committee.

H. Paul Rico, now in his late seventies, was called before the committee and asked why he had allowed—in fact, had instigated—such a gross miscarriage of justice.

"What do you want from me?" he snarled. "Tears?"

Whitey Bulger hadn't even been released from prison at the time of the murder that had led to the wrongful imprisonment. But the committee chairman, Dan Burton of Indiana, decided he needed to hear from Billy Bulger. Billy was subpoenaed to testify before the committee in Boston. There would be one witness, Billy Bulger. Through

his six-figure university flacks, Billy floated the suggestion that he might defy the subpoena and blow off the entire appearance.

As soon as that story broke, governor-elect Mitt Romney called a press conference to publicly tell Bulger that he had better be there for the committee hearing. And so he was, on a Friday morning in December 2002, at the John W. McCormack Courthouse in Post Office Square, named after the former Speaker whose name Whitey had dropped all those years ago in the air force, the same building where Johnny Martorano once ran down eleven flights of stairs to escape the U.S. marshals.

Billy's lawyer first asked that the hearing be closed to the press and public. Burton took a vote of his members. It was unanimous to keep it open. Among those voting against Bulger's request was the new congressman from South Boston, Steve Lynch, who had defeated Billy's son for his old state senate seat six years earlier. Now he had succeeded Billy's pal, the late Joe Moakley, as Southie's congressman. Steve Lynch—yet another Gypo Nolan, at least as far as Billy was concerned.

With the cameras rolling, Billy began by reading a statement in which he quoted from a nineteenth-century Ohio court decision about men of good character who sometimes find themselves in "ambiguous circumstances."

Chairman Burton listened politely. Then he asked the first question.

"Mr. Bulger, do you know where your brother Whitey is?"

Billy took the Fifth.

SIX MONTHS LATER, in Washington, Billy appeared before the committee once more. This time he had to answer their questions. He had been given a grant of immunity. As long as he told the truth, he couldn't be prosecuted. Billy Bulger had cut the same deal as Martorano, Weeks,

Salemme, and the rest of them. The irony escaped his rumpswabs in the media.

In the basement of the Rayburn Office Building, Billy was trying to save not only his own job but also those of all his otherwise-unemployable payroll patriots in the university system. The C-SPAN feed was being carried live by every major television station in Boston. Billy seemed almost contrite as he began by reading from a prepared statement about his fugitive brother.

"I now recognize that I didn't fully grasp the dimensions of his life. I am particularly sorry to think that he may have been guilty of some of the terrible things of which he is accused. I do still live in the hope that the

Whitey's brother Billy testifies before
a congressional committee in Washington
investigating FBI corruption in 2003.
Two rows back, left, is the author, Howie Carr.

worst of the charges against him will prove groundless. It is my hope."

This time Burton's first question to Billy Bulger was, What did you think your brother did for a living?

"Well, I know that he was for the most part . . ." Billy's voice drifted off. He started over. "I had the feeling that he was, uh, in the business of gaming and, and, uh . . ." He stopped again. "Whatever. It was vague to me but I didn't think, uh —for a long while he had some jobs but uh ultimately uh it was clear that he was not uh um being um uh you know he wasn't doing what I'd like him to do."

Burton asked, "Did you know anything about the Winter Hill Mob?"

"The what?" Bulger said.

"The gang he was connected to."

"No, I didn't." Pause. "I don't think I met anybody from that."

"You didn't know Flemmi?" Burton asked incredulously.

"I did know Steve Flemmi, yes."

"Well, he was part of that gang. You didn't know he was part of that gang?"

"No."

"Did you know what Steve Flemmi did for a living?"

"I thought he had a restaurant somewhere. And I thought he had a club, or something like that."

It was the Marconi Club, in Roxbury, into which Johnny had once invested $20,000. Stevie sold the club and eventually the Boston police got a search warrant and dug up its basement, looking for more bodies.

"Any indication," Burton said, "your brother was involved in murder?"

"Someplace," Billy Bulger said, "I saw it in the paper."

A lawyer for the committee finally brought up the name of Johnny Martorano. He reminded Bulger of Martorano's sworn testimony that Whitey had once told him

how Billy had asked Zip for a favor—keeping Whitey out of trouble.

"He said that?" Billy asked. "And was Mr. Martorano there when I did this? Was he present?"

"He understood," the lawyer said, "that you had done it at some point."

"I see," said Billy. "Well, if I ever did say something like that, uh, influence him to stay on the straight and narrow, if that's what's meant by it I could well have said it . . . I think it's a pretty innocent comment, if in fact I made it. I have no recollection but I don't want to quarrel with that source."

As soon as the hearing ended, Governor Romney let it be known that he would begin appointing known enemies of Billy Bulger to the UMass board. Billy took the hint and decided to call it quits. He got a severance package of $960,000 from the state, in addition to a state pension of just under $200,000 a year.

IN OCTOBER 2003, a few weeks after Billy Bulger's resignation as president of UMass, Stevie Flemmi pleaded guilty in U.S. District Court to ten counts of murder. The prosecutor read the agreed-upon statement of facts, listing the murders in order. As he reached the paragraph about the strangulation of Deb Davis in 1981, one of her brothers stood up in court and screamed at Stevie, "Fuck you, you fucking piece of shit!"

IN DECEMBER 2003, the City of Somerville began foreclosure proceedings on the old Marshall Street garage, out of which the Winter Hill Gang had operated. Howie Winter had fallen more than $11,000 behind on his tax payments.

That same month, H. Paul Rico answered a knock at his front door of his condo in Miami Shores. He was wearing a cashmere World Jai Alai cardigan sweater. When he

opened the door he saw several uniformed police officers as well as Mike Huff, the Tulsa homicide detective he'd snubbed so many years earlier. They told the seventy-seven-year-old retired FBI agent that they were there to arrest him on a murder warrant from Oklahoma. They read him his Miranda rights. Then Huff took a pair of handcuffs out of his coat and asked "Mr. Rico" to put his hands in front of him.

First, Rico asked them if they were joking. They told him they were not. When they informed him that he would now be taken to the Miami/Dade jail for booking, H. Paul Rico defecated in his trousers.

In January 2004, Rico was extradited to Oklahoma to stand trial on charges of arranging the 1981 murder of his boss, World Jai Alai owner Roger Wheeler. He was flown from Miami in an ambulance jet. As the plane landed in Tulsa, Rico again shat in his pants. At his arraignment at the county jail, Rico pleaded not guilty from his wheelchair.

On January 16, 2004, Rico died, alone in a Tulsa hospital room, with guards standing outside his room.

IN JUNE 2004, Johnny Martorano was again flown back to Boston to appear before Judge Mark Wolf. Almost ten years after his arrest in the parking lot in Boca Raton, he would finally be sentenced.

That morning, columnist Mike Barnicle, forced out of the *Globe* following allegations of fabrications of quotes and plagiarism but still working occasionally for the *Herald,* dusted off the old discredited Zip Connolly story line that Johnny Martorano still hadn't admitted to all the murders he'd committed.

"For those of you keeping score at home," Barnicle wrote, "his career record of kills far exceeds the modest number—twenty—he admitted to."

The only difference between this and so many other

pro-Whitey columns Barnicle had written over the years was that now even Barnicle had to admit that "Jimmy" and Stevie were "two total degenerates."

The feds had asked Wolf to impose a twelve-year sentence. As prosecutor Wyshak wrote in his motion, "While the government makes no excuses for Martorano's criminal activity, the sad truth is none of the murders in which he had been involved would have ever been solved had he not confessed."

But Judge Wolf wouldn't go for twelve years. He described Martorano as a "calculating opportunist" who had only decided to testify against Stevie Flemmi because he was concerned that Flemmi would testify against him. Nevertheless, Wolf acknowledged Johnny was no longer the killing machine he had once been.

"I'm not a prophet," Wolf said. "But you seem to have gotten the message. You're too old to initiate this all over again."

Before the sentencing, Martorano stood and read his own prepared statement.

"I've confessed to my family, my friends, and my priest. I've been forgiven and given a second chance. I will not embarrass anyone who stood up for me and supported me. As they say, actions speak louder than words. I'm hoping the risks I've taken to turn my life around and accept responsibility prove my sincerity."

The survivors of the victims were likewise allowed to address the judge. Barbara Sousa, widow of James Sousa, murdered at the garage in 1974, his body never found, said, "It is very hard to understand how a man who has admitted to killing twenty people can be regarded as giving 'valuable assistance' to anyone."

Tim Connors, son of Eddie Connors, shot to death in a phone booth on Morrissey Boulevard in 1976, said, "He's not sincere. No, not at all. It's just something doctored up by his attorneys."

But David Wheeler, son of Roger Wheeler, shot between the eyes in Tulsa in 1981, also wrote to Judge Wolf: "The irony that the hit man who murdered my father possesses more integrity than the FBI and the United States government will trouble me until my death."

The survivors sat on the right side of Judge Wolf's courtroom; Johnny's family sat on the left side. After a four-hour hearing, Judge Wolf sentenced him to fourteen years. He would be eligible for parole in 2007.

JOHNNY WAS SENT back to Florida. With Rico dead and Flemmi having pleaded guilty, most of his work as a government witness was done. If Whitey was ever brought back to Boston, Johnny would of course be called as a witness. And in 2008, he would have to testify in Florida, when Zip Connolly went on trial for second-degree murder in the 1982 John Callahan slaying.

But basically, all Johnny Martorano was doing now was completing his sentence, his bit. Back in Boston, the old gang continued to fade away. Fat Tony Ciulla died in 2003. He'd been in the Witness Protection Program for years, living in Southern California as Tony Capra—his wife's maiden name. But near the end, he moved back to Boston and was living with a relative, still looking for a writer to tell his story. As one writer noted, Fat Tony was predeceased by most of the tracks where he'd fixed races—Hialeah, Green Mountain, Narragansett.

Alvin Campbell died in 2005, Sonny Mercurio in 2006. One by one, the Angiulo brothers passed on, and John Hurley, and Joe McDonald's older brother Leo. . . .

As the date of his release neared, back in Boston Frank DiMento was getting calls from reporters, wanting the first postprison interview with Johnny Martorano.

Frank called me and says another reporter had called him. I told him, "Just another guy looking for a

story." And Frank says, no, I don't think so, not this one. Frank asks me, did you ever go to a private school in Rhode Island called Mount St. Charles? Of course I did, so Frank says, well, this guy Ed Bradley called, from CBS, and he says he was your best friend on and off the football field and he'd like to do whatever he can to help you.

Now, I only remember him as "Big Ed." I didn't even know Big Ed's last name back then. But he's been following my case, putting it all together. And he was fascinated by how strangely it had all turned out. He's black, he comes from a poverty-stricken background and ends up one of the biggest TV reporters in the country, and me, I'm white, from the suburbs, and I end up as . . . well, as what I ended up.

So Ed Bradley tells Frank, he wants to do a story on why and how it all happened the way it did, to both of us, him going one way and me the other. Big Ed says he figures this isn't just one segment on *60 Minutes,* this is the whole hour.

I said, "Good." I wanted to maybe get him into the prison, do the interview there. But they wouldn't let him come in with a camera crew, so he was going to meet me as I walked out the prison door. We'd shake hands and hug and then sit down and talk it through. I never spoke to him directly, but through Frank I promised him I'd do the interview.

But it was not to be. Bradley, who enjoyed doing Boston organized-crime pieces for *60 Minutes,* did his final one in early 2006 on Kevin Weeks, whose book about his career as Whitey's gravedigger was about to be published.

Within a few months, though, Bradley was stricken with a rare blood disorder. He died about four months before Johnny was to be released. But Johnny would fulfill his promise to Ed—he gave his first postprison interview

to *60 Minutes*. Steve Kroft ended up doing the story, asking all the right questions—even going back to Mount St. Charles, now a coed school, for some of the interviews. But somehow, without Big Ed, it just wasn't the same for Johnny.

FINALLY, ON MARCH 22, 2007, it was time for Johnny Martorano to go home, not to Boca Raton, but to Boston. He was offered the Witness Protection Program, but declined. Who exactly did he have to worry about back in

Carmen DiNunzio, aka the Cheeseman,
was the alleged boss of the Boston Mafia when
Johnny was released from prison in 2007.

Boston? The Hill was gone, Whitey and Stevie's successor crew scattered, and what beef did what was left of the Mafia have with Johnny? The guy the newspapers said was the new boss in Boston, Carmen DiNunzio, had been twenty years old when Johnny went on the lam. DiNunzio ran a cheese shop on Endicott Street in the North End and weighed 450 pounds. His nickname was "the Cheeseman."

In all factions of the Boston underworld, it seemed, no one had anything but gratitude for what Johnny had done. He'd avenged them all, living and dead. No friends of Johnny, or anyone else, were in prison because of his testimony. Only Stevie and Zip . . . and maybe, someday, Whitey.

Peter Limone, one of the guys who did thirty years in

Johnny Martorano's favorite photograph of himself.

prison for the Deegan murder he did not commit, would soon succeed the Cheeseman as the new boss, or so the papers and TV stations said. Limone, too, had sent a letter to Judge Wolf before Johnny's sentencing in 2004, pointing out Johnny's role in finally establishing his innocence.

No, Johnny would have no problems in Boston. At his sentencing in 2004, Eddie Connors's son had mentioned something about "street justice," but Johnny was not concerned. He just wanted to get to Boston, see his children, and try to do something he'd never done before— live a normal, straight life.

I had a friend, a guy I met on the lam in Orlando. John Pierce. He had a nightclub, then a redneck bar in Tampa, then a steakhouse in north Georgia. He used to visit me at the prison, so the day I got out, he drove down to pick me up. I walked out the door and got in his car and we drove 400 miles straight, to Hartsfield Airport in Atlanta. No stops. I just wanted to get home.

We get to the airport. John says, do you want me to come in with you? And I said, nah, I can handle it. So I go in there, and everything is different. I haven't been on a commercial airliner except as a prisoner since 9/11. I have no driver's license, only a prison ID. The guy looks at it and says, that's not good enough. I said, hey, what do you want from me? I just got out of prison, that's all I got. Finally they let me on the plane. JetBlue.

At Logan, my brother and my cousin Joe picked me up. If you've never been in prison, it's hard to explain what it's like, getting out. It's like coming out of a spaceship, everything seems a little off.

They took me to Santarpio's Pizza, right near the airport there in East Boston. I had pizza and lamb.

Must have been cheese pizza—Jimmy's a vegetarian. We finished dinner, and then they drove me to Woburn. I was staying with my cousin. I was tired, I got a good night's sleep, and the next morning I started making phone calls. I told everybody the same thing. I'm back.

Epilogue

Whitey Bulger was finally captured by the FBI on June 22, 2011.

He and Catherine Grieg had been living as Charles and Carol Gasko in Santa Monica, California, for at least fifteen years in a $1,165-a-month rent-controlled apartment three blocks from the beach. On the door of the Gaskos' 800-square-foot apartment was a hand-printed sign that said DO NOT KNOCK UNDER ANY CIRCUMSTANCES.

At about 5:45 on a Wednesday afternoon, the apartment building manager across the street from Whitey's third-floor apartment was instructed by FBI agents to call "Mr. Gasko" and tell him that his storage unit in the garage had been broken into.

When Whitey arrived at the garage a few minutes later, he found himself surrounded by FBI agents and local police. The feds ordered Whitey to get down on his knees, but he refused.

A neighbor and acquaintance who watched the arrest later told the *Boston Globe,* "He looked old; he looked dejected. He looked at me and he was sort of ashamed. He looked down."

One of the FBI agents handed him a cell phone and told him to call Catherine Greig.

"Carol," he said, "stay in the apartment. I've been arrested."

And thus it ended, not with a bang but a whimper.

IN THE END, it was a stray cat that led to the capture of America's most wanted criminal. An elderly neighbor in the apartment building had died, leaving behind a striped cat named Tiger. Tiger still hung around the complex, and several residents tried to feed him, but he only responded to Carol Gasko.

Gasko would feed the cat twice a day, just before sunrise and then at dusk. One morning at 6 A.M., an Icelandic model and cat lover named Anna Bjornsdottir came by and asked her what she was doing. Carol Gasko and Anna became friends—an odd pairing of a gangster's moll on the lam and a former Miss Iceland who had been one of the models in the famous Noxzema "Take It Off" television shaving-cream ads of the 1970s. Bjornsdottir spent months at a time in Los Angeles with her second husband, working as a top model. According to *People* magazine, she was making $2,000 a day as early as in 1980.

On May 1, Osama bin Laden was killed in Pakistan by U.S. Navy Seals. Whitey was now at the top of the FBI's Ten Most Wanted List, and he sensed that the heat was about to be turned up on him. Greig began telling neighbors that he was suffering from Alzheimer's. He seldom left the apartment.

And the FBI soon decided to begin a new campaign: a fourteen-city media buy aimed at older female viewers of daytime television, the demographic group that might have bumped into Catherine Greig at a beauty parlor. The ad never ran in Los Angeles, but the story was picked up by CNN, and in Iceland, Anna Bjornsdottir saw the photo

of the woman she knew as Carol Gasko. She called the FBI.

THE ARREST OF a Ten Most Wanted fugitive in a fashionable neighborhood was front-page news in Los Angeles, but back in Boston, it was the only story in the media for days. Inside the apartment, Whitey had exercise equipment, including a punching bag that he put in his front window with a hat on top of it, to make it seem from the outside as if someone was standing in the window. The police also found an old-style Boston "hide" built behind a wall, just like the one Whitey had installed on Silver Street when he had lived in South Boston with Teresa Stanley. Inside the wall, cops found more than thirty firearms, hundreds of rounds of ammunition, and $822,000 in cash.

Whitey cut other holes in the wall as well. In the master bedroom, where he slept alone (Catherine slept in the spare bedroom), Whitey left behind a hole, with a message above it. In pen, he wrote "Mice," beneath which he drew an arrow to the words "All done." And beneath that, in Spanish, he scrawled *"Fin. Muerte."*

End. Death.

The Gaskos had lived a quiet life, to say the least. The aging couple took twice-daily walks, in the morning and evening, often heading over to the Third Street Promenade, a touristy area on the beach. Besides Tiger the cat, they also fed squirrels. The Gaskos had no car, and Catherine walked eight blocks to do their grocery shopping. They apparently hadn't left Southern California in at least a decade, when they took a brief vacation in San Francisco, where Whitey had spent all those years on Alcatraz. Carol paid the rent every month in cash, across the street at the Embassy Hotel, which was owned by the same family that owned the apartment building, the Princess Eugenia.

Reports from the Gaskos' neighbors were mixed. Whitey was described by one woman as a "rageaholic." He watched TV until late in the night, and put up black curtains throughout the apartment.

One neighbor later told reporters she wanted to pass on a message to the survivors of Whitey's victims.

"Just let them know he did not have a nice life. He lived afraid in his little apartment with the curtains drawn without any opportunity to spend his money and enjoy his life."

BACK IN BOSTON, the story continued to dominate the news. After all the revelations over the years, no one in the Boston media, not even at the *Globe,* lauded Whitey anymore for "keeping the drugs out of Southie." But several elderly Southie residents did, in the inevitable man-in-the-street interviews, and they also mentioned Whitey's purchase of turkeys every Thanksgiving for the Town's down-and-outers.

In several news stories that first week, Whitey was compared to Robin Hood.

But what most people talked about was the FBI's account of being tipped off by a woman in Iceland. After the decades of lies and crimes and cover-ups, the credibility of the Boston office of the FBI was nonexistent.

By Friday, as Whitey was being flown back east, the Boston FBI office was forced to issue an extraordinary statement:

"Any claim that the FBI knew about Mr. Bulger's whereabouts prior to the FBI's publicity efforts this week are completely unfounded. When we learned his location, he was arrested promptly."

If anything, that statement increased the cynicism in Boston. So finally, in early October, Anna Bjornsdottir, who had already received a $2 million check from the U.S. Treasury, was outed in a front-page story in the

Boston Sunday Globe. When approached by *Globe* reporters in Iceland, she had run inside her house in fear. Despite the fact that Whitey's mob no longer existed, another uproar erupted in Boston, with the FBI accused of leaking its informant's name to the *Globe* to end the lingering suspicion that the story had been concocted to somehow protect the Bureau.

Within days, the FBI was forced to issue yet another unusual statement, denying it had either given up its informant's name or that it had tacitly informed the *Globe* that it was not opposed to the release.

Once again, few people believed the FBI's explanation.

WHITEY BULGER HAD grown up in St. Monica's Parish in South Boston, and was apprehended in Santa Monica. He lived on Third Street; back in Southie, he'd buried at least three bodies in the basement of a house on Third Street. His apartment was about four blocks from the offices of GK Films, which had produced the film most often associated with Whitey, *The Departed*. The FBI office in Los Angeles was less than four miles from the Princess Eugenia.

But more than coincidences tied other Bostonians to Santa Monica. His niece, Mary Hurley (Billy's daughter), had also lived on Third Street in the early 1990s, a couple of miles away from Whitey's apartment. She was unavailable for comment after her uncle's arrest.

Within walking distance of the apartment is a Boston Irish bar, Sonny McLean's. Naturally everyone there suddenly remembers seeing Whitey stop in to watch Celtics playoff games. A sign was quickly posted over the bar, WHITEY WUZ HERE, and the soundtrack from *The Departed* plays endlessly on the barroom's sound system. Back in Boston, producers for a sports-radio talk show recalled getting the occasional call from Boston tourists who had found themselves in Sonny McLean's. On a few

occasions, they'd even mentioned that someone who bore an amazing resemblance to Whitey Bulger was sitting at the bar. *Yeah, sure,* the producers would tell them before hanging up.

Then a cop in San Diego gave an interview to the *Herald.* He'd been quoted in the paper before, in 2006, after he had left a showing of *The Departed* in San Diego and spotted Whitey leaving the theater. He tailed Whitey until he jumped on a trolley, headed south toward Tijuana.

At the time, the feds had dismissed his story out of hand. Now Whitey was telling his captors that he and Catherine had often parked on the American side of the border and then walked into Tijuana to buy Atenolol, a prescription high-blood-pressure medication in the United States but available over the counter south of the border.

There had been other unconfirmed sightings of Whitey in Southern California. In 2000, a tipster reported seeing Whitey in a car outside a hair salon in Fountain Valley while Catherine had her hair done inside. That case took its place in Bulger lore when the L.A. office of the FBI sent out a fax announcing a definitive sighting of the fugitive, only to be followed an hour later by a fax from the Boston office announcing there had been no such sighting.

In 2005, an elderly man who bore more than a passing resemblance to Whitey was recorded by surveillance cameras robbing three banks in Orange County. But he was never seen again, and that sighting, too, was soon forgotten.

The most recent sighting had come in 2008, right after one of *America's Most Wanted*'s sixteen segments on Bulger. A family vacationing from Las Vegas spotted him sitting on a bench near the Third Street Promenade. They watched as he began chatting with another pedestrian wearing a Boston Celtics' shirt. The Vegas tourist had called in a tip to *America's Most Wanted* on June 30, 2008, and it is still listed in the *AMW* logbooks.

• • •

INSIDE THE APARTMENT, agents discovered that Whitey had collected fifteen different aliases, as well a book on how to forge fake IDs—*Secrets of a Back Alley ID Man.*

The most enduring of his fake IDs, however, belonged to an Irish-American street drunk named James William Lawlor. Taking a walk in the late 1990s, Bulger saw him sitting on a bench in downtown Los Angeles, noticed his resemblance to him, and quickly struck up a friendship.

Whitey set up Lawlor in a cheap downtown hotel and got him sober. In return, all Whitey asked for was the use of Lawlor's California driver's license, his birth certificate, and his Social Security number. Those were what Whitey needed for such mundane daily chores as buying prescription drugs, renting a car, or renting a safe-deposit box at a bank.

Of course, Lawlor was seven years younger, shorter, and much heavier than Whitey, and had hazel eyes. But eventually Whitey obtained new California state documents, which added four inches to Lawlor's height, and changed the color of his eyes to blue.

AT THEIR FIRST court hearing in Los Angeles, Whitey and Catherine joked and spoke to each other in whispers. A double mug-shot photograph made them look like the couple in the classic *American Gothic,* missing only the pitchfork.

Whitey spotted the reporters from Boston and Los Angeles, and he began scribbling into his hand, as if he were taking notes. When the magistrate asked Whitey if he'd read the indictment, he spoke for the first time since his capture, in what *The New York Times* described as "a thick Boston accent."

"I got them all here," Whitey said. "It will take me quite a while to finish these. But I know them all pretty much."

Both Whitey and Catherine waived their rights to fight extradition to Massachusetts and the next day they were on the way back to Boston. Prosecutors in both Tulsa and Miami issued statements asserting their eagerness to try Whitey for murder in their states, both of which have the death penalty.

Billy Bulger was no longer answering the door at his home on East Fourth Street, but he did issue a statement to the press: "I wish to express my sympathy to all the families hurt by the calamitous circumstances of this case."

BOTH BILLY AND Jackie Bulger showed up at their brother's first court appearance in Boston. With them was Billy's son, Chris, Whitey's favorite nephew, who had been recently been fired from his $100,000-a-year job with the state probation office in the midst of a patronage scandal.

In two other courtrooms that day, victims of Whitey and their survivors were asking judges to place liens on any of Bulger's loot that turned up. Among the plaintiffs were two brothers of Michael Milano, the bartender mistakenly machine-gunned in 1973. The bullet holes from that hit could still be seen in the stone wall of the nunnery at the corner of Sparhawk and Market streets in Brighton. Some of the Rakes were also in court. They had already won a judgment of $23 million against Whitey for stealing their liquor store, but had yet to see a penny of the money.

The federal courthouse was packed with victims, their families, cops, and reporters, but the center of the action was the courtroom where Whitey would be pleading. Minutes before Whitey was brought in, marshals pushed aside the throngs for the Bulgers, saying: "Step back, the senate president is here."

When Whitey was brought in, he smiled and nodded at his brothers, who did the same.

In what was becoming a tradition among high-profile

defendants in Boston, Whitey claimed he was indigent, and J. W. Carney, a well-known Boston lawyer, was appointed for him. Over the years, Carney's clients had included the Brookline abortion clinic shooter, John C. Salvi, who was later found dead in his prison cell. Another client was James Keown, a radio talk-show host who'd fatally poisoned his wife with antifreeze-laced Gatorade. Carney also represented a Muslim pharmacy student convicted of conspiring to blow up a suburban Boston mall.

Whitey's court appearance was brief, and he said little more than "Not guilty, Your Honor." None of the victims' names was read aloud—another bit of salt in the survivors' wounds. Afterward, outside the courthouse, on Northern Avenue where Whitey had gunned down Brian Halloran and Michael Donahue twenty-nine years earlier, reporters and camera crews chased Billy into the street. Chris tried to elbow them aside, but there were too many. Finally Billy was cornered, and a TV reporter noted that in the courtroom he had appeared somewhat "emotional."

Billy nodded, choosing his words carefully. "These are," he finally said, "unusual circumstances."

WHITEY WAS INCARCERATED at the Plymouth County Correctional Facility—where Johnny and Stevie and all the rest had been locked up in the 1990s. A correctional officer was stationed in a chair outside Whitey's cell twenty-four hours a day, and Whitey apparently spent most of his waking hours in one-sided conversations with the guards sitting in the hall.

"He won't shut up," one of them told the *Herald*. "They get pissed and think he's annoying, so they hold a book or magazine in front of their face and pretend to read and not hear him."

One of Whitey's more far-fetched claims: that he had allowed the feds to capture him.

·   ·   ·

THE MEDIA HAD their one *American Gothic* mug shot, as well as drawings scrawled in the federal courtrooms, but they still needed new video of Whitey. So in early July, the feds decided to bring him to the courthouse in a helicopter, after alerting all the newspapers and TV stations where the chopper would be landing. Whitey's descent from the clouds was carried on live TV, and millions of New Englanders saw a spry, bearded, bald eighty-one-year-old man step from the chopper in handcuffs and leg shackles. He was wearing the usual inmate's orange jumpsuit, wire-rimmed sunglasses, and headphones—apparently to protect his hearing on the short hop up from Plymouth.

In December 2011 Whitey returned to Boston in an ambulance after complaining of chest pains. He was checked in to Boston Medical Center under a famous fictional alias—Perry Mason—but refused treatment and was quickly returned to jail.

WHITEY KNEW HE'D never make bail, but Catherine Greig dreamed of getting out of the federal detention center in Central Falls, Rhode Island. Her lawyer would be paid for by Billy Bulger, she announced. The veteran defense attorney, Kevin Reddington, immediately pronounced her "an excellent bail candidate. Where's she going to go?"

As of early 2012, she remained in federal custody, with no bail set.

Reddington also told reporters that she would be not cooperating with the feds "while I'm representing her." This infuriated the victims, many of whom had been attending every court session. They were already angry that she was only facing a five-year rap for harboring a fugitive. Debbie Davis's brother told the papers, "Maybe if she was facing a couple of life sentences she'd talk."

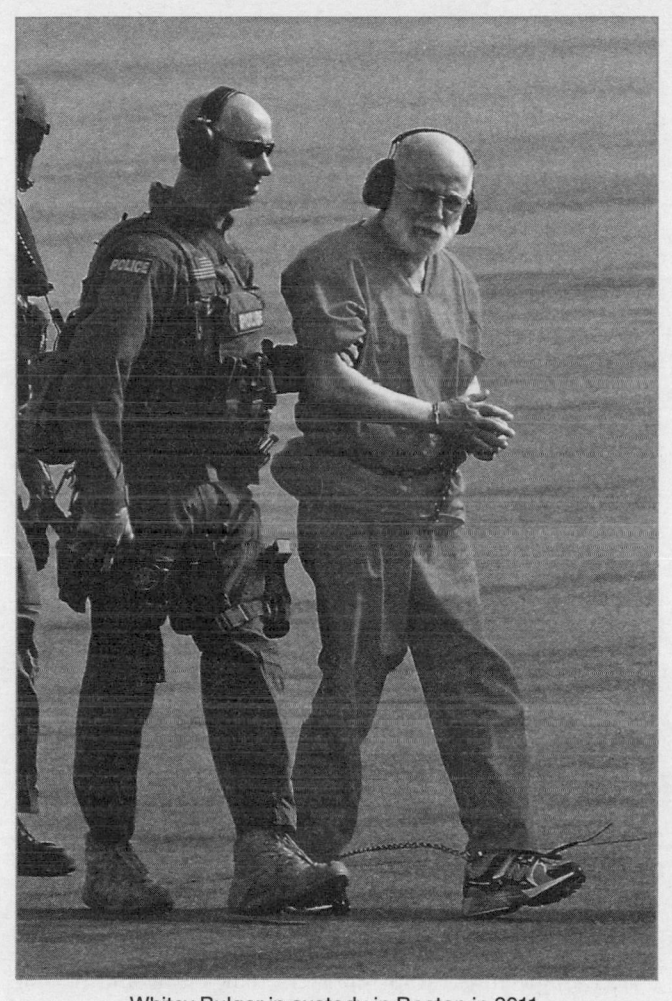

Whitey Bulger in custody in Boston in 2011.

Among Bostonians, questions remained about Greig: Whose numbers were on those two cell phones of hers that the feds had found in Santa Monica? And perhaps even more important, could she lead the cops to all the other safe-deposit boxes where Whitey had stashed his millions in ill-gotten gains?

Her twin sister, Margaret, who had offered to put her own home in Southie up as bail, gave a sob-story interview to the *Herald* about her gun-moll sister, saying, "She's all I have. I want her home. She just says, 'Don't worry about me. You have your own lives.'"

In the story outing the FBI informant, the *Globe* included an interview with the building's maintenance manager, who had gotten to know Whitey relatively well. Whitey wrote him a letter from the Plymouth jail in September, in which he said, "For me, it's over."

According to the *Globe,* Whitey also told his friend that Greig, who was jailed in Rhode Island, had somehow gotten a message to him.

"She told him she doesn't regret the sixteen years she lived with him. And he doesn't, either."

IN JANUARY 2012 federal prosecutors asked a judge to set a trial date for late 2012. Whitey's lawyers, though, argued that they couldn't possibly be prepared to go to trial before 2014, the year Whitey turns eighty-five.

Back in Santa Monica, his apartment has been repainted and rented to two men. The rent has been increased to $2,772 a month.

Where Are They Now

JOHNNY MARTORANO: Age seventy, retired, living in Boston; is spending all his time with family and friends and says that he has found a good woman and has finally settled down.

JIMMY MARTORANO: Age sixty-nine, living in Quincy, working as the winemaker at the Boston Winery in Dorchester.

HOWIE WINTER: Age eighty-one, retired, living in Millbury, Massachusetts, married to the former Ellen Brogna.

STEVIE FLEMMI: Age seventy-six, serving a life sentence without possibility of parole at an undisclosed federal location, believed to be in Otisville, New York. Sends a Christmas card every year to Tulsa detective Mike Huff.

JOHN "ZIP" CONNOLLY: Age sixty-nine, currently serving a racketeering sentence in federal prison in Butner, North Carolina, until June 2011, after which he will

begin serving a life sentence in the state of Florida for second-degree murder conviction in the death of John Callahan. Appeals continue in the Florida case. Screenplay, *Only the Ghost Knows,* remains unsold in Hollywood.

GENNARO "JERRY" ANGIULO: Former Mafia boss of Boston, died a free man in August 2009 at age ninety. Buried out of St. Leonard's in the North End with a full U.S. Navy honor guard, Hells Angels pallbearers, and a lengthy funeral procession led by a flat-bed truck carrying 190 floral bouquets. His son finished his eulogy to his father by saying, "In the words of Frank Sinatra, Jerry did it his way."

WILLIAM M. BULGER: Age seventy-six, younger brother of Whitey, continues to receive a state pension of $16,517.16 a month.

PAT NEE: Age sixty-five, former member of both the Mullens and the Winter Hill Gang; still living and working in South Boston.

DENNIS CONDON: FBI agent, partner of H. Paul Rico, died at age eighty-five in 2009. Paid obituary referred to his "illustrious career in law enforcement."

JEREMIAH O'SULLIVAN: Longtime federal prosecutor and former head of the Organized Crime Strike Force, who never publicly answered why he treated both Bulger brothers with such kid gloves over the years, died at age sixty-six in February 2009. The *Globe* described him as a "brilliant . . . straight arrow."

MICHAEL FLEMMI: Stevie's youngest brother, former Boston police officer, now serving his sentence in a

federal penitentiary in Elkton, Indiana. Scheduled to be released in September 2011, when he will be seventy-four.

JOHN BULGER: Whitey's youngest brother, paroled in April 2004, now seventy-two, continues court appeals to regain his $3,500-a-month state pension, arguing his crime of lying to a federal grand jury had nothing to do with his duties as clerk of what was then called the Boston Juvenile Court.

BILLY BARNOSKI: Winter Hill associate, now serving life sentence at MCI-Shirley medium security facility for the murder of Jackie McDermott. Continues to maintain innocence, and is appealing.

KENNY FISHMAN: Stevie Flemmi's attorney, now a Massachusetts Superior Court judge. Testified by videotape in the murder trial of Zip Connolly in 2008.

DIANE KOTTMYER: Former federal prosecutor, joked with Zip Connolly at his retirement dinner in 1990 about Whitey Bulger's South Boston Liquor Mart. Now a Massachusetts Superior Court judge.

CARMEN "THE CHEESEMAN" DINUNZIO: One-time Mafia boss of Boston, pleaded guilty to state and federal racketeering charges in 2009, currently serving his sentence in Morgantown, West Virginia. Scheduled release date: January 2015, when he will be fifty-seven years old.

JOEY YERARDI: Associate of Johnny Martorano, now serving federal sentence for racketeering at penitentiary in Otisville, New York. Is scheduled for release in 2012, when he will be fifty-eight years old.

ARNOLD CAMPBELL: Now seventy-five; only surviving member of the Campbell gang, retired in Phoenix, Arizona. Lives with daughter, collects Social Security pension of $920 a month, and another $120 a month from the state of Arizona, for which he once worked. Says, "I love Johnny and Jimmy. Johnny's my brother—100 percent."

PETER LIMONE: Now seventy-six; one of four men framed by the FBI for a murder he did not commit, was released in 2001 after thirty-three years in prison. In 2007, a federal judge awarded Limone and the others (or their estates) a total of $101.7 million for wrongful imprisonment. Arrested in December 2008 on state charges of extortion, loansharking, and gambling.

GEORGE MCLAUGHLIN: Now eighty-one, last of the McLaughlin brothers of Charlestown, imprisoned for murder since 1964; serving his life sentence at Bay State Correctional Center in Norfolk, Massachusetts.

FRANK SALEMME: Now seventy-six, reportedly released from federal prison in 2009 and living on Cape Cod.

ANTHONY "THE SAINT" ST. LAURENT: Now sixty-nine, as of 2010, imprisoned at Devens Medical Facility in Ayer, Massachusetts. According to authorities, has twice tried to hire hitmen to murder his Rhode Island Mafia rival, Robert DeLuca, telling one wired wiseguy: "Shoot him in the fucking head. Say, 'This is from the Saint.'" Most recently charged in February 2010 with attempting to shake down bookies in Taunton, Massachusetts. His seventy-three-year-old wife, Dorothy, pleaded guilty in September 2010 to being the Saint's "primary collection agent."

WILLIAM DELAHUNT: Age sixty-nine, former classmate of the Martorano brothers at St. Agatha's School in Milton, retired from the U.S. House of Representatives after completing his seventh two-year term in 2010.

JAMES J. "WHITEY" BULGER: Age eighty-two, captured by the FBI in Santa Monica, California, on June 22, 2011. Currently incarcerated at Plymouth County Correctional Facility in Massachusetts, awaiting trial on federal charges in Boston. Ruled to be indigent, is represented by a public defender.

Index